NETNOGRAPHY

⑤SAGE | 50 YEARS

SAGE was founded in 1965 by Sara Miller McCune to support the dissemination of usable knowledge by publishing innovative and high-quality research and teaching content. Today, we publish more than 750 journals, including those of more than 300 learned societies, more than 800 new books per year, and a growing range of library products including archives, data, case studies, reports, conference highlights, and video. SAGE remains majority-owned by our founder, and after Sara's lifetime will become owned by a charitable trust that secures our continued independence.

Los Angeles | London | New Delhi | Singapore | Washington DC | Boston

NETNOGRAPHY:
REDEFINED

2nd Edition

Robert V Kozinets

Los Angeles | London | New Delhi
Singapore | Washington DC | Boston

Los Angeles | London | New Delhi
Singapore | Washington DC | Boston

SAGE Publications Ltd
1 Oliver's Yard
55 City Road
London EC1Y 1SP

SAGE Publications Inc.
2455 Teller Road
Thousand Oaks, California 91320

SAGE Publications India Pvt Ltd
B 1/I 1 Mohan Cooperative Industrial Area
Mathura Road
New Delhi 110 044

SAGE Publications Asia-Pacific Pte Ltd
3 Church Street
#10-04 Samsung Hub
Singapore 049483

Editor: Mila Steele
Assistant editor: James Piper
Production editor: Ian Antcliff
Copyeditor: Christine Bitten
Proofreader: Kate Campbell
Indexer: David Rudeforth
Marketing manager: Sally Ransom
Cover design: Shaun Mercier
Typeset by: C&M Digitals (P) Ltd, Chennai, India
Printed and bound by CPI Group (UK) Ltd,
Croydon, CR0 4YY

MIX
Paper from responsible sources
FSC
www.fsc.org   FSC® C013604

Library of Congress Control Number: 2014956935

British Library Cataloguing in Publication data

A catalogue record for this book is available from the British Library

ISBN 978-1-4462-8574-9
ISBN 978-1-4462-8575-6 (pbk)

At SAGE we take sustainability seriously. Most of our products are printed in the UK using FSC papers and boards. When we print overseas we ensure sustainable papers are used as measured by the Egmont grading system. We undertake an annual audit to monitor our sustainability.

TABLE OF CONTENTS

ACKNOWLEDGMENTS

This book was a labour of love. And there are a lot of other people who love what they do and love why they do it that I want to thank. Ideas continue to grow, like children do, and even to sprout off and find their way to play with siblings and cousins in sister fields. It is immensely gratifying to see that and so, to you, the Reader, I offer my deep and genuine thanks for taking a chance on this book. I want to thank you first, because you are the Future of Netnography, if you choose to read and use and believe in this book.

At Oxford I met Katie Metzler, who ably took over from Patrick Brindle as the Managing Editor at Sage for this book. Thank you, Katie, for your patience, insights and support for my vision of this book. It would have been easy to do the same old thing again, but you understood that was not what netnography required. The staff and hired professionals at Sage have been very helpful, including Lily Mehrbod, Ian Antcliff, Christine Bitten and Sally Ransom. Among academics, Maria Xenitidou and Nigel Gilbert were among the first to notice my netnographic work in the UK, and opened the doors to participate and have a presence at the ESRC in Oxford. Andrew Bengry-Howell reached out to me from across the Atlantic after that, and along with Rose Wiles, Graham Crow and Melanie Nind shared ideas and contributed to the development of netnography.

My supervisor, Steve Arnold at Queen's, who is now retired, was an amazingly influential force on my thinking and early scholarship. He encouraged me to go deep into the Internet and technology, and while he was using sophisticated models to analyse Wal-Mart's entry into the Canadian market, we semiotically analysed their flyer advertising and institutional positioning. Eileen Fischer, who was there for me when I was a PhD student, has been a tirelessly perfect colleague in every way. John Sherry in Chicago, as my Kellogg mentor, but increasingly always in his writings, along with Brian Sternthal, Dawn Iacobucci, Alice Tybout, Greg Carpenter, Angela Lee, Hiroko Osaka, Phil Kotler, and other colleagues were very supportive of the early netnography ideas. Henry Jenkins contributed so much at the beginning and was such an influence through his scholarship. Craig Thompson, Doug Holt, Eric Arnould and Russ Belk have always been incredibly helpful to me and helped me to find options and lifelines of various sorts, to pull myself to shore, and to them I must add Morris Holbrook and Sidney Levy's unwavering support, even during my most difficult career phases.

Ingeborg Kleppe from NHH in Bergen, Norway was one of the earliest colleagues to start building coursework on a foundation of teaching netnography to undergraduate and graduate students as part of their explorations of the social and psychological realities of the social media experience today, and to bring me over to Bergen to train European scholars in netnography and social media; workshops from which a number of terrific new researchers, like Mina Askit, Carol Kelleher, Wolfgang Kotowski and Andrew Whalley have emerged. Andrea Hemetsberger was early on board in Innsbruck, as well as Kristine de Valck in Holland. John Deighton at MSI helped promote netnography in 2003, and Kaan Varnali, Aysegul Tokker and Tacli Yazicioglu were early adopters and proponents in Turkey. Galit Nimrod was a pioneer in Israel who invited me to conduct a netnography workshop there. Shortly after that, Maribel Suarez and Leticia Casotti in Rio de Janeiro co-created the first of two Brazilian netnography workshops. Debora Figueredo, Bernardo Figueredo and Tatiana Tosi have long been ceaseless supporters of netnography in Brazil, and on the web. Pablo Sanchez Kohn was an early social media active adopter in South America. Andreina Mandelli has fostered netnography education in Italy. Annouk Lievens in Antwerp organized the first Belgian netnography workshop. This is just the academic work – industry work will come in another format. I am certain to leave out far too many people, although in industry Patti Sunderland, Rita Denny, Patrick Thoburn, Michael Osofsky, Malcolm de Leo, Lisa Joy Rosner, Hans Gebauer, Oliver Gluth, Stephen Denny, Francois Gossieaux, Sean Moffitt and Darryl Silva stand out.

My colleagues in the field of marketing and consumer research have been tremendously supportive and collegial through the years. I feel truly blessed to be working in a field with scholars that have so much intelligence, heart and soul. It has been wonderful to see a global network of fellow scholars like Johann Füller, Hans Muhlbacher, Beth Hirschman, Stephen Brown, Pauline Maclaran, Miriam Caterall, Margaret Hogg, Simone Pettigrew, Jennifer Sandlin, Hope Schau, Susan Beckman, Al Muniz, Michelle Nelson, Roy Langer, Cele Otnes, Bernard Cova, Janice Denegri Knott, Douglas Brownlie, Avi Shankar, Robin Canniford and Paul Hewer become early adopting co-authors or authors, or mid and late adopters.

There are many new friends in these pages whose works I have enjoyed and am enjoying, people publishing from outside my immediate field who I have not met yet, some of whom I lightly chastise, most of whom I gesture at with great respect; too many individual authors to thank here, but I thank them in the pages of this book, and I hope that those of us working together in this virtual area will soon have a chance to meet in person.

Netnography must continue to benefit from energy infusions by gaining the attention of new young scholars and continuing netnographic efforts and developments from top-of-their-game and near-top-of-their-game scholars such as Markus Giesler, Joonas Rokka, Gachoucha Kretz, Daiane Scaraboto, Sarah Wilner, Marie-Agnes Parmentier, Pierre-Yann Dolbec, Henri Weijo, Joel Hietenan, Handan Vicdan, Ece Ilhan, Richard Kedzior, Fathima Saleem, Mariam Sudyam, Rachel

Ashman, Katharina Hellwig, Luciana Walthers and Luciana Velloso. With every passing month, with every conference, brilliant new scholars enter the field and develop, and keep the field evolving. As well, Master's students of all kinds, as well as PhD's in all programmes from around the world are beginning to tell me the tales of their netnographies. The netnography word is spreading. With this edition, netnography will become its own clear set of practices. MSc students, MBA students, MA students, MFA students. It is for all of us I write this book.

My Schulich colleagues are endless sources of assistance and inspiration, colouring everything I do. Peter Darke, Theo Noseworthy, Marshall Rice, Don Thompson, Joe Fayt, Ashley Konson, Steve Pulver, Alan Middleton, Aleem Visram, Roz Lin-Allen, Mark Silver, Alex Arifuzzaman, John Milne, Kelly Parke, Peter Zak, Bruno Moynie and Jessica Langer enrich my intellectual life, and life in general. Sheila Sinclair and Vilda Palmer, and also Maria Rizutto, keep me on track in so many ways. Monique Lim provided vital research assistance.

To Ulli, my constant sounding board and long-distance companion throughout the writing of this book: I adore you beyond words.

My mother and father, Anne and Michael Kozinets, and my sister and brother-in-law, Jennifer and David Rosen, relentlessly supported me through the redefinition of self that occurred since the last edition was published.

Aaron, Cameron and Brooke: everything I do is for the three of you. You are the lights of my life.

ABOUT THE AUTHOR

Robert V. Kozinets is widely recognized as the inventor of netnography, and a social media marketing and research authority. He has authored and co-authored over 150 pieces of research, and hundreds more Tweets (@kozinets) and blog posts (kozinets.net), usually about the intersection of technology, media, brands, methods, institutions and social groups. This includes four books – three of them Sage Method books. Currently, Kozinets is Associate Editor of the *Journal of Consumer Research* and the *Journal of Retailing*, an Academic Trustee of the *Marketing Science Institute*, and is the Industry seat on the Board of Directors of the *Association for Consumer Research*. On the industry side, he has extensive speaking, training and consulting experience with a range of global companies and organizations, including HSBC, TD Banking and Financial Group, American Express, Merck, Sony, Nissan, eBay, Campbell Soup and L'Oréal. He is Professor of Marketing at York University's Schulich School of Business, where he is also Chair of the Marketing department.

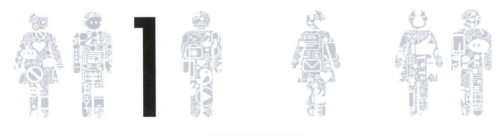

INTRODUCTION

The world with all its riches, life with its astounding achievements, man with the constant prodigy of his inventive powers, all are organically integrated in one single growth and one historical process, and all share the same upward progress towards an era of fulfillment – Tielhard de Chardin, *The Divine Milieu* (1957: 15)

Billions of individuals joined into networks partake in a complex world that not only reflects and reveals their lived experiences but is also, itself, a unique social phenomenon. Netnography can help you to understand that world. It can help you understand the various contexts that make it possible, the new social forms it advances, and the old forms it replaces. There are many challenges you will encounter when undertaking to research the world of online social interaction. This book offers solutions.

Netnography: Redefined uses social science methods to present a new approach to conducting ethical and thorough ethnographic research that combines archival and online communications work, participation and observation, with new forms of digital and network data collection, analysis and research representation. With this edition, I continue my focus on the practical workbench level, focusing on how netnography comes together as specific sets of research practices, but I amplify, specify and extend the overall approaches in light of the rise of social media, critiques of community and culture, the various tensions between the networked individuals, the proliferation of online ethnographic methods, and the maturation and spread of netnography. *Netnography: Redefined* is a discontinuous break from the past, a second edition that develops a radical new stance in the service of clearly differentiating the approach. In order to accomplish this, an introductory overview chapter is required. First it overviews the changing and always contested terrain of ethnographic inquiry. Secondly, it surveys the nature of online social experience and interaction: the phenomenon we wish to study.

- How can we understand human to human and human to machine interactions and experiences? What is the cultural and social phenomenon manifesting as social media, and how does it relate to concepts we already know such as networks, communities and culture?
- What are the research practices that guide, inform and structure netnography? How do historical precedent, extant theory and adaptive reasoning support them? How do the applications of these practices lead to cultural understanding?

As we outline and examine notions of online sociality and grapple with some of its vexing and important issues, it becomes apparent that simply opening a mobile phone and typing in some search terms is not, in itself, netnography. Netnography is, instead, specific sets of research positions and accompanying practices embedded in historical trajectories, webs of theoretical constructs, and networks of scholarship and citation; it is a particular performance of cultural research followed by specific kinds of representation of understanding. Thus, as a methodological primer, and not simply a book on method, this book must traverse and map some craggily shifting terrain, namely, the evolving, novel and challenging developments surrounding ethnography, technology research and social media.

In the former edition of the book, social media and online communities were still a bit of a novelty. Currently, with Facebook's active monthly users numbering over 1.3 billion, and social media and the Internet already widely recognized for changing politics, business and social life, there is little to be gained in belabouring the point that the study of social media is widespread, important and worthy of research attention.[1] However, because of its timing, the former book misses much that is currently of operational interest to ethnographic Internet researchers, such as direct applications of netnography to Facebook, Twitter, Instagram and Pinterest, and examples of successful tactics for doing so.

Applications and publications that use netnography are burgeoning across fields as diverse as Geography, Sociology, Media Studies, Travel and Tourism, Sexuality and Gender Research, Nursing, Addiction Research, Game Studies and Education. In the field of library and information studies, for example, Sally Burford and Sora Park used netnography to study how mobile tablet devices and their apps change young adults' access to information (Burford and Park, 2014). In the field of food sociology, Cronin and colleagues (2014) used netnography to examine discussions of over-consumption of food and alcohol and to then illustrate and develop a theory of their 'carnivalesque' qualities. Contributing to the language studies field, Sultana and colleagues (2014) used a netnography of Facebook groups to study the use of the 'linguistic, social and cultural practices' of young Bangladeshi and Mongolian adults. In economic geography, Grabher and Ibert (2014) used their netnographic study of online hybrid professional–hobbyist communities to conclude that the physical 'distance' in these communities should not be considered a deficiency, but rather an asset that helped them to collaboratively learn in ways different from face-to-face learning.

Across academic fields, netnography has been found immensely useful to reveal interaction styles, personal narratives, communal exchanges, online rules, practices, and rituals, discursive styles, innovative forms of collaboration and organization, and manifestations of creativity. This book captures the waves of exciting new social media research appearing across almost every academic field since the publication of that first edition. At the time of the last book, most of which was written in early 2009, there were few examples of the diverse forms that netnography was beginning to take, and the book contained very little systematic discussion of the various methodological and operational choices made by ethnographers seeking to use online archives and Internet communications as their main field site. This is remedied by the book's current edition.

University of Amsterdam professor Richard Rogers (2009) traces the trajectory of Internet research and attempts to distinguish between digital and virtual methods, largely concluding that appropriate or superior digital methods should be native to the digital environment, and use such affordances as crowdsourcing and social network analysis, rather than trying to adapt extant 'offline' techniques to the digital environment 'online' (see also Caliandro, 2014; Marres, 2012; Wesch, 2009). The idea that blind application of extant techniques to online social interactions will not work has been a founding principle of netnography, which explicitly seeks intelligent adaptation. However, intelligent adaptation means considering all options and not simply throwing out past approaches because they have already been done. Even in revolutionary times, and perhaps especially in revolutionary times, history and continuity are important to the making of wise decisions. In this edition, netnography remains rooted to core ethnographic principles of participant-observation while also seeking to selectively and systematically incorporate digital approaches such as social network analysis, data science and analytics, visualization methods, social media research presence and videography.

The current edition of this book seeks to provide a text that:

- engages with, describes and illustrates netnography that uses the different social media sites and forms, such as Facebook, Twitter, Instagram, YouTube and others;
- offers various up-to-date examples of successfully conducted and published netnographies across a variety of academic fields, including Library and Information Studies, Education, Nursing, Media and Cultural Studies, Anthropology, Sociology, Game Studies, Tourism and Travel, Urban Studies and Geography;
- grapples with sophisticated anthropological critiques of ethnography and provides suggestions for an evolution of its approach;

- develops and promotes a nuanced view of the online social interaction that is aligned with current cultural and social theory; and
- gives particulars regarding the different choices of netnographic form and focus, including other forms of online ethnography, that are available to researchers.

WHY NETNOGRAPHY IS NEEDED

Research is, at root, a set of practices. Boil a flask over a burner. Inject a substance into a vein. Write up a study with many impressive equations, tables and statistical analyses. Read a paper at a conference. Each recognized, legitimate particular form of research has clear affiliations, roots and sets of practices. If we do not know the affiliations, roots and sets of practices that govern a significantly different research approach, then we leave it up to individual authors to, so to speak, 'reinvent the method' every time they use it, and to claim (or have claimed for them) a uniqueness of their findings making them difficult to generalize because of their lack of specification. Uniform adherence to a standard set of practices simplifies communications, or at least helps to aggregate common knowledge so that the wheel of method turns smoothly even as it is – inevitably – being reinvented.

A set of postings on my blog debated the necessity of a separate term for ethnography conducted online. The debate benefitted from the insights of a number of commenters, especially those of Jerry Lombardi, an applied anthropologist with considerable marketing research experience. Although Jerry initially questioned the need for yet another neologism, eventually he wrote that:

> the worlds of research and intellectual innovation are strewn with neologisms that might've sounded odd or wrong when brand-new: cybernetics, psycholinguistics, software. So yes, new mappings of reality sometimes call for new names, and sometimes the names take a while to settle in.

We must consider, then, whether online sociality is different enough from its embodied variants to warrant a 'new mapping of reality'. Is online ethnography – whether we call it by this more generic term or by more specific terms such as virtual ethnography, digital ethnography, web ethnography, mobile ethnography, smartphone ethnography, or ICT ethnography – actually, significantly, different from other methods or from anthropology conducted face-to-face? In practice, the proliferating set of terms and practices is itself evidence that new adaptations are needed to differentiate online ethnography from its face-to-face predecessor.

In fact, online access to vast amounts of archived social interactions alongside live access to the human beings posting it entirely changes the practice of ethnography and, in fact, all of the social sciences. Into this vast and evolving ecosystem of social and individual data and captured and emergent communications, netnography is positioned somewhere between the vast searchlights of big data analysis and the close readings of discourse analysis. At times, it is more like a treasure hunt for rare marine species than a standard fishing trip or an activity like trawling the sea. Actual netnographic data itself can be rich or very thin, protected or given freely. It can be produced by a person or by a group, or co-produced with machines, software agents and bots. It can be generated through interactions between a real person and a researcher, or by sitting in digital archives. It can be highly interactive, like a conversation. Or it can be more like reading the diary of an individual. It can be polished like a corporately created production, or raw and crude, full of obscenities and spelling errors.

In addition, netnographic researchers are not dealing merely with words, but with images, drawings, photography, sound files, edited audiovisual presentations, website creations and other digital artifacts. Netnography provides participative guidelines, including an advocacy of the research web-page, the inclusion of Skype interviews, and in-person participative fieldwork, in order to migrate the refined perceptivity of ethnography to online media. With methodological rigour, care and humility, netnography becomes a dance of possibilities for human understanding of social technological interaction. Netnography requires interpretation of human communications under realistic contexts, in situ, in native conditions of interaction, when those human communications are shaped by new technologies.

When an approach is significantly different from existing approaches, it gains a new name and becomes, in effect, a discipline, field or school in itself. There are very few, if any, specific, procedural guidelines to take a researcher through the steps necessary to conduct and present an ethnography using social media data, attending to the scrupulous preservation of a humanist perspective on online interaction.[2] With its first presentation in 1996, netnography is certainly one of the first. With this book, I aim to make it the most lucid, defensible, differentiated and supportable.

Consider the system of academic research and publication. When undertaking a research project in an academic setting, such as research funded with grants, or Masters or PhD dissertations, it is customary for the researcher to provide proposals for the research that reference commonly accepted procedures and standards. Further, institutional review board or human subjects research review committees must be informed of research approaches and their utilization of reputably ethical methods. On the publication side, which is what makes the academic world go round, it greatly helps to have clear standards and statements so that editors and reviewers will know what to look for in the evaluation of such research. If the method is reputable, then the reviewers and editors can concentrate on the utility and novelty of the theoretical findings.

These are the multiple roles played by methodological standards in the conduct of normal science: they assist with evaluation at the proposal, ethics review and publication evaluation stages. Standards and procedures are set and, as terms regarding them fall into common usage, these standards make evaluation and understanding clearer. Social scientists build an approach that, while maintaining the inherent flexibility and adaptability of ethnography, also has a similar sense of procedural tradition and standards of quality. Although experimentation and critique is welcome and useful, the consistency of 'methodological rigour' benefits scholarship, providing clarity, better theory-construction, minimizing heedless replication and, in the end, generating greater recognition and increased opportunities for all scholars working in the area.[3]

For an interesting overview and assessment of netnography and its adoption as a methodological innovation in the social science, I recommend Bengry-Howell et al.'s (2011) NCRM Hub research report (see also Xenotidou and Gilbert, 2009; Wiles et al., 2013). In particular, I draw on one poignant critique of netnography contained in Wiles et al. (2013: 27; see also, among others, related critiques by Caliandro, 2014; Rokka, 2010; Weijo et al., 2014): 'What I can't see from where I'm standing is a very distinctive perspective that makes netnography different from Hine's virtual ethnography or different from the kind of work that lots of people are doing …' This is an important critique, and I believe that it emanates from two aspects of my past writing. First, the fact that the social media field has grown, and online or digital ethnography methods have proliferated, including virtual ethnography. Second, that netnography has been cast more at a 'workbench' and 'how-to' level which insufficiently discussed and developed its epistemology. With the next section of this chapter, I seek to begin to ameliorate this deficiency by discussing recent discussion and developments in anthropology and considering how they must impact and alter the conception and practice of netnography.

REFORMULATING ETHNOGRAPHIC FOCUS FOR SOCIAL MEDIA STUDIES

What exactly does netnography study? Traditionally, anthropologists and sociologists studied culture and community. Thus, these constructs would seem the most worthwhile foci for netnographic investigations. Indeed, my writing on netnography has consistently focused on constructs of online community and online culture, or 'cyberculture' (e.g., Kozinets, 1997, 1998, 2002a, 2010). However, with this edition that focus changes. Culture and community have become increasingly unstable concepts in anthropology. They are particularly unstable, as we shall see in this chapter, when used to reference online social phenomena. To develop a more subtle sophisticated foundation to guide netnographic practice, we begin with the nuances of destabilized (online) culture and community. Summarizing historical notions of online culture and community, this section problematizes these two concepts prior to a more in-depth examination of the core concepts of culture and community in the section following.

How did notions of community and culture appear historically in relation to computer and networked computing? In the 1950s, when the main image of a computer was a centralized corporate or government mainframe, many descriptions of computers compared them to giant brains. Later, as computers became smaller and more 'personal', entered people's homes, and were connected together into networks, the guiding metaphor for this construction was 'the information super-highway'. The term dates to at least 1988 and, if former American Vice-President Al Gore is to be believed, to 1979. In an intriguing book on the archetypes, myths and metaphors of the early Internet, Mark Stefik (1996) presents four then-prevalent metaphors of the information superhighway:

1. *Online Library*: a repository for publishing and storing collective knowledge, a form of communal or collective memory.
2. *Digital Communications Medium*: a place for email and, eventually, many other forms of communication.
3. *Electronic Marketplace*: a location for transactions of goods and services, including digital commerce, digital money and digital property.
4. *Digital World*: a gateway to new experiences, including new social settings, virtual and augmented reality, telepresence and ubiquitous computing.

Even in this early work, positioned in the same year I introduced netnography to the scientific community, we can clearly distinguish the different communicative modalities and possibilities offered by the Internet. There is a discernible 'Tale of the Internet' that proceeds through the four stages as follows. Early in its development, during the 'Dark Age' of computing, the creaky early computer peer network period that has sometimes been called 'Web 1.0' was born. With Web 1.0, the online experience was often (but not always) more like the reading of a book than the sharing of a conversation. Hence, the online library metaphor is still a powerful one. With major web-pages, online archives, and a vast majority of social media 'participants' simply reading or 'lurking', we could argue that the Internet retains much of this 'read-only' quality. Indeed, much of the big data stream now is rather unintentional: the never-really-random clicks and searches of everyone's everyday life. To be human today is to make approximately one hundred and seventeen discrete choices on our devices every day – more or less.

The plot thickens as we are slyly told that the Internet has evolved some-how. It has become much more than this. Some time around 2004 or maybe 2003 the so-called 'Web 2.0' revolution began to occur. The Internet forever after became based upon a backbone of software that increasingly enabled and empowered people to use the technology to interconnect in seemingly grass-roots ways. This enabled a type of online consumer choice, one that was driven in a person-to-person manner. All sorts of new styles and modes of interconnection blossomed as a result, including ones which facilitated new relationships (think eHarmony and online dating, TripAdvisor and hotel recommendations) as well as ones which helped manage existing and older relationships (think social networking sites such as Facebook and LinkedIn for existing personal and business contacts).

Of course, relationship-management notions have been a part of Internet and World Wide Web lore almost since its inception. Interconnection between people in a decentralized manner was the idea of Arpanet in the first place, and certainly a part of the Web that had long been emphasized by Tim Berners-Lee (the Web's creator), David Weinberger (co-author of the *Cluetrain Manifesto*), John Perry Barlow, the Electronic Frontier Foundation and other thoughtful Internet influentials and organizations. In fact, I used the Compuserve and Prodigy networks in the late 1980s and self-organizing groups such as fan and creative writing communities were easy to find. These networks allowed you to make contact with new people who shared your interests, and to start new groups at will. Even at that time, one did not need to know computer programming to join a group or start one. All one needed was to learn a few easy commands.

Whether we call the resulting sites social media, communications forums, marketplaces or virtual worlds, the guiding metaphor and concept for quite some time has been the community. The use of the term seems likely to have originated in 1978, when a husband and wife team, computer scientist and programmer Murray Turof and sociologist Roxanne Starr Hiltz, wrote one of the earliest books about how people were beginning to use computer networks (or 'computer conferencing') to socialize, congregate and organize. Published 12 years before both the invention of the World Wide Web by Tim Berners-Lee, *The Network Nation* (Hiltz and Turoff 1978) clearly predicted a world where social media were commonplace, and even ubiquitous. Clearly, the web was social from its beginnings.

As the Internet grew through the 1980s and early 1990s, a prevalent form of communication was the so-called 'community' forum, usually manifest as an interest or location-based bulletin board that assembled multiple attributed textual posts, and contained different, but centrally related, topical threads and active discussions. It was in this era of the community forum that Internet pioneer Howard Rheingold (1993: 5) continued the work of Hiltz and Turoff (1978), defining virtual communities as 'social aggregations that emerge from the net when enough people carry on … public discussions long enough, with sufficient human feeling, to form webs of personal relationships in cyberspace'. Based on his observations of online interest-based forums, support groups and role-playing games, Rheingold noted that people in online communities 'exchange pleasantries and argue, engage in intellectual discourse, conduct commerce, exchange knowledge, share emotional support, make plans, brainstorm, gossip, feud, fall in love, find friends and lose them, play games, flirt, create a little high art and a lot of idle talk' (1993: 3). And Rheingold was right. People in those forums did indeed seem to be enjoying the support and camaraderie we usually associate with in-the-flesh communities like neighbourhoods and religious groupings. However, the types of emotional depth and interconnection were not evenly distributed. His book depicts a range of forms and depths of human social interconnection. The use of the word community is highly significant. For as soon as we use this word, we find its critiques. Some of those critiques are now so substantial that they force a significant redefinition and reconfiguration of netnography.

Culture, Community and its Critics

Contested and Shifting Notions

How are we to understand notions of community and culture in the context of netnographic research practice? In the field of anthropology, the questioning of the underlying notions of stable community and culture which begun strongly and in earnest in the crisis of representation in the 1980s (see, for example, Clifford and Marcus, 1986), continues. Vered Amit and Nigel Rapport's (2002) *The Trouble with Community* interrogates 'the ethnographic enterprise and its ethnographic subjects' when they are 'no longer fixed conveniently in singular places' (Amit and Rapport, 2002: 1). As they explain, the notion of collectivity or community has long served as an anchor for sociological and anthropological research. Where location is unspecific, as in transnational or multi-sited cultures, then collective identities, including nation, ethnicity, occupation or political movement have been conveniently invoked.

Poet, novelist and anthropologist Michael Jackson (1998: 166) relates his encounter with self-styled Australian historian Frank Ropert whose dismissive and ridiculous accounts of Aborigine history were intended to demonstrate how they had 'lost their tradition culture'. However, Jackson (ibid.) uses the incident to demonstrate how the notion of culture is 'frequently invoked as an essentialized and divisive notion … [which] militates against the recognition of the humanity we share, and the human rights to which we have a common entitlement'. The meaning of aboriginal culture and aboriginal identity is no more uniform, mono-lithic, fixed or stable in time than that of, say, British identity. It would be absurd to say that British people had 'lost their traditional culture' because they did not speak, believe and behave the same as British people did 400 years ago on that same territory. The salience, for example, of my status as a Canadian, a professor, a *Game of Thrones* fan is not a constant, permanent, nor a central aspect of many of my social dealings in person, but one which shifts and is fluid. This is even less the case when I am projecting my identity through the misty, ever-shifting image-ethers of the Internet. Yet, like Frank Ropert, some scholars still seek cultural and communal constancy even as many of the processes they study – of dislocation, displacement, alienation, plurality, hybridization, disjunction, compartmentaliza-tion, escape and transgression – continually toss its possibility into doubt. We must be cautious not to assume as fixed and permanent those identities and inter-connections we observe in temporary, perhaps even transitional, form.

Similar critiques can and should be levelled at 'mechanistic, social-structural notions of culture and society as organically functioning and evolving wholes' (Amit and Rapport, 2002: 108). Michael Jackson (1998: 16) reminds us:

> That which we designate 'culture' … is simply the repertoire of psychic patterns and possibilities that generally have been implemented, foregrounded, or given legitimacy in a particular place at a particular point in time. But human culture, like consciousness

itself, rests on a shadowy and dissolving floe of blue ice, and this subliminal, habitual, repressed, unexpressed, and silent mass shapes and reshapes, stabilizes and destabilized the visible surface forms.

We should not underestimate the fluidity and instability of the human social realm. Culture adapts quickly to technologies and becomes technoculture perhaps because it is always in liquid motion, transforming and transformative. When studying online interaction, we surely wish to identify clear cultural categories such as nationalities, ethnicities, localisms, religiosities and occupational identities. However, we must strive to view them less as solid states of being than as liquid interactional elements that individual members bring to life as mental meanings. Rather than manifesting steadfast conditions of constancy, stability, functionality, reliability, timelessness, emergence and boundary, the processes at work in this post-structural and post-functionalist conception of culture are more about multiplicity, contradiction, randomness and unpredictability. Such a conception reminds us that there are degrees to which individuals choose their cultural identifications and opt to act as its standard-bearers and members. Cultures, on the other hand, do not own or have rights over their individuals or members.

Joonas Rokka (2010), building on his work with Johanna Moisander (Rokka and Moisander, 2009), conceptualizes online communities as new 'translocal sites of the social … i.e. not global or local but as contexts which are both transnational and local' (Rokka, 2010: 382) and calls for more analytic attention from netnographies, particularly by paying close attention to 'cultural practices'. With radical, but translocally resonant, implications for Durkheimian sociology and our understanding and use of the concept, practice-based analyses such as the one Rokka (2010) recommends can help us to move further in the direction of realizing the extents and ways in which culture is adopted rather than ascribed.

Society and culture can no longer be conceptualized in fundamentalist fashion. The realist tellings of ethnographic tales are outdated (Van Maanen, 1988). No longer can cultures be represented as reified, holistic, discrete, internally integrated and ontologically secure things-in-themselves. Instead, they must be portrayed as fluid processes, liquid Baumanite identities (Bauman, 2003), Appadurian transnational flows of complex translocal scapes (Appadurai, 1990). They are animated, borne, maintained, mutated, dispersed and transformed by individual consciousnesses. Although cultures and communities may be represented by members as homogenous, monolithic, and thus *a priori* this is, as Benedict Anderson (1983) reminds us, only an 'imagining'. It is idiom.

Interacting human beings are neither gigantic social machines nor vast evolving organisms, but symbolic constructions that assume different patterned forms depending upon which method we choose to use to study them. Cultures and communities are 'worlds of meaning' that exist purely because of their continued adoption and use 'in the minds of their members' (Cohen, 1985: 82). Individuals, with all their multiplicity, heterogeneity and unpredictability, come before cultures and communities, ontologically and morally. The traditions, customs, rituals, values and institutions of cultural communities all depend upon 'the contractual adherence of interacting individuals' for their continuation, meaningfulness, maintenance and value. Adopting this perspective, we might see that any given cultural community exists as an 'assemblage of individual life-projects and trajectories in momentary construction of common ground' (Amit and Rapport, 2002: 111). This more fluid perspective on online culture and community leads almost effortlessly to the notion of consocial identity and interaction.

Consocial Identities and Interactions

Rather than the tight bonds of community, an important form of contact guiding human relations in contemporary society seems to be consociation. We can think of consociation as a commonplace, largely instrumental, and often incidental form of association, one that we often take for granted because it has become so natural. It revolves around incidents, events, activities, places, rituals, acts, circumstances and people. For example, we might socialize with the people we are sitting next to at a play or a concert because the context creates conditions for this type of temporary, bounded, yet affable relationship. We are consocial with most of the people we work with, with other students, with other conference or trade show or festival goers, with many of our neighbours, with our parent's friends and their kids, with the parents of children at our children's schools, and so on (see Dyck, 2002). Some may become close friends. Some may join with us in groups of lasting relations. These close relationships and lasting relationships are not consocial, but social. But in many cases, as with neighbours and workmates, we see these people repeatedly but are unlikely to feel that they are close or important to us in a way that extends very far beyond the place- or event-based and ephemeral relationship. Although these relationships can be important and meaningful in the moment, they are entirely contingent upon our continued involvement in a particular association or activity. When we get up from our seats at the play, we may say goodbye, but we do not exchange phone numbers. When we change jobs or move, the friendly relationship with the co-worker or neighbour dissolves. Perhaps it only appears through Facebook. It remains dormant until an occasion occurs when we again need the person for one reason or another.

The ties that bind consociality are thus friendly, but not particularly strong. Consociality is conceptualized 'first and foremost by reference to what is held in common by members rather than in oppositional categories between insiders and outsiders' (Amit and Rapport, 2002: 59). Consociality is about 'what we share', a contextual fellowship, rather than 'who we are', an ascribed identity boundary such as race, religion, ethnicity or gender. The two forms are distinct and, even though one can shade or lead into the other, we should be careful not to systematically confound them. Applied to online social spaces, we might use this notion of consociality to wonder if the widely used terms 'online community' and 'virtual community' are, indeed, strong examples of this conflation of ascribed and achieved communal identity. Simply because one registers as a 'member' and then posts to an online group, seeking a particular kind of interaction, does this then mean that one becomes a 'member' of that 'community' online? Not, it seems, in any way similar to that of communities such as those based upon race, religion, ethnicity or gender.

A Netnographic View of Ascribed Culture and Community

This critique of culture and community suggests that collective entities such as community and culture are considerably less stable than some prior theory makes them out to be. Instead of more fixed and permanent communal identifications, more consocial forms of contact may occur, perhaps prevalently. Consociality eschews notions of inside-outside boundaries in favour of an emphasis on what is shared between people. Similarly, in a world of flowing cultural scapes transfigured by translocal qualities (Appadurai, 1990), cultural categories such as religion and ethnicity must be considered to be more fluid, multiple and unpredictable than ever before. In fact, this liquidity of culture and interaction may be one of the defining elements of our time. Hastened by technology and the exigencies of capitalism, dividing and connecting people from each other, people are liberated from ascribed culture and community. As Sasha Baron Cohen's ridiculous comic figure of Ali G suggests, being black is now a matter of individual choice. It appears that this freedom to choose even such hardwired identities as race and gender becomes ever more flexible on the Internet.

Relatedly, and drawing on Paul Ricoeur (1996), Amit and Rapport (2002: 116) suggest that we reconceptualize ethnography as a setting for responsibly reconstructing, representing and recounting entangled individual stories. We would do this by a 'respectful exchange of life narratives', a 'genuine labour of "narrative hospitality"' in which we write 'existential narratives – rich in subjectivities and interpersonal relations' (Amit and Rapport. 2002: 116). The outcome would be ethnography – and netnography – that portrays individuals who are free to choose a range of identities and subject positions doing just that. Emphasizing agentic identity over social structure, Amit and Rapport (2002: 117) counsel us to write about these individuals as free to believe in, adopt, evangelize, disbelieve in, function ironically within, and drop all sorts of communal, cultural and consocial identities and relationships.

What are the research implications of this view of culture and community as achieved, rather than ascribed? In the first place, it becomes incumbent upon netnographers and all other cultural researchers to analyse attachment to a community or adherence to cultural norms as, at least to some extent, a matter of individual choice rather than necessity or duty. The existence of communities, online or otherwise, should be treated analytically as an expression of an ongoing negotiation between individuals. Online cultural and community identities are adopted by people, sometimes temporarily, and often to varying extents. Can it be entirely acceptable to assume that someone who posts on YouTube is also partaking in YouTube 'culture' or is a member of the YouTube 'community' and shares some sense of common 'identity'? To do so stretches the limits not only of the terms, but also strains the credibility of the netnographer. We can see the practice of YouTube posting as significant, surely. We can analyse the content of the posting, its relation with other posts, attendant 'minding' behaviour such as tagging, offering keywords, linking and replying to others' YouTube comments and posts. But it would be questionable to assume that this set of practices says anything more about the poster's lasting identity or loyalties unless we found further evidence of this in connected research.

Relatedly, anthropologist Roy Wagner (2001) charts an 'anthropology of the subject' that uses the holographic worldview and perspectives of Melanesians to explore the relationship between the part and whole, intersubjective relationships in general and the anthropological and ethnographic endeavour itself. Among his core ideas are that anthropologists do not learn from culture members, but teach themselves to these members, that meaning is 'an insidious mental contagion' and that 'artificial reality is nearer to life than life itself' (Wagner, 2001: xiii–xiv). We will pick up a number of these important themes as we traverse the methodological development and upgrading of netnography in Chapters 2 and 3.

In a relevant article, Henri Weijo and colleagues (2014) note that my methodological development of netnography has had to increasingly acknowledge the fragmentation, proliferation and delocalization of online communities. They find a situated individualism and delocalized performances that benefit from a netnographic attention to introspection and re-emphasize the importance of researcher participation and reflexivity. These comments are astutely on target. With a more firm sense of the multifaceted social experiences we encounter when we observe online social experience, we can then proceed to a more macroscopic view of Internet use and online social behaviour, beginning with global figures.

Behold the Online Human

Almost 3 billion people around the world currently crank the handle daily on some kind of Internet box in their homes, whether via a laptop, desktop, or mobile device.[4] In 1995, that number was less than 15 million. This is, without a doubt, the single most important, rapid change in communications, learning and interconnection in human history. It is leading to some of the most tribal and primitive acts in our history, alongside some of the most utopian and militarily advanced. The Internet's interpersonal interconnections are an amplification of everything, a self-and-other reflecting reflection that ramifies through the rapid infiltration of the world into boxes in everyone's homes, purses, cases and pockets.

Table 1.1

INTERNET USAGE STATISTICS
The Internet Big Picture
World Internet Users and Population Stats

WORLD INTERNET USAGE AND POPULATION STATISTICS
December 31, 2013

World Regions	Population (2014 Est.)	Internet Users Dec. 31, 2000	Internet Users Latest Data	Penetration (% Population)	Growth 2000-2014	Users % of Table
Africa	1,125,721,038	4,514,400	**240,146,482**	21.3%	5,219.6%	8.6%
Asia	3,996,408,007	114,304,000	**1,265,143,702**	31.7%	1,006.8%	45.1%
Europe	825,802,657	105,096,093	**566,261,317**	68.6%	438.8%	20.2%
Middle East	231,062,860	3,284,800	**103,829,614**	44.9%	3,060.9%	3.7%
North America	353,860,227	108,096,800	**300,287,577**	84.9%	177.8%	10.7%
Latin America/ Caribbean	612,279,181	18,068,919	**302,006,016**	49.3%	1,571.4%	10.8%
Oceania/Australia	36,724,649	7,620,480	**24,804,226**	67.5%	225.5%	0.9%
WORLD TOTAL	7,181,858,619	360,985,492	**2,802,478,934**	**39.0%**	**676.3%**	**100.0%**

NOTES: (1) Internet Usage and World Population Statistics are for December 31, 2013. (2) CLICK on each world region name for detailed regional usage information. (3) Demographic (Population) numbers are based on data from the US Census Bureau and local census agencies. (4) Internet usage information comes from data published by Nielsen Online, by the International Telecommunications Union, by GfK, local ICT Regulators and other reliable sources. (5) For definitions, disclaimers, navigation help and methodology, please refer to the Site Surfing Guide. (6) Information in this site may be cited, giving the due credit to www.internetworldstats.com. Copyright © 2001-2014, Miniwatts Marketing Group. All rights reserved worldwide.

As Table 1.1 shows, as of 2014, over 68% of the population in Europe, over 67% of Oceania, and almost 85% of North Americans are home Internet users. In Asia, there are over 1.2 billion users. Although about 60% of the world's population do not have home Internet access, this number is skewed by the large numbers of people in Africa and Asia without such access, many of whom are likely not currently to have infrastructure that can support such activity. Yet, for much of the world, the Internet and social media have fully arrived. Excluding (for calculation purposes only) the almost five billion people in Africa and Asia, the total number of people in the Middle East, Latin America, North America, Oceania and Europe combined who are not connected to the Internet sinks to only 37%. Yet it is also important to remember that Asian users currently account for almost half of all Internet users worldwide, about 49%. And although the number of non-English websites is spreading rapidly, with Chinese, Spanish and Japanese the three next most commonly used tongues, about 55% of the most visited websites across the entire Internet still use the English language.

The Pew Internet Report, which surveys United States' citizens about their Internet usage, has repeatedly found Internet use to be strongly correlated with age, education attainment and household income. Although only 15% of United States' adults do not use the Internet or email, it is clear that those who use the Internet most tend to be younger, more educated, and to have higher household income than those who do not. These user characteristics seem to be global. Technologies such as laptops are still expensive beyond reach for many world-wide; similarly, computers and their operating systems require literacy and can be found difficult to operate. Hence it is rather unsurprising that countries with lower income levels have less Internet usage. However, this fact is partially offset by the effect of mobile phones with Internet access. Younger people worldwide are turning to the Internet and to social media. Netnographers should be attuned to the contextual cues surrounding technology usage, which help us to more appro-priately conceptualize the various uses and users of Internet connection.

The power to connect is an authentic social power. As well as enabling and empow-ering, it threatens and disrupts. In recent history, we have seen multiple instances of connective technologies fomenting revolutionary ideas that have turned into polit-ical action. Consider the Twitter-based organization in Libya and YouTubed beating to death of its former leader in 2011. These are incredible social media outcomes, regardless of their cause. Breaking news stories around the world have revealed just how extensively all of our social media communications are monitored by intel-ligence agencies around the world, in particular the National Security Agency in the United States.[5] In terms of state censorship, Saudi Arabia and China still censor Internet content heavily, including social media.[6] Other countries, such as Russia and India censor selectively. The censorship situation is in flux in a number of other countries, including Turkey and Australia. These social situations are particularly sensitive in the Middle East, with its so-called social media led 'Twitter revolutions'. A country such as Turkey provides an excellent example of the simultaneous fra-gility and political power of open and democratic social media access, with waves of support and suppression of social media Internet tools and platforms and apps constantly ebbing and waxing. Hence, netnographers must also be attuned to the legislative, state surveillance, and regulatory context limiting or facilitating both the use of social media and its users' self-surveillance and self-censorship.

Social Media as Social Life

Already in 2006 a survey found that 52% of American online community members went on to meet other online community members in the flesh (The Digital Future Report, 2008). In 2008, that number went up to 56% (ibid.). By 2010, the question of in-person interaction and its answer had become meaningless because almost everyone on Facebook meets some of their closest Facebook friends every single day. This is the way of social media and the Internet. It has evolved from anomaly and nerdy pastime to mainstream with lightning-like rapidity. Past research must be constantly questioned in the light of the present. Current research must be constantly reviewed in light of the past.

Similarly, the questions asked in 2008 about people's sentiments towards 'their online communities' seem dated already. How should we interpret the figure of 55%

who declare their devotion to online communities, professing that they feel every bit as strongly about their online communities as they do about their real-world communities (ibid.)? In an age of social media, where, for example, I am socially and consocially linked to my children and cousins, workmates and significant other, closest friends and parents on Facebook, does such a comparison have any meaning? Of course, the fact that this was 2008, and these were almost certainly blogs and forums that were being compared to immediate social, religious and neighbourhood-based relationships is rather revealing. Coming from a time before the major social media sites hopelessly conflated physical and virtual social connections, this research finding speaks to the depth of involvement and connection imparted by early instances of Internet connection. Although Facebook makes efficient increasingly global relationships, it can often be an intensely local experience.

Now, we move to the effects of Internet communications among existing relationships: a most interesting thing if we consider that most Internet-mediated interactions are conducted with people we know well, good friends, or are related to, or married to, or are otherwise joined into some sort of close relationship. As of 2014, 67% of American Internet users credit their online communication with family and friends with generally strengthening those relationships; only 18% say online access generally weakens those relationships (Fox and Rainie, 2014). That rather overwhelming difference points to how deeply people in America, at least, feel that online communications have strengthened their existing social ties rather than weakened them. Interestingly enough, there are no significant demographic differences tied to users' feelings about the impact of online communication on relationships (ibid). Equal proportions of online men and women, young and old, rich and poor, highly educated and less well educated, Internet veterans and relative newbies say by 3-to-1 or better that online communication is a relationship enhancer, rather than a relationship detractor.

As of 2013, a full 73% of online American adults use a social networking site of some kind, with Facebook clearly dominant at 71%, followed by LinkedIn, Pinterest, and then Twitter (Duggan and Smith, 2013). Facebook has become a part of many people's daily routines as well, with 63% of users visiting the site at least once a day, and 40% doing so multiple times throughout the day. Facebook and other major sites have both mainstream and specific elements or areas containing particular interest and identity groups. These reports chart the qualitative shift in social media consumption – a term preferable to online community membership in many ways. As more Americans have adopted social media – and Facebook in particular – it has become inevitably more mainstream and more demographically representative.

Although Facebook is a mainstream site, appealing to a wide demographic cross-section, this is not the case with other sites, which are more stratified and either appeal or cater to specific groups' needs. For instance, a Pinterest user is four times more likely to be a woman than a man (ibid.). LinkedIn appeals much more to college graduates and members of higher income households. Twitter and Instagram user bases tend to overlap, and to skew to younger adults, urban dwellers and non-whites (ibid.). As well, a plethora of other sites cater to all sort of local, identity, activity and interest-based tastes and social configurations. An entire ecosystem of other 'targeted' sites and online meeting places has developed. Netnographers have unprecedented choice and unprecedented opportunity. In addition to the more professionally oriented LinkedIn, consider the relationship-facilitating Tinder and Couple, and the more urban hipster oriented Foursquare. As well, we still have over 170 million blogs, a vast and literally uncounted space of many hundreds of thousands or even millions of forums and wikis.

We must also not forget visual and audiovisual sites such as YouTube, with a billion users per month watching a mind-blowing 6 billion hours of video (40% of them accessing the site from mobile devices). Instagram, owned by Facebook, has 200 million active monthly users as of 2014 – as many as Facebook did in 2009 and only about 50 million less than Twitter has in 2014. By the time you read this on paper, or in an ebook, there is little doubt that these numbers will be significantly higher: the growth rates are incredible. What they mean, what we are doing with them, and what we do with them as a civilization – one with challenges running the gamut from ideological and religious wars mutating with Internet interconnection and tribal instincts, to virulent diseases increasingly spreading, to inequality, hardship, poverty, ignorance, climate change and inhumanity – is part of the purpose of netnography.

The social media space is complex and varied, with sites that range from the social to the informational, specific sites for specific purposes and interest, and particular sites targeted to the needs of particular groups and also targeted to idio-syncratic needs. In netnography, we must be aware of this landscape as we seek to match our research interests to available sites, procedures. We will pick up and develop further these ideas in Chapter 7 when we discuss the quest for data. More people are connecting through more sites in more ways for more purposes than ever before. Chatting and checking in with others about one's day or about the news, or before or after a purchase, a doctor's visit, a parenting decision, a political rally, or a television show is becoming second nature. For many people around the world, online sociality is a part of their overall social behaviour, even their everyday social behaviour. It is already familiar, mundane, taken-for-granted. Normal. Natural. The latest technologies, it seems, have become natural, even 'human nature'.

Through social media, we can learn about this phenomenon, of technological adoption and adaptation. Though their media shall ye know them: from posts and updates, Twitter poetry, YouTubery, and of course blogs, we can learn about real concerns, real meanings, real causes, real feelings. We can learn new words, new terms, new techniques, new products, new answers, new ideas. We will encounter genuine concerns, genuine needs, genuine people. As I wrote in 1998, 'These social groups have a "real" existence for their participants, and thus have consequential effects on many aspects of behaviour' (Kozinets, 1998: 366). Online social experiences have authentic consequences for social image, social identity.

In fact, they can 'amplify' causation in social connection: they *are* interconnection. Even before you can have communication in this same point-to-point manner, you must have interconnection.

THE CONSTRUCTS INHABITING THIS BOOK

This book is arranged as a series of logical steps to lead you from a conceptual understanding of netnography and theories about online social interaction and experience to learning the specific research practices, codes of behaviour, epistemological and theoretical orientations, representational styles and different forms of netnography. The book positions netnography within different approaches used by social scientists. It provides tools, framework and many examples. In its concluding chapters, it explains and illustrates the four essential kinds of netnography: symbolic, digital, auto and humanist. The way that this journey unfolds in chapter structure is detailed below.

The opening chapter will explain the function and need for netnography, for a redefined, fully updated, and upgraded version of netnography, and for the book as a whole. Chapter 1 will begin the reformulation of netnography by incorporating anthropological critiques of culture and communities and then by exploring notions of consocialities. An overview will follow of some soon-to-be-outdated statistics that nonetheless provide a current snapshot and benchmark for the future and against the past.

In Chapter 2, we will examine online social interaction and experience that transports us from cultural conceptions to archetypes of network structure, prefiguring the more synthetic and hybridizing forms of the latter part of this book. On the cultural side, Chapter 2 first discusses technoculture, ethnographic approaches, sociality and the cultural-communal debate. It conceptualizes four ideal types of online social experience and relates them to a variety of extant social media sites, which are also contexts for our research. Next, the chapter moves into social structural types of social media understandings. It provides six quantitatively generalizable archetypes of network structure: polarized and tight crowds, brand and community clusters, broadcast and support networks. The chapter will then extend this to a full discussion and incorporation of networked individualism that concludes with its 12 principles. As it fades to give way to Chapter 3, Chapter 2 will begin to circle around some preliminary thoughts about the human, the social, the story and the plenitude.

Chapter 3 will delve into different methods considered complementary with netnography. It will begin by taking a macroscopic look at the choice of method. Netnography is about obtaining cultural understandings of human experience from online social interaction and content, and representing them as a form of research. Complementary methods include social search 'big' data analytics survey data and findings, interviews and journal methods, and social network analyses. We will find in this chapter that, compared to traditional ethnography, netnography has six essential differences: alteration, access, archiving, analysis, ethics and colonization. The chapter explores the implications of these six differences to the research practices of netnography before turning to one of the most key chapters in the book.

Chapter 4 will redefine netnography as a specific set of related data collection and creation, analysis, interpretive, ethical and representational research practices, where a significant amount of the data collected and participant-observational research conducted originates in and manifests through the data shared freely on the Internet, including the myriad of mobile applications. Its emphasis on significant amounts of Internet data will differentiate netnography from approaches such as digital ethnography or digital anthropology that are more general in orientation and can include more traditional ethnographies. The chapter will then proceed to a discussion of Hine's virtual ethnography, the roles of materiality in digital anthropology, the creeping mundaneness of technologies and the importance of storytelling. The chapter then will provide an overview of the state of netnography today, examining the growth and development of netnography as an interdisciplinary research field. From this, a portrait of the spectrum of netnographies resolves. Key elements of this portrait are its voyeurism, quest for intimacy and engagement. The chapter concludes with a new 12-step process for netnography: introspection, investigation, information, interview, inspection, interaction, immersion, indexing, interpretation, iteration, instantiation and integration.

Chapter 5 will begin to get you ready to conduct a netnography. The chapter opens with a reminder that our state of readiness is not always as prepared as we think it might be and that many types of decision and research practices may be needed before we can initiate our data collection. Researcher introspection begins the netnographic journey, and several exercises lead you onto that path. Next, the axiology of netnography will be explained and detailed as a guiding principle. The heart of the chapter will help you formulate a research focus as well as research questions that can be answered using a netnographic approach. Netnographies of online social interaction and experience tend to focus on sites, topics and people.

In the next chapter, you will be given a general overview and set of specific guidelines for the ethical conduct of netnography. The netnographer has choices when it comes to research practices, and being informed about Internet research ethics procedures and accepted human subjects research protocols is important to netnographic undertakings in academic settings. This chapter follows a model of territorialism and spatial metaphor in online social relations. Public versus private debates will be reframed as being about how we treat people's digital doubles in our research. Informed consent will be discussed as well as the general principle of doing no harm with our research. The chapter will then proceed from these ideas and principles to offer guidelines for ethical netnographic practice: stating your name, being honest, using your existing social media profiles, following personal branding principles to represent yourself, asking permission when needed, worrying about terms of service when necessary, gaining clear consent for interviews, citing and giving credit, and potentially pursuing proposed procedures for concealing and fabricating. In summary, Chapter 6 will provide you with the up-to-date foundations and specific guidelines for the ethical conduct of netnography.

Chapter 7 will treat a central practice within netnography – data collection. In netnography, data are found in archives, co-created and produced. This chapter elaborates the various important choices in data 'collection'. What are data? How should we 'collect', co-produce, find and produce them in netnography? This chapter will provide the guidelines pertaining to, searching for, finding, filtering, selecting and saving data. It will provide the criteria you need to decide which sites to search in depth, and which data to collect and curate. It concludes by providing fundamentals behind the actual workbench level of capturing, collecting and storing data from archives and online social interactions and experiences.

Under the guiding injunction to participate in online social experience, Chapter 8 will continue the discussion about data collection. This chapter will discuss the creation of interactive and produced netnographic data from online social interaction and other participation. It will provide detailed and illustrated examples to guide researchers interested in using the recommended netnographic practice of a research web-page. A section will follow on the use of interviews in netnography. Next, the chapter considers the production of reflective data, often called fieldnotes. Reflective data is reconceptualized as an ethnographic affordance and guidelines given for its conduct. As with the prior chapter, technical advice and examples will be provided throughout.

In the next chapter, we will explore the essence of netnographic data analysis and interpretation through hermeneutics and deep readings. Chapter 9 deploys the word 'interpenetration' and the metaphor of the collage to discuss the ways that analysis and interpretation may cohere and conjoin. It provides and describes seven analytic movements: cultural decoding, re-memorying, visual abstraction, tournament play, abduction, imagining and artifying. Next, the chapter discusses hermeneutic interpretation as well as holons and holarchic systems and relates them to the analytic and interpretive needs of netnographers working in complex social media spaces. A detailed example from Facebook coverage of a new story about an Ebola outbreak follows. Data is displayed and interpreted. The final section provides the nuts and bolts of three types of data analysis and interpretation: manual, semi-automatic and using algorithmic software. The use of analytics in digital netnography is discussed. In closing, the chapter offers some thoughts about the unique elements of netnographic data that might guide its analysis.

Anthropology has been at the centre of issues of scientific representation since the Crisis of Representation in the 1980s. Chapter 10 will open with a history lesson focusing on ethnographic representation. It will then provide the four ideal types of netnographic representation: symbolic, digital, auto and humanist. These forms constitute an approach to the ethnography of online interaction and experience that ranges from the reflective, subjective and personal to the statistical, expansive and descriptive. The choice of final research product form determines choices about data collection and analysis. Symbolic, digital and auto netnographies are explained in this chapter.

In Chapter 11, we explore the final of the four types of netnography: humanist netnography. Humanist netnography takes netnography's representational challenge to the highest level. Humanist netnographers focus on human interactions and experiences with and through technology in the contemporary, global, corporate-run and government surveilled landscape. They seek resonance, verisimilitude and polyphony in their representations, and embrace multiple methods. Inspired by developments in the digital humanities, netnographers producing a humanist netnography will seek a widening audience to share and collaboratively build ideas that work for positive change in the world. This chapter overviews the vision and standards for humanist netnography and provides one possible example of the kind of work it seeks to inspire.

In the social media era, scientific representation in netnography is a public, deliberate and ethically charged act of self-presentation that is closely related to academic goals of successful scholarship and career advancement. With this introduction to the book now complete, we will turn to an examination of some of the theories and conceptions that guide our understanding of online social interactions and experiences.

SUMMARY

Technology use becomes more invisible and natural to us with each passing day, with the Internet and mobile becoming increasingly seemingly indispensible. This book considers social and machine interaction from a human perspective, discussing the implications of online social interaction and experience in the context of conducting and representing academic ethnography. In this chapter, we overviewed anthropological critiques of the notions of cultures and communities, and learned about the need for a redefined and updated version of netnography. The reformulation of netnography began through exploration of notions of networks, socialities and consocialities. We also began to examine the field sites of ethnographic interaction, overviewing research and statistics that provide a current snapshot of online social experience. Finally, we learned about the structure of this book and its approach to netnography.

KEY READINGS

Amit, Vered and Nigel Rapport (2002) *The Trouble with Community: Anthropological Reflections on Movement, Identity and Collectivity*. London: Pluto.

Duggan, Maeve and Aaron Smith (2013) 'Social Media Update 2013', Pew Internet & American Life Project, 30 December. Available at: http://www.pewinternet. org/2013/12/30/social-media-update-2013/ (accessed 15 October 2014).

Wesch, Michael (2009) 'YouTube and you: Experience of self-awareness in the context collapse of the recording webcams', *Explorations in Media Ecology*, 8(2): 19–34.

NOTES

1. In the first chapter of the last edition of the book, which I wrote in early 2009, I thought I might be overstating when I wrote that there are at least 100 million, and perhaps as many as a billion people around the world who participate in online communities as a regular, ongoing part of their social experience. Currently there is no doubt that social media touches numbers far greater than this through ubiquitous mobile technologies. At last count, there were 6.9 billion mobile phone subscriptions worldwide for a world population of 7.1 billion people. These subscriptions potentially connect billions to the Internet and social media sites. I feel more assured that I am not hyperbolizing this time when I write that, although currently not quite there, social media has the near-term potential to be ubiquitous.

2. I herein formally acknowledge important and useful books such as Hine's (2000) *Virtual Ethnography*, Boellerstorff et al.'s (2012) *Ethnography and Virtual Worlds*, Horst and Miller's (2012) *Digital Anthropology* and Underberg and Zorn's (2013) *Digital Ethnography*. In fact, all of these books have usefully influenced and guided my own thinking about netnography. My statement is intended to point out that, although these books may offer theoretical overviews, general advice, examples and case studies, they tend to be focused on particular field sites (e.g., virtual worlds, such as Second Life), or particular approaches (e.g., eliciting and collecting online storytelling narratives). They are examples of different forms or sites of netnography. With this edition, new practices like introspection and personal academic branding exercises are intended to clearly differentiate the method from all other approaches to online or digital ethnography.

   Netnography remains a pragmatic and workbench-level explication of an approach, and as it branches out and extends far beyond what physical ethnography could ever do, it also maintains a strong connection with the anthropological and sociological ethnographic past. With this edition, I also hope that it benefits from increasing conceptual sophistication and cross-disciplinarity.

3. Some scholars have suggested adaptations, for instance, of netnography's ethical standards. Others have opted to use those adaptations, and cited the adaptive work. I present as many diverse viewpoints as I can in this book, while still oh-so-gently suggesting particular standards and practices as netnography, or, more accurately, as 'appropriately netnographic'.

4. We have barely begun to count television screen and videogame consoles, although clearly they must at some point be included.

5. NSA surveillance is empowered by the fact that so much data flows through the Internet. Also, because the American intelligence agencies were able to collaborate so closely with so many social media companies, such as Facebook, Apple, Skype, Microsoft and Google, there should be little doubt that surveillance by state intelligence agencies is both widespread and global. We can and should get into debates about whether this is a good or a bad thing, as we are a free society facing many security challenges and Internet surveillance is a key matter pertaining to both our safety and our freedom. We should always listen to both sides, but proceed as true social scientists with evidence and with viable, peer-reviewed research. The Internet is a far more effective and insidious surveillance tool than even George Orwell's hideous telescreens: we should know as much as we can about this side of it as well as the side that advances our knowledge and reveals our humanity.

6. Yet I find it interesting to note that Saudi Arabia also has the most avid YouTube users, with 90 million views of the online video channel per day.

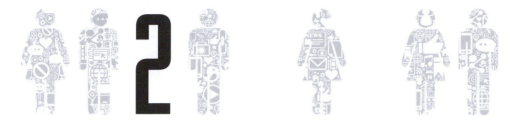

2

NETWORKED SOCIALITY

TECHNOCULTURE

Almost four decades before Facebook and Twitter, the Canadian media theorist Marshall McLuhan predicted that the 'cool', participative and inclusive 'electric media' would 'retribalize' human society into a collectivist utopia (see, for example, McLuhan, 1970). McLuhan considered individualizing to be a negative societal trend, initiated by the rise of the phonetic alphabet, which we might consider an early social media invention. To McLuhan, privacy, nationalism and individualism were negative outcomes of various technologies that would eventually become things of the past. Electronic retribalization would rectify these problems, as lone and isolated human beings would become part of a vast collectivity that synchronized their minds and nervous systems through integrative interactive technologies.

Throughout history and into the present, many seers and theorists have predicted this technologically mediated 'coming together'. These predictions often have a mystical iridescence to them that connects them to thinkers such as Catholic philosopher-priest Tielhard de Chardin whose quote opens the former chapter. Predictions abound that intermingle utopia, apocalypse and the Godlike achievement of a world consciousness Supermind.[1] 'For Tielhard ... technologies are not simply human tools, but vessels of the expanding noosphere, the body and nervous system of a world consciousness striving to be' (Davis, 1998: 296). Kevin Kelly, Mark Pesce, Jennifer Cobb Kreisberg and Pierre Lévy are but a few of the influential contemporary scholars and writers adopting this notion that technology will assist human evolution towards some sort of a positively utopian collective mind. Are the dense, in-the-moment interconnections of our mobile phones, Twitter and Facebook mutating our species into a de-individualized collective? Are social media inexorably transmuting us into a hivespecies?

Reading the work of these authors, we feel the leaden gravity of their technological determinism, the impression that technology is acting to shape our evolution as a species. However, this is certainly not the only framing we can place on the rise of Internet technology to its near-ubiquitous current status. Other scholars have assumed a technocultural view. At an early stage of the Internet's development, cultural theorists Constance Penley and Andrew Ross described a technocultural view as follows:

> Technologies are not repressively foisted upon passive populations, any more than the power to realize their repressive potential is in the hands of a conspiring few. They are developed at any one time and place in accord with a complex set of existing rules or rational procedures, institutional histories, technical possibilities, and, last, but not least, popular desires. (Penley and Ross, 1991: xiv)

The insight that technology does not determine human social behaviours, but that technologies and human beings are co-determining, co-constructive agents is a crucially important one to anthropologists who study science and technology. With our ideas and actions, we choose technologies, we adapt them, and we shape them, just as technologies alter our practices, behaviours, lifestyles and ways of being. As E. Gabriella Coleman (2010: 488) writes in her review of digital ethnographies in anthropology, wherever people communicate and deploy these technologies

> there will be circulations, reimaginings, magnifications, deletions, translations, revisionings, and remakings of a range of cultural representations, experiences, and identities, but the precise ways that these dynamics unfold can never be fully anticipated in advance.

Our actions cannot ever entirely control the technologies that we use. There are always unintended side effects (such as global warming resulting from mass global industrialization). The way that technology and human cultures interact is a complex dance, an interweaving and intertwining of actants.

Technologies of every type constantly shape and reshape our bodies, our places, our institutions and our social identities. Simultaneously, technologies are endlessly shaped to our needs. Understanding this transformative interconnection makes us accountable for particular and general contexts – specific times and places, distinctive rules or rational procedures, institutional histories, technical possibilities, practical and popular uses, as well as fears, hope, ambitions, ideologies and dreams. A thorough understanding of these concepts requires ethnography of both online and technology-enabled physical spaces, such as homes and workplaces, and even human bodies in interaction and motion. Fields including anthropology, sociology, education, communications, health and addiction, food studies, media studies, management, geography and sexuality research have begun to use netnography to study and unpack the rich significance of new, technologically mediated social behaviours as they are presented through online communication.

For anthropologists, there is a growing corpus of 'ethnographic approaches to digital media' scholarship that Coleman (2010) divides into broad and overlapping categories. Considering ethnographies of 'digital media' to include ethnographies related to 'a wide range of nonanalog technologies, including cell phones, the Internet, and software applications ...', Coleman (2010: 488) surveys the following three areas:

1. Cultural Politics: ethnographies concerning 'how cultural identities, representations, and imaginaries' are 'remade, subverted, communicated and circulated through individual and collective engagement with digital technologies.' Included in this category are 'digital ontologies' that look at a cultural group's digital productions as a map of their 'overall structure of priorities and issues' (Srinivasan, 2006: 510); examinations of how online social experiences relate with topics of identity, ethnicity and race (e.g., Nakamura, 2007); studies of the digital divide (e.g., Ito et al., 2005); and studies about how technologies such as smartphones help to extend sociality and kin networks (Horst and Miller, 2006).
2. Vernacular Cultures: ethnographies examining different phenomena, genres, and groups 'whose logic is organized significantly around, although not necessarily determined by, selected properties of digital media'. Included in this category are ethnographies of software hackers and developers (e.g., Coleman, 2009), digital activism (e.g., Sreberny and Khiabany, 2010), government surveillance (e.g., Morozov, 2009), 'informational capitalism' involving technology workers (e.g., Biao, 2007) and technology's toxic aftereffects (e.g., Maxwell and Miller, 2008), as well as linkages between digital media and language, ideologies, change, informality, virtuosity, revitalization, play and morality (e.g., Jones and Schieffelin, 2009).
3. Prosaics: ethnographies which look at 'how digital media feed into, reflect, and shape other kinds of social practices' and in so doing illuminate 'how the use and production of digital media have become integrated into everyday cultural, linguistic, and economic life'. This category uncovers people's lived experiences with digital media; the conditions under which they are made, altered and deployed; their genres; and their material and ideological functioning. For example, it includes studies of digital journalists (Boyer, 2010), digital piracy (e.g., Larkin, 2008), digital media influences on perception and awareness (e.g., Wesch, 2009), affect and addiction (e.g., Chan, 2008), how various places and spaces sustain virtual technologies and spaces (e.g., Fuller and Narasimhan, 2007), and how digital technologies magnify the speed, spread and exploitation potential of contemporary capitalism around the world (e.g., Schull, 2010).

Considered as a body of work, these studies cover a wide swath of contemporary human engagement with technology. Although some of this work is recognizably netnographic, such as Daniels' (2009) study of racism online, much of it expands the scope of investigation to consider human experiences with technology as broadly as possible. Online and offline engagements with the gamut of digital media have become their focal point. Netnography, as we shall discuss in upcoming chapters, is different from digital anthropology in that it has as its core the analysis of data collected through participant-observation over the Internet, including the use of laptops, tablets, mobile communication devices and their various applications. However, netnographic investigations should engage with the relevant findings of digital anthropology in order to strengthen our comprehension of the larger networks in which all online social experiences are embedded. This chapter seeks to open and broaden netnography's focus, while also overviewing and providing essential theoretical background to serve as its base.

Media Have Never Not Been Social

Researchers have been curious and interested in the effect of technological mediation on communications since the radically disruptive introduction of the telegraph and, later, the telephone. So, almost from the beginning of the Internet in the early 1970s, scholars had been studying its effects on social relations in various ways. Alongside the important and insightful observational work of Hiltz and Turoff (1978), early work on online social interaction was based on social psychological theory and experimental tests. This was early media theory: it studied the medium and media of communication. Some of this work hypothesized that, considered as media, online media were too 'thin', or socialcue impoverished, to serve as a foundation for meaningful social activity (e.g., Daft and Lengel, 1986). Because textual online social experiences originally missed the immediacy of voice inflection, accents, facial expressions, directions of gaze, gaze-meeting, posture, body language and movement, and touching, they were theorized to be less meaningful than face-to-face social experiences, and their relationships to be shallower and less satisfying (e.g., Dubrovsky et al., 1991; Short et al., 1976; Sproull and Kiesler, 1986; Walther, 1992, 1995).

The early Internet environment was viewed as a social environment with leery suspicion and cynicism. It was not a social place, but a context that created task-oriented, 'impersonal', 'inflammatory', 'cold' and 'unsociable' interactions (Kiesler et al., 1984, 1985; Rice and Rogers, 1984; Rice and Love, 1987; Sproull and Kiesler, 1986; Walther, 1992: 58–9). When these suppositions were tested in laboratories or in workplaces under highly controlled scientific conditions – contexts that also may have helped spawn a task-oriented and coldly unsociable environment for social interactions – they were borne out to levels of statistical significance.

Related to this was another set of theories that posited a 'status equalization effect'. Hierarchy was the name of this game. How, they asked, could authority be maintained in the anonymous and chaotic social space of online communication? It was hypothesized that if you could not tell your boss or your boss's boss from your underling then this, added to technologically induced anonymity, would result in a reduction of social differences. Across the barriers of class, gender and age, people would simply communicate in an uninhibited way without the need to dominate. People would also be more individualistic, more self-absorbed and narcissistic – favouring a culture of me, myself and I (Dubrovsky et al., 1991; Sproull and Kiesler, 1986). Many of these behaviours were already observable in online interactions, such as 'flaming', or insults, petty discursive wars with rude, crude, hostile, aggressive and outright cruel language as well as the use of profanities. WTF? Scientists came to the world of online social interaction with ideas that technology-based interactions undermined, even subverted, the existing social structure.

And this may be where Victor Turner's notion of communitas comes in. For Turner believed, in common with many of the other anthropologists we have already discussed in these pages, that there was something to be gained by distancing his terminology from the more popular term 'community'; he expressly rejected its connotation as a geographical proximity 'area of common living' (Turner, 1969: 96). Instead communitas is a deeply human connection. Communitas is 'an essential and generic human bond, without which there would be no society' (Turner, 1969: 97). Communitas is a sense of being equal with your comrades, having kin, being a member of a group, and also an internalized sense of membership as connection, a way to fulfil needs for belonging, affiliation, acceptance and love. Turner saw communitas as linked with liminality, with the grey nether regions that lay inbetween social positions in a rite of passage, as a force of anti-structure, disorder, disruption and chaos. These transformative forces become absorbed by, or at least alternate with, forces of social order, of structure, of the 'hierarchical system of politico-legal-economic positions' (Turner, 1969: 96), worlds of authority, elders, rules, laws, traditions, values, shamings, feeling inferior, status, feeling superior, punishments, conditioning, enforcement and sometimes brutal acts of 'religious' 'education'. This is communitas and hierarchy, structure and anti-structure, chaos and order, played out on a human cultural scale.

Keep Turner's ideas in mind. For as soon as work emerged which empirically examined how people were actually using technologies, these early but no less social media (and is there ever a time when media had not been social?), we found that people were able to 'develop an ability to express missing nonverbal cues in written form' (Rice and Love, 1987: 89). Symbols, emoticons, avatars, moving gif files, intentional misspellings, corrections and capitalization – all are examples of the successful human struggle to overcome the limitations of allegedly 'thin' media (Danet, 2001; Sherblom, 1988: 44; Walther, 1992, 1995). So the lived world of people, when we peered into it using data from early Internet users, rather than simulated users in a lab, began to demonstrate the emergence of personally enriching social worlds well before the clever avatars of Second Life, the photo albums of Facebook, and the detailed professional profile pages of LinkedIn. 'The characterizations of CMC [computer-mediated communications] born from experiments on groups seem contradictory to the findings of CMC in field studies' concluded Walther (1992: 53). For the most part, social cues and thin media did not hold up outside of one-off experiments in the lab. The reality of online social experience was not thin, but thick. It was social, long-term, long tail, complex, processual and evolving. It showed human beings adopting to technological limitations in their social experience, and developing adaptations that enhanced it, sometimes in novel ways.

Initial concerns that Internet use might corrode groups, families and community life are asserted and contradicted in pendulum fashion, with significant minorities holding, in surveys, that this is true for them (Fox and Rainie, 2014). On the other hand, surveys as early as the year 2000 – the Dark Ages before blogging and social media as we know it – revealed that people believed the Internet enabled them to keep in touch more effectively with their friends and family, and even to extend their social networks. The fact that people positively viewed email, bulletin boards, and the few other affordances of the age validates the immense value simply of the power to connect with others and share communications with them, even if it was primarily written text. Communitas. We hunger for it. We strive for it. We flock to it.[2]

We value social capital as well. As a result of their study of the impact of online communities on social capital and involvement in local communities, Kavanaugh and Patterson (2001: 507) suggested that 'the longer people are on the Internet, the more likely they are to use the Internet to engage in social-capital-building activities'. We can see some of these larger social capital building processes highlighted in more focused studies of smaller communities. Valenzuela and colleagues (2009) surveyed over 2600 Texan students and found significant, positive, but relatively small relationships between their Facebook use and their life satisfaction, social trust, civic engagement and political participation. Mathwick and colleagues (2008) studied a software forum's peer-to-peer problem-solving community and found norms of voluntarism, reciprocity and social trust underlying the community's employment of social capital. Working in a German venture capital context, Vasileiadou and Missler-Behr (2011) find different forms of social and relational capital being effectively deployed in a variety of virtual social interactions. Although their findings suggest small positive correlations between social capital and social media use, Valenzuela et al. (2009) warn us that social networks are not panaceas for the generational disengagement from civic duty decried by Robert Putnam (2000) among others. Yet, somehow, viewed over time and combined with survey results, the weight of evidence seems to tip us towards the notion that people's social lives are enhanced by online contact more than they are diminished.

Ethnographic and naturalistic observations of people's interweaving of Internet communications with their social behaviours have been critically important to our accurate understanding. Examining how people actually deploy communications technologies in their own social worlds over the long term, as they increasingly use them to spin webs that meaningfully interconnect, turns out to be quite different from what people were doing in short-term situations with the technologies in laboratory situations. Like large stones dropped into lake water, when information and communications technology is cast into the world, it ripples outward, manifests in many ways, begetting different forms of sociality that continue to spread outwards in their influence. There are definite patternings in these forms. Effective netnography contains theory that is aware of these subtle and complex arrangements. We now continue to discuss additional arrangements and configurations in this world of online sociality.

SOCIAL MEDIA BETWEEN THE COMMUNAL AND THE COMMERCIAL

Burning Man is a countercultural grassroots happening that grew out of the Cacophany Society in San Francisco, California, becoming first a happening and then an internationally recognized super-event. In the early days of the Burning Man Project, as it is often called by its organizers, event co-founder Larry Harvey used to compare the event to the Internet. The comparison evokes the social media and pre-corporate colonization-like aspects of the early Internet. Like the Internet, Burning Man consists of many individual, decentralized parties. Like the Internet, Burning Man is uncensored and authentic. Like the Internet, Burning Man is hyper-textual and intertextual – it connects to many other things: art, design, science, high technology, spirituality, dance, primitivism, utopianism, polytheism, polyamory, Marxism, the survivalist movement, and almost any other social group or gathering containing a whiff of social movement about it. Like Burning Man, the motivation for social media participation can often include interest in social change enacted through involvement in major collective projects. And through this involvement, participants in both worlds hope to learn from and commune with an interesting diverse group of other people who are currently unknown to them, but who come in a similar spirit of giving. Communitas. We hunger for it, online and deep down in our bodies. We go out in the desert looking for it.

A great sacred quality somehow seems to descend in the miraculously commonplace selfless acts occurring during Burning Man, such as the first moment someone you have never seen before, someone costumed up like a weird clown just for fun to make you smile, runs up to you while you are parched and dry in the 107 degree Black Rock desert heat and hands you a cool blue popsicle. The process channels ancient and sacred communitas, almost as a palpable force. Yet we might wonder if acts of communitas may be the hardest to transfer over to Internet exchanges.

'Abstractions appear as hostile to live contact' wrote Victor Turner in *The Ritual Process* (Turner, 1969: 141). The person who would try to do good to another person 'must do it in Minute Particulars; General Good is the plea of the Hypocrite and the

Scoundrel' said William Blake (Maclagan and Russell, 1907). It may be that some physical quality inheres in direct, embodied, human contact that we do not want to surrender, for to abdicate this 'immediatism', as Sufi philosopher Hakim Bey (1994) calls it, this embodiment of human being as contact between co-located human bodies, is to abandon something vital and essential about our humanness. Perhaps, also, there is some quality immanent in the gift itself. It may be that communitas inheres in the generous and selfless act of sharing, whether online or in person. Perhaps it is the gift which breaks us out of the confining and isolating bonds of individuality and selfishness that we tend to associate with modern society and its capitalist marketplaces. Perhaps the gift frees us to emerge into the wider world of creativity and contribution that we still link with communal and social ideals.

The futurist Marina Gorbis sees exactly the same sort of tension between the social and the commercial enacted in the world of social media. She envisions a future that she calls the 'socialstructured' world 'as a way to build a better future by de-institutionalizing production, infusing social ties and human connectedness into our economic life, [and] in the process redefining established paradigms of work, productivity, and value' (Gorbis, 2013: 208). She draws upon a long tradition of theorists, from Ferdinand Tonnies to Lewis Hyde, who have separated the social logics of belonging, togetherness and sharing from those of marketplaces and transactions.

> Although most scholars recognize communities as extremely diverse, a certain type of community has often been held up as an ideal. This communal ideal can be characterized as a group of people living in close proximity with mutual social relations characterized by caring and sharing. Tönnies ([1887] 1957) evoked this ideal in his notion of 'Gemeinschaft,' ... The origin of this caring, sharing communal ideal is in the deep trust and interdependence of family relations. Markets are different. The ideal market is seen as more of what Tönnies (1957) termed a 'Gesellschaft' type of phenomenon; it provides more formal, contractual, socially distanced relations. These relations are transactions-based and occur for the purpose of exchange (Weber [1922] 1978; Williamson 1975). In market transactions, the object is to increase one's advantage, to get more than one gives. To simplify the contrast, ideal communities are about caring about and sharing with insiders while ideal markets are about transacting with outsiders. Although both involve power relations and although they are interrelated or embedded in one another (see, e.g., Biggart 1989; Frenzen and Davis 1990; Granovetter 1985), marketplace exchanges focus more than communal exchanges on monetizing the exchange value of goods and services, and extracting excess value, or profits, from transactions. Throughout human history, markets have generally been constrained to particular places, times, and roles, and largely kept conceptually distinct from other important social institutions, such as home and family. With the rise of industrialization and postindustrialization, however, the influence of the market has increasingly encroached upon times, spaces, and roles previously reserved for communal relations. As the self-interested logics of the market have filtered into communal relations, they have been accused of increasingly undermining the realization of the caring, sharing, communal ideal. (Kozinets, 2002b: 21–22)

Along with a number of other scholars, Gorbis (2013: 3–6) believes that social media are creating a new kind of network or relationship-driven economy, where individuals join forces in order to create and share knowledge, services and even products that existing institutions such as corporations, governments and educational establishments are unable or unwilling to provide. According to Gorbis, these technologies are helping individuals create groupings around interests, identities and shared personal challenges. Socialstructuring is a process of moving away from the depersonalized world of 'institutional production' – Big Business, Big Government, and Big Education – into a new economy of social connection and social rewards (ibid.: 3). She sees the new social media technologies as enabling people to coexist simultaneously in both market and social economies and links this idea to philosopher Lewis Hyde's notion of 'the Commerce of the Creative Spirit' (ibid.: 202–203).

In *The Gift*, Hyde (1979) recounts how the inspiration of the artist is widely perceived to be a gift. For inspiration to be maintained, the artist feels the desire, the need, and even the compulsion to make the work and then offer it to an audience at little or no profit: 'The gift must stay in motion ... So long as the gift is not withheld, the creative spirit will remain a stranger to the economics of scarcity ... [whether it is] salmon, forest birds, poetry, symphonies, or Kula shells ... to bestow one of our creations is the surest way to invoke the next' (ibid,: 146). Hyde counsels us to give our gifts away, and perpetuate the magic circle of community. Yet, although all cultures and all artists have felt the tension between the moral economy of gift exchange and the transactional pressures of the marketplace, there have been some unique aspects to modern capitalism. Hyde finds, for instance, the exploitation of the arts in modern capitalism to be 'without precedent' and their 'high finance' approach to create a commodification that diminishes creativity and turns arts into industry (ibid.: 158).

Drawing on Hyde's work, media scholars and theorists Henry Jenkins, Sam Ford, and Josh Green also link their ideas about media creation to British historian E.P. Thompson's (1971) notion of the 'moral economy'. Their book, *Spreadable Media* (Jenkins et al., 2013), sensitively and adroitly traces the many complications arising from corporate, group, and individual negotiation of the hybrid gift-commercial space of social media. They chastise those who rhetorically embrace an 'architecture of participation' online. This stance can naively gloss over the conflict, choices and compromises that are often required of participants. Zwick et al. (2008), as well as Cova and Dalli (2009) provide critical views of the social media economy of free and exploited labour, casting them as a political form of Foucauldian govern-mentality, a self-disciplinarily fueled pathway to creating docile, duped and compliantly creative consumers (see also Andrew Keen's 2007 *The Cult of the Amateur*). Wise from their long engagement with media fan communities, Jenkins et al. (2013: 55) certainly do not go this far. They do, however, caution that 'it's crucial not to diminish the many noncommercial logics governing the engaged participation of audiences online' (Jenkins et al., 2013: 55).

Their advice is more about how not to kill, and how to resist theorizing the premature death of, the collective geese that keep laying social media's golden eggs.

In netnographic research my co-authors and I conducted on how word of mouth marketing was spread by bloggers in a mobile phone giveaway campaign, we identified in the patterns of blogger narratives the clear presence of a similar type of communal-commercial tension (Kozinets et al., 2010). In such social media-based marketing 'the consumer is required to be a type of consumer–marketer hybrid [and thus] the traditional social contract that maintains marketplace relationships at a distance from communities is violated, creating great tension' (2010: 83). This tension remains dormant in some contexts, but blooms into explicitness in other. A process of translation occurs as a result of the tension. Marketing messages are altered to become more believable, relevant and palatable to the particular group. As the marketplace interrupted the social experiences of social media users, participants felt compelled to translate and transform 'persuasion oriented, market-generated, sales objective-oriented "hype" [into] relevant, useful, communally desirable social information that builds individual reputations and group relationships' (ibid.).

A precautionary note is sounded by Campbell (2005) in his examination of lesbian, gay, bisexual and transsexual (LGBT) online communities. He depicts gay Internet portals openly courting the gay community online with promises of inclusion and an authentic communal experience. However, they also simultaneously reposition gays and lesbians in a commercial panopticon that places them under corporate surveillance. He wonders if 'all commercial portals purporting to serve politically marginalized groups beg the question of whether there can be a harmonious balance between the interests of community and the drives of commerce' (2005: 678; see also Campbell, 2004; Campbell and Carlson, 2002). These are central themes, of import to our understanding as corporate actors like the publicly traded Facebook, LinkedIn and Twitter corporations' attempts to further their own interests by increasingly influencing and monetizing people's online social experiences.

On the other hand, Jenkins et al. (2013) describe the many ways that DIY and fan labour is self aware, taking pleasure, gaining capital and esteem and finding many sources of value from the economic outputs that they are contributing towards in social media. Seeing such labour as 'engaged' and even gift-like rather that exploited recognizes that participants 'are pursuing their own interests, connected to and informed by those decisions made by others within their social networks' (Jenkins et al., 2013: 60). Scholars who continue to see the media participant, including the 'engaged' and creative social media participant, as a passive or exploited dupe must confront the evidence that, at least for some people and in some circumstances, such participation provides a panoply of benefits, although these benefits may not include the strictly economic exchanges of the market economy.

Gorbis sees social media as the antidote, the bridge between the two worlds of the social and the commercial. Indeed, Gorbis' ideas are very closely related to those of Yochai Benkler, Henry Jenkins and Manuel Castells, although she fails to cite any of them. Harvard University law professor Benkler (2006: 117) for instance finds that 'sharing is everywhere in the advanced economies' and that studies on social capital, trust and the social provisioning of public goods 'point to an emerging understanding of social production and exchange as an alternative to markets and firms'. As examples, he gives SETI and Slashdot. Benkler's conclusion is optimistic, arguing that the new network economy of social media provides us with an opportunity to alter the way that 'we create and exchange information, knowledge, a culture. By doing so, we can make the twenty-first century one that offers individuals greater autonomy, political communities greater democracy, and societies greater opportunities for cultural self-reflection and human connection … [possibly resulting in] a true transformation toward more liberal and egalitarian societies' (Benkler, 2006: 473).

We can postulate a world where the Maker Movement, The Internet of Things and the proliferation of Artificial Intelligence, robots and bots take over much of industrial production and traditional work, and enormous economies of scope and scale enable massive amounts of things and services to be produced and provisioned by only a few people. The economics of the gathering, the Wikinomics that Don Tapscott and colleagues research and write about (e.g., Moffitt and Dover, 2011; Tapscott and Williams, 2007), also lead to greater and greater efficiencies of scale, and the scope of Chris Anderson's (2008) 'long tail' economies provides more diversity in the marketplace than ever before. Thus, as Gorbis, Hyde, Benkler and these other authors advance, we may increasingly need to turn our collective attention to questions of how the commerce of the Creative Spirit will play out for us in science, government, media, education, arts, health, tourism, consumption, or any other social domain.

VARIETIES OF ONLINE SOCIAL EXPERIENCE

We can conceptualize different types of online social experience partially by relating them to the type of site in which we find them. For instance, we might expect a social networking site such as Facebook to provide a different type of online social experience than that of a forum like 4Chan, a blog like Mashable, a tagging service like Reddit, or a fan wiki like *The Big Bang Theory*. In the last edition of this book, and based upon earlier work (Kozinets, 1998, 1999), I theorized a more functional 'ideal type' typology of different forms of online sociality, which I now revise and update as represented in Figure 2.1.

This updated typology presumes that the nature of online social relations varies from the intensely personal and deeply meaningful – i.e., Gemeinschaft-like caring and sharing communal forms – to those that are quite superficial, short-lasting and relatively insignificant – and more Gessellschaft, market-and-transaction oriented exchange. They can also vary from those that are oriented strictly around a

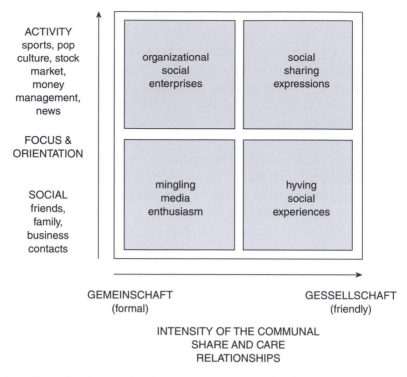

ACTIVITY
sports, pop
culture, stock
market,
money
management,
news

FOCUS &
ORIENTATION

SOCIAL
friends,
family,
business
contacts

organizational
social
enterprises

social
sharing
expressions

mingling
media
enthusiasm

hyving
social
experiences

GEMEINSCHAFT
(formal)

GESSELLSCHAFT
(friendly)

INTENSITY OF THE COMMUNAL
SHARE AND CARE
RELATIONSHIPS

Figure 2.1   Four ideal types of online social experience in sites

particular activity, such as hydroponic tomato cultivation or discussing *America's Got Talent*, or a location or destination, such as TripAdvisor, to those in which a unifying activity or interest is often completely irrelevant, such as on Facebook.

Although there seems to be a correlation between the type of online site and the type of online social experience (for example, Facebook providing predominantly interpersonal rather than activity-based experiences), there is by no means a perfect correlation. Any site, or type of site, can be used for any purpose. These purposes and exchanges may vary over time even with the same individuals on the same online site. Rather than to suggest any sort of simplistic determinism, when we have found so much evidence to the contrary of such principles, the intention of the classification is to draw the netnographer's attention to the type of social experience rather than to propose any technologically overdetermining structural effects of a site, app, or software form on social actors' agency. The four proposed ideal types of online social experience are mingling, bonding, sharing and organizing. I explain each type of experience in turn.

An experience that one has online in interaction, information reception, or exchange that are socially weaker or only for business or necessity, such as the proverbial person–clerk interaction at a retail checkout counter, might be known as a *mingling media enthusiasm*. Twitter experiences can often be like this, and

Facebook or LinkedIn is like this when we meet new people or have the opportunity to find or otherwise electronically experience other people. Particular virtual worlds, chat-rooms, and certain gamespaces provide this mingling social experience. They tend to satisfy people's relatively superficial, short-lived and weak tie 'relational' and 'recreational' need; they are consocial more than communal experiences.

Online social experiences that can create strong social ties between members, resulting in more meaningful or longer-lasting relationships, but where the participants are not firmly or lastingly focused on a shared or unifying focal activity, purpose, project or interest, might be termed *hyving social experiences*. Social networking sites such as Facebook, dating sites like OKCupid, communications apps like WhatsApp or Tinder, and virtual worlds like Second Life can often provide this type of online social experience and fulfil their members' relational needs.

A third type of online social experience is online interaction for the express purpose of sharing targeted information, news, stories, images, photos, jokes, expertise, information and techniques about some particular activity or interest which is the raison d'être of the interaction. These are *sharing social expressions*. Many blogs like TMZ or the Huffington Post, wikis such as Wikia or Wiktionary, newsgroups such as alt.coffee, website forums, social content rating and tagging services like Digg or Reddit, photo and video-sharing communities like Instagram, Vine or YouTube would all be loci of such sharings. They offer participants and readers a bank of shared content, but not necessarily the promise of a deep engagement in social relationships. The modes of interaction on these communities are predominantly consocial and friendly, consisting of broadcast-to-person, shared, rebroadcast or peer-to-peer based exchanges of content and information.

Finally, we have online social experiences that offer a chance to create social ties between people as well as focusing on sharing information and intelligence about some central, unifying interest, project, theme or activity. These experiences I term *organizational social enterprises*. Although blogs, wikis, Social networking sites (SNS) interest groups and other forms of online gatherings certainly can and often are used as *organizational social enterprises*, I have seen many more of these experiences grow from microblogs such as Twitter, meeting sites such as Meetup.com or the group function of sites such as LinkedIn, website forums, evolved zines such as Boing Boing, user-based creative communities such as devoted websites and projects such as *Star Trek Phase II* (see Kozinets, 2007). A good example is provided by open source software experience in all of its various manifestations, such as slashdot (Hemetsberger and Reinhardt, 2006). The mode of interaction in these gatherings is supportive, informational, content-based and also can be relational. Our understanding of these different social types can now be enhanced by a deeper understanding of the types of social structures that pervade the Internet.

Analysing Social Network Structures

An interesting and useful technique to incorporate into netnography for understanding these types of social relations is social network analysis. It is neither necessary nor would it be desirable for all netnographers to adopt social network analysis techniques in their studies. However, netnographers would be wise to familiarize themselves, at least on a basic level, with social network analysis techniques, procedures and general research findings. This is especially important for the many scholars who are conducting what I will, in later chapters, refer to as Digital Netnographies. Although we will overview the technique in more detail in the next chapter, a fundamental understanding of the technique is useful for understanding some of the concepts and theory that this chapter will proceed to present.[3]

Social network analysis is an analytical method that focuses on the structures and patterns of relationships between and among social actors in a network (Berkowitz, 1982; Wellman, 1988). In social network analysis, there are two main units of analysis. The social actors we are interested in are called the 'nodes' and the relation between them is called the 'tie'. A network is composed of a set of actors connected by a set of relational ties. The actors can be persons, teams, organizations, technologies, non-human actors like bots, ideas, messages, products, cities or other concepts. Examples of ties would include sharing information, an economic transaction, transfer of resources, shared associations or affiliations, sexual relations, physical connections, sharing ideas or values, and so on (Wasserman and Faust, 1994). A group of people who are connected by particular social relationships, such as family kinship, friendship, working together, a shared hobby or common interest, or exchanging any sort of information, can be considered to be a social network.

Social network analysis has its foundations in sociology, sociometrics and graph theory, and in the structural–functionalist line of 'Manchester anthropologists, who built on both of these strands to investigate the structure of "community" relations in tribal and village societies' (Scott, 1991: 7). Social network analysis thus deals in relational data and, although it is possible to quantify and statistically analyse these relations, network analysis also 'consists of a body of qualitative measures of network structure' (Scott, 1991: 3). There is, thus, a very natural relationship between a structural approach to ethnography, or netnography, and the approach of social network analysis.

Over the last 35 years, the social network analysis approach to research has grown rapidly in sociology and communication studies, and has spread to a range of other fields.

Social networking analysts seek to describe networks of relations as fully as possible, tease out the prominent patterns in such networks, trace the flow of information (and other resources) through them, and discover what effects these relations and networks have on people and organizations. (Garton et al., 1999: 75)

Social network analysis is structural. Its unit of analysis is the relationship, and what it finds interesting in relationships are their patterns. There is, therefore, considerable overlap with certain kinds of netnography, which can be focused upon relationships and the structured patterns of exchanges of things like language, symbols, discourse, values, power, and other symbolic and material resources. Social network analysts consider the various resources that are exchanged in communications between people online, and these can include communications which are textual, graphical, animated, audio, photographic or audiovisual, and can comprise sharing information, discussing work-related rumours, sharing advice, giving emotional support or providing companionship (Haythornthwaite et al., 1995). Netnographers also consider those resources, viewing them in and from various and overlapping contexts, which might include as multiple and shared sources of significance and also as bearers of interpersonal connection.

There are many opportunities for synergies between the structural analysis of social networks and the more identity-, story-, discourse- and meaning-centred analyses of netnography. Consider as a nuancing adjunct to the mingling, bonding, sharing and organizing functional types of online social experience, the following ways to think about the social structures present within the social media forms that netnographers aim to understand and explain. We consider several important and influential ideal types of online social experiences in the following section.

SOCIAL UNIVERSES AND NETWORK ARCHETYPES

There are many ways to conceptualize the universe of social media forms in order to gain a basic view of the variegated types of connection that people have with one another online. Two essential and interrelated ways that people connect with one another are socially and through topics. In social network-based research that analysed the maps of thousands of different Twitter conversations and their related social exchange patterns, a 2014 Pew Internet report identifies six archetypal forms of network structure that emerged from the way people shared topics and messages with one another: polarized crowds, tight crowds, brand clusters, community clusters, broadcast networks and support networks (Smith et al., 2014). These six distinctive structures are not intended to be exhaustive. However, they inform us about some of the various forms that online sociality can take, depending upon the topic of the conversation, the type of the connections between individual actors in the network, the information sources and other resources (for communication also leads to access) that are used, the precise kinds of computer, corporate, transactional and social networks that are involved, the leaders of the conversation, and the structure of the conversation.

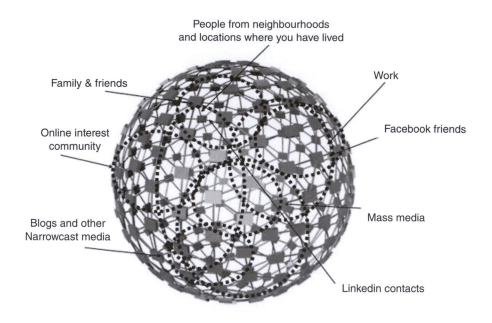

People from neighbourhoods
and locations where you have lived

Work

Family & friends

Facebook friends

Online interest
community

Blogs and other
Narrowcast media

Mass media

Linkedin contacts

Figure 2.2   Your personal social network core

In Figure 2.2, I use these structures to think about the way that individuals can connect with one other. The centre of Figure 2.2 is a particular individual's online social network, which links them socially to friends, family and co-workers, many of whom they already know personally, but also more distantly to organizations and interest groups who they may not know in person.

Relationships in these communities can assume different structures and shapes depending upon the nature of these conversations and their different social experiences. These experiences vary in their social and consocial characteristics. They can be unified, fragmented, divided, polarized or clustered in their dispersion and arrangement, as we visualize them. The network becomes its visualization, and the visualization of networks can quickly be acted out on the human social stage, when that stage is online.

Two are highly centralized, appearing with hub and spoke lines. In the first, the lines go inwards, towards the broadcaster, for this is an audience model. It is the structure that people assume when they are audiencing something. They do it in groups, in couples and individually. Each is qualitatively different, of course, and requires a human interpretation, but they are also all an audience. They are all sharing information they see on the screen, treated with the voyeur's gaze, the screen gaze that my co authors and I (Kozinets et al., 2004) saw in ESPN Zone in retail themed Mag Mile Chicago circa 2002. Online, think of a powerful broadcast network like BBC World News. It has influence because it is being linked to by many individuals and groups, and then shared among them. They comment on it in Twitter. Some have a lot of person-to-person interaction, and others do not. People can have many types of social connections as well as topical connections, and at many times the two will interact. Twitter tends to simplify so that we can see the basic structures. In reality, with other media like Facebook, we will likely see more complex hybrid forms of audience and network structure.

Figure 2.3 is a riff upon Smith et al. (2014), a reconceptualization that alters names, labels and even definitions while seeking to portray some dimensionalization and classification. This Figure offers a typologization on the theoretical ideal level of the complexity and diversity of interaction in the online universe of social experience. We can look to connect to resources like information, service, material connections, cultural resources, styles and identities for our identity projects, props for our life roles, brands to show where we belong. When we look for resources we can either become an audience, or we can ask for help. These two are collectively expressed, for they are common between individuals; they are the Audience and Customer Support Network forms. The following points describe these six forms trapped in two dimensions in Figure 2.3.

Resource Connections: Audience and Customer Support Networks

Audience networks possess a distinctive structure based upon the re-broadcasting of major news and media organizational information. The Twitter network forms into an audience shape when it re-tweets breaking news stories and the output of well-known media outlets and pundits. Most members of the Broadcast Network audience are not really conducting conversations between one another, which is why their level of intercommunication is low. But some are gathering through their audiencing, there is no doubt of this either.

So they are more than a network, acting, instead, as conduits. They themselves become like information distributors, intermediaries who bring the fresh news from on high, and then distribute it to their immediate network, socially. Instead of everyone buying a newspaper, or a specialty newsletter, or the various information sources people used to use, or everyone watching television, these people act as conduits and value-adding media re-broadcast channels. They transfer, and probably sometimes translate, news and information from major media outlets to their own more immediate and localized ones. The cynosure of all ears and eyes is the retweeting re-broadcaster. Smaller subgroups of densely connected people – which Pew's people termed 'subject groupies' – hang out repeatedly holding conversations with one another about the news.

Audiences can be very disconnected from one another. They link only to the hub news source. Yet there are others, some who form discussion groups based on the news, some who do this regularly. So there is no true ideal form, there are only tendencies.

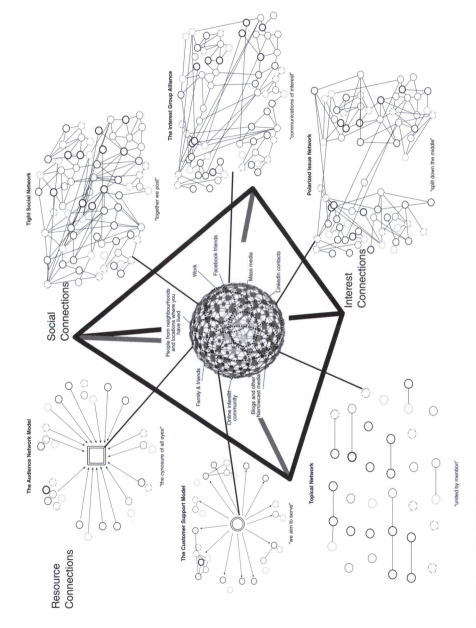

Tight Social Network

"together we post"

The Interest Group Alliance

"communications of interest"

Polarized Issue Network

"split down the middle"

Social
Connections

Interest
Connections

Work

Facebook friends

Mass media

People from neighbourhoods
and locations where you
have lived

LinkedIn contacts

Family & friends

Online interest
community

Blogs and other
Narrowcast media

The Audience Network Model

"the cynosure of all eyes"

Resource
Connections

The Customer Support Model

"we aim to serve"

Topical Network

"united by mention"

Figure 2.3   Social types of networks

And in this underdetermined tendency, the network assumes the shape we see in Figure 2.4. The one central account, the one information resource distributor, which is the agency like a popular YouTube blogger like Nardwuar, the BBC or CNN.com, becomes the hub, and the many spokes are audiences and individual audience members. They are all reaching in to contact Nardwuar, Bethany Mota, or whoever the resource is, and to then share it with their networks.

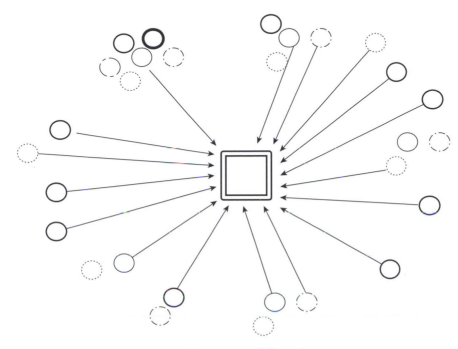

'the cynosure of all eyes'

Figure 2.4   The audience network model

Customer support networks are also surveillance networks, where one central agent monitors and responds to the transmissions of network members. Customer support networks are the product of so-called 'social care' customer service and support exchanges. In this case, it is the company calling the person. Hello, I overheard you complaining about my company. Is there something bothering you about my company that I can help you with? The shape that is assumed as customer complaints lodged against major businesses become handled by corporate customer service representatives is the one we see in Figure 2.5.

The contacts are outbound. The one hub connects outward to the individuals it is monitoring. This form becomes increasingly important as government, businesses, and other groups such as non-profits and NGOs try to provide centralized services and support through social media and also to reach out very close and

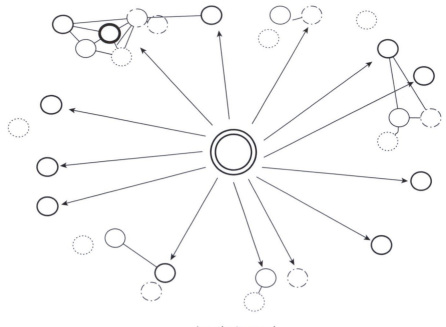

'we aim to serve'

Figure 2.5   The customer support (and consumer surveillance) network

learn as much as possible about people, since data is inexpensive and easy to sort, and acting on it for fundraising, sales and volunteer networks is important and fairly easy to do now with social media.

Connections of Interest: Topical and Polarized Issue Networks

Another important source of connection is the sharing of particular interests. If I do not know you, and you do not know me, but we both use the same hashtag #JohnOliverForPresident, then we share something. If we know each other only through some topic, and that topic is very polarized, a type of us-versus-them arrangement exists where your beliefs determine very quickly whether you will feel comfortable on one side of this issue rather than the other. These connections are both full of mutual interest, as we will explore in the following sections.

Topical network cluster is the shape assumed by a social network when a non-interactive type of conversation occurs about the same topic, conducted by many disconnected participants (see Figure 2.6). This is the form assumed when established products and services, such as Apple technology products, and media and sports celebrities are discussed on Twitter. Examples would include Tweets about things such as a goal in World Cup soccer, or the introduction of a new iPad by Apple. The larger was the population discussing such a topic, the less likely that

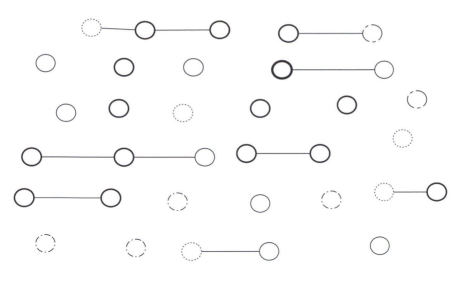

'united by mention'

Figure 2.6   Topical cluster network

the participants were connecting to one another. This form stands in stark contrast to Muniz and O'Guinn's (2001) theorized notion of the 'brand community' that brings people together through shared conversations about a brand. Instead, the participants in brand clusters broadcast information about a topic without really connecting in a communal way with one another. Often, this information is a simple re-broadcast (in this case a retweet) of corporate or institutional information, advertising or publicity. Unlike the participants in the tight or polarized crowd social form, they do not have much in the way of a continuing conversation with one another.

Polarized issue networks are connected, tight, and unified together; however, they are divided and partisan with one other large group (see Figure 2.7). They feature two large and densely interconnected groups that have little connection flowing between them. When topics were divisive and related to heated political subjects, such as European EU-led immigration policies, the social network assumed this form. As indicated by the slight interconnection between the groups, these groups do not argue directly with one another. Even though they are talking about the same topic, they ignore each other, like two large and independent continents, or they reference them mockingly, or mock their hashtags. Generally, they point to different web resources and use different hashtags. They build their own separate sets of resources. In the Pew study, liberal groups in the United States tended to link to mainstream media sources, while conservatives linked to a different set of resources. We could think about parallels among Facebook groups, blogs or websites.

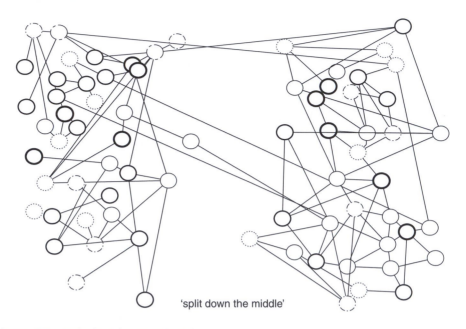

'split down the middle'

Figure 2.7 Polarized issue network

For example, conversations on the two-climate change websites ucsusa.com (the Union of Concerned Scientists) and skepticalscience.com also are likely to contain polarized crowds. The form is almost built into the Internet in some cases.

Social Connections: Tight Social Networks and Interest Group Alliances

Finally, we catch two of the most social of the social forms of online connection. When people want to interact with one another about something they all feel strongly about, then we can say that this is a tight network, with lots of interconnections, close and interlinked. Another way that this can happen, certainly not different or exclusive from tight social networks, but even possibly like a broadening out of that field, is that the group you are in is composed of people you know well, and that group is joined by others you don't know as well, and your group is linked to many other similar groups in many different locations which you do not even know. But you all share resources and you have opportunities to connect. We should be, in such cases, far more interested in the hierarchies and power-interest-resource access related structures of these arrangements. Rarely are they far from political and corporate interests and projects. Yet their emancipatory power, and enablement of activism and alternative ideologies is almost now without its sceptics.

Tight social networks are composed of the most highly interconnected people with very few isolated participants (see Figure 2.8). Tight crowds look much more like the

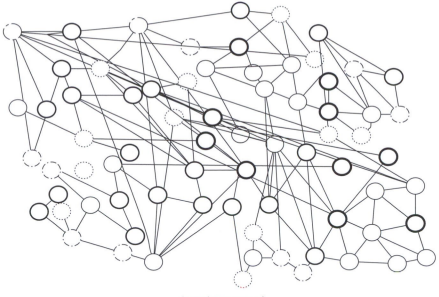

'together we post'

Figure 2.8 Tight social networks

traditional definition of 'online communities' than many of the other forms. They conduct large and open conversations about similar topics, responding to one another in a form that resembles the coherent threads of a newsgroup or forum. The ties between people indicate mass and widespread practices of sharing and mutual support provision. Online versions of conferences, professional topics, hobbies, interests, media and sports fan groups, and other subjects that attract large amounts of common interest assume the form of the tight social network. It mimics in many ways family, kinship and friend structures. A tight social network could also happen in particular workplaces. It may be that different networks have begun substituting for one another: work for religion, friends for family, hobbies for neighbourhoods, and so on.

Interest group alliance networks are more complex forms in which popular and widely shared topics unite multiple smaller groups. Each of these groups forms around a few social hubs (see Figure 2.9). Each of these hubs has its own largely separate audience, set of influencers and sources of information. They generally form for a little while when people have an interest in something, then they dissipate. Interest group alliance networks have multiple centres of activity. They are not as unified as the tight social network. However, a relatively small number of people are in those multiple centres, responsible for an inordinately disproportionate amount of social media activity. The conversations surrounding major global news stories, such as the recent coverage of the missing Air Malaysia flight 370 are the sort of interest groups that arise, bubbling up from the underground, to last for a while,

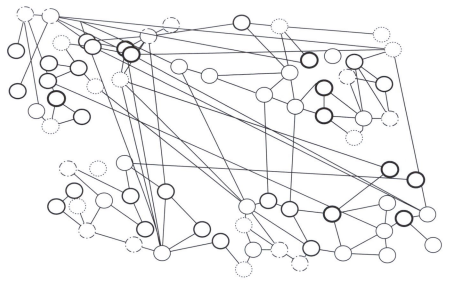

'communications of interest'

Figure 2.9   Interest group alliance network

their stories stoked by mainstream news and information outlets, national, local, global and different interested communities, such as travellers, Chinese expatriates, engineers, conspiracy theorists, and so on. Each of these groups has its own following, which is long lasting but shifts from topic to topic. This network is a portrait of that topic. Thus, revealing the multiplicity of conversations and viewpoints on a single topic shared through social media, a collection of medium-sized groups will manifest along with a fair number of isolates.

Several relevant patterns and ideas are present in this research to help us understand our topics. For example, studying a single large online site dedicated to climate change denial, such as Skeptical Science, may be sufficient in order to illuminate the topic of climate change denial sites, their functions, processes, structures and roles. Such a site would likely have much in common with interest groups or tight social networks.

However, to understand the ideological ecosystem in which such a site operates, you would likely need to broaden out to other sites or locations of information. You then might find the site partaking in the polarized issue form. It could be that the audience network model is being formed. Netnographers may need to shift their discernment of online experiences from notions of communities to those of particular network structures which govern repeat interactions that are topically, temporally and locally based. Whether we should be studying one single site, several interconnected sites, one person as the centre for many site-lines, or a set of many sites is another important research question. We will consider this question of research questions much further in Chapter 5.

Studying the findings of social network analyses such as this one tells us something about the structures we are dealing with. Knowing structures is very helpful to seeing the bigger picture. We, through these shapes and structures, see the continued, perhaps amplified, influence of major broadcast media. The continuing social media significance of corporate actors such as advertisers, public relations people, celebrity endorsers and customer service personnel is an indication about where the true power centres of the network reside.

The findings underscore hierarchy. Online 'influentials' are a powerful force given superpowers by the Internet. Everett Rogers identified the importance of the offline variety of the influential market agent years ago. But in the age of YouTube and Twitter it is virtually unlimited how many people one person can reach out towards.

Caroline Haythornthwaite (2005: 140) notes how technological change is merging with what she calls 'social mechanisms'. Ongoing online social interactions conducted through forms such as interest group clusters and polarized issue networks can help turn strangers into friends. Trusting relationships, linked to strong social ties, are relevant to understanding and planning the online provision of many types of public information. Other uses include facilitating: peer exchanges such as couchsurfing's hospitality exchange service; economic exchanges such as eBay's trust-dependent online marketplace; social activism such as Greenpeace's campaign against Nestlé; and political campaign management, such as the 2008 social media campaign for American President Barack Obama. Materializing within all of these forms, and all of the structures we have just examined, is a predominant tendency that our next section treats in some detail.

THE THEORY OF NETWORKED INDIVIDUALISM

As we continue considering theory about the Internet's impact on social groupings, we must consider the research findings of University of Toronto Professor Barry Wellman. Wellman (2001: 2031) convincingly argues that 'computer networks are inherently social networks' and that, as computer networks proliferated, we find ourselves in a network society that is 'loosely bounded and sparsely knit'. Wellman's influential notions are based in his social network analyses of Internet and computer network data. They parallel, detail, enrich and inform the understanding of core concepts of culture, community, individuals and participation articulated above. Wellman, along with a range of colleagues, has been developing the idea of 'networked individualism' since before most scholars had heard about the Internet. His ideas have been adopted by other major Internet scholars such as the influential Internet philosopher, Manuel Castells (1996). Castells articulated further the potential for social media to enable and enhance people's individualistic tendencies in the new society of technologically mediated networks that he viewed as the new basic unit of human society (Castells, 1996).

According to Wellman's co-authored book with noted Internet scholar and researcher Lee Rainie (Rainie and Wellman, 2012: 11), networked individualism is a shift in people's social lives 'away from densely knit family, neighbourhood, and group relationships toward more far-flung, less-tight, more diverse personal networks'. Coming as a result of the social network, Internet and mobile 'revolutions', networked individualism means that 'people function more as connected individuals and less as embedded group members'. Members of a family may now act more like participants of multiple networks – only one of which is the family – than solely or primarily as members of that family. Their home may no longer be mainly a place where they congregate together as a family and pursue common family activities. Instead it becomes more of a base for their individual networking with the outside world, with each family member maintaining their own separate personal computer, mobile phone, set of contacts, and so on. Wellman's results and examples illustrate a shift to the sort of more fluid, open and individual-centred conceptions of culture and community espoused by anthropologists Amit and Rapport (2002) and reviewed in Chapter 1 of this book.

From Rainie and Wellman (2012: 12–18) we can reiterate the following 12 principles regarding networked individualism:

1. Networked individuals increasingly meet social, emotional and economic needs by tapping into dispersed networks of diverse associates instead of relying on more intimate connections with a relatively small number of core associates.
2. Networked individuals maintain partial membership in many networks or social groups and rely less on permanent membership in established groups.
3. Technology is accelerating the trend toward networked individualism by accelerating the growth, accessibility and diversification of these kinds of arrangements.
4. The Internet is the new neighbourhood, increasingly containing some of the networked individual's most important social contacts.
5. Networked individuals are empowered by the Internet to project their vision and voice to extended audiences, and invite them to become a part of their social world.
6. The lines between communication, information and action have become increasingly blurred as networked individuals use the Internet, mobile phones and social networks to instantly get information and act upon it.
7. Networked individuals move easily between relationships and social settings to construct their own complex identities, depending on their passion, beliefs, lifestyles, professional associations, work interests, hobbies, media habits, subcultural inclinations and other personal characteristics.
8. Less formal, more fluctuating and more specialized peer-to-peer relationships are more easily sustained at work, and the benefits of hierarchical boss-subordinate relationships are less obvious.
9. Home and work are far more intertwined than in the past.
10. The public and private spheres of life are far more intertwined than in the past.
11. New expectations and realities are emerging regarding the transparency, availability, and privacy of people.
12. In this new era of less hierarchy, more information and looser relationships, there is greater uncertainty than ever before about which information sources to believe and who to trust.

And yet, as with all matters human and social, there is balance. Although extremely helpful to recognize that the rise of the network society is enabling a form of networked individualism, we also must attend to the many ways that people are also using that technology to build new social forms. Our concluding section to this chapter provides a brief overview that reorients us in this connective direction.

TECHNOGENESIS

Technogenesis is the idea that human beings and our technologies coevolve together. Paleoanthropologists have long accepted that human beings coevolve with their tools, for example, bipedalism and more flexible opposable digitry coevolved along with tool manufacture and transportation (Hayles, 2012: 10). As we change our human, social and physical environment through technology, our technological environment also changes us, selecting people who are more capable of succeeding within it. Netnography is intellectually emplaced within this study of coevolving human-technology transformation and adaptation.

As more researchers conduct ethnographies of online social experiences, we learn just how much – and how little – these phenomena are changing society. Coleman's (2010: 489) comments are pertinent in this regard: 'The presumption that digital technologies are the basis of planetary transformations is widespread, but unfounded'. There is no question that these technologies and their online social experiences have massive scale and global reach, and that global financial capital, national intelligence agencies, and transnational corporations are deeply involved in their production, maintenance and inner workings. Yet it is also easy to overstate technology's impact in, say, 'producing a shared subjectivity or a wholly new sensorium, still less a life world that might characterize a vast population', such as with the use of the term 'digital native' (Coleman, 2010: 490).

Online sociality and consociality reveal both the 'modern' and the 'postmodern' condition: the constant appearance of flux, movement, speed, change and progress. We see this progress as technological change – a constant dynamic in our human world. New hardware, new software, new abilities to communicate, entertain, inform, broadcast, listen and learn. Our world has become one of never-ending adaptation, ever-increasing rates of change. Our netnographic investigations, although clearly cognizant of the reality that digital technologies 'have cultivated new modes of communication and selfhood; reorganized social perceptions and forms of self-awareness; and established collective interests, institutions, and life project' (ibid.), must also be sceptical of claims of widespread change and the autonomous and overdetermining power of technology and digital media. In some cases, as Miller and Slater (2000) discovered, digital technologies facilitate social reproduction, reinforcing a tendency to favour old and comfortable views of self and culture over novel ones. Sometimes, it may be that the forms of living change, but the ways of life remain the same.

Studies of online social experience reveal how our existing worlds of human relationships, work relationships and structures of power are reinforced, extended,

developed and changed. As technological systems change, human systems adapt, and institutional arrangements shift. Netnography has helped reveal how rating services, such as those of TripAdvisor, create a new accounting system online. Social media networks are assemblages that become plugged into extant social norms and systems that inspire trust and interpersonal connection; they can thus rapidly assume a role in decision-making that was previously accorded to institutional actors (Jeacle and Carter, 2011). Netnographies of social experiences online inform us about alterations in our core notions of self – the heart of the psychological atom. Lysloff (2003) is cautiously optimistic about the online social experience's expressionistic, exhibitionistic and existential impacts on our individual lives as human beings. She relates online experience to the postmodern notion of the fragmented, multiple self as well as to a Situationist sense of voice:

> When we go online, the computer extends our identity into a virtual world of disembodied presence, and at the same time, it also incites us to take on other identities. We lurk in, or engage with, on-line lists and usenet groups that enable different versions of ourselves to emerge dialogically. The computer, in this way, allows for a new kind of performativity, an actualization of multiple and perhaps idealized selves through text and image. (Lysloff, 2003: 255)

Online social experiences possess a paradoxical quality that simultaneously liberates and constrains. They reveal tensions between powerful commercial structures and the communal forms that they promote. They tell us about the promotion of cultural transformation and the creation of change agents. Investigations expand into activism, as social media for social change become a matter increasingly on the transnational agenda. In their study of YouTube videos about the Israeli navy interception of a Gaza-bound flotilla, Sumiala and Tikka (2013) find that:

> YouTube served as a platform where various operators had the opportunity to construct their meanings of reality and where the emphasis shifted from journalism-centered to user-centered, from monological to plural, from media houses to grassroots-level citizen journalists and/or activist groups, and from journalism of facts to journalism of attachment and events (see also Boczkowski, 2004; Chouliaraki, 2010) ... YouTube also gave ordinary people the opportunity to tell their own story, to raise their own individual voices, and to share their accounts of that reality on the same platform (p. 330).

As the following chapters will explore through multiple examples, the truth of many netnographies lies in this notion of maintaining, even amplifying, the power of the story. The way that stories intertwine with other stories in the process of people interconnecting with one another through online social experiences is a thread that runs through word of mouth to oral history and tradition to the study of folklore. Folklorist Anders Gustavsson (2013) studied memorial sites on the Internet for the deceased in Sweden and in Norway. He performs a culturally comparative netnography that uses a collection of individuals' online social expressions about life-after-death and any supernatural beliefs surrounding death to comparatively analyse the two national cultures.

> The messages posted on the websites are both shorter and less emotional in Norway than in the case of their counterparts in Sweden, who observe more a diffuse, general religiosity that reminds us of New Age modes of thought, in which individuals and the brightness of a coming existence have a prominent position. In Sweden people tend to regard what is new as being positive, to focus on cheerful events. Life's darkest moments can be given a brighter shape. In this respect, Norway can be seen as being more realistic in its preservation of older traditions and in not merely rejecting life's darker sides without further discussion. (Gustavsson, 2013: 113–114)

Because of the interactions of social media and the Internet, so many aspects of our life change – even the social experience of death. Manuel Castells (1996: 31) wrote that the novel form of the technologically mediated network society is 'fundamentally altering the way we are born, we live, we sleep, we produce, we consume, we dream, we fight, or we die'. It is as if the force of evolution itself has turned its full attention to the digital realm, more than happy to use technology to run human social lives in fast forward and thereby reveal to us an endlessly shifting new wardrobe of diverse social experiences. And whether those costumes are comfortable or awkward, the changes to our way of being strong or weak, easily outnumbered by embodied experiences or at times absolutely overpowering and intimidating, they require our careful study and critical attention.

In 1997, Grant McCracken wrote, in a creatively masterful gem called *Plenitude* (1997: 17–18), that 'Our diversity is the plenitude of society. What Plato found astounding was the sheer number of plants and animals in the world. This book is concerned with the sheer number and variety of social species'. McCracken (1997: 18) could have been predicting the future of social media companies, types of social experience, types of online experience, or types of interactions with people mediated by technology, when he wrote:

> It overflows even the most agile of our classificatory schemes. We may enjoy a moment's illusion that the world has been restored to order. And then we look around us. Everywhere there is diversity, variety, heterogeneity. And we wonder: what set of categories can comprehend so many species of social life? What typology will embrace them all?

The Internet has increased social diversity, for it makes individualism, particularly patterned individualism, incredibly easy to share, especially in the current market-driven milieu's bottomless hunger for new styles, trends and change. These changes and styles, and the structures and sites that form them, cry out for taxonomizing. Historical thinking and analysis, the comparison of taxonomic forms of human practice and their evolution so vital to ethnography, have also thus far been largely absent from netnographies (including my own), perhaps because the field and what it deals with are still so very new. I would hope that upcoming studies, informed by this book, would rectify this sin of omission.

SUMMARY

Our discursive dive into extant theory on online sociality has taken us from cultural conceptions to archetypes of network structure. On the cultural side, we have moved from technoculture to technogenesis, through ethnographic approaches, sociality and cultural-communal hybridizations and divides. We conceptualize four ideal types of online social experience and relate them to a variety of extant social media sites, which are also contexts for our research. After this we move into structural types of understandings of online interaction. We outline and overview social network analysis in order to provide the six archetypes of network structure. Finally, we close with a full discussion and incorporation of networked individualism, which plays into our development of more introspective elements to netnography, and even auto-, netnography through this book. Networked individualism's 12 principles follow to introduce the end to a chapter that offers a cultural network theory backbone to the social interactions and structures of online experience.

KEY READINGS

Coleman, E. Gabriella (2010) 'Ethnographic approaches to digital media', *Annual Review of Anthropology*, 39: 487–505.

Rainie, Lee and Barry Wellman (2012) *Networked: The New Social Operating System*. Cambridge, MA and London: MIT Press.

Smith, Marc A., Lee Rainie, Ben Shneiderman and Itai Himelboim (2014) 'Mapping Twitter topic networks: From polarized crowds to community clusters', *Pew Internet & American Life Project,* 20 February. Available at: http://www.pewinternet. org/2014/02/20/mapping-twitter-topic-networks-from-polarized-crowds-to-community-clusters/ (accessed 15 October 2014).

NOTES

1. For detail on these many mystically founded technology predictions and the relation between technology and mysticism more generally, I highly recommended Erik Davis' excellent 1998 book *Technosis*.

2. And this might be why we are so quick to call things 'community' that are often little more than a set of temporary, obligatory, opportunistic social practices.

3. Relatedly, we have computationally assisted visualization being used within the field of Digital Humanities, and most certainly just as much within the visual arts. This is the idea of 'digital forensics' from work such as Matthew Kirschenbaum's physical book called *Mechanisms: New Media and Digital Forensics* (2008). As Hayles (2012: 32) notes, 'The idea is to bring to digital methods the same materialist emphasis of bibliographic study, using microscopic (and occasionally even nanoscale) examination of digital objects and codes to understand their histories, contexts, and transmission pathways.'

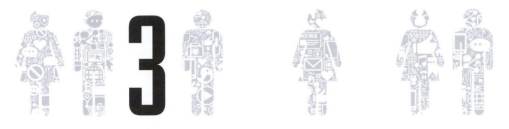

3

RESEARCHING NETWORKED SOCIALITY

An individual trained in technical, scientific writing, statistics, and computer statistical programs and familiar with quantitative journals in the library would most likely choose the quantitative design. On the other hand, individuals who enjoy writing in a literary way or conducting personal interviews or making up-close observations may gravitate to the qualitative approach – John Cresswell, *Research Design*, 3rd edn (2009: 19)

CONSIDERING THE CHOICE OF METHOD

One of the fundamental choices that any researcher can face concerns what method to use. In contemporary academia, researchers can become wedded to particular techniques when they decide to enter particular scholarly fields, work with particular dissertation chairs or supervisors, or publish in particular journals. This narrowing of scope and interest, accompanied by a narrowing knowledge of the theories and methods that lie outside one's chosen field, is unfortunate. However, the depth of knowledge and skill required for many of these highly specialized fields necessitates, at least for a time, that students and professionals focus their knowledge and attention.

One of the first major choices faced by a researcher-in-training is whether to use a quantitative approach, a qualitative approach, or an approach that uses mixed methods. Creswell (2009) helpfully complicates the neat division between qualitative and quantitative research. From a netnographic viewpoint, I continue his efforts. Consider that the images, words, Facebook profiles, Twitter hashtags, sounds and video files flowing through the Internet are composed of binary signals and various electromagnetically charged and uncharged blips of electrons and photons riding wires between various distant servers. Ultimately, they are zeroes and ones, already numerical and, in their own way, quantitative. We thus see fluidity and transferability, as analogue human experiences such as sitting and talking to a camera are transferred into digitally coded signals, shared through a platform like Vine or YouTube, then decoded into densely pixelled moving images on screens and sounds emanating from speakers and headphones. This experience of audiencing can be captured as qualitative words and images experienced by a human listener and watcher, coded into fieldnotes or captured as a text file or visual screenshot, and immediately or subsequently optionally coded and transferred into a quantitative reading. Quant becomes qual becomes quant in this slippery shifting example.

Creswell (2009: 4) offers that the key difference between these approaches is that qualitative research is useful for exploring and understanding meanings, whereas quantitative research is used for testing theories by examining the relationships between measurable variables. However, Sudweeks and Simoff (1999: 32) question 'this neat qualitative and quantitative dichotomy', arguing that 'each methodology has its own set of costs and benefits, especially when applied to Internet research, and that it is possible to tease out and match the strengths of each with particular variables of interest'. It is this matching process between approaches and questions that should interest netnographic researchers, and with which this chapter will mainly concern itself.

Although this chapter is mainly used to explore and set up ethnography as the direct historical predecessor and source of the core practices of netnography, it is crucial that netnography be viewed more as an approach to guide analysis and understanding than a strictly bound set of principles and practices. Netnography is about obtaining cultural understandings of human experiences from online social interaction and/or content, and representing them as a form of research. Thus, what distinguishes netnography from all other methods is two matters. First, an axiology – the purpose is to explore, reveal and understand human realities and social worlds as they change in a coevolutionary process with technoculture. Second is a central source of data. Netnography focuses primarily on the artifactual and communicative realities of online social exchange. Within these bounds, many paths and forms of understanding are usefully employed, centring upon but not limited to participant observational techniques.

In netnography as in all science, method should relate to the type of data and analysis capable of answering the research question that you want to investigate. This is why netnography begins with a stage that seeks to clarify the relevant research question to be investigated. From that decision about research question, a data quest proceeds. From that stage, other method considerations flow.

In a new or constantly changing field such as Internet studies, we can think of the pool of variables, and perhaps even constructs as dynamic and growing.

When I began looking at online social interactions in the mid-1990s, as a place where media fans gathered to discuss and share their fascinations and fantasies, it seemed rather obvious that they were providing something like a new context. *What can we learn from Star Trek fans' online discussions about how meaningful Star Trek-related social interaction is in their daily lives?* This was one question which interested me. It viewed online communications as a place to learn generalizable principles about all *Star Trek* fans' relations with what I called *Star Trek*'s 'culture of consumption' (Kozinets, 2001). However, as I began building theory about what happened through these online social interactions, they become theoretically relevant as a construct. The questions evolved to something like '*what are the social, policy-related, or strategic implications of online social interactions*?' (see, for example, Kozinets, 1999). By the late 1990s, online community and other conceptions of online social experiences had become constructs of interest in their own right.

The analogue world we inhabit contains almost infinite qualities. Living in that world and experiencing it as a human being involves myriad, almost second-by-second acts of classification and categorization, many of which, as our psychologist colleagues demonstrate so well with their concepts of heuristics and peripheral routes to information processing, take place below the threshold of our conscious deliberation. As we theorize and abstract from experience to research representation, however, these acts of classification and categorization become focal constructs of our conscious concentration. As we concatenate, obviate, synthesize and abbreviate elements of our so-called genuine experience of the allegedly real world that appears so naturally before us – and which now includes mobile smartphones with Internet access, ubiquitous tablets, and endless laptops and desktops, all of which would have been very strange sights just a decade or two ago – we build the required abstractions for our theories. In rapidly changing social realms, we need to maintain the ability to define and classify the heretofore undefined and singular. For example, we want to be able to creatively explore the relationship between various types of technologically mediated communication and the experience of ending a relationship, as did Gershon (2010).

By attending to large numbers of distinct qualities, qualitative techniques can help draw (or re-draw) the map of a new or rapidly changing terrain. Doing so can also help identify what may be the most interesting constructs and relationships at work in a social phenomenon for other researchers who will come later. As thinking becomes more developed about some of these topics, quantitative and more confirmatory analyses are generally employed to refine knowledge of the way that small sets of constructs interrelate with one another. Yet, at any point in this investigative process, qualitative research can 'stir things up' by questioning definitions, re-operationalizing constructs, or by introducing new and overlooked constructs and relationships. This is the process often at work with netnographic theorizing, as it is everywhere within the scientific enterprise.

My general advice to scholars is to read in an area of scholarship that interests you, and become as familiar with the researchers, constructs and theories in use as you are with the members of your own friend network. However, and continuing the metaphor, do not be blinded to making new friends, for some of your new friends may be even more helpful to you as you move to new contexts than the old ones you already know. Netnographic immersion, which we will discuss in the next chapter, implies that you stay attuned to the way online social experiences manifest in particular instances and situations as much as you can in your own research project. From immersion you must constantly ask yourself what you notice, where your attention is drawn, to which areas do you gain an intellectual energizing, an unexpected empathy and a more heartfelt understanding? Of course, within this more intuitive approach, you are also asking which theories or constructs fit or do not fit into the actual social worlds you experience and cognize? If you find new or under-explored constructs, new construct combinations, new inflections, or even new phenomena to detail and describe, you may follow these energizing and illuminating aspects to new theory constructions. The relationship between research practices that result in the collection or construction of 'data' are interlinked with extant theoretical conceptions (such as the illusory division between the virtual and the real, for example, or the unsupportable inferences that the digital is immaterial and that the physical is becoming digital). As well, and as we will discuss at length towards the end of this book, your research is intertwined with the desired output of produced and performed research representations.

Many other approaches are complementary with netnography. In its questing for rich insight and understanding, netnography, like its older sibling, ethnography, is promiscuous. It attaches itself to and incorporates a variety of different research techniques and approaches. Thus, the comparison and contrast that follow are not necessarily a sign of one technique being better than another. Instead, the differences are those of one tool being better at driving in a nail and another being useful for removing a screw. Do not believe unreflective methodological–ideological evangelists. Despite what anyone might tell you, one research method cannot be inherently superior to another research method. It can only be better at studying a particular phenomenon or at answering particular types of research questions.

BOX 3.1

What considerations should you consider in broadening your investigation to include multiple techniques?

- Methods should always be driven by research focus and research questions.
- Match the type of data you need to the type of question you are trying to answer.
- Use the methodological approach best fitted to the level of analysis, constructs and type of data you can collect.

SURVEYS, SURVEY DATA AND SURVEY FINDINGS

Netnographies rarely include surveys. However, surveys such as the Pew Internet report might be used before or during netnographies to inform relevant questions about online social experience. Surveys have been useful for providing overviews about online social experiences, from which we have been able to speak with confidence about large-scale patterns. Once researchers have determined adequate categorizations and classifications, such as online dating, social networking sites or microblogging, surveys can assist in understanding how popular these categorizations might be. Similarly, surveys can tell us much about people's online social activities, and also about the way that their online activities influence other aspects of their daily lives. Surveys can also be used after online interviews in order to confirm or verify particular kinds of local understanding among more general populations.

What is the average size of an online social network in Brazil? How many people around the world Tweet at least once per day? How many Spanish teenagers check their Facebook account less than once a week? What is the age profile of users of the Chinese microblog Weibo? Are there more women than men actively using Instagram? All of these questions might use survey research in order to provide answers.

The application of surveys using web-pages or other online formats is called the online survey method. Online survey methods have grown rapidly in the last decade (Andrews et al., 2003; Lazar and Preece, 1999; Wright, 2005). From practically a standing start, online surveys have become the major method for investigating a wide variety of social questions. Online surveys are an excellent way to gain a particular kind of understanding about online social experience.

Whereas the traditional mail or telephone survey excluded a lot of potential researchers from large-scale data collection (Couper, 2000), online surveys are far more accessible and easy-to-use. For example, the online service SurveyMonkey.com is simple to set up and use and includes a ready group of participants. The service is also currently free to use for students or others doing small-scale samples. It has been very popular with students in my courses. Other popular online survey systems and companies include Surveywiz, SurveyPro, SurveySaid, Zoomerang and WebSurveyor, and there are many others.

Online survey research can be quite inexpensive when compared with mail surveys (Weible and Wallace, 1998). Research by Watt (1999) even demonstrates that the cost per respondent can decrease dramatically as the online sample size increases, something that does not happen with any other form of survey. In terms of accuracy, research thus far indicates that the results of online surveys seem not to differ significantly from the results of postal surveys, but offer strong advantages in distribution and turnaround time (Andrews et al., 2003; Wright, 2005; Yun and Trumbo, 2000).

Online surveys are unique. They have distinct characteristics – such as their technological features, the particular demographic characteristics of the groups they survey on the Internet, and the particular patterns of respondent responses. These unique characteristics alter the way that survey designers must write their questions, when the surveys can be used, how to involve traditional non-responders or Internet 'lurkers', and how to analyse the survey results accordingly (Andrews et al., 2003; Sohn, 2001).

The Pew Internet Reports are valuable sets of data that help us to understand the rapidly changing world of online activity that are the direct results of survey research. Many researchers interested in the overall complexion of the Internet and its online cultures and communities employ these data. They use them in order to understand the frequency, popularity and changes in the activities of people as they interact and communicate online, use blogs, social networking sites and other social media tools. These survey-based studies also illuminate interesting patterns of usage by different demographic groups, such as men and women, different ethnic groups and races, and different ages and generational cohorts. Similarly, educational institution-based surveys of online panels such as The Digital Futures Project at the USC Annenberg School for Communication and Journalism are useful as tracking studies enabling us to discern changing general patterns in online interaction. Forrester Research also uses survey information to form various ideas, such as its clustering segmentation of the 'Social Technographics Profile' (Li and Bernoff, 2008). In order to get a 'big picture' view of an online social phenomenon, to compare behaviour on one site to that of other sites, to talk about demographic constituencies, to provide numerical estimates of population or influence or provide other comparative information, a netnographer may need to incorporate survey-related data and analysis. Online surveys are therefore good for research on online social experience in which you want to:

- draw conclusions about online interactions and uses that are representative of a particular population
- draw conclusions about changing patterns in online social interactions or usage
- gain a sense of the correlations between various factors, such as demographics, attitudes and online social interaction and usage
- gain retrospective accounts regarding what people recall about their online social experiences and actions
- gain a sense of people's attitudes and opinions about their online social experiences and uses
- learn about people's self-reported representations of what they do, or intend to do, in regards to their online social activities.

Online and other surveys can help to set up netnographic studies by answering online social experience related research questions such as:

- How many people around the world participate in online social experiences?
- How many people use Pinterest on a daily basis?
- Which social media sites are visited by more men than women?
- What are the most popular online social activities?

- How many people in Finland have logged on to a virtual world in the past month?
- How has the time that Polish teenagers spend using email versus social networking sites changed over the last five years?
- How many people say they have met their spouse through social media?

Surveys are not particularly appropriate for research that must:

- explore a new online social experience topic about which little previously was known
- investigate an online social experience whose characteristics are only dimly understood, or about which we do not know the relevant questions to ask
- understand what people actually did or said in the past
- precisely specify relationships or social structures
- gain a profound and multifaceted understanding of another person's point of view
- learn the unique way that language and practices are used
- exhibit a complex, nuanced understanding of a human social experience, event or phenomenon.

INTERVIEWS AND JOURNAL METHODS

Internet Interviewing

At its most basic, an interview is a conversation, a set of questions and answers between two people who agree that one will assume the role of the questioner, and the other the role of the answerer. The only difference between an online interview and a face-to-face interview is that the online interview occurs through the mediation of some technological apparatus. That, however, is a big difference.

In the physical world, the topic of interviewing is so intertwined with the conduct of ethnography that the two are virtually inseparable. So it is with netnography and online interviewing. The online interview has become a staple of online ethnographic research, present as part of the method from the very beginnings of work in this field (e.g., Baym, 1995, 1999; Correll, 1995). In this chapter, I will overview the conduct of online depth interviews. Although, as we will see in the next few chapters, it is possible to conduct a purely observational netnography, the recommended participant-observational stance very often dictates an interview component (whether online or off). Speaking of purely textual interviews, Bruckman (2006: 87) opines that 'online interviews are of limited value' and asserts that face-to-face or phone interviews offer far greater insight. Barring some way to contextualize the social and cultural data beyond the self-evident fact of the online encounter, the data can be difficult to interpret. Yet although online interviews have traditionally been hindered by the lack of individual identifiers and body language, in the age of the Skype interview, online interviewing offers considerably more social information than traditional phone interviews.

Synchronous, text-based, chat interviews often can offer a thin, rather rushed and superficial interaction. Telephone interviews have a long history and are established throughout the social sciences. But other online means now include email, audio (as in voice over IP or phone-like online communications) and audio visual connections, such as Skype, Facetime or Google Hangout (which I generically and without brand prejudice group into the category 'Skype interviews'). These media are valuable and can simulate in many ways the advantages of face-to-face interviewing. These advantages include providing a verifiable visual and auditory sense of the physical presence of the previously unidentified other and their immediate physical surroundings (see Deakin and Wakefield, 2014; Hanna, 2012; Kivits, 2005; Weinmann et al., 2012). Chapter 7, which examines netnographic data collection methods, will feature a detailed discussion and set of guidelines to help plan and conduct online interviews, including those conducted over Skype. Even using chat or email for interviews can be valuable, if interpreted carefully. Meeting this interpretive challenge can mean a greatly enhanced confidence in the data's utility for understanding other social and cultural contexts. In Chapters 7 and 9, we will discuss these issues and provide some data collection and interpretive strategies for dealing with them.

Of course, conducting an interview through your computer means that your communications are going to be shaped by the medium you use. Yet to think that a face-to-face interview is somehow unmediated and free from the frames of self-presentation is a case of naïve neglect. Consider, for example, Erving Goffman's considerable body of work on the matter. 'In anthropology there is no such thing as pure human immediacy; interacting face-to-face is just as culturally inflected as digitally mediated communication, but, as Goffman (1959, 1974) points out again and again, we fail to see the framed nature of face-to-face interaction because these frames work so effectively' (Horst and Miller, 2012: 12). It may well be that moving to Skype interviews returns us to a set of social frames that appear more effortless and natural, despite the fact that they are equally as constructed as those of chat or email interviews.

It is highly relevant that many stigmatized behaviours have been effectively studied using netnographic methods. These stigmatic behaviours include drug use and addiction (e.g., Mudry and Strong, 2012; Tackett-Gibson, 2008), anorexia and body image disorders (Dyke, 2013; Smith and Stewart, 2012), various sexual orientations and behaviours (e.g., Berdychevsky et al., 2013) and cosmetic plastic surgery (Langer and Beckman, 2005), to name a few. Humphrey (2009) studied Russian chat rooms and concluded that the online social medium was enormously empowering, allowing participants to express more fully their passion and spirit. Stories of disabled people coming alive and expressing what they believe to be their more genuine selves through online social experiences are also common in the literature (e.g., Ginsburg, 2012). In all of these cases, the online social experience was found to be liberating to the expression of the fully authentic self rather than constraining. Not only is the real world virtual and mediated in many ways, but the virtual world also is absolutely real in many of its effects.

The Internet Journal

Researchers seeking to understand the subjective impact of Internet connectivity can also collect documents from research participants. These documents may take the form of diaries or journals in which participants record day-to-day or even hour-by-hour events, reflections, or impressions of experiences. For example, Andrusyszyn and Davie (1997) describe the interactive journal-writing study they undertook. In a way, interactive reflective writing is like having fieldnotes from participants, and thus multiplying the numbers of subjective perspectives on the focal phenomenon of online social experience. Journals can be kept in physical form, in notebooks, on paper, on people's handheld devices like tablets or laptops, on mobile phones, or located on the cloud and accessed through multiple devices. The online format of journal writing or diary keeping has several inherent advantages. Participants can be reminded or prompted automatically for their entries. Entries can be automatically saved. As well, participants can enter their journals in a form that is easier to read and expand upon than handwriting. It is recorded in computer-readable text form, and in a way that can facilitate the addition of photos, drawings, screenshots, recordings of verbal material, video, or any combination of these. Many of the advantages of online interviewing can also pertain to the data arising from online diaries or journals. Maintaining a diverse collection of such materials can lend depth and increased resonance to netnographic datasets.

Depending on your research focus, you may or may not need the sort of detailed, open-ended, descriptive, reflexive personal understanding that can be gained from journals or depth interviews. As with in-person ethnography, a simple in situ conversation, or a quick exchange of information, might suffice to inform your research question. As with research in general, the recommended type of interview is going to be determined by the type of data that are required. For the type of nuanced phenomenological understandings of online social experiences that are usually sought in a netnography, depth interviewing is usually the method of choice. Most online ethnographers in cultural studies, anthropology and sociology employ depth interview techniques.

Depth interviews allow netnographic researchers to broaden their understanding of what they observe online. For example, in a depth interview, one can try to understand the social situation of the research participant – their age, gender, nationality, education level, linguistic orientation, ethnic orientation, sexual orientation, and so on. They would seek to understand how the participant's social situation influences their online social participation, and is also influenced by it. Depth interviews also allow netnographers to question the relationship between online social interactions and other online activities and relate them to one another and to the wealth of other social interactions, affiliations and activities in the person's life. In this way, a fuller and more complete portrait of human social experiences can be drawn.

Depth interviews and journal methods are appropriate for research on online social experiences in which you must:

- include a detailed subjective recounting of people's lived experiences of online social experience (i.e., a phenomenological understanding)
- deepen the understanding of the relationship between a person's own unique sociocultural situation and their online social interactions and experiences
- gain a detailed, multifaceted, grounded, subjective sense of a person's perspective and sense of meaning as it relates to their social experiences, including the online
- witness and share people's recollections, recordings and interpretations of experiences, interactions and events.

Online interviews and journal methods can help answer research questions about online social experience such as:

- How do people relate to the information, experiences and connections from online social interactions and apply them in their lives?
- What are the most common metaphors that people in China use to understand their online social experiences?
- How do family members experience their loved ones' behaviour in online interactions?
- How do people use their online social experiences to moderate their emotional states throughout the day?
- How are narratives about online relationships related to important health care topics in people's lives?
- What impact do the stories that people hear through online interactions have on the way that they connect with their spouse, parents, children and other family members?

Interviews are not necessarily useful when you want to:

- make conclusions that are representative of a particular population
- generalize findings to distinct and divergent other populations
- determine what actually happened in particular places or with particular events
- understand the causal relations between events
- quantify relationships.

SOCIAL NETWORK ANALYSIS

An Overview

As introduced in Chapter 2, social network analysis is an analytical method that focuses on the structures and patterns of relationships between and among social actors in a network. Netnographers should first realize that the relationships and ties studied by social network analysis result, in general, in different descriptive approaches. The first looks at these relationships from the 'personal' or 'ego-centred' perspective of people who are the centre of their network. As Rainie and Wellman

(2012: 55) explain, each person is 'at the center of his or her own *personal network*: a solar system of one to two thousand and more people orbiting around us. Each person has become a communication and information switchboard connecting persons, networks, and institutions.' Conceptualizing this personal network can be enormously helpful to our analysis of the networked individualism phenomenon discussed in Chapter 2. It relates to a range of interesting theoretical questions about topics such as consociality, networks and communities against which netnographers may often come up.

The second and more familiar descriptive approach is often called the whole network approach. This approach considers an entire social network based on some particular research definition of the boundaries of that network. The whole network approach also helps researchers to identify the relative positions that members occupy within a network as well as suggesting the very important partitioning of subgroups or 'cliques' within the group.

The boundary of a social network might be the online site that hosts the online social experiences and interactions, such as Facebook, Twitter, Dropbox or Skype. Alternatively, the boundaries of the social network might be focused around a particular activity, interest or goal. So, for example, the phenomenon of social exchanges regarding kite-surfing could be studied across many venues including Facebook groups, tweets, web-pages, forums, email mailing lists, physical locations such as Greek Islands, magazine subscription lists, corporate-sponsored competitions and events, YouTube videos, and documentary television shows and films. We could also conceivably study online kite-surfing social interactions as one whole network. Because the consideration of group boundaries is so critical, netnographic investigations can be useful for conceptualizing the boundaries of these social networks for social network analysis. Conversely, social network analysis can identify bounded social networks for netnographers to engage with and investigate.

Each social tie in a social network belongs, at its most basic level, to the 'dyad' formed between two actors. Relations refer to the resources that are exchanged, and these relations can be characterized by their content, their direction and their strength. Online social exchanges can include sharing a picture on Facebook, sharing a blog link on Twitter, or posting a news story on LinkedIn. They can include telling people about your favourite TV show, remarking on a sports score, criticizing someone else's status update, or answering an open question. Strong ties appear to include 'combinations of intimacy, self-disclosure, provision of reciprocal services, frequent contact, and kinship, as between close friends or colleagues' (Garton et al., 1999: 79). Often, ties will be referred to as either weak or strong. In general, because definitions of weak or strong will vary by context, a weak tie is one that is sporadic or irregular, and has little emotional connection. An example might be people who are regular visitors to the same blog, but who have never communicated or commented on each other's comments. People who are friends with solid sharing privileges on Facebook would be a good example of ostensible, possible strong ties.

The strength of ties can be operationalized depending upon the type of community. Peers may communicate more or less frequently; they may exchange large or small amounts of information or goods; the information that they share might be important or trivial. It is worth noting that these judgements tend to vary with the cultural situation of social actors – whether information is important or trivial is a socially constructed determination of value.

There is a range of interesting units of analysis used in social network analysis. To understand the relationships created by these ties, social network analysis focuses on the properties of the relationship. Two actors could have a tie based on a single relationship – such as belonging to the same *Comedy Nights with Kapil*-discussing online forum. The pair could also have a multiplex relationship based within a number of different relationships, such as working for the same company, living in the same part of Mumbai, belonging to the same Hindu temple, and being a member of the same Akshay Kumar-devoted Facebook fan group. Multiplex ties are more supportive, long-lasting, voluntary, and intimate and are also maintained through more different forums or media. Multiplexity is one of the properties of social ties, as are directionality, reciprocity and symmetry, strength and homophily.

The 'dyadic' level is only one possible level of analysis. Analysing 'triads' and even larger networks, such as those that comprise online communities, involves consideration of the structural properties of those networks as well as the structural properties of individuals within those networks. One important measure to netnography is centrality, a measure that reveals the actors that may be the most important, prominent, or influential ones in a network. There are several different kinds of centrality. Degree centrality looks at the most popular active actors in a network. It focuses on measuring how many other actors a particular actor is in direct contact with. Eigenvector centrality measures how much a node is connected to other nodes that are also tightly connected to one another. Eigenvector centrality is more concerned with power and influence than popularity. Betweenness centrality measures an actor's sphere of influence. A central actor in this context is truly in the middle of things. The more influence an actor has over the flow of information, the more power and control that actor can potentially wield (Wasserman and Faust, 1994). Finally, closeness centrality looks at aspects such as reach and reachability instead of power or popularity.

In summary, social network analysis helps us learn about how social networks manifest through computer network connectivity. It is often a useful complement to netnography and can be combined with or worked in to a netnographic study. Social network analysis is suitable for research on online social experiences in which you want to:

- learn about the structure of a community's communications
- discuss patterns of social relations or 'ties'
- describe different types of social relations and exchanges between members of an identified social network
- investigate the patterns of online communication and interaction

- study the flows of communication and connection through particular or different online sites and networks
- compare community structures and communication flows between various types of social networks, interactions and experiences.

Social network analysis will allow you to answer research questions such as:

- What is the structure of the communications in a particular online site or network? Who is communicating with whom? Who communicates the most?
- Who are the most influential communicators in this online social network?
- Is there a core group and a peripheral group in this particular network?
- How is this individual connected to other individuals in and through social networks?
- What are the various subgroups in this social network?
- How does information flow through this particular network?
- How does communication on one online site or platform differ from communications in another online site or platform in terms of who uses it and what is communicated?
- What are the overall patterns in information spread between one or more particular online social networks?

Social network analysis, by itself, is not generally appropriate for research that seeks to:

- gain a detailed, nuanced understanding of the lived experience of people engaging in online social interactions and communications
- understand the social practices and related systems of meaning and value that manifest through online social interactions and exchanges
- convey and compare the unique ways that language is used to manifest culture through online social interactions and experiences.

ETHNOGRAPHY AND NETNOGRAPHY

Preaching to the Choir

Interviewer: What is ethnography, exactly?

Research participant: Ethnography is an anthropological approach that has gained popularity in sociology, cultural and media studies, nursing, geography, marketing and management research, and many other fields in the social sciences.

The term refers both to the act of doing ethnographic fieldwork and to the representations based on such a study. Dick Hobbs provides a cogent definition of ethnography, defining it as:

a *cocktail* of methodologies that *share* the *assumption* that *personal engagement with the subject is the key* to understanding a particular *culture or social setting*. Participant observation is the most common component of this cocktail, but interviews, conversational and discourse analysis, documentary analysis, film and photography all have their place in the ethnographer's repertoire. *Description* resides at the core of ethnography, and however this *description* is constructed it is the *intense meaning of social life* from the *everyday* perspective of group members that is *sought*. (Hobbs, 2006: 101, emphasis added)

Ethnography's popularity probably flows from its open-ended quality as well as the rich content of its findings. Ethnography's flexibility has allowed it to be used for over a century to represent and understand the behaviours of people belonging to almost every race, nationality, religion, culture and age group. Ethnographies have even been conducted of the local ways of life of non-human 'tribes' of gorillas, chimpanzee, dolphins and wolves. Ethnographers in the last two decades have also become increasingly concerned with the acknowledgment and inflection of their own reflexivity as researchers. This is because ethnography relies very heavily on what consumer anthropologist John Sherry (1991: 572) calls 'the acuity of the researcher-as-instrument'. Good ethnographies are the creations of good ethnographers. The nature of the ethnographic enterprise, its techniques and approaches as well as its requirement for subtle, metaphorical and hermeneutic interpretation, rapidly renders transparent the rhetorical skill of the researcher.

And if there is one thing that ethnographies of the social sciences such as LaTour and Woolgar (1979) have taught us, it is that ethnography is grounded in context; it is infused with, and imbues, local knowledges of the particular and specific. In fact, I would argue that anthropology emerged from the Crisis of Representation stronger than it ever had been because of the opening created by experimental ethnography. Experimental ethnography gave anthropologists license to play with media and message. Popular culture around the world has become increasingly in focus for anthropologists, and, arguably, digital media along with the Digital Humanities is moving towards a more central place within cultural anthropology, as culture itself becomes global and digital, both one and so very different (Horst and Miller, 2012).

Ethnography is thus an inherently assimilative practice. It is interlinked with multiple other methods. We give these other interlinked methods names: interviews, discourse analysis, literary analysis, semiotics, videography. They have other names because they are sufficiently different from the overall practice of ethnography that they require unique new designations, even though all of them came after or in some sense were derived from the larger more specific practice of anthropological writing. People who perform semiotic analyses within an ethnography, or who do videography will need special, new, unique and often authenticated training. Although their work relates to ethnography, they pursue it in particular ways, capturing data in specific ways, dictated by specific, agreed-upon standards.

Any given ethnography, therefore, already combines multiple methods – many of them named separately, such as creative interviewing, discourse analysis, visual analysis and observations – under one term. Sirsi et al. (1996) followed their ethnography of a natural food market with a series of social psychological experiments, which they fed into a causal equation model. Howard (2002) offered a 'network ethnography' that pragmatically combined social network analysis with ethnography. Because it is attuned to the subtleties of context, no two ethnographies employ exactly the same approach. Ethnography is based on adaptation or *bricolage*; its assemblage-based approach is continually being refashioned to suit particular fields of scholarship, research questions, research sites, times, researcher preferences, skill sets, methodological innovations and cultural groups. Netnography is a component of this reality of assemblage-based ethnographic research.

Netnography is participant-observational research based in online hanging-out, download, reflection and connection. Netnographers use online and mobile data sources for social data to arrive at ethnographic understandings and representations of online social experience. Therefore, just as practically every ethnography will extend almost naturally and organically from a basis in participant-observation to include other elements such as interviews, descriptive statistics, archival data collection, extended historical case analysis, videography, projective techniques such as collages, semiotic analysis, and a range of other techniques, so too will it now extend to include netnography. And so too will netnography branch out and grow into its own, as it is already doing. And from netnography we extend into all manner of new quantitative and qualitative and combined techniques. This book explores four different forms for these combinations and extensions. There are, however, many more hybridizations that are both happening and possible.

It would be right, then, to see in a method section of an ethnography a line stating that the method included participant-observation as well as interviews, videography and netnography. The use of the term netnography in that case would represent the researcher's attempt to acknowledge, first and foremost, the importance of techno-culturally mediated communications in the social lives of members of the network. From there, it signals the inclusion in their data collection strategies of the triangulation amongst different and similar sources of sociocultural understanding, such as Internet archives, recorded conversations, and reflective fieldnotes. Next, the use of the term would acknowledge that, as with other approaches like interviews or semiotics, netnography has its own uniquely adapted set of practices and procedures, combining digital archival skills with digital analysis and even, as this book will elaborate, personal academic branding theory.

Never, ever, again should you think of something as either a netnography or an ethnography. Instead, what you must explain is prevalence and origin of data, alongside data collection strategy. The data collection strategy of netnography, like ethnography, always centres upon the researcher. For an ethnography is the story of a particular place at a particular time, inhabited by a particular person who conveys the research. It transpires at a human level, the story of an individual human, acting among other human beings in an enacted world of concretized beliefs and values. This is also what netnography chronicles, and how it chronicles: stories of our own digital, digitizing, human and humanizing uses of technoculture and the daily life it constantly changes in every domain – medical, industrial, military, commercial, educational, societal.

And because it is based in participation, a netnographer should reach out in some sense, a human voice trying to find another human voice amidst the technology, and then write about the experience. It must be perhaps the most sacred and important part of the ethnography: the part called entrée. We linger upon it because it is the liminal space within the netnography. It is the place where we go from being outside of the network to increasingly inside of the digital network. It is an experience of Being-Through-Technology, Dasein durch Technologie. Entrée is where the transitions happen that are so subtle that if you don't pay close attention and monitor them, you miss them.

Netnography is about paying attention to those transitions. In context. From the centre of your own network. You operate from your own social researcher brand, because you truly cannot be out in social media space conducting research openly unless you have a legitimate brand of yourself on Facebook, Twitter, YouTube and LinkedIn at least, if not also on Instagram, Pinterest and Vine. You cannot hide behind your researcher identity and only publish in dying specialist top-tier peer-reviewed paper journals. Although acceptance within them still grants the keys to the kingdom, at some point many of us believe that only publishing in these obscurantist forms will be widely recognized as a losing game. Netnography is one way we can all envision what comes next.

Ethnography and netnography can be conceptualized to be as flexible as red clay upon the village potter's wheel. Netnography is the work of the privileged few. Those of us doing it without censorship or oppression or restrictions that are unacceptable to the freedom to speak the truth have an obligation to use this amazingly rare academic power for social and self-betterment. In so doing, we may be able to see our own consumption of social media for what it is, and to centre our ethnographies, introspectively, upon this reality.

The reality of netnography as a social media superpowered descendant of ethnography lies in its dual nature. The dual nature of netnography's participant observational research is reflected in the two core qualities of online network information: that it is archival and that it offers live communications. It offers a research experience that is asynchronous and somewhat distant from the human sense of immediate social and personal contact, and that also is or can be synchronous and close from a human point of view. It has nodes and ties. It has digital archives that are recordings and snapshots. These elements flow by at the supercharged pace of popular culture for all of us now, researchers included. Ethnography of social media is a reading of humanity's newest and most incredible hallucinogen for collective dreaming, and its sense of 'direct' communication and participation. The Internet is archives and communication, together.

REALITY AND NETNOGRAPHY: WHY IDEAS OF COMBINING ONLINE AND OFFLINE ARE NONSENSICAL

The technocultural experience of human social communications. If we consider McLuhan's and others' contention that language is, itself, a technology, then technology and humanity have never been far apart. Language is the technology of culture, and technology always contains within it the language of culture. Language is endlessly and ineluctably technocultural. It should come as no surprise, then, that what people consider discrete categories of 'online' and 'offline' social worlds are, of course, hopelessly intermeshed in interwoven human practice and social worlds. The two are as interconnected as are the speaker and the spoken, the tool-user and the tool, the individual and the cultural. If we wish to study the various aspects of living and being a particular type of person today, then we must study communication and the production of communication. This means that our studies of particular types of people in the current age must be technocultural.

The semiotics of indexicality are salient in human level interpretations of online social worlds. Netnography is stuffed firmly into the world of technocultural communications, and holds special interest in the products and process of technocultural communication. Drawing inspiration from the semiotics of indexicality, Boellerstorff (2012: 42) convincingly argues that 'the idea that online and offline could [first be separate and then could] fuse makes as much sense as a semiotics whose followers would anticipate the collapsing of the gap between sign and referent, imagining a day when words would be the same thing as that which they denote'. Despite many temptations to view and analyse events in the human world as a convergence of the allegedly once separate realms of the embodied and the online, 'the virtual and the actual are not blurring, nor are they pulling apart from one another. Such spatial metaphors of proximity and movement radically mischaracterize the semiotic and material interchanges that forge both the virtual and the actual' (Boellerstorff, 2012: 56). And so we are back to a virtual ethnography, like Hine (2000), but in this strange sense, encapsulated one within the other, the virtual is no longer a partial piece of a wider reality better represented by 'real ethnography' or an 'ethnography of the real'. Instead, it is an entire slice of a reality-in-itself.

The dataset is deep and wide, selected through mainly human intelligence. Netnography concerns itself with data: data from the Internet, from participants in the research and from the researcher. The human researcher generates four types of data: interactions with others, interactions with things (including and especially actant technology), a network of connections and measurements accompanied by analysis and discussion about how they change, and an introspective element, the Deep N of One which reflects uniquely and binds these separate stories together along with a scientific purview into a single story, which in some sense is our individualized story. However, just because the so-called subjective reality of the researcher can be described and represented uniquely, cordoned off from other types of research understanding, does not mean that it is actually separate in practice from so-called objective scientific understanding. This is true of all research. All analysis in netnography deliberately and consciously reflects the human perspective of the researcher. Otherwise, this could not be netnography.

In human social worlds, meanings are communicated via messages encoded within other messages. Contemplate the meaning of a profession. How are the members of that group reflected in the representations of others? How do they reflect their acts and meaning to themselves? Let us consider that the profession is the occupation of nursing. We can wonder about how nursing is reflected in popular culture and also how nursing 'culture' reflects itself to itself.

We can conceive of a range of methods to investigate the topic. These might include interviewing nurses and others and asking them directly about the associations they have connected to nursing. We might look at television or YouTube images of nurses and nursing and analyse them. However, we now might consider that global human communication has all become a part of one communication stream: an omnichannel, or polymedia. We are cultural and communicative astronauts piloting our journey through laptops and smartphones, our lives now docked here, now there, often at several screens at once, at home and at work, on the road and in your home city. Netnography is the captain's log of that journey through Internet sociocultural experience of cyber social space. We play a game when we do this as well. We imagine that when we communicate this way we do it in a kind of shared social 'space'.

Popular culture, commercial advertising and creative works are interrelated with communications media and social influence at fundamental levels. We will continue thinking about how to investigate sociocultural reflections of nursing. Another method might be to think about symbolic representations of nursing in art, poetry, or music. What about an analysis of creative works by nurses? Or the work of nurses who also write and perhaps perform poetry? Or we might consider the representations of nursing-themed tattoos. To gain access to a bank of tattoos themed around nursing we might turn to the Internet, with its stores of information. This is exactly the course of action undertaken by Henrik Eriksson and colleagues in their 2014 article in the journal *Nursing Inquiry*.

The line is often impossibly blurred between what is virtual and what simply makes permanent an image taken of another image of another image. Clearly, tattoo photos are pictures of physical events, traces of material and symbol etched into flesh. They are, thus, impossible without the existence themselves of a range of different technologies and practices, such as skin dyes, hypodermic needles, paramedical practitioner industries, and the entire social and semiotic structure around body decoration traditions and norms. A tattoo is an embodied reality of symbolism. It is an emotional language we choose to permanently inscribe upon our bodies. Tattoos are enabled by material industries that change and maintain bodies in social space and through individual time and experience. Tattoos are images. Social media shared images of tattoos are images of images.

Yet the method used to study them is an adapted version of symbolic netnography; Salzmann-Erikson and Eriksson's own rebranded rendering of netnography previously published elsewhere. It is the symbolic translation of traces and talking, of communications as events in and of themselves as well as for what they save, archive, collectively categorize, taxonomize, folksonomize and syncretically signify. Eriksson et al.'s (2014) study is not, then, merely a study of 400 images found online, but a study of the culture underlying those images. As symbolic netnographies often do, it finds common cultural themes. In one, nurses are Janus-faced demon-angels, 'angels of mercy and domination'. In another, technology itself is a type of monster, perhaps one fully realized in the isolating nightmare of working in the Belly of the Great Beast that is contemporary nursing. Bespeaking, perhaps, the sample, we see a militaristic or para-militaristic 'embodying the corps' that may tell us not only about the Marine and mass media origins of tattoos spreading thoroughly throughout global culture, but also about the background and professions of those who get nursing tattoos and who post them online. Images were analysed, facilitated by the Internet. But there are questions. Is this really an entire netnography? What sort of participant observation occurred? Was it self-reflective? Who is the ethnographic 'self' reflected given that the article is written by five authors? Does it really matter if there is participation, or what kind of participation matters? Although the authors probe deeply underneath the skin of the nature of tattooing, and how it reflects nursing's deep paradoxes and ambivalences, their analysis leaves largely unpenetrated the way this ritual interacts with online interaction, sociality and consociality.

Does a symbolic netnography such as this one worry about the sample? About the nurses who would choose to get tattoos thereby being included in the research? About which subset of tattoos would their bearers choose to share with others? About those who found websites? About which photos and which tattoos were excluded, and which included?

In the symbolic netnography, for the most part, we consider it, and it should inflect our analysis. But representative sampling is most certainly not a crucial matter. We rely upon the skill of the netnographer-as-instrument, the interpretive skill of the cultural researcher and their ability to use scientific skill and semiotic imagination to sample both broadly (400 complex images is not a minor dataset) and deeply (for a profound reading of multiple images is not a minor undertaking). Thus does netnography move easily from studies of sites, such as nursing communities, to topics, such as popular themes in shared representational images of nursing shared online. Particular research practices harmonize with particular questions and areas of interest, exemplifying the much-lauded flexibility of ethnography and, in this specific case, netnography in action. And yet, the thread of a personal story is something that future work in the area might delve into more deeply. Who are the authors? What drives their interest in the topic? Are they, themselves linked? Compelling netnographies are strung with the beads of personal stories, decorated with tales and images of human artifacts. They are careful curations of others' creative creations.

SIX FUNDAMENTAL CONCEPTUAL CONSTRUCTIONS ABOUT THE DIFFERENCES BETWEEN TRADITIONAL ETHNOGRAPHY AND NETNOGRAPHY

Although they are often intertwined, online interactions and groupings and physically embodied social interactions and gatherings possess some fundamentally different characteristics that necessitate and influence the approach of netnography. There are six fundamental differences: alteration, access, archiving, analysis, ethics and colonization.

Alteration

First is the alteration of communication to suit the technological medium, be it a Facebook page's formatting requirements, a Twitter post's restrictive 140-character limit, YouTube's requirements of some video literacy, or the simple transmission behind the translation of a speech act into a textual post. There is nothing inherently 'unnatural' about technologically mediated social interaction, no more, ultimately, than television, the telegram, the book, organized art or religion. And yet, it is different. Just as the changes in our vocabulary indicate, where 'selfie' becomes an accepted word featured in the dictionary, that difference is dynamic, a cultural moving target.

History teaches us that the new ages heralded by the introduction of new technologies are not always as revolutionary as they at first may seem (Schivelbusch, 1986: 36). Technological innovations are usually greeted with utopian glee, only to become disappointments after their early failures. In our impetuous impatience, we barely notice their gradual improvements. After a time, they change and their changes may miraculously change everyday life in radical new ways. As a universal archive and the ultimate communication experience, both of them incredibly amplified, the Internet has grown so far beyond its predecessors that it is technologically something entirely Other.

Just as the railways rapidly altered peoples' subjective perception in almost no time of what was possible in terms of covering a certain distance in a certain amount of time, so too did networked computing radically transform people's ideas. It changed how they thought about with whom they could communicate. When, how, how often, how many, and even why. The meaning of a breakup by text message or WhatsApp is entirely different from the meaning of a breakup by Skype (Gershon, 2010). It is this subjective sense of personally grounded understanding that is in many ways so significant to a cultural understanding of the Internet, because with it comes reflexivity, awareness and the resonant enactment of archetypal narratives.

We now have so many choices: even in a single application like Facebook we can text, message, share photos, talk in videophone, post to our network, comment, like and interact in a number of ways. We have many choices, just as we do in person and with spoken communications, a range of social innuendo online, a symbolic and temporal cartography and topography to the social interaction. In many ways, we can see a more sophisticated and considered self-presentation, frames that are stronger than the ones we might see in ordinary daily life. It is one of the jobs of netnography to try to understand how communications are altered. It is one of the netnographic tasks to understand a particular group by following the trail of rapid but somehow taken-for-granted technological changes, in different situations, with different groups.

Access

Second is a very different level of access, where existing friends can communicate more intensely, where online interactions may gain attention over physical ones (think of the person on a date checking their Facebook account constantly), and where access to the public, to marginal groups, or to complete strangers who may or may not share some interests, become commonplace and simple. The participatory, egalitarian ethic of the Internet apparently originated from its contact with academic and hacker communities whose ethos was 'information should be free'. Online social interactions manifest this ethos through the general democracy and inclusiveness of many, if not most, online social sites. All of the major social networking and social media sites, many newsgroups, forums and boards, blog and newspaper comment pages, offer open membership, and also provide informational guides to help neophytes join their network to the network. New blood enriches the system.

Language is still an issue. Mandarin speakers tend to remain with Mandarin speakers, and only very rarely partake in conversations with, say, Portuguese speakers. Prior studies told us that large online groups are less communal, social and friendly than small groups (e.g., Baym, 1995; Clerc, 1996), but this was exactly the problem that the social networking sites solved with Friendster and MySpace. By breaking up the board and disregarding topics as the central organizing principle in favour of social networks, the evolving Internet facilitated a different kind of mix of intimacy and excitement, the new and the familiar. The opportunities for dyadic relations are everywhere, from every link of Facebook and LinkedIn. With Twitter, Instagram and Pinterest, so many brands and personal brands are now within a moment's reach.

Anonymity is still present in the age of Facebook and LinkedIn, but it is increasingly unnecessary for many. Anonymity can confound and trouble researchers seeking to fix a particular demographic onto textual and other productions posted online. Who *is* one communicating with in an online social interaction? Often it is not a particular person, but more of a particular imagined and intended audience. Is it different with an online Skype interview, which is recorded, stored, archived and shared as the dataset? Bound up in the network, the dataset reveals that person's network and simultaneously the centre of that person's network. Like the sun in a solar system, we can discern the most non-anonymous figure in the netnography, the most present being in the text. Anonymity and its close cousin pseudonymity make the netnographic approach necessarily different from the approach of face-to-face ethnography.

We have known for a long time that online social interaction is a unique public–private hybrid that offers participants the allure of stepping into the global spotlight before an 'audience'. They potentially become celebrities, micro-celebrities, and perhaps we should talk of macro-celebrities, or meso-celebrities. And perhaps we might even one day scale celebrity on a hundred point scale, with different descriptions of all the types and intensities of celebrity-hood. For, make no mistake, along with Bitcoin, celebrity is one of the new Coins of the Realm. Multiple institutions, from government to research to industry are happy to see the boundless opportunities inherent not only in assisting people as they exhibitionistically share or even broadcast their most private stuff, but also to publicly help them voyeuristically partake in the private information of others. The surveillance state is a multi-panopticon. People are watched by institutional actors, and watch institutional actors, but they also watch each other. This new level of voyeurism and exhibitionism is substantially unlike anything a face-to-face ethnographer would encounter. Accessibility is therefore another key difference to which the netnographic approach must be tuned.

Archiving

Third is the record keeping and archiving functionality of social media. Although in-person social interactions can be memorable or even noted, usually they evaporate as they occur, leaving only memories. Online social interactions often leave a more permanent trace. In fact, as 'Twitter sexter' and perfectly named American politician Anthony Weiner discovered, online social interactions are automatically archived, easily shared and create permanent records.

The Internet is an archive, an incredible one. The term persistent world has been coined to refer to the lasting qualities of virtual worlds online, and changes made to them by users, even after a user has exited the site or software program. This persistent quality applies equally well to the social aspect of the Internet that captures interactions. Back in 1996, Newhagen and Rafaeli (1996) were already noting that 'communication on the Net leaves tracks to an extent unmatched by that in any other context – the content is easily observable, recorded, and copied. Participant demography behaviours of consumption, choice, attention, reaction, learning and so forth, are widely captured and logged'. Almost 20 years later, considerable sophistication has been added in our ability to sort, find and monitor these records.

Efficient search engines make accessible every interaction, every hashtag, every mention including misspellings, or every posting on a given topic. The physical analogy would be to have access to recordings of every public social contact. The recording of synchronous conversations and interactions does not present much of a technical challenge. For netnographers, it presents enormous opportunity.

Analysis

The fourth difference relates to the many more and different forms of analysis that we can bring to bear against this range of diversified cultural material and its information. As we will discuss in Chapters 7 and 8, this wealth of information creates enormous challenges and temptations for ethnographic research study. The tradeoffs of mass data capture and analysis are unique to netnography and perhaps more than any other characteristic mark a distinct divide with the traditions of in-person ethnography. The ability to mine, scrape, capture, automatically code and monitor data flows is a novel capacity of which traditional ethnographers such as Herodotus could never have even dared to dream.

Ethics

This leads to a fifth difference: a range of ethical and social questions about these new modes of interaction, regarding governance and rights within this communication form, questioning whether it is a private or public space, or some unique hybrid. The legal and connected moral systems of the world are struggling to adapt to ever-changing technologies and their impact on individuals, culture and society. These ethical differences are captured and treated in depth in Chapter 6 of this book.

Colonization

Finally, large corporate and organizational interests have intensely colonized online interactions, and this has changed and continues to change the nature of social interaction, and even society, in a way not seen with earlier forms of in-person social interaction. Throughout this book, we will mention and sometimes examine the distinct differences that corporate involvement in social media and the Internet make on the research enterprise. The discussion of communal and commercial tensions from Chapter 2 is one such example.

And, Finally, the Choir Breaks into Rapt Song

The analysis of existing online conversations and other Internet discourse combines options that are both naturalistic and unobtrusive – a powerful combination that sets netnography apart from focus groups, depth interviews, surveys, experiments and in-person ethnographies. As we will detail in the next chapter, netnography can only compliment and hope to complement existing legitimate methods such as social network analysis, big data approaches, smart data and predictive modelling and psychological experiments. It is apparent that many of these techniques can easily work in concert with one another. Results from one type of study can simply and usefully inform the research questions of any other type of study.

For example, a netnographic charting of the contours and classifications of new online social experiences from the inside out will inform the survey work done to confirm and to quantify these classifications of different types. Similarly, netnographically derived assertions about the relationship between different types of online social interaction and involvement in participatory culture can be studied with further survey work. The social structures underlying these divergent networks can also be analysed using social network analysis. In conjunction with one another, a fuller portrait can be painted of the mulitifaceted nature of online and, increasingly, even offline phenomena. I counsel the scholar to remember these possibilities as they go forward and to remain ecumenical and open-minded when it comes to questions of the truth or superiority of one method over another. The question, instead, is one of collaboration. No form of collaboration should be impossible in this exciting age of intertwining technique.

SUMMARY

This chapter delved into different methods that would be considered complementary with netnography. It began by taking a big picture look at the choice of method. Should one choose qualitative or quantitative? In most cases, these differences were found to be false or politically maintained distinctions. Netnography is about obtaining cultural understandings of the experiences of people and groups from online social interaction and content, and understanding them scientifically. Some of the complementary methods that were discussed include the use of survey data and findings, interviews and journal methods, and social network analyses. The chapter concluded with a long section comparing traditional ethnography to netnography, noting similarities and differences in a systematic and organized manner. Online and off, online communicative participation and online archival download and observation, ethnography and netnography are all concepts that are embedded within particular, situated, local and contextualized research practices. Individual social media interactions, experiences and identities are brought to life as we enact them online.

KEY READINGS

Eriksson, Henrik, Mats Christiansen, Jessica Holmgren, Annica Engstrom and Martin Salzmann–Erikson (2014) 'Nursing under the skin: A netnographic study of metaphors and meanings in nursing tattoos', *Nursing Inquiry*, 21(4): 318–326.

Garton, Laura, Caroline Haythornthwaite and Barry Wellman (1999) 'Studying on-line social networks', in Steve Jones (ed.), *Doing Internet Research: Critical Issues in Methods for Examining the Net*. Thousand Oaks, CA: Sage. pp. 75–105.

Wright, Kevin B. (2005) 'Researching internet-based populations: Advantages and disadvantages of online survey research, online questionnaire authoring software packages, and web survey services', *Journal of Computer-Mediated Communication*, 10 (April).

4

NETNOGRAPHY REDEFINED

ON(WARDS) NETNOGRAPHY

Netnography is the name given to a specific set of related data collection, analysis, ethical and representational research practices, where a significant amount of the data collected and participant-observational research conducted originates in and manifests through the data shared freely on the Internet, including mobile applications. This emphasis on significant amounts of Internet data differentiates netnography from approaches such as digital ethnography or digital anthropology that are more general in orientation and, for example, can include more traditional ethnographies examining how national cultures inflect mobile Internet use (e.g., Miller and Slater, 2000), technology use within the home (e.g., Silverstone and Hirsch, 1992), or occupational cultures of software developers (see Tacchi, 2012; see also the overview of Coleman, 2010).

Yet, as described in Chapter 3, the notion of significant amounts of research data originating from the Internet absolutely does not preclude extending netnographic data collection to interviews conducted via email, Skype, in person, or using other methods. It does not obviate the need to ground, emplace and contextualize data through the analysis of other related archives and sites, including ones that include fleshy contact. It opens up the possibilities of incorporating and blending computational methods of data collection, analysis, word recognition, coding and visualization. It most certainly does not limit analysis to content analysis. Netnography's focus and forte has always been the myriad communicative acts and interactions flowing through the Internet. These can be textual, graphic, photographic, audiovisual, musical, commercially influenced and sponsored or not. They can be collectively or individually produced. They may be situated in and through single or multiple sites and formats. Netnography begins and ends with an explicitly human window into the rich communicative and symbolic world of people and groups as they use the Internet, the Web, and social media, leaving its traces and transmissions for us to discover and decode.

FROM VIRTUAL ETHNOGRAPHY TO REAL NETNOGRAPHY

My thinking on netnography and online netnography are increasingly enriched by repeat engagements with *Virtual Ethnography* (Hine, 2000). In this important and influential book, Christine Hine charted some of the key ontological and epistemological challenges that a researcher faces when applying the notion of ethnography to the study of online community. In the first place, Hine (2000: 9) notes that the Internet can be viewed as both a type of 'place, cyberspace, where culture is formed and reformed' and also that it is 'a product of culture' or a 'cultural artefact'. Online ethnography must take account of these disrupted boundaries, and be able to accommodate the fact that the Internet manifests culture as both setting and product, as simultaneously placelike and artifactual.

Comparing the online and face-to-face variants of ethnography, Hine (2000: 63–6) suggests that ethnography online is deficient in some important ways:

> virtual ethnography is not only virtual in the sense of being disembodied. Virtuality also carries a connotation of 'not quite', adequate for practical purposes even if not strictly the real thing ... Virtual ethnography is adequate for the practical purpose of exploring the relations of mediated interaction, even if not quite the real thing in methodologically purist terms. It is an adaptive ethnography which sets out to suit itself to the conditions in which it finds itself. (Hine, 2000: 65)

What exactly are we to make of Hine's (2000: 10) suggestion that an ethnographic narrative is presented as authentic when it contains 'Face-to-face interaction and the rhetoric of having travelled to a remote field site'? Perhaps this is an early response that charts where a particular conceptual boundary stood at a particular time. Clearly, by definition, an online ethnography cannot have these qualities. The location question is especially vexing because 'the concept of the field site is brought into question. If culture and community are not self-evidently located in place, then neither is ethnography' (Hine, 2000: 64). As a result, 'virtual ethnography is necessarily partial. A holistic description of any informant, location or culture is impossible to achieve' (Hine, 2000: 65). Online ethnographies are therefore always 'wholeheartedly partial' in virtual ethnography: they are 'almost but not quite like the real thing' (Hine, 2000: 10).

Yet surely the notion of a 'real' ethnography, an online ethnography, a virtual ethnography, and a netnography are as socially constructed as the notion of an ethnography itself. All constructions of 'reality' and 'authenticity', practicality, and even 'adequacy' and 'holism' are contextually determined, consensually maintained, collaboratively enforced, and contingent upon standards that we deem or do not deem to accept.

There is no *really real* ethnography, no *de facto* perfect ethnography that would satisfy every methodological purist. It exists not as some perfect practice, nor, as for Rogers (2009), as some outdated technique. Nor does there need to be. As John van Maanen (1988) illustrated, there is a vast variety of different types of ethnography, from realist narratives to fantastic travelogue adventures, from reflective auto-ethnographies to polyvocal polylogues, from impressionistic tales to starkly statistical large-scale portraits and even vivid videographies. There is no reason why, amidst all the choices and flexibility of ethnography, we could not include 'face-to-face interaction' – through Skype, for instance, or embodied with someone we met through Twitter and then email – or travel to a 'remote field site' consisting of a foreign language online social space with extremely eclectic and highly coded social practices. In fact, as the last chapter asserts, there is no reason why a netnography interested in, say mobile phone rituals in rural China would not also travel to rural China – a perhaps remote field site. We have almost unlimited potential for inclusive, resonant and creative expression of ethnography that would include polyvocal polylogues of polymedia (Madianou and Miller, 2011).

Miller and Horst (2012: 24) emphasize the role of materiality in digital anthropology, arguing that studying what it means to be human also means studying how human beings socialize 'within a material world of cultural artefacts that include the order, agency, and relationships between things themselves and not just their relationships to persons'. We thus have three forms of materiality to contend with in any anthropology of the digital: the materiality of technology and the digital infrastructure itself, the materiality of digital content itself, and the materiality of the digital as context (Miller and Horst, 2012: 25). Hence, the use of the term virtual itself seems to lend gravity to what Blanchette (2011) terms 'the trope of immateriality', where digital 'culture' or 'community' also partake of a sort of presumed ephemerality that empirically does not and philosophically cannot exist. Yet it does exists still as a belief, both emic and etic. '[C]omputers are unique in the history of writing technologies in that they present a premediated material environment built and engineered to propagate an illusion of immateriality' (Kirschenbaum, 2008: 135). The Internet looks and feels virtual because it has been designed this way. However, we must realize that it is as immaterial as the various smokestacks, batteries and wind farms that partially power it.

From founding father Bronislaw Malinowski we learn the lasting good advice that 'The fieldworker must spend at least a year in the field, use the local vernacular, live apart from his own land, and above all make the psychological transference whereby "they" becomes "we"' (van Maanen, 1988: 36). With netnography and online social experience, these criteria are seemingly hopelessly compromised, leading Hine (2000) to assert that ethnography online will always be a narrative of concession, immaterial and inauthentic, perhaps a tale of the long tail of humanity, rather than a true story of the field. However, Hine (2000: 10) suggests that we might shift our evaluation of ethnographic authenticity to one that seeks an ethnographer who has 'similar experiences to those of informants, however those experiences are mediated'. The key to a virtual ethnographer's legitimacy in virtual ethnography, then, is researcher participation: 'gaining a reflexive understanding of what it is to be part of the Internet' (Hine, 2000: 10). As it stretches to accommodate the virtual, Hine sees ethnography changing, 'opening up', to transcend 'holistic' studies of 'bounded culture' and instead becoming a place where ethnographic engagement with a field site is replaced with 'an experientially based knowing' that 'draws on connection rather than location in defining its object' (Hine, 2000: 10). This is immensely helpful theorizing that helps us to undergird netnography, and any online ethnography, differently than traditional ethnography. The principles of virtual ethnography thus provide a useful launch point for a discussion of the conceptual underpinnings of netnography. Hine (2000: 63–65) offers ten 'principles for virtual ethnography' which I interpret and summarize here:

1. Ethnography is based on the sustained physical presence of an ethnographer in a cultural field site, combined with intensive engagement with the everyday life of culture members.
2. Interactive media, such as the Internet and social media, question the notion of a field site of interaction because they must be understood as both culture and cultural artifact.
3. Ethnography in a culture of mediated interaction, such as the Internet, makes the notion of location unnecessary.
4. Ethnography moves from a conception of location and boundary to one of flow and connectivity.
5. Cultural, social, ontological, epistemological and other boundaries in virtual ethnography are not to be assumed *a priori*, but to be explored through the course of the research.
6. Temporal dislocation accompanies spatial dislocation in virtual ethnography.
7. Virtual ethnography is necessarily partial because it cannot achieve descriptions of informants, locations, or culture in their entirety. (However, I would add that this is an impossible ideal. I would also add that online ethnography in return makes visible many interactions and relations which would be difficult if not impossible to discern in any other manner).
8. The ethnographer's intensive and reflexive engagement with mediated interaction and the technologies that influence it are a valuable source of insight.
9. The shaping of the ethnography by the use of technology forms the backbone of the ethnography.
10. Virtual ethnography is adequate for exploring technologically mediated interactions.

From all of the aforementioned principles and ideas, I formulate and synthesize my guidelines for netnographic inquiry. I also keep closely in mind Miller and Horst's (2012: 29) important contention that 'the key to digital anthropology, and perhaps to the future of anthropology itself, is, in part, the study of how things become rapidly mundane'. It is to a recognition not that the virtual is immaterial, but precisely because it grows to seem immaterial, that our research practices must be specially attuned. Around the globe, Internet based communications, interactions, information exchanges and experiences are achieving not merely acceptance, but the 'moral incorporation' written about by Silverstone et al. (1992) where radically new technological innovations become taken for granted, and norms prevail to guide their usage. Based in the latest thinking about notions of culture, community, ethnography, and networked individualism, these guidelines ground the ontology and epistemology of netnography, especially as it affects immersion.

CITATION, SITUATION AND STORYTELLING

Everyday life and myriad studies reveal a Cambrian period-like expansion of forms of online social being. Netnographers are akin to Old World biologists when scientists discovered the New World: all of a sudden the world was teeming with new forms of life again, some familiar, some strangely different. The netnographer's task is to chronicle living life in these times, in these particular contexts, and then to analyse it to understand key questions about our humanity. As we begin to see patterns of freedom and enslavement, agency and structure, system and individual, in notions of belonging to multiple online social networks, ideas of social structure in and of themselves liberate us and constrain us in certainly somewhat predictable ways and in particular circumstances more than others. Technoculture is the terrain we traverse. Who lives in it? How? How do they connect? How is their identity altered by the technocultural engagement? What do people do with and to and through it? What does it reveal about the groups to which they belong? How can we get to know them deeper through their communications? These are some of the questions of the netnographer.

And yet the terrain is shifting so quickly that we might wonder if our theories and tests can completely keep up with changes such as new technologies, new social forms, new forms of business, new forms of economy and exchange. Are we actually moving closer to our imagined futures, our intended better places, our utopias – as we seem to always say when any new technology, even a website or an app, is launched? All the while, it sometimes does seem as if many technological Pandora's gift-boxes are being opened all at the same time. We need sober thinking to help us to understand these rapid and simultaneous changes. And so, onto this steep and muddy cliff, which calls for the charting of new online social realities, steps the netnographer.

For it is the netnographer's job to chronicle and storytell in a lasting, memorable and honourable way the emerging cultural memes and consocialities that replace notions of self, notions of other, notions of small kin groups and larger friendship groups, collegial networks and professional networks as we transfer more and more of our attention and identity onto the digitizing of our lived experiences in various ways. These choices often revolve around our selves, our self-presented shot, the selfie at the core of our personal profile. And thus our own personal networks serve as a very solid basis for study, but by no means more than a powerful starting point. If networked individualism is the core of the network, we must first seek the Deep N of One. Auto-ethnography is at this core, poetry, self-reflection or, as has been developed in theories of consumer behaviour and culture: introspection.

Then, we must turn to our friends, new and sometimes old, and we must tell their stories. It is entirely within the ethnographic storytelling context to change names and grant 'pseudonyms'. Reaching out, one voice calling to other voices is necessary. It cannot be a one way suctioning of data: this is not netnography. This is instead data mining, or automated qualitative coding and perhaps big data analysis/analytics. These techniques rely heavily on machine intelligence to look at massive amounts of data in unprecedented ways. But reaching out and participating in a research project with a human voice is the basis of the practice of netnography. This is what I advocate: working on your profile and social media profiles as what you are: netnographic researchers performing digital anthropology into people's social experiences and interactions in web and mobile social media sites. Interactions with other living and breathing people. I advocate the method of the research web-page which could also of course be a mobile app. However, networks should join other networks as we also venture out to observe and perhaps ask community members directly, on their own sites, while they are doing their own thing, for help with our research.

Immersion is key. Centring in the now of cultural being is essential for the netnographer: it is this essential core of her 'doing' of netnography that links her in real and human time, in the timing of drums and breath and walking, to read the words, to hear the stories, to learn the terms, and understand them, of the groups and the people she seeks to understand.

IMMERSION IN NETNOGRAPHY

Netnography faithfully exports anthropology's set of ontological, epistemological, and axiological commitments to the study of online social experience. The contours of this experience influence and inflect extant ethnographic practices – such as making cultural entrée, keeping fieldnotes, interviewing participants, using hermeneutic interpretation, ensuring consent and providing human, humane and resonant representations. In addition, the experience adds specific and detailed new topics and practices that include locating communities and topics, narrowing data, handling large digital datasets with digital forms of analysis, navigating difficult online ethical matters and procedures, and using the digital medium as a representational research affordance.

In netnography, ethnographic immersion is more like the immersion of professional divers in the giant aquariums of big cities, where they dip in and dive about for a certain amount of time, swimming with rays, sharks and the many multicoloured fish before returning to the other 'reality' of land breathing animals that they know. Then, the netnographer might make more appointments to do that. It is not necessarily the traditional immersion of the culture member, or more accurately the researcher studying the people and structures that identify openly with them. It may be that shared identities do not even come into it. Some netnographies are purely reflective, or reflexive, or refractive. Some do not need to transcend beyond the most particular: our selves, our inner thoughts and sense of feeling that can be expressed purely as poetry, video, or any other deeply understood text. It can be hard to study an actual gathering of people, and appreciate it in a human sense, without gaining this fully 'human' appreciative understanding, one which comes when you are actually communicating with other people. However, there are many ways to gain this understanding. For some it can mean broadcasting a message out there to the world that talks about you or something you care about as your research topic, then charting the social and human response from the personal level, then extrapolating out to explore topics in social media. The approach has many choices within it.

Netnography as a process partakes in the ethnographic quality of moving from outside to in. The netnographer, like the ethnographer, begins her investigation socially outside a group or notional space or set of interactions and then moves increasingly inside of it to finally return out again to explain what is happening on the inside. It can happen through interaction or through inaction, through activity or through passivity, but it must be reflected upon to be part of the netnographic enterprise: the reflective field noting is thus a central part of the technique. Fieldnotes, in fact, become a central core of this new netnography, a netnography built as much of one's own story and stories (relating much of this through the magic of abstraction to 'theory generation' and 'theory development' including frequent 'theoretical synthesis') as the stories of others.

NETNOGRAPHY: STATE OF THE ART

Looking at Netnography Today

What is the state of the art regarding netnography in the social sciences today? When Bengry-Howell et al. (2011: 8) searched Google Scholar for research using netnography, they found 'in the region of 1,300 results'. They offer several conclusions from their early research overview of the method. First, '42% of the citations for netnography were direct applications of netnography' and 'most applied the steps that Kozinets outlines and claimed to be following his method' (Bengry-Howell et al., 2011: 11). At that time, they found that 24% of netnography's citations were already coming from outside areas related to business. The use in these areas was growing rapidly as netnography diffused to other fields, even prior to the publication of the first edition of this book. 60% of the citations about netnography came from outside of the USA. Bengry-Howell et al. (2011) concluded that

> there has been a steady increase in citations referring to the method. The majority of citations relate to applications of netnography but there are also a high number of citations where Kozinets and/or netnography is referenced or referred to ... There is some evidence of take-up or interest in the approach from wider social science disciplines .... there are citations from authors in a wide range of other countries; there are a high number of citations by authors in Europe, particularly the UK. There are also some citations from Australasia and Hong Kong. This certainly indicates some global spread of the approach.

In their analysis of netnographic citations, Bartl et al. (2013) assert that their study's population was the 284 hits for netnography in total that showed up in major databases that were published between 1997 and 2012, which they weeded down to 116 articles for study. The study does not seem to include books, trade magazines and journals, conference proceedings, dissertation papers or online journals. Still, it seems a reasonable sample even if it is not comprehensive, and certainly tells us about the way that journals that are listed on big databases view and receive netnography. It should be noted that business and management perspectives have heretofore been entwined with netnography as a research method, because these papers needed to move through an academic top-tier journal review process in order to contribute to my own career aspirations to be a full and tenured professor.

Aside from a handful or two of publications in the centre of marketing, most netnographies are not yet appearing in top tier journals in various other fields such as nursing, education, communications, women's studies, geography, political science, Internet studies, game studies, addiction research, health care, anthropology, sociology, library sciences and religious studies – although they are appearing at the periphery, and in increasing numbers. I believe that experienced netnographers – and yes, this certainly means you if I have cited you here, or even if you think that I should be citing you right now – only need to ramp up the quality and imagination of their efforts. In henceforth unpublished research that Daiane Scaraboto and I conducted at the Schulich School of Business, we found that, of ranked publications which had published netnographies, 23% were top-tier publications, with 16% second-tier, 29% third-tier and 32% fourth-tier (according to the ABAS journal rating scale). This is a fairly even distribution, which seems promising. We also found that the fields that cited it included the ones listed in the first sentence of this paragraph.

Almost 60% of the work published as a netnography included multiple methods as the netnographic approach, demonstrating that the adaptability and flexibility associated with ethnography have transferred to netnography. The most commonly combined method was interviews, online, phone or in person. Next were surveys, archival data, focus groups, case studies, diary methods, introspective storytelling, sketch or 'mind' maps, and student discussion. 65% say that they investigate more than a single online site. And so we find that the method is being used more as a grounding for multimethod improvisation and a branching out into online social space in search of research experiences and answers.[1]

We also find some interesting methodological insights. A full 75% of papers do not mention or utilize field notes. This leaves a perfect quarter, 25%, who are using the method as a source of reflective network outbranching. And it is also interesting to note that almost 20% of research publications mention the use of a 'research web-page' as originally used and noted in some early netnography work, and described in the first edition of *Netnography*. 27% of articles refer to the use of a search engine, and Google dominates those mentions, followed by specialized tools like Medline, Technorati, PubMed and channels like YouTube.

It seems that, as we do analytics to determine the core keyword area searches for netnography articles, we find the biggest cluster around the category 'Definition and Procedure'. The next biggest category is that related to the study of consumers and to culture or country. Then there were technology and innovation associations. And then huge, overarching and difficult to categorize categories of brand, sports and entertainment, tourism, and healthcare and food. These search results bespeak a huge diversity of topics and keyword associations for netnography, beyond that it is a technique. And this is exactly as it should be. Pick up on the legitimacy of the approach, the existence of common and established standards, and then study something specific, in context. That is, for many, it seems, the heart of netnography.

I think that the best netnographies most definitely have not been composed yet. I do think that they will be more like compositions than like texts, and I would expect that video in fact would be the choice of medium for expansive and high quality netnography – video accompanied by a paper manuscript. Old and new, coexisting.

For a book chapter on qualitative data analysis in netnography, I considered performing a netnography of sites dedicated to netnography and ended with some short illustrations and an analysis of postings on the dedicated netnography LinkedIn group (Kozinets et al., 2014). A netnography of netnography sites has a certain recursive appeal. Today, in October 2014, when I search Google Scholar for netnography, my search yields about 4000 results. As I examine the results of these searches, it seems that netnography continues its spread to a range of social science disciplines, and to countries outside of the United States. In fact, the first edition of this book, which was published only as Bengry-Howell et al. (2011) were conducting their research, has garnered hundreds of citations and attempts to offer a more general research approach to an international audience, as you must already know because you are reading this book.

A SPECTRUM OF NETNOGRAPHIES

In this section, we will overview and attempt to make some sense of the considerable number of netnographies that have already been written and published to date. I have worked with Daiane Scaraboto and Monique Lim on related projects that looked at the body of work published using or directly related to netnography, and benefited from the work of Bengry-Howell et al. (2011) and Bartl et al. (2013). My findings here draw upon and attempt to significantly extend this work. I will thus discuss several patterns in the extant netnographic literature. These are not intended to be comprehensive or exhaustive overviews of the literature – those were provided in the section above. Instead in this section what I would like to do is comment on the present of netnography prior to introducing an updated netnographic research approach, one that has evolved by responding to the challenges of the social media space and the potential that I believe to be inherent in the method. They are as follows:

- That netnography has often been used to reveal discourse about hidden and stigmatic behaviours that may be more difficult to study in person, giving it a voyeuristic quality.
- That netnographies tend to be conducted at some degree of researcher distance, with site immersion and engagement rendered opaque.
- That some netnographic researchers tend to constrain their datasets to a smaller amount of data, focusing on their research question's frame, and using depth techniques like discourse analysis.
- That some netnographic researchers tend to open their datasets to large amounts of data, sometimes vast amounts or 'big data' and integrate computational analysis and visualization tools into their netnographies.
- That data collection and analysis are framed by academic disciplines, and the resulting research is disciplined by this framing.
- That many netnographies do not focus exclusively on particular groups or sites, but tend to focus more on topics that are related to groups, sites, or multiple sites.
- That site selection often involves some sort of negotiation process with site owners or data managers.
- That the use of netnographic research is often justified in terms of emphasizing its concern over having identifiable stages in a process, steps in a procedure, and among these one of the most often cited is guidelines for research ethics.

We now proceed to discuss these observations in the context of published netnography. In later chapters, this spectrum of netnographies will inform the development of four ideal types of netnography: the linguistic and cultural translating Symbolic Netnography, the computationally assisted method embracing Digital Netnography, the introspective and revealing Auto-netnography, and the praxis-driven, resonance seeking, and to some extent publicly accessible and shared Humanist Netnography. These representational forms of netnography will be detailed in Chapters 10 and 11. For the next few sections, we explore various facets of extant netnographies with some examples and discussion.

REVELATIONS OF STIGMA AND A PENCHANT FOR VOYEURISM

In the first instance, there is a clear pattern of netnographic investigation being used to reveal ideas, opinions and behaviours that have some degree of stigma to them. The optional anonymity and the feeling of freedom in Internet communications combine with people's strong needs to connect, share, as well as find information and emotional support from other people who can understand them. The result is that researchers who seek insights into normally hidden behaviours such as drug addiction can find amazing treasure troves online of discourse, shared advice, and even personal connections to further their understanding of these critically important areas (see also van Hout, 2014).

How do people talk about their recreational use of very dangerous drugs such as ketamine, a psychedelic used as a general anaesthetic, in online forums? Addiction researcher and theorist Melissa Tackett-Gibson (2008) conducted a netnography of ketamine forums and found that their discussions nuanced, provided culture-level detail, and generally supported Beck's risk society theories. In particular, the data revealed how Beck's framing of risks relies on experts, while online social exchanges provide new experts and expertise that must be considered in contemporary society.

In the second instance, the participative stance of the netnographer in published works still seems to be at a considerable distance from the phenomenon she or he studies. Consider the stance within the story of the netnographer in the netnography in this citation from Tackett-Gibson's (2008) ketamine forum study:

> 'Research into the long-term impact of K use is still in its infancy, much like the research into MDMA use was a decade ago. Now the evidence is strong that MDMA is a harmful drug, and it's looking like K will be the same. Having said all that, I like K very much' (The Harder Stuff, 2001). Ketamine, like many other drugs discussed at DrugSite was considered potentially harmful. However, its harmful effects were believed to be (in comparison to other hallucinogens) minor and quite manageable. ... Ketamine risks were associated with physical health effects, environmental causes of injury or harm, and social harm. Even so, the harmful effects of ketamine were not considered a serious concern of those who infrequently used small amounts of the drug and controlled their use and use environment.

In this set of quotes, the netnographer's narrative voice sounds like a fellow scientist citing another scientist's voice, another online scholar's statement that she is quoting. The person cited has expertise status, and discussed 'research into the long-term impact of K'. This person declares the research in its infancy and finding the drug's results similar to MDMA, in that the drug is clearly harmful. The netnographic narrative effect is a bit like etic piled on top of etic, as the netnographer details the perspective shared by online social interactants. The etic form of citing another scholar, to the scholarly readers of the journal, sounds emic. So what we have in this case is actually an emic-sounding narrative of the participants, which is actually composed of etic terms of expertise – the inverse of a Malinowski-style ethnography that translates the language of natives into the abstractions of scientists. Nonetheless, the author's voice is authoritative, a recognizably realist tale upon which I can only imagine John van Maanen (1988) would expostulate.

It seems from Tackett-Gibson's methodological narration that her research was challenged by the difficult topic and all of the ethical concerns it raises. Her work needs to be not only etic, but ethical. I can detect volumes in a single, passively worded sentence: 'While the original research design called for the use of ethnographic methods, much like those described by Kozinets (1998), efforts were limited to observing online interactions' (Tackett-Gibson, 2008: 249). Earlier, she has explained that the research required her to collaborate and partner with 'large online drug information websites' – two companies refused, presumably because of fear of US drug law enforcement. On a site where anonymity and confidentiality were difficult but deeply desired, the researchers were directed to try to protect anonymity in a variety of ways. The following description gives some sense of the pragmatic tradeoffs involved in working with the corporation:

> The parameters of research activities were generally established by website administrators and moderators. At their request, our data collection activities were limited to reading, archiving active forum discussions and searching website content and archives. The presence of a researcher/lurker in the forums was not disclosed to participants, nor was it made explicit that the website was collaborating in the project until the survey was administered. Moderators believed that the disclosure of the project might hinder the free exchange of information and impact perceptions of trust in the community, albeit one that interacted in a medium that was publicly accessible online. Although participants were not notified of the project or provided an opportunity to consent to participation, DrugSite users were required to register with the site and 'agree' to terms of use. These terms explicitly notified users that forum communication was the property of the website and nonconfidential. (Tackett-Gibson, 2008: 248)

So although the researcher entered the field intending to perform a netnography as a full participant-observer, her research activities were limited to a more observational, archival, lurking style of data collection. Corporate moderators, who controlled access to the data, made this decision. There is also a falling back to legal and regulatory definitions of correct research ethics, as the terms of use for the site invoking data ownership and the lack of confidentiality are used as a form of proxy for research consent. Nonetheless, the result is a satisfyingly cultural tale after all: a story told at the level of the widespread group. What we find is that 'lay knowledge' – that ever-slippery inverse dotted-line slope between the emic and the etic – is eroding the clear workings of the established risk society of doctors, drug companies and other pharmaceutical experts. No wonder, perhaps, that it was difficult to find drug companies willing to partner the research. The wide and open access of these sites spawns a mutating, mitigating malformation of information we might think of as a cultural gene. This cultural gene is not the fixed, stable, unchangingly viral Dawkinist or Blackmorean kind of a meme at all but more of a living and organic thing. It is culture-generating, culturally generative, and also can be a hallmark of a particular cultural generation. The message of this cultural gene is simple: ketamine is risky, but worth it; you can mitigate the risks by playing it smart; this site and this thread will tell you what you need to do it safely and easily if you decide, after knowing the risks, that you want to do it. It is an incredibly seductive message. There is no hiding it. And its implications for other online sites of seductive subversion and addiction, from how-to-do and how-to-join guides to risky sex habits to bomb production to religious fundamentalism and terrorism, are generalizable and obvious.

Netnographies are framed by their researchers and their researchers' core disciplines in interestingly subtle and gross ways. In this case, the research on ketamine use is framed through a medical world of culture and language. It is intertextually culture-linked to chemical production and pharmacies, drug companies and the medical scientific research education industry establishment. What is the concept that makes the most sense to this framing? Risk, of course. Adopting a particular theoretical worldview and then seeing 'constructions of risk and harm in online discussions of ketamine use' is an entirely appropriate way to frame what is occurring with online social experiences and interactions in this site. It may help that Tackett-Gibson (2008) is affiliated with a College of Criminal Justice in Texas. She articulates her key concerns theoretically around this risk society. She uses a particular data lens to collect the data among two psychedelic and hard drugs discussion forums, finds 120 ketamine titled threads, and then theoretically focuses the data only on 59 discussion threads. She uses 'predefined thematic categories congruent with the research question' to code the data, but also allows for emergent categories, although we do not have a sense of what constituted those emergent categories.

'Having said all that, I like K very much'; the expert turns out to be the addict. Neophyte addicts rely on online experts and systems. Of course, a netnography of a mystical psychedelic site that used ketamine conducted by a religious studies scholar and published in a journal of religious experience scholarship would likely look very different and reach entirely different conclusions. A pharmacy scholar's netnographic look at the same website could reveal a veritable overflowing horn of plenty, a great thanksgiving day of abundant theoretical topics to explore. A sociologist interested in youth culture might find the board resonant with linguistic forms and imagistic functions of the psychedelic past. But in this case, the insights are generally framed, as they rhetorically and epistemologically should be, as relating directly to 'addiction': the first word in the journal's title.

NETNOGRAPHY AS AN ARCHIVE OF LIFE AND WINDOW INTO HIDDEN WORLDS

Netnography's utility in revealing hidden worlds seems a major advantage to studies of private life as well. For example, Small and Harris (2014) considered the touristic topic of 'Crying Babies on Planes'. As a data source, they considered the debates surrounding the phenomenon as it manifested through the archives of public online news sites and discussion boards, and also through the responses of airline websites. They find considerable detail concerning the contours of the social field of discussion surrounding the issue. These include passenger rights and responsibilities, the multiplicity of disciplinary gazes at work in contemporary society, and the many coded practices of travel and tourism. Their analysis reveals that airlines may be oblivious, ignorant of, or simply negligent in addressing the discursive and sociocultural practices and norms surrounding the evaluations of crying babies on airplanes.

Another way that netnography has been used is to try to pry open the door between the public and the private. For example, is there a wider social setting to addiction and addictive behaviours? Do the interactive and confessional forms of discourse on social media give us opportunities to audience more unvarnished accounts of the social exchanges surrounding and perhaps facilitating negative behaviours such as the binge drinking of teenagers? Simone Pettigrew and her colleagues in Western Australia position netnography as a solution to aid with the self-report biases, colloquial language barriers and ethical issues involved in researching teenage binge drinking utilizing other methods. Instead, they used netnography, which they gloss as 'a blend of ethnography, content analysis, and discourse analysis' (Pettigrew et al., 2013: 32) to listen in on teen discussions of their parents' role in their own binge drinking (Pettigrew et al., 2013).

Unlike Tackett-Gibson's study, the researchers did not require extensive collaboration and negotiation with corporate websites to collect their data. Also unlike Tackett-Gibson, Pettigrew et al. (2013) examined a broad range of different sites (but no social networking sites like Facebook, which is full of alcohol related information); they explored the topic of teenage binge drinking across sites, rather than focusing on one topic within one site. As with Tackett-Gibson's study, we learn very little directly about the researcher's own motives or inclination to perform the study, and the participative role is limited largely to a type of focused collector, sorter and reporter of 824 pages (single or double spaced?) of data.

It turns out that, in online discussions found on 14 different websites, adults are a predominantly negative influence. Vigilance was largely absent; tolerance and ignorance were found to be widespread. We do not know much about who is sending these messages, or how representative they might be of general attitudes and actions by Australian teens and their families. We learn little about the reception of these interactions, and what experiences prompt and result from them. In fact, had the four authors to the study reflected upon their own alcohol use as teens, and the use of alcohol by teen members of their family and friend network, perhaps with their own experiences with teenage children, perhaps using their own Facebook contacts as raw material (but reported in only the most general and shielded way), we would have been treated to a more profound and personal portrayal of the phenomenon. Even the addition of a Deep N of One would add colour and insight that is missing from the netnography. The result of the study is a report that suggests there is a problem to address, and that involving parents may be part of the answer. We still do not see the entire picture, but this study certainly unlocks the portal to learning more about the wide range of social influences on drinking and other harmful behaviours that are reflected and developed through online social interactions and experiences.

INTIMACY, ACADEMY AND EXHIBITIONISM

I want us to consider Katrien Jacobs' (2010) ethnographic and auto-ethnographic study of web users' sexual behaviours and self-representations on Adult Friend Finder. AFF, or Adult Friend Finder, is a massive online site dedicated to sexual self-display and finding sexual partners. Jacobs was interested in a set of five questions, several of them quite causal, which included why people in Hong Kong would use the USA-based AFF to find and seduce one another, and why people adopt certain identities and personas on the sex site. Following on the patterns of the two research projects above, we might assume that the researcher in this case would assume an observational research stance, gain AFF's permission to download text and then begin finding relevant threads of data to collect, code, conceptualize and then communicate.

However, Jacobs is inspired to 'maintain empathic and reflective voices to facilitate social knowledge and intimacy' (2010: 693). Jacobs (2010: 693–694) discusses how she 'created the profile of a scholarly sex machine to attract people and to negotiate a sexual-intellectual kind of cooperation' for her ethnographic research.

In August 2006, I uploaded the profile of Lizzy Kinsey, a 40-year-old Caucasian bi-sexual woman and the imagined granddaughter of American sexologist Alfred Kinsey. Alongside my scholarly ambitions to garner data and interview people, I wanted to experiment with my own sexual self-display. I wanted to attract web users and photographed my naked body, while trying to give a hint of my underlying research goals. The picture I selected shows a close-up of my naked torso and breasts, while sitting down on my knees with a pen lying on top of my legs ... Lizzy Kinsey was cast as an outgoing and sexually active female who uses a pen as a reflective tool. The pen could be seen as an instrument to play with sexually or to record stories … In the written part of the profile, people were asked to send me their erotic secrets and stories, or to share experiences in a face-to-face encounter. The response was overwhelming as Lizzy Kinsey received five to six responses on a daily basis. The profile was rewritten a couple of times but it was always generic so that people would have to guess about the underlying motivations. By using the profile, I attracted and teased people who were interested in sex and in picking me up or chatting online, but I slowly revealed to them that I was a researcher who wanted to share and record experiences. Many people simply disappeared at that point, or they masturbated their way through these negotiations and then dropped off, but some remained on board and were willing to share more in-depth information.

Jacobs' article begins to dig deeper into the local sexual personas of the many people she meets. Her dataset flows easily between her electronic interactions and her in-person interviews, which dominate the findings and provide some sense of the social situation of participants and their sexual preferences, such as a Chinese man's Charlie's Angels inspired desire for a blonde white woman or the Chinese woman's desire for a larger Caucasian penis. As a white woman on display and gathering responsive information, Jacobs finds herself entering into a highly racialized zone of sexuality, where culture, community, dreams and preconceptions meet through sexual categories of physical types, body parts and sizes.

Katrien Jacobs' study is part of a larger project, so it offers more of a tempting taste than a full-blown ethnographic engagement. Yet, like the teasing promise of sex with the researcher, the study offers a tantalizing potential that is merely hinted at rather than fulfilled.

As Lizzy Kinsey, I was investigating and playing with a desire to become part of this network, which to me also represents a realm of cross-racial desire to transcend my local alienation. I constructed my own persona with a bad girl flavour to be a sex machine on the site, yet a rebel within the context of academic research. (2010: 700)

The netnographic researcher must take her or his personal social network and combine it with other persons' social and personal networks through online networks. This is a key happening in 'Lizzy Kinsey and the Adult Friendfinders: An ethnographic study of Internet sex and pornographic self-display in Hong Kong'. The ethnography is partial, but successful, because it is a familiar ethnographic tale of familiarization and defamiliarization. Jacobs becomes caught up in a local scene that involves her foreignness, both Hong Kong and AFF, and she struggles to learn and adapt to both. Fieldnotes are primarily used to describe and contextualize interview data.

But we do not catch more than a fleeting glimpse behind Jacobs' academic journal author profile, such as her own deeper impressions, emotional engagements, fears and desires. Was she tempted to act, and if so was she constrained by the research context? What did she learn about her own identity as exotic Other, not only as a sexualized Caucasian woman among Asians, but also of authority-figure, intelligent female, reflexive and interrogative academic among practitioners and experiencers? What is left behind, I find, is a deeper exploration of how her work positions her as 'a rebel within the context of academic research' and especially feminist research such as, for example, that of my adventurously innovative York colleague Shannon Bell (see, for example, Bell, 2010). Jacobs completes her article by speaking about her 'journey of sexual and cultural discovery' (2010: 701) and yet in the article we learn almost nothing about it.

ENGAGEMENT

I understand how hard this self-realizing reflectivity and revelation can be. I am not asking a minor thing. Holding a mirror up to ourselves is not something that comes easily to academics or, indeed, to people. Somehow the 'I' of our work, the core of the network, the researcher and the researcher-as-instrument continue to be written out of almost all netnographies. Even those which seek to include it. Mea culpa.

I have already related the study of nursing tattoos conducted by Erikkson et al. (2014). Complex attitudinal images are important to ascertain as well, and quite amenable to netnographic investigation. When accounting scholars want to know how accountants are portrayed in popular jokes (if they are portrayed at all), they go to www.skp.com.au/humour/ahshort.htm (Miley and Read, 2012). The skill of Miley and Read (2012) in this article, however, is not in data collection, but in their interpretation and metaphorically adept theorizing. Exemplifying a theoretical engagement with the contents of the site, they find that the accountant's popular culture image as portrayed in the online forum are related to the 'comedy of skills' performances of fifteenth century Italian improvisational theatre.

Similarly, Alang and Fomotar (2014) use 1421 messages posted in 236 message threads from a forum for same sex families on a single online website dedicated to a broad range of pregnancy, birth and childcare topics to study post-partum depression in lesbian couples. They describe their research as a 'purely observational' netnography. Studies such as these build out netnography from studies of particular sites and microcultures to studies of topics, social experiences and interactions. They are situated not simply in the 'communal', a term we contested to the point of rupture earlier in this book, but in a notional space of interaction and information exchange around particular topics located on and through particular online sites. What we must consider, however, is the role of researcher engagement in such enterprises. How can netnography remain personal when all that may seem to be required is the download, coding, analysis and reportage of this publicly available data?

I barely acknowledge my own role in some of the netnographies I have written. Although netnography originated as an outcropping of my dissertation research's prolonged and immersive personal and participative engagement in fan communities and extended into the lived experience of coffee consumption, worlds of food connoisseurship, café culture and the discrimination of taste (Kozinets, 1999, 2002a), I eventually came up with the opaque term 'observational netnography' – a moderator that downplays or even eliminates the participative element of the technique – in Brown et al. (2003). Yet there was a certain arbitrary opportunism in this rhetorical move. For, as I wrote the *Star Wars* section of the Retro-Branding article for the *Journal of Marketing* (Brown et al., 2003), there was much of the fanboy persona about me, a person I wished to distance myself from because of my existing identification as a fan scholar.

This article was clearly an early fan netnography of the *Star Wars* fan community, and although it was published under the guise of the *Journal of Marketing*, it was really about a more general and powerful social notion which now extends far beyond business into consumer culture and translocal culturescapes themselves, that of the brand and its stories. What it found was that brands have stories, and the most complex and powerful brands are brands of stories. In 1995–1996, as I was involved in media fan ethnography and writing my first papers about netnography, I was interacting with *X-Files* fans and attending my first *X-Files* convention. In 2001–2002, while writing the retro marketing paper, I was engaging personally with the in-person and online social activities surrounding seeing the classic and newer prequel *Star Wars* films, including seeing them with my young sons. Those films were part of my home, my office, my collections, my life. Researching and writing this article resonated with a particular time in my life when I first saw the first *Star Wars* movie on the big screen. Very retro, on a personal level. Very participative and ethnographic. And also squelched, denied and invisible in the text.

If I had it to do over again I would have built a *Star Wars* fans site and forum. I would have told people that I was a researcher doing research on *Star Wars* topics and this site was my contribution to people who also had interests in that topic. And my site would be new and interesting, well designed, tasteful and professional looking. And my profile would also be new, interesting, well-designed, tasteful and professional looking. And the site would be modest, giving some background on me, my connections, links to some of my work, and then offer a purpose in talking about this particular research project, and providing some context of other academic and scholarly work that have looked at *Star Wars* and *Star Wars* fan communities. And my article would have featured this first personal connection to the *Star Wars* brand, past and present, as part of my research into retro brands.

In the world of science, we seek to keep sharpening and honing our theories, testing them and finding out how and why and when they work, and when they do not. So I can learn publicly, it seems, from my errors in applying netnography. I have taken it more into a direction of unengaged content analysis rather than in a more human-centred, participative, personally, socially and emotionally engaged vector. Now, I have the privilege of redefining netnography, refocusing and redirecting it, two decades after its inception.

This book tries to further elaborate and develop netnography as an approach dedicated to intersubjective mappings of our social media interconnections with one another. A key element of this is to manage not to forget the participative, reflective, interactive and active part of our research in which we use the communicative functions of social media and the Internet. We balance this with the observational aspect of our research activities. This observational aspect is incredibly significant, engaging with a vast and growing set of archives about various topics. We think about engagement with single and multiple sites. We consider the foci that netnography draws us towards, rather than relying upon the types of physical sites, self-identified groups and personal gatherings that simply present themselves conveniently to us. We decide which other research methods will be used along with netnography, and how and when they are combined. We contemplate data analysis. And we consider how the research is to be presented and represented. In all, these considerations lead to a reformulated process for conducting netnography.

THE 12 PHASES OF NETNOGRAPHY

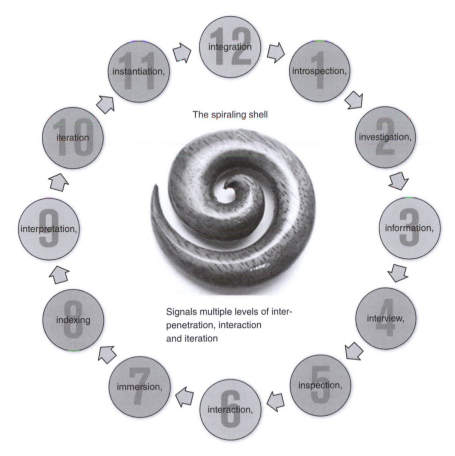

Figure 4.1

We can and should think about netnography as being something that happens during times, and that shows us difference faces during different phases. It is the netnographer's job to make sense of people's current state of being, their social lives, their identities, their values, rituals, language, beliefs, constraints, passions and current technological and cultural messes. These are dynamic, variable matters. More than this, it is the humanist netnographer's duty and, as we will see, her undying passion, to express and help others express and share, at the most fundamental of levels, what our collective hopes and dreams for the future are, what our fears are about the past and what is being lost, and to help organize and share and legitimately and prolifically spread those thoughts about what is going on?, what are our alternatives?, and what can we do about it? It is netnography's job to study the lifeways and lifeworlds of regular people and groups while still minding and modelling the institutional roles of this impossibly interconnected tangle of knots and invisible mendings which needs our consideration, thought, cogitation and solution finding. Let the words on the face of our clock, our reminder of the limits of our time, guide us through the journey through the many faces and phases of humanity appearing over the Internet.

As research practice, netnography has 12 roughly temporal, non-exclusive and often-interacting process levels to help us achieve these lofty objectives:

1. An introspection phase where the researcher must reflect upon the role of the research in her current life project and life themes, and her actual life story as it unfolds.
2. An investigation phase where the researcher crafts and hones the netnographic question, basing it upon the study of sites, topics or people, posing it appropriately, such that it could be reasonably answered by a netnographic research design (otherwise why deploy netnography and not some other approach?).
3. An informational phase, where ethical considerations are raised early, and foreknowledge of acceptable research ethics practices are followed.
4. An initial interview stage where either people or sites are found and then investigatively interviewed and found to match to various online forms of sociality and satisfaction. Search engines and good comprehensive guidelines are key to finding a good range of sites to investigate. This investigation has the purpose of informing our later stages, including interaction, where we will design our interaction research website. Interviews add to the informational phase.
5. A choice that must be made of particular site or sites comes at the phase of inspection, as evaluations and different sorts of site, topic, person and even group combination schemes are possible and useful. Ethnographers of fleshy interactions do not have so many alternatives to choose from in simultaneous and interlinked format. As netnographers, the tradeoffs and key synergies are unique and important.
6. An interaction entrée strategy that plots out the extent of the researcher's participation in online social interactions with other human beings (it may be minimal or zero, but it may also be considerable). In this stage, you should strongly consider creating an interaction research website in order to interact with people in a way that is open, generous and ethical.

7. Immersion in the data, topic or site on a frequent basis constitutes the seventh phase. Depth of understanding in netnography grows organically in a natural unfolding of what feels like 'human' time. This can take many shapes.

8. An indexing data collection strategy, which ensures that an adequate but not overwhelming amount of data is collected from a relevant variety of relevant sources, is the eighth phase. The role of this data is not to encompass the entire great masses of all data on the topic and to reflect, in some sense, the general. Instead this is small data. It reflects some sort of a connoisseurship and then careful weighting of data. This is a strategy that carefully selects lesser amounts of very high quality data that are then used to reveal and highlight meaningful aspects of the particular.

9. Once data is collected, interpretive analysis, or 'interpenetration', should begin in depth immediately and then continuously, as a striving for depth of understanding becomes the key regard. Humanistic, phenomenological, existential and hermeneutic methods are favoured in the interpenetration stage, and a variety of language theories usefully applied.

10. A number of iterations may of course take place, as this is qualitative research. Iterations are phases within phases, the spiralling back centre of the clock's face. We are interpreting continuously and seeking insights, general rules, patterns, research question saturation. We go back to the field site and the data. We return to the literature in a spiralling-in cycle looking for contributions, answers, representations, ideas and questions; a meeting-in-the-middle (see Belk et al., 2013). As answers resolve from our close encounters with the data, literature, imagination and site, we begin to build the representations that we will use to carry it to the research world. For starters, netnography is about using the media we have and also about expanding traditional scholarship into more accessible forms. This means simplifying and sharing stories at times, but also not sacrificing our academic integrity by 'dumbing down' and making compromises.

11. In the penultimate phase, netnography is instantiated somehow, in space and on time. Any given netnography is a research project presented on different stages in different manners. One of four ideal types might be used to guide this instantiated representation: symbolic, digital, auto or humanist. These representations and instantiations have methodological implications. Method guidelines help you to focus and streamline the making of research design decisions.

12. Finally something should happen. Some change that might occur and be detected or measured as a result of this netnography having been performed. Is publication the goal? Wild applause at a conference? One million views on YouTube? A story in the national press about the topic? Regardless, the end result is in some sense an integration: integrating research answers with research questions, integrating research representation with research site and presentational format, integrating decisions and actions with needs for wider frames of understanding and empathy and requirements for procedures. The 12th and final phase of netnography is part of its ongoing life in the world. It deals with the integration of findings and discussion with recommended action in the wider world. What is the end game of your own pursuit and sharing of netnographic research? This phase does not stop when a journal article is published.

The remainder of this book now proceeds to describe in nonlinear fashion, in embedded detail and with examples, these 12 process levels, these faces of phases and times, and beginning in the next chapter with the early introspection and investigation stages.

SUMMARY

Chapter 4 redefined netnography as a specific set of research practices related to data collection, creation and analysis, ethical, and representational concerns, where a significant amount of the data collected and participant-observational research conducted originates in and manifests through the data shared on Internet and mobile networks. Netnography is ethnography for online networks of social interaction and experience. Netnography's definition makes it more identifiably specific than digital ethnography and digital anthropology. The chapter discussed virtual ethnography, materiality, the mundaneness of technologies and the importance of storytelling. It overviewed the state of netnography today, examining the growth and development of netnography as an interdisciplinary research field, and then provided a voyeur's gaze into a spectrum of netnographies characterized by voyeurism, quest for intimacy, and technology user engagement. The chapter concluded with a new 12-step process to guide us through the changing phases and faces of netnography.

KEY READINGS

Boellstorff, Tom, Bonnie Nardi, Celia Pearce and T.L. Taylor (2012) *Ethnography and Virtual Worlds: A Handbook of Method*. Princeton, NJ: Princeton University Press.
Hine, Christine (2000) *Virtual Ethnography*. London: Sage.
Miller, Daniel and Heather A. Horst (2012) 'The digital and the human: A prospectus for digital anthropology', in Heather A. Horst and Daniel Miller, *Digital Anthropology*. London: Bloomsbury. pp. 3–35.

NOTE

1. This is from my research with Daiane Scaraboto on an early subset of 73 netnography articles all published before 2010.

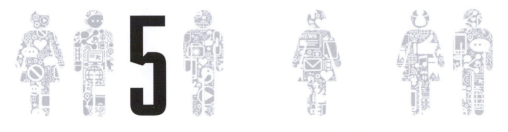

5

PLANNING AND PREPARATION

[Not] only are the natives uninterested in helping and sometimes aggressive if you ask them to, they probably aren't even around. Blink, and you'll miss them ... Trying to find a stable structure, a static form will result in finding either nothing at all or merely a trivial trace. – Alf Rehn, on his experience of the Warez scene relating to conducting an online ethnography, in *Electronic Potlatch* (2001: 38-39)

READY? SET? ...

Are you ready to begin a netnographic research project? Pull that smartphone out of your purse or pocket. Flip open your laptop or uncover your handy dandy tablet. Double tap that app. Type some keywords into that search engine, pick your site and you should be good to go. You are just a few clicks away from finding a fabulously free-flowing online conversation about just about anything. And then you are off, entering the wonderful world of netnography. Or maybe not.

Before you take action, begin interacting, recording, experiencing and reflecting in the semi-structured modalities of netnographic research, there are just a few important things you need to get straight. You need to decide what you are going to be studying. How you are going to study it. What will constitute 'data' for you. How you will collect them. How your ongoing analysis will be conducted. How it will guide you. How you will represent yourself. How you will handle this project ethically. What are the benefits? What are the risks?

The risks of poor planning are real. We can usefully start this section with an illustrative example of a poorly conceptualized and rapidly entered netnography. This tale of the field begins with a new and overly eager adjunct professor initiating a research project on online boycotts. After a fairly short amount of time thinking about the project, this budding netnographer posts a message to an online board that says something very much like the following.

Hello Everyone

I am a professor at [University X] in [location]. A colleague and I have begun to research boycotts from the consumer's point of view. We are very interested in finding out more about individual's [*sic*] involvement in boycotts and we are currently using the Internet to try to gather some information.

The information we are trying to gather we believe will help everyone who has a stake in helping to understand how boycotts are perceived and understood by the people who are persuaded (or not persuaded) by them. This would include anyone who organizes or supports boycotts, and might contribute to helping make future efforts maximally effective. We would be happy to share our findings with you on an individual basis, if you are interested in becoming involved in this very important research area.

All responses will be totally confidential. If quoted, you will be given a 'pseudonym' so that you always remain anonymous. *If* you have ever been involved in a boycott, we would greatly appreciate it if you would take a few minutes to email me [at eageradjunct@email.com] with your answers to these THREE, fairly short, sets of questions: [3 questions here].

Thank you very much for your participation in this 'cyber-interview'. Again, please send the answers to [email] (or, if you like, you can post them publicly on this newsgroup). We will respond to everyone who answers our request for help.

Sincerely,

[eageradjunct, name anonymized]

P.S. If you have any questions about this research, please feel free to post them on the group or send them to me.

The approach taken here seems, at first sight, reasonable as well as eager. Eager adjunct professor introduces himself, gives his affiliation, accurately conveys the research focus, and offers some questions. He seems polite. He talks about participant anonymity and the use of pseudonyms in the final research report. The researcher even tries to suggest that there will be some benefit to those interested in the topic of boycotts from participation in the research.

So what is the response from this posting? For instructional purposes only, let us have a look. The first response is friendly and positive. Written by 'Josphh' (a pseudonym), this post is a detailed and useful set of answers to the questions, posted to the entire newsgroup. It is exactly the sort of set of answers that the eager adjunct seems to be hoping for. We could score it, if we were keeping score, as a research victory. The next response, from 'Father Wintersod' (another pseudonym), a regular poster on this community bulletin board, is not nearly as positive.

Father Wintersod states that he is completely convinced that research like this is part of a system of mind control. He suggests that the research is under the control of the government, large corporations and other institutions. Research like this helps them to learn how to psychologically manipulate the public. For example, large corporations could use this research to try to make their immoral marketing practices more resistant to boycotts; it could be employed to help those corporations counteract and counter-argue boycotts. Father Wintersod suggests, in no uncertain terms, that this research seeks out useful intelligence to use against good people.

Father Wintersod, it seems, is a person with some status on this online board. He is an active poster with a particular point of view. He is what we might term an 'influential' member of the board. So when he then advises the other members of the community to 'boycott this research on boycotts', this move must be taken seriously as a threat to the research project. Father Wintersod claims that boycotting the eager adjunct's research is important to the members of the board and says that he is 'deadly serious'. In large capital letters, he writes 'BOYCOTT ALL RESEARCH', then analyses the negative intentions of the original questions and the harmful uses to which they might be put, terms the research a 'cyber-interrogation' rather than a cyber-interview, and finishes with a large, banner-like posting of three lines in capital letters, surrounded by rows of asterisks, urging fellow newsgroup members to 'BOYCOTT THIS RESEARCH'.

I can tell you that this response completely caught that new netnographic researcher off guard. I know, because that eager young adjunct professor – who had just gotten a black eye and bloody nose – was me.

In the initial stages of netnography, context is everything. The information intentionally left out of my description of my activities was that I was posting to a newsgroup called alt.gathering.rainbow. Alt.gathering.rainbow had shown up among my search engine results as a group with some interesting boycott and consumer activism related posts. In 1997, they were one of several newsgroups that contained messages and conversations discussing boycotts. However, I had rather ignorantly not performed any investigation into this online group. Had I done so, my investigation would have revealed that alt.gathering.rainbow is a group for the members of the radical countercultural environmentalist group The Rainbow Family of Living Light, a utopian group with hippie roots which eschews commercialism and has had major run-ins with government organizations. Because I knew little if anything about the group, my entrée was overly heavy-handed. Beginning with my academic credentials, I was assuming an establishment perspective in which members of the group would see degrees, research and education as legitimate, rather than institutional symbols to be viewed with scepticism. Knowing that this is an anti-establishment group would have directed me to other online groups, or else at least suggested that I invest the time to educate myself about the Rainbow Family's unique beliefs and countercultural values before I attempted to communicate with them.[1]

Context is everything, and context is constantly changing. With a quick scan of the Internet, you will find numerous examples of missteps by over-eager and under-informed online researchers. On a popular shopping newsgroup, a student researcher 'Alexandra34567' (an assigned pseudonym) posted a message that opened with a research question asking newsgroup members about 'the influence of family and peers' on their levels of trust of 'a brand online'. Alexandra34567 explained that she was a student from a certain university involved in research about brand trust online, and that she would be using what she called 'a rather new research method called netnography'.

'Lloyd' replied. He informed Alexandra34567 that 'we have already heard this before'. It turns out that this newsgroup has been receiving postings like this, using the same basic question, for five years. This might not be Alexandra34567's fault; it could be that her instructor had given this assignment to her class every year. She may have suggested that her students proceed directly to this newsgroup or its related website. The fact that he belongs to a group that is useful to a university class does not seem to move Lloyd at all. He critiques her question, which is the same one he has seen, year after year, posted and reposted to the community (see Bruckman, 2006 for valuable insights about student projects using netnography).

One of Lloyd's major critiques seems to be in Alexandra34567's approach to research. Lloyd calls it 'spamming' newsgroups. What is the implication of this term? Essentially, it means that the members of online groups generally believe that they have better things to do than to answer some anonymous person's research questions. It means that they resent the intrusions and interruptions of online researchers. This resentment obviously grows when the intrusions are repeated or not particularly mindful of the group and its norms. In our times, it means that they have almost certainly seen quite a bit of this sort of interference, and they are not interested in seeing it again.

It is a testament to the good nature of people that graceless questions such as these still often end up yielding considerate answers. I have even seen culture members rewrite students' awkward research questions for them and then offer lengthy, helpful answers. However, increasingly common encroachments mean that online participants are cautious and often unabashedly negative about being contacted by researchers (see Bruckman, 2002). Yes, this is a shame. But, yes, this is the reality all netnographers are faced with today.

Consideration, as you begin your netnography, is everything. And so is your own attitude and approach. This is where notions of immersion and participation become relevant, and where a self-examination leading to increased self-under-standing must begin. Whether I was aware of it or not, I had adopted a default approach strategy that could be labelled 'experience-distant'. In fact, I was posting essentially the same set of questions and explanations to multiple online groups. These groups had in common only that according to my searches they seemed active in boycotts, and included such diverse gatherings as rec.sport.jetski, rec. running, alt.music.hardcore, alt.food.mcdonalds, and news.admin.net-abuse. email. I had no knowledge of the values and history of any of these groups.

However, I did start to learn about the Rainbow Family after I received the mixed set of responses from them, the helpful and useful answer followed by the digital tarring-and-feathering. The responses prompted some soul searching. In the spirit of participation, I tried to start a conversation. I offered a careful, rational reply to Father Wintersod's critique of my research and its intentions that began by acknowledging the often-skewed power dynamics of the research role and industry. I knew my response was a public representation, so I disclosed something of my background for doing this research. After introspecting about my own motivations, I related the research to my identity 'as a long-time environmentalist and animal rights supporter'.

A few members of the newsgroup posted some supportive comments, including an affirming 'I believe you'. 'Reg' invited me to attend a Rainbow Family gathering. 'Paulie' suggested that I consider how inescapable 'the system' is and how guilefully it is able to use broad-minded people such as him, or me, to achieve its own ends. The lesson I learned is that intention and motivation count in netnographic participation, and that it is valuable and important to ascertain and explore the catalysts of your own interest before you share them with others through online social experiences. Remember that this is a social experience, and being social means communicating, connecting and making contributions.

Related to the sociality of interaction is the importance of language. Alexandra34567 began her incursion into the online shopping group's ongoing conversations with some advanced vocabulary and, as I did, also offered up her academic credentials. These rhetorical moves could be interpreted negatively, as signals of presumed superiority and outsider status. When we use our own terminology to speak to people online, rather than their own, it is a linguistic turn reminiscent of colonialism. It signals not only that we are uninterested in learning their language, but also that we believe our terms to be superior. In 2008, 'Ricardo', a university student working on his dissertation, posted a very specific and jargon-laden query to the alt.coffee newsgroup, which included the following: 'For my dissertation, I am conducting a netnography study on the authenticity of Starbuck's emotional brandind [sic] strategy.'

The response to the query was immediate, and quite likely not what Ricardo was expecting. First, the highly literate members of the group critiqued Ricardo's writing skills, careless typos and grammatical errors. Members then began to speculate on his status as a non-native English speaker and to guess which global region he was from, probably East Asia. Then, 'Tim Boulder' offered the following astute assessment of Ricardo's deployment of obscure academic language:

Oh, and on top of that, a lot of academic fields are overrun with jargon – 'netnography', 'emotional branding', etc. It is the nature of any guild that they develop their own terminology which is often opaque to outsiders. It may seem as if the purpose of this is to keep the hoi polloi mystified and excluded from the discussion but there are natural reasons for doing so – to those versed in the art, a single word can explain a lot and all the 'insiders' know exactly what that word means. If you read alt.coffee it has its own jargon that isn't obvious to outsiders coming in and asking about 'the handle thing', what is a HX, etc. Unfortunately, in modern academic writing, jargon often becomes a substitute for clear thinking, especially in the social 'sciences' – there was the famous experiment where someone wrote a paper that consisted of random gibberish in strings of academic buzzwords and the paper was accepted for publication by an academic journal.[2]

What is remarkable about Tim's post? First, it identifies the insider–outsider tension which Ricardo's use of terms such as 'netnography' and 'emotional branding' represents and relates that tension to the presence of populace-mystifying guilds. In fact, Ricardo later elaborates that he seeks 'to highlight some aspects of Starbuck's doppoelganger [sic] brand image and analyse how these meanings are incorporated into consumer preferences, lifestyles, belief systems and identities'. Second, it equanimously compares the alt.coffee group's own use of jargon with its use by academic writers. I find it equally noteworthy that a student such as Ricardo, who claims to be conducting a netnography, and chooses to do so on a community that I have already studied and written about, does not choose to benefit from the linguistic and stylistic translations in that published work before undertaking a new investigation. Similarly, Lloyd offers several linguistic and convention-related correctives to Alexandra34567's post, including a gentle correction that netnography is not particularly new.

Ricardo, Alexandra34567, Tim and Lloyd are our educators as we begin discussing the many research practices of netnography. For as scholars, students, academics and other researchers, we must assume a stance of humility and docile self-understanding. I strongly object, for example, to Ricardo's outburst in which he tit-for-tats one of his critics by copying and pasting a post of one of his critics that contains a couple of typos. He then proceeds to tell the members of the forum that they disappoint him, are 'not willing to co-operate' and are 'being immature about it'. Finally he accuses another poster of 'racism'. This tantrum is counter-productive not only for Ricardo, but for all who seek to practise netnography. It threatens to poison the well for all of us who seek knowledge through online social interaction. Remember that the intrusive, interruptive and interrogative form of netnography that Ricardo is practising is analogous to telemarketing or knocking on someone's front door and asking them research questions during their dinnertime! There should be absolutely no assumption that the people who are communicating using social media should 'co-operate' with us or even tolerate such intrusion. In my opinion, the members of alt.coffee were acting entirely appropriately and very true to the group's character when they lightly teased Ricardo.

Rather than responding to such taunts by resorting to the use of language that might indicate your academic superiority, I propose two things. First, try to minimize the intrusiveness of your own participation. I will offer details on this idea later in this chapter and the next. Second, assume instead that the participants in your study are, in fact, superior to you in their knowledge of their own conduct. You are their inferior. Genuinely attempt to approach them with humility, assured in the knowledge that they know much more about their online social experiences and interactions (and very likely many other things) than do you. Remember in your own research that just about anyone you contact can become a researcher themselves. If you use a term like 'netnography' they can quickly search it on Wikipedia and discover its meaning and background. The same is true about almost any specialized professional or academic term. Some of them may indeed be professionals, professors or researchers themselves. We do not know. And we cannot assume.

These illustrations may seem difficult and painful illustrations – even negative. Yet I find them thoroughly authentic. Netnography is neither neat nor is it clean. Like much of social life and like ethnography, it is messy. It forces you to consider the intelligence of others, to treat them as social equals and not subjects or objects of study. It also forces you to confront your own pre-understandings, motives and prejudices. It draws your attention to the need for genuine conversation.

As we proceed through this chapter, you must consider all of the factors you will need to consider as you prepare to conduct your netnography. Building on the 12-step process of netnography introduced in Chapter 4, these planning factors include:

- You need to consider the netnographic question that guides your project, introspecting and designing your research from your own profound sources of motivation (Stage 1: Introspection). This will also involve:

  o Understanding and meaningfully communicating your interests, motivations and pre-understandings of the topic and question.

- Knowing your research topic and initial research question (Stage 2: Investigation).

  o Locating and reading related research studies and if possible connecting with other researchers in your topical domain.

- You must think about the ethical and other social implications of your work, and build personally and professionally acceptable research practices (Stage 3: Information).

  o Relatedly, you must gain ethical approval for your research project (if this is academic research), and ensure that you are meeting or exceeding all ethical, professional and legal standards that apply.

- You need to familiarize yourself with the type of online social interactions and experiences you seek to investigate (i.e., which relate to your topic and question) and the sites of these interactions and experiences (Stage 4: Interview).

  o This investigation process should become featured in your fieldnotes from the very beginning of your research.
  o You need to have already started keeping fieldnotes, and be ready to add to them every time you contact, think about, or do something else related to your online social experience.

- You must evaluate and then choose from among the many possible sites of interaction and experience (Stage 5: Inspection).

- You should plan the participative elements of your online social interaction with other people (Stage 6: Interaction).

  o For this, you should understand in advance the type of interactions and experiences you will require for your project, and how you will undertake those interactions and experiences or allow them to organically emerge.
  o As an output, you should have a clear, written set of guidelines representing decisions you have made that will structure and supervise your on-going social participation.

- You must temporally plan for a regular engagement schedule (Stage 7: Immersion).

- You need to have a data collection strategy (Stage 8: Indexing).

  o This involves the elaboration of particular data collection, co-creation, and creation practices.
  o As an output, you should have a clear, written set of guidelines representing decisions you have made that will structure and supervise your on-going social observations.
  o These should be informed by your research focus, question and your end point in a type of netnographic representation (see Chapter 10 for information about the four ideal types of netnography).

- You must plan for interpretive, and interpenetrative, analysis (Stage 9: Interpretation).

- You must schedule for and accommodate continuous repeated incursions into theory and field site as well as reconceptualizations of major elements of your project, such as the research question (Stage 10: Iteration).

- You should keep the representational form of the final product of your project in mind, while also allowing it to emerge and evolve. What is to be your representational end-point? Which of the four types of netnography will you pursue – symbolic, digital, auto, humanistic – or some hybrid, combination or new variant? (Stage 11: Instantiation)

- Think about what you would like to be the end effect of your netnographic research presentation? What are you aiming for? Publications? Mentions in the popular press? Social change? Retweets and shares in the social media sphere? Think about how you will access and measure your success at reaching these goals (Stage 12: Integration).

The remainder of this chapter will offer additional detail on these 12 elements to consider as you begin to plan your netnographic research project, with special emphasis on the stages of Investigation, Interview, Inspection and Interaction. We thus proceed to consider the first aspect of preparing to investigate, which involves an introspective examination of the researcher's own motivation and understanding.

RESEARCH INTROSPECTION: BEGINNING WITH RESEARCHER SELF-UNDERSTANDING

Why would we begin our netnography with an introspective look at our own selves? The reason is both axiological and rigorous. If we accept that the ultimate purpose of a netnography is to explore parts of the human experience, what it means to be a person, a member of a group, to hold an identity, a role, in a particular cultural context, and that this exploration happens both through an examination that centres upon particular online social experiences and interactions and through one in which we, as participant-observers play a key role, then becoming conscious and aware of our own social and psychic position in the research is the very foundation of the netnographic endeavour. This section looks at the role of researcher introspection by synthesizing a range of relevant writing on the topic.

In a whimsical and wide-ranging article entitled 'Stalking the amphisbaena', Sidney Levy (1996: 172) notes that:

> introspection is an inevitable part of [all] research, used by all research workers, as it merely means looking within one's self to know one's ideas and feelings. That is, introspection is another word for being self-conscious, aware, thoughtful, having ideas, and knowing what they are.

Levy then proceeds to interpret a single quantitatively focused article, which could have been any scientific article at all, and shows how many times the researchers make introspective assumptions, subtly express doubts or intentions, and otherwise bring their own subjective viewpoint into the allegedly objective scientific narrative. He uses the example to suggest that even though social scientists often rhetorically 'strive for the appearance and security of objectivity, this should not obscure the fact that all our thoughts are introspective-comments and stories about what we observed, what we did, what we thought, and why we thought it' (ibid: 173).

In his article, Levy seems to agree with Heidegger's notion that authenticity comes from self-reflection. However, he also describes a more deliberate, extreme and 'brooding' form of introspection, in which our own truth represents in some sense the only truth, and which leads to egocentricity, fanaticism and ostensible solipsism (1996: 173). For Levy, a balanced and curious perspective is best. This humanistic scientific point of view is one which acknowledges that our belief and certainty in our own and others' knowledge is, ultimately, internalized and introspective, but is influenced by the dance between our subjective impressions, motives, deductions and decisions, and the stimuli we inductively receive from the external, empirical world. How we do this, procedurally, he leaves somewhat under-developed.

In their article on developing a research role for 'philosophical hermeneutics', Stephen Arnold and Eileen Fischer offer additional ideas about the role of introspection in research. They explain the notion of researcher 'pre-understandings' or 'pre-judgements' (also sometimes called 'prejudices') as our usually unnoticed implicit presuppositions and perspective, 'the accumulation of the beliefs, theories, codes, metaphors, myths, events, practices, institutions, and ideologies (as apprehended through language)' that precede our research work (Arnold and Fischer, 1994: 56). An awareness of our pre-understandings is empowering, it enables the research to be consciously created and the researcher to be creative and expansive. It leads to self-examination of our own prior beliefs, theories, models and metaphors that help us to systematically gain an ongoing reflexivity about our research. The ideal result seems perfect to the humanist goals of netnography: hermeneutic self-understanding. 'Hermeneutic understanding' combines 'self-understanding, self-reflection, and self-development' and 'is an action-oriented, practical-moral knowledge brought to, and derived from, a specific situation or problem' (Arnold and Fischer, 1994: 59).

Introspection researcher Stephen J. Gould (2012: 453) notes the many types of researchers, including sociologists and ethnographers, who have engaged with introspective techniques, and the many forms that these approaches have assumed, including:

> introspection, researcher introspection, subjective personal introspection, reflexivity, self-reflexivity, introspectionism, autoethnography, auto-netnography, narrative introspection (also storied), metacognitive introspection, meditative introspection, systematic self-observation, self-experimentation, spiritual, and synthetic.

Gould (2012) conceives of an introspection theory that is driven by the intensely personal experiences of each researcher, but which also evolves as part of a reflexive system that is constituted in the flow of community and cultural development, negotiation and debate. Perhaps most usefully of all, Gould (2012) conceives of introspection not merely as a static ideational concept that concerns researchers but as a research practice itself. He vivifies the notion with a series of practical exercises that inspired me to adapt them to the purposes of initiating a netnographic research project (see Boxes).

BOX 5.1

Who Are You? Introspective Exercise 1

Before beginning to focus your netnography, it is important to first focus on the most important research instrument you have in your arsenal. Yourself. The researcher-as-instrument. I prefer to think while writing, and my visual sense appreciates seeing what it is that I think I know. You may prefer to conduct this exercise purely as a mental task. However, I do think that having a written visual-textual document as a takeaway may be valuable as you ground yourself in your research project.

Write down your name. Find a few recent photographs of yourself, and then put them into a document, and/or focus on them on a screen. If you have a recent bio, read it. Dissect it. Do the same thing with your curriculum vita or resumé. Now, ask yourself, 'Who am I?' Who are you as an individual being? What makes you unique? What is captured in your photo, your name, your CV and bio? What is not captured?

Take a few moments to breathe. Close your eyes. Focus upon your thoughts and feelings. Follow their trails. Where do they come from? Which ones repeat? What do they say about you as a person who is unique and uniquely alive, right now, in this place, in this time?

What do they say about your sensations, your perceptions, your experiences? What meanings pervade them? Are you drawn to certain words, senses, colours, faces, places, emotions, moods or actions? What constitutes some of the elements of the molecule of you?

Open your eyes and try to capture what you thought and felt about your own unique social situation. How do you relate your introspective inner self with multiple extrospective cultures, such as your gender, age, sexual orientation, lifestyle groups, hobbies, consumption tribes, national, ethnic, religious, political and family connections and affiliations?

What is your personal narrative? What stories do you tell yourself about yourself? What stories do you tell certain other people about yourself? What do you tell those who are closest to you? What do you not tell them? What do you tell your professional colleagues? What do you not tell them? What do you tell the people you do research with, including those who you seek to portray as objects of your research? What will you tell the people in your netnography about yourself? What will you write about yourself?

What, then, is your perspective? What is your unique combination of perspectives? What are the inescapable and glorious essences of you that you inevitably work within, and which simultaneously empower and constrain you? How might this affect, emplace and situate your approach to research? How might it affect how you represent yourself to colleagues, to readers, to people you meet through online social experiences and interactions?

At the end of this thought exercise, write down the answer to this single question: what is the unique essence of your individuality and intellectual curiosity, today, here and now, that you will bring to this research project?

BOX 5.2

What Do You Want? Introspective Exercise 2

Find a comfortable position, sit upright and simply breathe. Close your eyes. Notice your breath for a while. Notice your body as it sits, upright and solid like a mountain. Now focus on your stream of consciousness, your thoughts and feelings. Watch them flowing and burbling. Notice where they move in your body. Notice what they do, what they say, what they tell you to do.

(Continued)

(Continued)

Notice what your mind says that you want. What do you desire? Where in the past did your mind go? What echoes repeat? Where does your mind reach out into the future? What visions do you pursue? What would you like, now? What form do your desires take? What emotions are attached to your longings? Are you planning to act on them? Where do they come from? How are they yours?

Now think about research. About your research project. What do you want from it? What do you want to know? What do you want it to do for you? What forces, people or values limit you? How is this research an extension of your desires? What sort of research are you considering? What topics? What people? What sites? Which ones arouse your passion? Why? How do they relate to you, your thoughts and your desires? Which ones constrain you and limit you? Which ones arouse fear? Which ones arouse love and joy? Which ones make you feel less of yourself? Which ones make you feel more of yourself? Why do you feel this way?

Finally, write down the answer to this single question: How will this introspectively gained knowledge change the way that you approach your netnography and its research topic?

BOX 5.3

Your Personal Statements: Applied. Introspective Exercise 3

Now that you are aware of the multifaceted social being that you are, can you commit to a more bandwidth-friendly version of yourself to represent you to the outside world? Who are you? What do you want? If you know the answers, somewhat, more so now because of exercises 1 and 2, then you are clearly ready to proceed to using them to plan your research strategy and practices.

Research strategy concerns: (1) who you will be speaking to (sampling), (2) what you will be looking for (attention to elements of social situation), (3) where you will be looking (site search and selection) and (4) how you will be collecting, co-creating or producing your own data. How will your research plan in netnography clearly state the who, what, where and how of your data finding, collecting, making and monitoring?

Your research practices can be nearly infinite in their detail. Any combination of particular research practices can become easily cultural in skilful hands, with nuanced, socially, psychologically and historically formed explanatory narratives. For example, even multilinear regressive nonparametric econometric modelling of scraped social media data can and should become a part of an ingenious netnography.

Your job in the initial stage of beginning your netnography is to create two research guides. One is a written-visual guide about the set of key and focused characteristics directing how you will represent yourself in your netnographic field research, which will have a participative component. The second is about your deep sources of motivation and founts of long-running and passionate intellectual curiosity. What do you desire? In the exercise, where in the future and past did your mind go? What echoes repeat into the shadowiest and eldest part of your psyche?

Think about research. Now think about netnography. Now think about the kinds of questions you can answer with a netnography. Think about the sorts of phenomena that netnography can potentially inform, both combined with other methods and also rowing solo down the sea of scientific knowledge.

Think about your self. Now think about research. These hold the keys. Now write out your personal research strategy statement, which will include (1) who is the audience for this research, (2) what you will be looking for, (3) where you will be looking for data and (4) how you will be collecting, co-creating or producing your own data.

When you have completed the three exercises in Boxes 5.1, 5.2 and 5.3, you are ready to move to harmonize and deeply consider them before moving to the next aspect of the Investigation stage.

Why are we doing this research at all? Is there a self-centred reason? Is there a social reason, or even a social adaptation of these methods that can seem overly internally focused? These are the guides of axiology and social introspection. Axiology answers why – the social and the self. Social introspection provides tools and a concrete and scholarly example. We will consider each in turn, with social introspection considered first.

SOCIAL INTROSPECTION

Introspection on a personal level can be powerful and essential for grounding your netnography in a deep sense of yourself, your desires and the role that this research will play in your life and in your unfolding as not only an inquiring academic scientist but also an expressive being. Yet if introspection is to faithfully guide us, how are we to avoid the idiosyncrasies and even solipsistic tendencies that can haunt the method? Minowa et al. (2012) consider group introspection methods between researchers working in a team in order to ameliorate this issue. Exemplifying and demonstrating their approach, they use their own cultural diversity – the researchers are Japanese, Italian and Northern Irish – to demonstrate how their individual differences can inform ethnographically driven introspection. Minowa et al. term their approach 'Xenoheteroglossic autoethnography' or XHAE and define it as 'ethnographically driven researcher introspection'.

> With multiple researchers from diverse cultural backgrounds, XHAE orients reflexivity towards the generation of insights about the researcher's subjective stance and his/her relation to the cultural stances of his/her research partners and informants instead of aiming to produce data to be used for theory generation. (2012: 485)

Therefore, this form of social introspection is usefully applied in multi-sited ethnographic contexts (as many if not most netnographies are multi-sited). It also benefits from the cultural and situational diversity of researchers in a research team. The insights from such social introspection are useful for improving research rigour, quality and relevance and, I would add, for building team rapport as well as gaining a sense of one's own self as a distinct social being. 'Engaging in this method from the preliminary stage of a full-blown multi-sited ethnography helps foster sensitivity, generates intra-and-inter researcher-reflexivity, and produces insightful conceptual founding for further study' (ibid.).

In terms of its execution, xenoheteroglossic autoethnography has four stages in which it impacts the research project. First, there is a type of introspective researcher-to-researcher entrée, in which cultural rapport with colleagues, scholars and with their representation of ethnographic informants and members of other cultures is established, taking one's introspective conceptualizing into and beyond the self. Second, XHAE impacts the gathering and documenting of data by researchers deliberately for their own collective use in the social introspection phase of the research. Third, the analysis and communication of the data at these early stages reveals earlier the need for cultural translation and disambiguation, as differing cultural contexts and individual idiosyncrasies emerge under collective analytic scrutiny. Finally, ensuring the reliability of the research process and product assumes many procedural forms. In more traditional autoethnography, a number of strategies are used to attempt to attain 'distance' – the dual perspectives of the emic and the etic, of being both a part of a social or cultural phenomenon, such as being a culture member in most autoethnographies, and being a part of a scholarly group or community of supposedly more objective and impartial scientists or investigators. Reliability or trustworthiness of results in XHAE is fuelled by a devotion to group and individual introspection as a continuous and ongoing process, to introspection continually incorporated into and within the data analysis stages, and to the established qualitative data analysis notion of theoretical saturation.

Group introspection offers some interesting ideas that may be applied to netnographic projects. It takes advantages of techniques of researcher collaboration and collective reflection that are well established in the procedures of qualitative research – for example, anthropologists meeting with advisors and supervisors – in order to gain a more nuanced sense both of cultural difference and of emic–etic tensions in analysis. Cultural nuance and reflexivity drive this form of autoethnography as they do ethnography and netnography. Circular relationships between metacognitive and narrative levels of introspection (Gould, 2012) are continually sought and these relationships are perhaps best captured through introspective essays such as the ones that this chapter's exercises are intended to help you create. The goal is to inspire and then share stories with one another that will lead to insights that inspire the creation and sharing of additional stories. The shape and form of these stories may, indeed, have a quality that seeks out social and self-betterment. The next section explores the role of this direction in netnography.

AXIOLOGY

What do we think of when we think of social media, of being out there on social media? We cannot help but think of ourselves as already out there as social actors, with all of our friends and family and co-workers looking at us. And acquaintances, who can now quickly find us using so many different ways. We are at the very height of the surveillance society. The monitoring of each one of us is at historically impossible levels. And we know this keenly well, do we not, fellow netnographers? For if you are not very active in social media right now, what are you doing trying to be an expert in this field? Your attention to research practice, to research as both a Learned Craft and an Innovative Art is of paramount import. It is at this level that netnography easily splits from social science and jumps directly into Digital Humanities. There need be no sudden seismic shifts if we realize that our representational methodologies are leading us squarely back, through our increasingly sophisticated analytic abilities, to representations through the arts, and through stories.

So can it be a major surprise to learn that the Number One World-Leading professional consulting company selling rigorous netnography projects, which combine text-mining, natural language processing, and deep meaningful cultural analyses – all very client-facing and applied consumer insight – uses artistic renderings of interesting cultural stories and themes, often gleaned from tiny datasets of single person postings (of immensely high relevatory quality), as well as interpreted creatively across data from many different social media postings by talented researchers? For Munich-based consultancy and research company Hyve, as for many companies, netnography can be part of a powerful market research business. For academic scholars, it must be more. This is not about self-betterment but instead about a search for the truth about human beings, groups, identities and social experiences in increasingly mechanical and instrumentalizing times. We must remember what always happens when we try to turn people into numbers, or we favour dead things over live ones. We must shake our fists at dystopian threats, and speak the truth to power. Netnography shares in this academic ethos. This is its axiology.

Technology changes the social control game, absolutely. Everything goes through networks, but many networks are wild and uncontrolled. Few netnographers have dared to set foot into these spaces, with exceptions of course. As a social science method with a real social setting, like all good anthropology today, netnography is keenly attuned to the role of large corporate actors – including not only corporations but also their governments, advertising agencies, consultants and other organizations such as nonprofits – who all seek in their own ways to own, exploit, monetize, develop or colonize online social spaces.

The space race of at least the next decade will be into online social spaces. There is little doubt of this when we look at the most sophisticated global measuring instrument ever devised: the global stock market. As the valuations of Amazon, Google, Apple, Twitter and Facebook indicate, the technological marvel and epistemic consumption object of the stock market values online social spaces ever more and more, as it becomes ever more clearly attuned through personal technology to the collective attention, and even perhaps awareness or consciousness, of the masses who are all wired into the network, into so many different networks of social connection, information, emotion and exchange.

Netnography considers the balances involved in the trade-off between large corporate actors, the abuses of power that typically trail such large corporate actors, and people's individual needs for and established human rights of privacy, dignity and freedom. It seems rather clear that, if communications online are consistently monitored, this further distances them from some of the human qualities of other types of communications; this is an empirical phenomenon worthy of further investigation and consideration.

Following established ethnographic practice as well as those concerned with 'praxis', a research-informed course of action 'designed to change social conditions and create a better society' in some way (Murray and Ozanne, 1991: 138), is important to the axiology of netnography, particularly humanist netnography as described in Chapter 11. As with Action Research, or Critical Ethnography, but applied specifically to contemporary and technologically mediated society, netnography seeks to expose hidden and taken-for-granted power relations present in social media spaces and to analyse the social and cultural effects of these relations. For example, Campbell's (2005) study of an Internet portal for gay men and lesbians demonstrates how a social medium is constructed on communal terms and then exploited for its profitability. Zwick et al. (2008) look at how the innovation-rendering processes and capitalist ideologies surrounding 'consumer generation' and 'consumer co-creation' may actually be exploitative mechanisms to use social media to drive unpaid labour. More recently, Ella Lillqvist (2014) presented results of a netnography examining company-stakeholder power relations as they manifest online at the micro-discursive level. Along with the usual emancipatory possibilities, her research locates many attempts by companies to silence expression, to manipulate the conversation, and to control thinking on particular topics. These social media instantiated power struggles are crucial topics for our times. For, alongside its aims of understanding culture and society through its social media manifestations, netnography seeks to confront questions of structure and agency in the realm of social media, noting how transformation of political, corporate and personal power are effected, hindered, managed and empowered by different social media networks, practices and forms. Respecting the history and social patterns of the Internet, this axiological emphasis on values aims to decolonize online communications and favour social movements that empower and liberate communication networks for the benefit of individual citizens rather than corporations and the people who sit atop and draw resources from their hierarchies.

When you have considered these elements and completed all of these exercises, you will be ready to move to the next part of the Investigation stage, which invites you to integrate your introspective research insights more formally into the development of your research question.

FORMULATING NETNOGRAPHIC RESEARCH
Finding your Focus

This section is dedicated to helping you construct and focus research questions appropriate for netnography. Our first set of exercises concerned your theoretical interests. These will inevitably be shaped by a variety of forces, not only the often-profound curiosity and desire for knowledge which you can explore through introspection, but also the extant current of interest and thought running through your academic field, your particular academic department and your colleagues. This topical interest will direct you to locate your netnography in certain areas. Thus, at the earliest conceptual stage of your research, the dance of theory and data begins.

What does it mean to find a site for netnographic research? My past descriptive work unnecessarily limited the siting of netnographic fieldwork to the location of particular online groups or distinguishable online sites. With this work, informed now by several years of working with these concepts in workshops around the world, and informed particularly by work I did in Norway, Belgium, Israel and Brazil, I examine and develop the assumptions underlying the siting of netnography. These notions require us to critique the idea of locating research in online social fields, and to closely examine claims of difference between social fields.

We might initially find it tempting to see online social fields as less real or more partial than other kinds of social fields, in the way that Hine (2000) suggests. However, this perspective requires us to demarcate in some meaningful way the nature of both of these social locations – for example, is a telephone call included in 'online'? Is a VOIP phone call received via tablet? Via mobile phone? How about an SMS message – or short email – received on a landline phone but sent from mobile?

Elaborating differences also requires us to distinguish meaningfully between the offline and the online. If we ponder its deeper significance, this ultimately means that we must make clear distinguishing boundaries between a communicative medium and its originators and receivers. This is difficult if not impossible. If our analysis stopped at the door of the person using their phone to send a text, then why would we not simply exclude speaking out loud as well? Although the two are very different in infrastructure and operation, they conceptually have much in common. If the alphabet and language, speech, books and telephones are all technologies, then technology is a fact of social being. Facebook, email, SMS, television shows, WhatsApp, YouTube, Twitter, LinkedIn and phone calls all combine into something indispensible, total and totemic. An omnichannel, if you will, of media that we use throughout our days and nights to send and receive information of various sorts. This is a concept which Madianou and Miller (2011) term polymedia. At many points, the lines distinguishing online and offline polymedia inconveniently blur and sometimes shift, as the digital becomes solid and the material world becomes rendered in light, as with the Maker Movement and the Internet of Things. At their margins, media, messages and messengers all meet.

Ethnographers consistently complicate the notion of field sites, because culture is borne through human beings and their communications (e.g., Amit and Rapport, 2002). Boundaries and types of sites are unstable, as people have always been nomadic in their habits. Yet an ethnography can be conducted of a particular event, such as Kumbh Mela in India or Burning Moose in Canada. An ethnography can even be conducted of a single park, a street corner, or a retail store. In netnography, the concept of 'a' 'field' 'site' becomes even more fluid and diffuse than it is with ethnography. Netnography does not need to be focused on a particular website or online location. However, it certainly can be. It need not correspond to a particular location, group of persons, or even topic that exists discretely in some sort of fully materialized manifestation in the physical world, such as San Antonio, Texas, first-time mothers, or amateur woodworking. Rather, netnography's topic matter is specific communications. It just so happens that these specific communications manifest as bits of charge collected on various circuits, caught and shared through electrochemical metal configurations.

In netnography, sites vary from bounded to dispersed. In the first consideration, we might be interested in examining a particular online community, for example, Wikipedia, alt.coffee, the Winter is Coming *Game of Thrones* news blog, the use of #addiction hashtags, or the Church of Satan's official Facebook group. Alternatively, a research topic can be considered to be manifesting in a widely dispersed manner among a wide number of online and offline social experiences. A site such as a *Star Trek* or Samsung Galaxy wiki can seem at first glance to be a straightforward single location of the type that my netnography work originally studied. However, even in early work my interest in a particular topic, such as *Star Trek* fandom, drew me to a variety of sites or groups. Sometimes, certainly, my entire study stayed on one site such as alt. coffee (e.g., Kozinets, 2002a), but this was as much topical as it was a response to the relative concentration of the early Internet prior to the explosion of blogs and other social media forms. The same seems true of other netnographies. For example, when Al Muniz and Hope Schau studied the online social experience of Apple Newton users, they located their study on a newsgroup (alt.fa.newton) and then added data from a listserv (the NewtChat Listserv). Citing Schau and Gilly (2003), they state that they expanded their data collection/online social site domain to 'user created Web-pages' and examined them 'for relevant narrative themes' (Muniz and Schau, 2005: 738). Thus we see how, in its application, netnographic site selection is driven not merely by attention to a particular group, but by the presence of 'relevant narrative themes'. These themes are relevant because they relate to the topic of interest, rather than to any particular identifiable group or person.

As another example, consider the netnography of Mkono et al. (2013) looking at tourists' social interactions regarding their food-related cultural experiences in Victoria Falls, Zimbabwe. This seems like a very focused topic, one that could be considered through a single website. And yet, after the three authors examined the available data sources, they decided to use three different (but similar) online travel review sites: Igougo.com, TripAdvisor.com, and Virtualtourist.com, because they wanted to sample more data. They then examined 285 tourist reviews of five Victoria Falls restaurants from those three sites. The researchers knew what type of online social interactions they were looking for, and what types of social experiences they wanted to learn more about. They found interactions and experiences relating to the topic of food-related experience in Victoria Falls on several sites, and so those sites became the loci of their research.

What if your research interest is in a particular group of people? We never know entirely who is posting to a particular site, although we usually have a very good idea. Facebook and Twitter to some extent have encouraged people to forsake anonymity and privacy for convenience, transparency, openness and mutual trust. Rather than originating in a site, and then trying to ascertain or speculate who is posting in it, some netnographies begin with a particular group of people and then look at how they are using technology-mediated communications. One example of this is Teresa Davis' (2010) sociological study of migrant identity as it is expressed through online social experiences. In this case, the author was a member of a group of South Indian university friends who, 20 years after their graduation, formed an online group to discuss their experiences and keep in touch. Because Davis knew exactly who was involved in the group personally, her confidence in the reliability of the data as able to speak about actual Indian migrant experience was high. Similarly, Olga Isupova (2011) wrote about the lived experience of Russian women undergoing fertility assistance treatment by joining a Russian forum dedicated to the topic, www.probirka.ru. Because the author was involved as a participant not only in the community but also in fertility assistance, her intellectual and emotional proximity to the topic, as well as her prolonged engagement of 5 years interacting through the site, served as a close check on the validity of the data.

In general, where the identity of the query is important, it may be very helpful for the netnographer to begin as a field worker (if not an ethnographer) interviewing people personally, perhaps on Skype, perhaps in their homes, using their own native devices, and following them where their interests and connections take them online. Then, we would follow up with netnographic explorations in further depth in the online field sites that were identified in the personal interviews, making them, at least for a time, the full site of the netnographic immersion.

In many realistic contexts, researchers are interested in some combination of things, such as how a particular topic manifests socially among a certain pre-defined group of people of interest. For example, consider a topic such as how young tweens are using social media to try to understand and cope with the upcoming challenges of being a teenager and then an adult, and how associated dilemmas and choices affect the sorts of social activities they will engage in now and in the near future. That latter topic could involve a range of sites and forums accessed across multiple locations and through many devices, guided by live inter-views with actual teens who direct the inquiry to specific practices embedded in artifact and text. Given the wide range of social media formats relevant to the top-ical group of interest (tweens), including social networking sites such as Facebook, microblogs such as Twitter, blogs, video games, forums and other communicative sites, the research study would inevitably be a communications-centred reading. It would be driven ultimately by the identified sites and artifacts at least and from there would extend to answer questions about how the practices come to be embedded and, in particular, to the patterns across research participant's acts, the social shapes of this particular group's shared practices.

SITES, TOPICS AND PEOPLE

Netnographic research is based upon studies of Sites, Topics and People. Sites are Locations. If a sign or marker of any kind points to it in the physical world, be it an http code or a street sign, a flashing marquee or a poster promoting an event, it is a Location. A study of a Site can include any sort of social site or field recog-nizable in the social sciences as a place or a space of one type of another, usually cultural, but also geographic and this would include notional and cyber 'spaces'. These spaces are places where imaginary worlds take root. Participation in such social sites is vital. Our job as reflexive netnographers is to chronicle membership and archive our perspective on this as an emic landscape that becomes part of our etic World.

Topics are Conceptual. They mainline directly into the nomologically net-worked world of the theoretical construct. You specify what you are studying. You shoot Topics into a series of search engines. You optimize the findings for maximum interest, and then follow where the short and long tails of the keyword snake leads you, deeper and deeper into the forest of social media wisdom, lore, magic and trickery. Similarly, the study of social media seems important to top-ics such as identity construction, values and worldviews, technology and media influence, social movements and social activism. Ethnographies of contemporary social existence, for most people and many groups in the developed world, are considerably richer when they can reference and analyse the content of emails, the presence of smartphones and their messages, Facebook, Twitter and blogs. The influence of social media on contemporary social movements has, for example, been often noted (see, for example, Varnali and Gorgulu, 2014). Topics follow researcher interests, and may be reflected in particular sites. But, overall, they are sites of attention rather than actual bounded sites themselves.

People are also legitimate topics of studies. Profiles can be treated historically and autobiographically. If we are to believe in the world of the micro-celebrity, then we must be willing and able to write biographically and historically about individuals who rise to social media fame. In fact, the emphasis on personal branding, the rise of networked individualism, and the deep storytelling presence of personal experience lend credibility to the notion that individuals, singly, multiply and deeply, constitute a key area of separate study within netnography.

The net effect is quite different from traditional ethnography. Ethnography is, traditionally, in-person participative-observational fieldwork that has been conducted in particular settings and with and among particular, identified or identifiable people and their social groups. It is a human enterprise, a human level writing project. As Herodotus did it, essentially we still do it. Anthropologists use ethnography to try to explain what it means to be human, and what it means to be human today. Digital anthropology looks at the spectrum of being human within a world of digital media. Ethnography is both an experiential doing – the ethnic ethnos of the culture – and a reflective writing and analysis. The (auto/ethno/netno/porno)graphic act becomes both a type of personal psychoanalysis and also one of cultural analysis. It partakes in a collision and a purification of the narrative and metacognitive process of online social experience. Particular people and peoples, groups and gatherings can be the foundational focus of netnographies. Yet all netnographies are also rooted participatively in their active scientist-author.

FORMULATING RESEARCH QUESTIONS

With a spotlight now placed on the sweet spot of netnographic inquiry lying in sites, topics and/or people, we can formulate an initial research question to guide our research. I should note here, as we do in several places in the Belk et al. (2013) book on qualitative research, that your initial research question may look quite different from the one that will appear in the final publication or presentation of your research. However, it is still useful to begin with one research question, or set of questions, that evolve during the process of the investigation. By the time the final research product is complete, that original set of research questions may have changed, sometimes quite dramatically, with new ones emerging in the process of further fieldwork and its interpretation. In fact, the ninth stage of netnography, iteration, explicitly recognizes and even incorporates the narrowing of research focus that can and must occur as theory confronts netnographic field-level data, and as that data is used to inform a deeper and more specific reading of theory.

A good place to start with is in general questions. And it is here that your earlier exercises about your own interests, desires, curiosities and passions may begin to serve you well – in addition to the many counterbalancing and enriching interests of your field, colleagues, journal editors, conference organizers, department chairs and Deans, potential reviewers, and so on. Broad questions can help begin your exploration of a particular site, topic or person. In addition, netnographies need not necessarily commence with entirely novel sites or topics. Instead, they can hone in, narrow, and focus on particular relationships or previously identified constructs, in order to provide us with a deeper or more detailed understanding of them, refining and validating existing theory. For example, we might be interested in how some aspect of online social experience changes an aspect of society or social relations. For example, West and Thakore (2013) decided to study how racial exclusion is extended into online social relations through studying an online group for adult toy collectors. For specific guidelines for formulating your netnography's research questions, please see Box 5.4.

BOX 5.4

Netnographic research questions: Guidelines

1. Formulate a single large, broad, guiding question (you can always narrow it down later).
2. Ensure that your question is amenable to netnographic inquiry. That is, does your question relate to the online social interaction and experience of particular sites, topics or people? If not, go back to the drawing board to reformulate.
3. Building on that large question, formulate no more than five related sub-questions that elaborate parts of your major question.
4. Try to focus on the question word you are using. If you are interested in people and topics or their locations in online sites, then 'where' may be important. If you are interested in processes, then 'how' and 'when' may be important. If you are interested in people who inhabit sites or discuss topics, then 'who' may be important. Your most useful questions often will begin with 'what', as they relate to descriptions of things such as types of online narratives, stories, topics, meanings or associations. 'Why' tends to be a very difficult question for netnographic evidence to conclusively answer.
5. Try experimenting in your question with exploratory verbs such as 'discover', 'understand', 'explore', 'describe', or 'report' (Creswell, 2009: 129-131).

In general, the five guidelines in Box 5.4 provide a solid foundation for narrowing your research approach and deciding upon your research question. However, prescriptions such as these are not to be slavishly followed. The idea of approaching fieldwork with a fresh set of eyes is a good one, but we can never fully achieve it. My own preference is to have a solid understanding of your general theoretical field, but to consistently attempt to be aware that your perspective is biased because of it. This should fit into your introspection process, where you seek to ascertain your pre-understandings and prejudices – knowledge and desires that direct your attention and cause you to focus upon particular aspects of reality to the exclusion of others. Inevitably, we enter our field site laden with 'theory goggles'. The key is to realize that we are wearing them and to try to guess how they are colouring our view. That realization, in many ways, is at the root of the scientific endeavour to see familiar things in an unfamiliar way. Galileo, Marx and Einstein had to remove their own theory goggles or they would have been unable to do anything but confirm or validate the existing theories of their times.

In particular, you should try to obsessively scour all written works, particularly scholarly academic works for conceptualizations related to your netnography's focal topics of interest – regardless of whether the exact same terms or framing have been used by prior scholars. So, for instance, if you are interested in 'media-related fantasy worlds' but others are writing about related ideas as 'spectacle' or 'hyperreality', then you would want to include the related ideas, perhaps organizing, comparing and contrasting them with one another, and show your readers how this literature is a budding, growing, vital field, rather than one in which you, alone, have the single, correct term.

Try to possess as much knowledge about what others have done and thought in related areas as you can, at every single stage of your research investigation, but also to treat this with some degree of scepticism, as only the current state of the art, subject to revision when you find something fascinating and new in your netnographic research. Remember as well that the future value of your new netnographically derived idea or theory will lie in how broadly and deeply others are able to deploy it in their own thinking and writing. Connecting your work with a larger frame of reference of scholarly thought helps you build conversational bridges with related literature in your area, which will be vital once you need to position your research representation.

In order to evaluate and extend your theoretical reach, scholars of online cultures and communities will find it very useful to consult past works in related areas and to network with scholars working in these areas. As noted by Silver (2006: 2), scholars of online communities and cultures, or the broader field of 'Internet studies to which it belongs', now have the benefit of drawing upon 'a community of scholars; conferences and symposia; journals, journal articles, anthologies, monographs, and textbooks; university courses, common curriculum, and majors; theses and dissertations; theories and methodologies; and academic centers'. A listing of these resources in book form goes stale almost as fast as a jug of milk, and so I leave it to you in this edition to use your favourite search engine to carefully search for these resources prior to undertaking your netnography.

The value of a single precise journal article in your area that clarifies your thinking and leads you to dozens of rich new references, or a single helpful scholarly contact, can never be overrated. Whatever effort you put into reaching out to other scholars and delving into related theoretical works will very likely be copiously rewarded.

Finally, you must realize that your research question and your research topic are going to influence your collection, or quest, for data. Your research question is also a data quest(ion): it tells you what information you will be looking out for. Further to this filtering function, you are inevitably classifying and coding information *as data*, as you collect it, and this leads to additional classification as you collect more, as it becomes more of an organized collection of data rather than simply an aggregation of disparate bits of information. We will return to examine these ideas more deeply in Chapter 7 when we examine the data quest.

Because netnographic procedures have always been finely tuned to their consequences, the next chapter will detail these matters and offer specific guidelines to help you incorporate established and accepted ethical guidelines into your research. With your research topic and question now formulated, you are more able to start formulating a plan for research that will achieve your research aims, and do it in a way that minimizes its disruption of people, online atmospherics and events.

SUMMARY

In this chapter, you began to prepare to conduct a netnography. The chapter opened with a pithy reminder that our state of readiness is not always as prepared as we might believe. Many types of decision and research practices may be needed before we can rigorously conduct our netnography. Researcher introspection began our netnographic journey, and several exercises guide you through a type of inner grounding process and then lead you to a social introspection exercise. The axiological principles of netnography were offered and held to be guiding foundations of the work. Next, you learned how to formulate a research focus and research question that are appropriately investigated through netnography. Netnographies of online social interaction and experience tend to focus on sites, topics and people.

KEY READINGS

Gould, Stephen J. (2012) 'The emergence of Consumer Introspection Theory (CIT): Introduction to a JBR special issue', *Journal of Business Research*, 65: 453–460.

Kozinets, Robert V. (1998) 'On netnography: Initial reflections on consumer research investigations of cyberculture', in Joseph Alba and Wesley Hutchinson (eds), *Advances in Consumer Research*, Volume 25. Provo, UT: Association for Consumer Research. pp. 366–371.

Silver, David (2006) 'Introduction: Where is internet studies?', in David Silver and Adrienne Massanari (eds), *Critical Cyberculture Studies*. New York and London: New York University Press. pp. 1–14.

NOTES

1. Showing just how public, accessible and long-lasting are these communications, you can easily locate my posting and its responses by entering some of the text of my initial posting into the newsgroup search engine at Google Groups. If you read the resulting thread of conversation, you may note how the members of the group educated me not only about their group and its values, but also about my own possible institutional biases. This sort of exchange of perspectives is one of the most powerful and valuable aspects of netnographic participation.

2. I believe that the reference in question is Sokal, Alan D. (1996) 'Transgressing the boundaries: Towards a transformative hermeneutics of quantum gravity', *Social Text, 46/47:* 217–252 (retrieved 3 April 2007) – a rather grievous, hyperbolic and exceptional – yet highly publicized – affair in which a noted physics professor submitted a jargon-laden, ideologically skewed paper about physics to a special issue of a postmodern cultural studies journal which did not practise peer review.

6

ETHICS

At least for the foreseeable near future, researchers must operate flexibly to adapt to continual shifts in perceptions, unstable terms of service, radically distinctive national and cultural expectations for privacy, and still steady growth of Internet use – Annette Markham, 'Fabrication as ethical practice,' *Information, Communication, and Society* (2012: 337)

ETHICAL TERRITORY

Notions of territoriality pervade online social experiences as people carve up communications and technologies conceptually into spaces that they can own. These notions of territoriality are very strong and instinctual within us, biobasic urges around which we have built language and culture. We all instinctively understand, at the very important and tacit level that is rarely discussed, the territory-defending grunts of large scary animals like bears and hippos, walruses and gorillas, or the frenzied panic of a chimpanzee, or the horrific feline majesty of the lion's roar. Territory and its importance is so deep within us that we could safely say it accompanied entirely the development of language out of those grunts, chirps, displays of tooth, horn and erect feathers. Territoriality is linked to anger, lust and fear, and intermixes them. These strong emotions, this incredibly articulate language of ownership and property and rights, extends throughout our dealings not only with the material world, but also and often even to other human beings.

If we look around at Internet data, at the various self-organized groupings of information and identity, we can see how the entire Internet has become a series of territories divided by language, by nationality, by traditional religions, regionally, governmentally, economically, financially, by kinship line, and on and on. Indeed, people regularly map them as if they were territories. They also seek to own eyeballs, attention, and customer loyalty, among other things.

All of this is because we carry our possessive nature with us, online. We bring in our need to own and make our own and defend. We treat Internet space as something we need to win over, to settle upon, protect. In this, even as netnographers, we all sometimes seek blindly to stake our claim, carve out our territory, and to own our own piece of the unownable Internet.

In the social sciences, ethics matter. Netnographers face a lot of ethical choices and probably load up a certain personal and legal responsibility even as they go online and then write up their research and publish it. But if we leave territoriality aside, we will see that research ethics is the area of netnography that is the most uncertain as well as the most public. I field many questions from people who are afraid that they might 'get it wrong'. They are right – answers are difficult and even big (business) school IRB-approved social media research projects have become examples of ethical disasters.

Many of the published descriptions of netnography provided in Chapter 4's overview invest considerable page space into providing detailed procedural accountings and assurances that appropriate ethical bodies have given their approval to the research, and appropriate ethical choices have been made to guide netnographic research practices. This is no coincidence. A considerable number of the research topics discussed in that overview – psychedelic drug use, sexual adventurism, adult facilitation of teenage binge drinking – are sensitive matters. Because research ethics are such an important matter, they cannot be left as an afterthought or treated in an *ad hoc* manner during or after the ethnographic entrée and collection of data. Instead, ensuring an ethical research stance must be an important and integrated part of planning the netnographic research project. Thus, it is imperative that you familiarize yourself with the state of the art in ethical research standards for this area. Decisions about how to approach people, how to collect and store data, and how the work will be represented should be acknowledged and contemplated well in advance of actually executing them. In addition, ethical decisions will follow you throughout the process of conducting your netnography, presenting it, and perhaps even afterwards.

In their method handbook about conducting ethnographies in virtual worlds such as *Second Life*, Tom Boellstorff and colleagues (2012) offer some useful general guidelines, which include:

- The Principle of Care: Following a general and 'ideal' principle of 'taking good care' of informants, such that the researcher ensures as much as possible 'that informants gain some reward from participating in research' (pp. 129-130).

- Informed Consent: keeping informants informed about the nature and purpose of our ethnographic studies, where possible, for example, by informing people in a Second Life profile that you are an anthropologist conducting, or changing one's virtual world avatar to a different image (such as one which includes a halo).
- Mitigating Institutional and Legal Risk: being aware of 'relevant laws that govern judicial access to fieldnotes' and our own research (p. 135), and also of the nature of contracts such as the Terms of Service (ToS) and End User Licensing Agreements (EULAs) that govern commercial virtual worlds (and, I might add, commercial social media).
- Anonymity: avoiding inappropriately revealing the identities of ethnographic informants, any other confidential information about them, or information that could lead to their identification.
- Deception: avoiding deceptive practices such as appearing in Second Life as a 'fly on the wall' or, say, as a disabled person or person of a different race in order to study such topics.
- Sex and Intimacy: avoiding, if possible, intimate and sexual relationships with ethnographic informants, and conducting any relationships that do occur with a high degree of integrity.
- Doing Good and Compensation: striving for a positive impact on the Second Life communities under study, which can include giving gifts or showing appreciation.
- Taking Leave: exiting the ethnographic research gracefully, by appropriately preparing informants for your departure.
- Accurate and Empathic Portrayal: forging an accurate and 'sympathetic depiction of informants' lives, even when discussing aspect of informants' lives that some might find troubling' (p. 149).

Not all netnography is as personally involving as the virtual world and Second Life ethnographies described by Boellstorff et al. (2012). However, netnographic incursions have the potential to be as invasive as their ethnographic equivalents. In their conduct, we make lasting impressions, leaving our own tracks and trails leading to other people. We are conducting a type of outreach during which we have the opportunity to learn, to share knowledge, to listen, to speak, to be enlightened, to outrage, to be offended, to challenge, to be confronted, and even to do harm.

Ethnography has always been active and activist. To 'observe' contains its own set of ethical risks, but to be active entails many more because you are visible. Perhaps it is the fact that we put our names on our research reports that we must be so careful about what we present as our reality. We represent our profession to community members and to the world.

Fieldwork means human-level research, analysing situations at the human level but using every scrap of knowledge and wisdom to do so. Fieldwork is thus an ineluctably propitious chance to reveal our true intentions. In academia, this means revealing ourselves and our colleagues as goodwill ambassadors, public servants, ignorant exploiters, ambivalent bystanders, attention-seeking posers, or many other positions. And each of us, ultimately, makes those choices and sticks with them on a daily, hourly, even minute-by-minute basis as we interact with a variety of social experiences in our lives. These experiences include the online social experiences that become a key focus as we conduct netnographic research on the various artifacts and through the various communication channels available to prompt, promote, idealize, utopianize, maintain and monetize online social experience.

With its mix of participation and observation, its often uncomfortable closeness, and its traditions of distanced description and cultural revelation, traditional ethnographic inquiry already possesses some of the thorniest bramble bushes in the research ethics jungle. When we add the need to understand technological complexities in both hardware, software and their synergistic interrelating, as well as people's many personalities, groups and quirks, and then multiply those quirks and traits by all of the unique cultures and all their procreative multiplications and subdivisions, these already-difficult issues become even more formidable.

Over the past ten years, significant amounts of new research and literature have emerged to enlighten our perspective on what constitutes ethical online research and ethical online versions of ethnography, including netnography. This chapter stands on the shoulders of some pioneering giants in this field, fellow scholars working in the areas of ethical philosophy, Internet legal issues, and online research ethics, only some of whose work is directly cited and developed throughout this chapter, but to all of whom I owe a considerable debt.

Full consensus on these matters will probably never exist. These are approximations. Ethics is a moving target. Although certainly not an exhaustive treatment of the topic of the ethics of online ethnography, this chapter is intended to provide you with solid grounding in understanding the ethical dilemmas you will confront. However, I will resist as much as possible giving the general advice to 'play nice' and platitudes about making endless adjustments and remaining flexible to the contingencies of the social scene. I will try to confront questions about practice with answers about practice. It is interesting to analyse research ethics challenges. But I believe that it is necessary to tell the netnographer how to approach people, what to say and do, how much to be involved in a community, what sort of ethical commitments might arise when using your own social network on Facebook or Twitter to do research, what to ask permission for, how to cite people, and to recommend protocols guiding these practices specifically that you can say you used to engage in ethical and legitimate netnographic inquiry. Although I will not specifically be able to overview advice for every single social media platform existing today, I do not think this much detail is required or desirable. This chapter will give a wealth of different examples for multiple sites and types of sites so that you can see a very good sampling of all of the current offerings out there, with attention paid of course to major players like YouTube, LinkedIn, Twitter, and Facebook.

To dig deeper into questions about your particular project, you are encouraged to consult the various citations and resources mentioned in this chapter as you are required or inspired to do so. Additionally, you would be wise to check online, in journal articles, and in books for the most current and up-to-date thinking about these rapidly changing topics, including among them the growing groups of netnographers on LinkedIn, Twitter and Facebook.

BOX 6.1

Aren't Social Media Public Spaces?

In presentations of netnography, I often hear from students or fellow scholars who insist that, when people post things on general Internet forums, pages, blogs or Twitter, they already know that it becomes public knowledge. 'Why would we go to all that trouble just to confirm what we already know?' Isn't this like quoting from a letter to the editor in a newspaper? As Zimmer (2010) notes in his examination of a careless research handling of Facebook data, many researchers simply assume that social media data is 'already public'.

It may be true at this point in history that most people do know that their online postings and information can be read in that form by members of the general public – and also, for that matter, by marketing researchers and members of intelligence agencies such as the NSA. However, the fact that people know that their postings are public does not automatically lead to the conclusion that they also grant automatic unspoken consent for academics and other types of scholarly researchers to use this data in any way that they please. A short example will suffice as I will develop this argument throughout this chapter.

In early research on *X-Files* fans, I began downloading information from the public bulletin board alt.tv.x-files. I thought it would be appropriate to ask people's permission before I directly cited them. When I did, everyone gave their permission except for one person. Of course, that one person composed a wonderful quote that I wanted to use. They had posted, using a pseudonym, an intriguing narrative about their own personal UFO sighting and how it related to their relationship to the *X-Files* television show. This person may have been embarrassed because paranormal activities and experiences – especially those outside of the institutional context of organized religion – are stigmatized in our society. Or, more likely, given the tone of their response to me, they were wary of further attention because they subscribed to the same cover-up and intelligence service conspiracy theory dramas that animate the television show. But because the data were so interesting and so closely related to my paper's themes of consumption of conspiracy and the supernatural, I decided after some internal debate about bothering people too much to write one more time to this person, tell them how interesting their post was, and ask them to reconsider letting me use it if I followed all the rules of ethical research behaviour and quoted them using a pseudonym in the research. I also noted that this would be a research publication, not a mass publication.

After my request to reconsider, this person again definitively declined. According to many guidelines, and to those who declare the Internet a public space, that person's wishes should not have determined my actions as a researcher. According to a more legalistic interpretation, just because someone in a public crowd surrounding a celebrity does not want to be photographed does not give them any rights to tell a newspaper they cannot publish a photo of the celebrity that also captures or even features their face. Public data means public.

However, netnography is human research, and I conceptualize it as attending to human feeling. Of course, if I did not ask, then he could not have refused me permission. I could

(Continued)

(Continued)

just have used his data without concern. But knowing as I did that this person did not want to be included meant that it would have felt very wrong for me to include their data.

I think that this stance has powerful ethical implications. Do other people's concerns about their postings matter to us as researchers? Have standards regarding privacy changed enough that we can now safely assume that people understand the public nature of their postings and, moreover, consent to the use of their postings as research data? Are we expected to let the individuals who post make the final determination about whether we can quote them or not? Would medical research, for example, be able to continue if there were no double-blind placebo studies?

Buitelaar (2014) considers the case of two convicted German murderers who sued Wikipedia, asking that the entry naming them as murderers should be taken down because there is a German law that such news stories cannot be carried after the criminals have served their prison sentences. Should we also be asked to rewrite history, then, on the basis of privacy and confidentiality?

Perhaps these notions of privacy and confidentiality are a function of the times. In 1996, the Internet was a very different place and the standards were clearly in flux. And yet, the same issues seem to remain almost two decades later. For example, LeBesco (2004) reported that, in a single month, eight researchers tried to gain access to a particular online community site and all but one was rejected by the group. Bakardjieva (2005) reported her frustration with recruiting respondents through announcements on online newsgroups, a tactic she later abandoned. They asked permission, rather than assuming it, and were refused. These are clearly not isolated examples, as you will read of many such cases, and other related compromises such as those regarding the use of corporate sites, throughout this book.

In an article pithily titled 'Go Away', James Hudson and Amy Bruckman (2004) relate that people in chat-rooms reacted with hostility when they were aware of being studied by researchers. When these people were given the opportunity to become part of the research, only four out of 766 potential participants chose to do so. In summary, Johns et al. (2003: 159) reported that 'many list owners and newsgroup members deeply resent the presence of researchers and journalists in their groups'.

Knowing this, can we proceed on the assumption that the members of various networks that we may contact or access are automatically granting us their consent to use their words, images, photos, videos and connections in our research? Or can we make a firm and supportable argument that we are engaging in research on public postings in a public space that may have some public benefit? As we will learn in the remainder of this chapter, the answer is not a simple one.

IRE, IRB AND NETNOGRAPHY

Among its many affordances, the Internet exists as a set of sophisticated tools that people use, a sociocultural phenomenon that changes people's lives and the ways that they socialize, and as a site for researchers to investigate. Internet Research Ethics (or IRE) is 'an emerging and fascinating research field', a sphere

of inquiry that 'has been growing steadily since the late 1990s, with many disciplinary examinations of what it means to conduct research – ethically – in online or Internet-based environments' (Buchanan, 2006: 14). Important guidelines have been advanced and developed through such leading organizations as the American Association for the Advancement of Science (Frankel and Siang, 1999), the Association of Internet Researchers (see Association of Internet Researchers Ethics Working Group, 2002, 2012), and the American Psychological Association (see Kraut et al., 2004). There are two excellent journals largely dedicated to these issues: *Ethics and Information Technology*, published by Kluwer Academic and the *International Journal of Internet Research Ethics*, published online by the Center for Information Policy Research, School of Information Studies, University of Wisconsin-Milwaukee. Alongside a number of special issues dedicated to the topic, seminars and conferences, a number of helpful edited and co-authored volumes have been published (see, for example, Boellstorff et al., 2012; Buchanan, 2004; Ess, 2009; Johns et al., 2003; Krotoski, 2010; McKee and Porter, 2009; Thorseth, 2003). However, as the authors of the AoIR Ethics Working Committee Report (2012) state, 'no official guidance or "answers" regarding Internet research ethics have been adopted at any national or international level'.

The issues that IRE deals with are dynamic and complex; they touch upon philosophical matters, commercial interests, academic traditions of research practice and method, and institutional arrangements, as well as the oversight of legislative and regulatory bodies. IRE must deal with a wide range of epistemological and logistical issues as addresses a panoply of divergent individual research approaches to the Internet. As a whole, IRE's concerns stretch from legal issues such as 'liability for negligence' and 'damage to reputation' to conventional research ethics notions of 'informed consent' and 'respect', to social issues such as autonomy, the right to privacy, and the various differences in relevant international standards and laws.

It is onto this shifting, complex ground of moral, legal, policy- and method-oriented decisions that every netnographer must step. For if we wish to conduct a netnography, we are going to have to answer to various institutional and regulatory bodies for the ethical standards of our research. In the United States, each university's Institutional Review Board, or 'IRB', governs and administers applicable research ethics standards. These IRBs in the United States are guided by the Code of Federal Regulations Title 45, Part 46, Protection of Human Subjects, which was inspired by the spirit of the Belmont report, which in turn was prompted by the research protocols emerging from international awareness that stemmed from the Nuremburg trails of Nazi experimentation on human beings. In other countries, the names and protocols may be different. In a number of countries, academic research ethics are governed by Human Subjects Research Ethics Committees, which in turn tend to be regulated by government agencies and bodies that offer academic research grants. Some countries have no such institutions governing university researchers, but international laws may still be in effect. For research practitioners, various industry associations have codes of ethics or guidelines that govern the practice of ethical research. Every academic researcher is likely to be governed by at least one and perhaps two ethical research institutions and their codes.

Obviously, the aspiring and practising netnographer does not need to be concerned with the history or entirety of the Internet research ethics literature. As netnographers, what concerns us most are those topics and guidelines pertaining particularly to the online conduct of participant observational research and interviews. We must grapple with some difficult and obscure questions before we can make defensible decisions about how to conduct our netnography. Although it is far from an exhaustive list, you may want to consult Box 6.2 for a list of some relevant questions.

BOX 6.2

Relevant Ethical Questions in Netnography

Conducting a netnography that is ethical and adapted to the unique environment of the Internet is far from simple. There are perplexing and difficult questions that scholars from philosophy, legal issues and various academic departments are working to answer. Some of the ethical questions that are relevant to netnographic inquiry include:

- Are online social interactions private or public?
- What roles do corporations like Facebook, Google, Apple and Twitter play in our research? Do they have a say in what is ethical, legal or moral?
- Whose consent do we need to gain in netnography?
- How do we gain the informed consent of the online other?
- Who actually owns the online data posted on social networking sites or micoblogs?
- How do we deal with the information on corporate websites and other online forums? Can we use it in our research?
- Should we use conversations that we participate in or 'overhear' in chat-rooms? Are there different ethical rules for different types and sites of online media?
- Do age and vulnerability matter online? In media in which identity is difficult to verify, how can we be sure about the age or vulnerability of research participants?
- Do international boundaries influence the way a netnographer collects data and publishes research?

These are vital questions. The answers will help you to formulate adaptable yet directive guidelines for your research. Of course, like the Internet itself, these issues and acceptable protocols are constantly changing. You are obligated as a researcher to stay on current with the topics that are relevant to you and your research interests, and to make the decisions that you believe to be correct in consultation with your colleagues and relevant regulatory bodies (for academics in the USA, this would be your Institutional Review Board). For others, you may need to consult your university department or legal experts.

Because ethical decisions need to be made at every stage of netnographic research, this chapter will cover several broad issues. First, as a general preparation for ethical decision making, we will discuss conceptions that see netnography as focused on data or people and transpiring within public or private spaces. Moving to the entrée and data collection phases of research, we consider issues surrounding informed consent. As data collection and analysis continue and turn into concerns about representations, we must plan our research to avoid unnecessary harm or maximize net benefit to culture members, which forms the next section. In the final introductory section, we will consider the ethical complexities of representation.

The chapter then proceeds to discuss and describe four general procedural areas to address these issues: (1) identifying yourself and informing relevant constituents about your research, (2) asking for appropriate permissions, (3) gaining consent where needed, and (4) properly citing and crediting culture members. Although certainly not an exhaustive treatment of the topic, this chapter should give you a strong general sense of the major ideas, accepted conventions, practices and procedures that you need in order to proceed ethically with your research, as well as to provide citations and resources enabling you to dig deeper into questions about your own particular netnography.

PUBLIC DATA *VS.* PRIVATE PEOPLE

Much debate about Internet research ethics is concerned with whether we should treat computer-mediated interactions as if they took place in either a public or a private space. This spatial metaphor is commonly applied to the Internet and seems, in fact, to be a fundamental human cognition (Munt, 2001). According to the Protection of Human Subjects, US Code of Federal Regulations Title 45, Part 46 (2009), which governs Institutional Review Boards in the United States, human subjects research is research in which there is an intervention or interaction with another person for the purpose of gathering information, or in which information is recorded by a researcher in such a way that a person can be identified through it directly or indirectly. Netnography in which the researcher interacts with another person in order to gather information clearly fits into the human subjects research model. However, Bassett and O'Riordan (2002) make a convincing argument that the notion of treating all Internet research as human subjects research draws from the faulty view that the Internet is a type of place or a social space, rather than a text. I have been arguing throughout this book that the Internet is actually text-like and spacelike, and that these qualities exist both separately and simultaneously. This does not make things simpler for matters of ethics.

> The Internet is not only a text-based medium made up of communities, newsgroups and email lists. It is also a medium of publication, and significantly one where users can take control of the means of production, create their own cultural artifacts and

> intervene in the production of existing ones. The Internet can thus be perceived as a form of cultural production, in a similar framework to that of the print media, broadcast television and radio. (Bassett and O'Riordan, 2002: 235)

Although this is certainly true, Skype can also be like a private phone call, Twitter like a personal text message, and Snapchat like the flash of a prying camera. These are quite unlike print media and broadcast television.

Earlier, we introduced the idea that netnographic investigations reside in these two core aspects of online social experience and interaction: direct communications with people, and the use of archival materials. Applied to the topic of Internet research ethics, this dichotomy leads us to see our ethical obligations with greater clarity. When we are engaging in placelike participation, communicating with other people through email, shooting them messages through Google Plus, and interviewing them through Facetime and on Google Hangouts, we are engaging in research with human beings (or, in unfortunately psychological ethics parlance, 'subjects') and we must comport ourselves accordingly. This means human subjects research protocols about informed consent and other related permissions pertain. A Google Hangout is clearly more like a telephone call than a public space and in that case the same privacy rules governing telephone interviews apply to the research conversation.

However, where the Internet has been used to give members of the public, in essence, their own 'megaphone' as Ed McQuarrie and his co-authors (2013) cleverly term it, as when they publish their own zine, blog, or other publication, and this would logically extend to include public Twitter feed, public Facebook and LinkedIn profiles, photos and status updates, as well as when they comment in public on news stories, others' stories, or a YouTube video, then we can think about this type of publication as a public document. Bassett and O'Riordan (2002: 244) suggest that

> If an individual or group has chosen to use Internet media to publish their opinions then the researcher needs to consider their decision to the same degree that they would with a similar publication in traditional print media. Overly protective research ethics risk diminishing the cultural capital of those engaging in cultural production through Internet technologies, and inadvertently contributing to their further marginalization.

The authors opine that citation or quotation of the clearly published and publicly displayed information – including, it would seem, previously private data, such as an author's name – is the correct and ethical course of action. They use their study of a lesbian website, which they decided to cloak with the name 'Gaygirls.com' to illustrate an alternative to their main point. Instead of showing how it is like a public forum, the Gaygirls.com example shows the possibilities of marginalization or pathologization by treating certain public and published texts by certain kinds of people as too 'sensitive' to cite or quote.

The presence of conversations that have been stored and saved in publicly searchable formats, including those that occur between the researcher and other people, are a bit murkier. Are these conversations more like transcribed and archived telephone chats (perhaps SMS or WhatsApp messages might be a more apropos metaphor) or are they like public conversations, a panel discussion or public debate? What about the practical matter of trying to hunt down the pseudonymous contributors to a ten-year-old but still fascinating and theoretically illuminating online conversation – a frustrating game I have played in deference to earlier, seemingly outdated, standards regarding obtaining permission. Bassett and O'Riordan (2002: 244–245) again have an answer:

> It is not always possible, for example, to gain the consent of a large number of participants who may have changed their email address or ceased posting to a website on which the material under research is located. This should not prevent research of textual material that they have chosen to output via the Internet anymore than it would for textual products in other print or broadcast media. Academic research ideally endeavours to reflect the range and versatility of the media that it considers and we should avoid any unintentional erasure of minority groups in research that might result from considering their textual output as private social interaction.

What I find most fascinating and useful about the stance of Bassett and O'Riordan (2002) is that the article points us to error of exclusion as well as errors of inclusion. By excluding data, and voices, we risk marginalization and also commit ethical breaches. Every decision in netnography has ethical ramifications, both what to include and what to exclude.

However, with a bit of digging this clearly becomes yet another grey area. If we automatically include conversations we find online because locating their posters is difficult, or because we think that the sensitive material that they shared should not be marginalized or excluded, do we not run a risk of causing these people harm? In fact, technology in the Internet age makes the realization of privacy increasingly difficult. Given a single direct quote from one of its postings, Gaygirls.com is almost too easy to identify.

And what of the case where we ask or prompt for questions in a public forum? Are we free from obligations? Guiding sets of standards are certainly appropriate. The Association of Internet Researchers recommends a case-based approach that addresses ethical concerns as they manifest and must be addressed at different stages of the research process. Their indispensible 19-page document is shared for free online and contains specific ethical questions about the particular research context that must then be balanced further with the disciplinary, institutional, legal, cultural, and other constraints facing the researcher (Association of Internet Researchers Ethics Working Group, 2012). As Lomborg (2012: 45) describes and illustrates it, following the Association of Internet Researchers' ethical guidelines leads to an inductive, case-based approach that takes as a starting point for ethical decision-making a careful examination of the ethical issues arising from the specific research project ... [and results in paying] attention to the specific details of a research project (i.e. research questions, methodology and data, analyses and publication of findings), as well as disciplinary standards, and cultural-contextual factors.

However, these guidelines still leave much for us to ponder.

Consider the fact that the research use of online conversations, if gathered in a publicly accessible venue, is not human subjects research according to the Code of Federal Regulations' definition. If the research involves collecting and analysing existing documents or records that are publicly available, this research qualifies for a human subjects exemption because it is more similar to a published text than a private individual exchange. According to Internet research pioneer Joseph Walther (2002: 207) people who post material on a publicly available communication system on the Internet should understand that it is public, not private or confidential. Analysing social interactions as they are carried on archives does not constitute human subjects research, more specifically, if the researcher does not record the identity of the communicators and if the researcher can legally and easily gain public access to these communications or archives. This 'does not record the identity' clause is actually very treacherous, because it is rather simple to use search engines to link texts to pseudonyms and pseudonyms to identities. The Internet records people's identities and makes them accessible, even if the researcher does not.

So, is the use of this data similar to the 'fair use' of copyright materials in the USA, subject to certain restrictions, but otherwise effectively waived as far as research purposes are concerned (Walther, 2002)? Even if this is so, many of these fair use exemptions *are not* in effect in international law. Those nations' lack of fair use laws may well impede the ability of researchers outside the United States to conduct netnography. In addition, researchers seeking to make use of social media resources located on local commercial websites may well run up against legal restrictions in terms of use and end user agreements. Individual researchers are advised to consider these guidelines, but also to check into the relevant laws, regulations and institutions pertaining to their countries.

Another important and emerging destabilization concerns the assumed separation of the text or data from the person. 'An essential element of informational self-determination is the control the individual has over the information that is available about her in the Internet environment, also known as her digital double' (Buitelaar 2014: 266). Digital doubles, also known as digital personae, are models of individuals built out of data, used as proxies for individuals, and often treated 'as an "extension" of the offline identity and personality of the individual concerned' (Bernal, 2012: 6). Not only has the line impossibly blurred between the public and the private, but so too has the distinction between a person's physical being and their social being as represented and captured through their

various digital traces and tracks as captured on CCTV cameras, in logs of mobile phone conversation, through Skype calls, LinkedIn profile updates, and Dropbox files, and in other online technologically mediated and captured personal and social interactions. Digital doubles are identities. Centring on individual biography and autobiography, Buitelaar (2014: 277) suggests that, in this world of digital doubles, Internet researchers – and in this context, that most certainly includes netnographers – should use narrative techniques and combine them with historiographical methods in order to uphold a principle of 'informational self-determination, with its constituent elements of human dignity and autonomy' and thus 'place the innate right of privacy in a fair position vis-à-vis the right to the freedom of expression'.

The Internet is not really a place or a text; it is not either public or private; it does not simply contain data but digital doubles of our identities and selves. It is not even one single type of social interaction, but many types: social network status updates, microblogged tweets, posted photos, comments, chats, likes, emails, podcasts, videos, telephone conversations shared using VOIP protocols, and many others. Issues of representation, misrepresentation and self-presentation mix into a confusing muddle as we consider that our netnographic work contributes to, but also partakes within and can be equally subject to, processes of exhibition and expression over which individuals increasingly strive to have some degree of control. I believe that we must devise equally powerful, adaptive, transforming, creative and bricolage-based solutions to these ethical issues, such as those of thought leader Annette Markham (2004, 2012). The models guiding our efforts in netnography need to be open to the vast and social interrelation of being and representation that is transforming society and culture, while remaining ever cognizant of the need to respect, affirm, and uphold fundamental human rights.

BOX 6.3

Deontological and Consequentialist Thinking about Internet Research Ethics

The netnographer has choices when it comes to research ethics procedures, but there are certain requirements that are well established such as informed consent and risks versus benefits. Both of these aspects are locked into a consequentialist moral form of reasoning. Consequentialism is built upon a foundation of estimated consequences, the notion that the end justifies the means. Consequentialism, for example, might conclude that it is all right to kill people (say, terrorists or suspected terrorists) to achieve some particular aim, such as making the world a better place. In deontological thinking, however, which is not seen as much as it used to be, you say that doing something is just wrong. It is wrong

(Continued)

(Continued)

to conduct adultery. It is wrong to disrespect your Father. It is wrong to kill another human being. It is simply wrong and it should not be done no matter the consequences, conditions or context. The Ten Commandments and most Biblical pronouncements are not contingent, contextual and consequential. They contain Absolutes. Deontological thinking in netnography gets us to a place in which some violations are simply not cool and others are unforgivable. We might, in future, need to revisit our foundations, and explore what is and is not all right to say and to do as we explore online social interactions and where they lead us.

INFORMED CONSENT

In a departure from traditional face-to-face methods like ethnography, focus groups, or personal interviews, netnography uses cultural information that is not given specifically, in confidence, to the researcher. However, using this data comes with some ethical questions. If gaining the informed consent of research participants is a cornerstone of ethical research conduct, should it not also be the case with netnographic data? In the early days of Internet research and Internet-based ethnographies, King (1996) recommended gaining additional informed consent from online research participants. Similarly, Sharf (1999) echoed this heightened sensitivity to the ethics of online fieldwork, even that which was purely observational. Yet, as Frankel and Siang (1999: 8) noted, even at that early stage, the 'ease of anonymity and pseudonymity of Internet communications also poses logistical difficulties for implementing the informed consent process' (see also Bassett and O'Riordan, 2002). Furthermore, as we discussed in the prior section, the collection and analysis of archived messages does not officially constitute human subjects' social research. Informed consent is a human subjects' ethical construct and constraint. We do not need to ask a book's author for permission to cite her in our research, or a set of speakers on a televised programme whether we can quote their conversations. Why would Internet data be so different?

Netnography goes further than unobtrusive observation and download. Netnographers are cultural participants; they interact. Perhaps the closest analogue to traditional ethnography that we find online, with its exotic locations and Others is the virtual world ethnography. Writing about the ethics of virtual world ethnography (which could, if it followed this book's guidelines, also be a netnography), 'we are obligated to do as much as possible to reveal to our informants the nature and purpose of our studies' and also to keep them informed about the research as 'an ongoing imperative' (Boellstorff et al., 2012: 133). Yet exposing yourself as a netnographer can be risky business, and may help account for the distancing drift of netnography away from more participative styles. If you act in a manner found to be irresponsible and disrespectful, that could lead to your public exposure and censure, and might even invite legal sanctions.

The AoIR Ethics Working Committee report (2012) counsels that we must consider how we will recognize in our research design the autonomy of others and acknowledge that they are of equal worth to ourselves and should be treated in this fashion. Four important factors help to influence whether we require informed consent in this case. First, what is the nature of the research involvement? Are personal interviews involved, or personal conversations, or is the nature purely one of accessing archives of past contributions or interactions? The former is clearly more deserving of informed consent than the latter. Do we have reason to believe that research participants believe that their online social interactions are private and protected (even if they are not so)? In the case that they do believe their interactions are private, following a principle of autonomy and respect would dictate that the provision of informed consent should prevail. What types of data are being used? Videos and photographs often have faces that can easily be identified by facial recognition software, and informed consent would be called for. Similarly, direct quotes are increasingly easy to identify through search engines. Even supposedly anonymized Facebook has been the source of major ethical troubles. In a helpful exploration, Zimmer (2010) analyses the use of Facebook data in a multi-year, IRB-approved, NSF-funded study of a cohort of 1700 university students. The author finds that

> the notion of what constitutes 'consent' within the context of divulging personal information in social networking spaces must be further explored, especially in light of this contextual understanding of norms of information flow within specific spheres ,,, [and the Facebook case] also reveals that we still have not learned the lessons of the AOL data release and similar instances where presumed anonymous datasets have been re-identified. (Zimmer, 2010: 323)

When we know that data can be traced, we are obligated to gain informed consent (or attempt to make the data truly untraceable).

Finally, we must consider the probability of harm to individuals or their groups. Walther (2002: 212–213) noted the cases where implied consent prevailed, which included 'many kinds of human subjects social research that do involve some kind of interaction or intervention'. These studies could be exempt from IRB concern 'due to the lack of harm the research presents' to those being researched. For example, researching anonymous person's normal day-to-day online social behaviours, not collecting any data that could be used to reveal their identities, and aggregating the results would serve as an example. Another way that implied consent can occur over the Internet is when research consent-related information is presented to the prospective research participant in some unobtrusive, electronic form. The participant might signal their consent by agreeing to continue in the study after reading a form or the text on a pop-up, and then clicking an 'accept' button on a web-page and/or by providing basic data such as their name and/or email. In a virtual world setting, one researcher approached participants asking for their 'blessing' for her project and then presented them with links, an email, and a posting to a description of her research and an online consent form; another researcher placed a halo over the head of her avatar to designate her role as an ethnographer (Boellstorff et al., 2012: 133–135). It is common in netnography for the researcher of a particular community to post information about their status as a researcher and the purpose of their study on their profile and often on forum boards. However, there may also be situations in netnography where gaining informed consent is desirable, but there are constraints that could render written consent impractical or even harmful. All of these factors should be considered.

We usually think about the consent process occurring at the beginning of a study, perhaps as we first begin to collect data. We might need to gain consent from companies, from moderators, from online system administrators, from parents or guardians of minors or other ostensibly vulnerable persons, groups or from individuals. There are many ways to obtain consent from informants or participants, including print or digital signatures, other identifiers, virtual consent tokens, or click boxes. Buchanan et al. (2010) usefully contextualize the consent process by suggesting that 'Sometimes it may be more ethical to get informed consent at the end when you want to present a specific case study or quote an individual or focus on a particular element. Therefore, informed consent should be always an inductive process'.

Although questions have been raised about whether an informed consent approach can be valid without certain knowledge of the competency, comprehension and even the age of the research participant, Walther (2002: 213) notes that many traditionally accepted methods such as mail and telephone surveys deal with the same sort of uncertain knowledge about whether people are actually who they say they are. In fact, there is no clear, indisputable link between face-to-face research and judgements of research participant competency and comprehension. Similarly, the fact that we have no steadfast guarantees that we can truly inform our participants about study risks should not deter us from doing our best to follow the required procedures.

DO NO HARM ONLINE

The same potential for harm present in face-to-face ethnographies – revelation of personal or cultural secrets, hurtful portrayals of culture members, disdainful treatment of customs – is present in netnography. Past methodological treatments have warned netnographers to be careful in considering the ethical concerns of privacy, confidentiality, appropriation and consent (Kozinets, 2002a, 2006), and to this we should add the 'fundamental human rights of human dignity, autonomy, protection, safety, maximization of benefits and minimizations of harms, or, in the most recent accepted phrasing, respect for persons, justice, and beneficence' (Association of Internet Researchers Ethics Working Group, 2012: 4).

In order to be able to make the consequentialist and utilitarian tradeoffs that guide ethical research decisions, we must work with a solid understanding of the terms risk and harm (see Box 6.3 for more on this). The US Federal Code Title 45 regulations define minimal risk as meaning that 'the probability and magnitude of harm or discomfort anticipated in the research are not greater in and of themselves than those ordinarily encountered in daily life or during the performance of routine physical or psychological examinations or tests' (Protection of Human Subjects, 2009). This definition is obviously tailored to a world of physical medical experimentation, not ethnographic exploration. It does not particularly help us to assess the impact of publication and exposure. However, we might wonder, and I might suggest, that just as Title 45 compares medical research tests with 'the performance of routine physical or psychological examinations or tests', so too might we compare the exposure of a netnographic research report to the routine exposure people have on social media to comments, exposure and critique, and also the routine exposure that people have to being highlighted and featured in traditional media, such as being interviewed for an article in a magazine or newspaper, or a story on television. Would publication in our article subject the person to stresses that would be significantly beyond those that they already routinely encounter in their daily lives as active social media posters and commenters? Would it be significantly more than if they were featured in a news story?

There are certain groups that are inherently vulnerable. For example if you are studying sites that feature or facilitate illicit or addictive drug use, marital infidelity, criminal activity or other illegal or stigmatized behaviours, the participants on these sites cannot be construed to be minimal risk. Even in the current day, there are large numbers of people using online social experiences for matters sexual who do not want their sexual orientation or tastes or online habits 'outed'. Yet the risk to these people is also a function of the goals of your study and must be weighed against its potential benefits. You may be studying a site related to tourism and discover a large and active area detailing how to illegally import poached items made from endangered animal species. Would you identify the site and the activity, but not the participants? Would you provide examples of the activity? Would you ignore it and study other areas of the site because of the ethical consequences? Each of these decisions will have consequences that are problematic in their own right. Because you now know about the role of this site in facilitating trade in illegal goods made from endangered species, do you now have an obligation – a moral one at least and perhaps even an ethical one – to report it somehow, even if not as part of your scientific research? Would you need to weigh the benefit to these animals and to upholding the laws protecting them, against the benefits of protecting your research participants from being exposed for their unethical criminal activities?

People may well have strong feelings about the research use of archives of their online interactions. Walther (2002: 215) opines that these issues warrant our careful consideration and further discussion; however, he suggests that they probably do not warrant 'the suspension of scientifically designed and theoretically motivated research'. Nonetheless, the general guidelines of the AoIR Working Committee (2012: 4–5) prove helpful. These guidelines consider fundamental an approach that:

1. Considers the vulnerability of the community, author, or participant, and considers the obligation to protect directly commensurate with vulnerability.
2. Applies ethical principles practically, contextually and inductively rather than universally, because 'harm' must be defined contextually (a process of 'phronesis').
3. Carefully thinks about how human subjects ethics principles may apply even to decontextualized anonymous data which can in many cases be de-anonymized and re-contextualized.
4. Appropriately balances the rights of subjects with the social benefits of research and researchers' rights to conduct research.
5. Considers ethical issues during every step of the research process, from planning to dissemination.
6. Consults as many people and resources as possible, including fellow researchers, research participants, review boards, ethics guidelines, published scholarship and legal precedents.

Consider the many netnographies we have discussed so far that deal with stigmatized topics such as psychedelic drug promotion and information or online sexual display and meeting sites. How do we handle netnographies about sites, groups, or individuals that may not be positive or flattering to the individuals or groups involved? For example, Katrin Tiidenburg (2014) performed online fieldwork studying self-shooters who take sexy exhibitionistic photos of themselves to share online. Her visual analysis of these sexy selfies includes visual images of the photographs. However, Tiidenburg adheres to ethical guidelines as follows:

> Because of the sensitivity of the topic, ethical choices and protecting my informants has been a priority throughout the research process. While I did acquire informed consent from all of my participants, I have gone back to them over the course of my fieldwork to make sure they are aware of and OK with me also analyzing and using their images in addition to their text, etc. I used ethical fabrication (Markham, 2012) in two ways in this article. I altered the wordings of blog outtakes to minimize their reverse-searchability, and I altered the images I included by running them through a sketching application, hiding watermarks, and placing a modesty block on one of Peter's images [a photo which reveals his penis].

We might, for example, consider that the spouses, parents, friends, children, family members and co-workers of people such as Peter might not be aware that they are sharing photos of themselves with their genitalia hanging out online. If the information in Karin Tiidenburg's netnographic study led to the identification of informants, might harm be done to them? The obvious answer here is yes.

Yet, as Bruckman (2002: 225, emphasis in original) notes, '*human subjects regulations do not prohibit us from doing harm to subjects*'. In this case, we might wonder if denying them another exhibitionistic possibility, with the audience of a journal, might harm people who are already sharing exhibitionistic photos online. In other words, we are forced by definitions of harm to impose our own standards onto others, as Tiidenburg does in her study. The relevant sections of the federal code relating to criteria for IRB approval of research suggest that risks to research participants should be minimized and that 'risks to subjects are reasonable in relation to anticipated benefits, if any, to subjects, and the importance of the knowledge that may reasonably be expected to result' (Protection of Human Subjects, 2009). This assumes, however, not only that these definitions of harm, risks and benefits are stable both for society and for the individual research participant, it also assumes that the researcher can accurately assess and compare these conditions.

In fact, 'to complicate matters further, as a lived concept, privacy is inextricable from its sister concepts: harm and vulnerability. To understand how potential research participants conceptualize one requires consideration of all three, separately and together, in context' (Markham, 2012: 337). There is thus a consequentialist, utilitarian ethical philosophy guiding academic research practice – not a deontological one founded in the idea of doing no harm. Susan Herring (1996) notes that, as scholars, we are not bound to adopt research methods or voice research results in order to please our research participants. In an ideal situation, the netnographic researcher 'would carefully weigh the public benefit of making the revelation, and balance this against the potential harm to the subject' (Bruckman, 2002: 225). Yet, bereft of the wisdom of Solomon, we are forced by the indistinct, dynamically unstable online social environment to make our own very difficult evaluations. Ethical procedures must be decided on a case-by-case basis contingent upon the topic matter, the research purposes and the research approach of your particular netnography.

TO NAME OR NOT TO NAME, THAT IS THE QUESTION

Annette Markham finds the notion of privacy online to be not only an ambiguous concept, but one which is eroding:

> Sociologists and journalists have long considered a person's words to be freely available - if uttered publicly or with permission - to analyze and quote, as long as we anonymize the source. Researchers operating in physical environments traditionally took for granted the ability to safely store field notes, interview transcripts, demographic data, and other information that might reveal the location of the study or the participants' identities. These methods of data protection no longer suffice in situations where social researchers need to design studies, manage data, and build research reports in increasing public, archivable, searchable, and traceable spaces. More and more, data mining technologies are used to link participants to the information they produce and consume via a range of mobile devices, game consoles, and other Internet-based technologies. In such research environments, there are few means of adequately disguising details about the venue and persons being studied. (Markham, 2012: 336)

There are a number of pertinent and interrelated points about this topic of anonymizing and disguising that we must consider. First and probably most importantly, there is no getting around Markham's fact that a direct quote from a public online interaction can be accessed through a full-text search in a public search engine. It is therefore a fairly simple procedure to enter the verbatim quote of participants used in research publications into a public search engine and to then link that quotation with the actual pseudonym of a culture member. So, for example, in my past research on the alt.coffee newsgroups, published in 2002, I need not have bothered anonymizing people's names. If I enter the full text from my published article into Google, the entire message pops up, in context, with pseudonym or real name (in many cases) intact. Pseudonym and actual identity are already interrelated and traceable. Online pseudonyms often function as real names. People may 'routinely disclose information linking their pseudonym and real name' (Bruckman, 2002: 221). Even if they do not, in the Facebook and Twitter age, most people are using their 'real name' and with API links and cookies everywhere, it is a relatively simple matter to link the use of one name with another.

A quick observation is in order. Although I definitely see these revealing practices as an undermining of the illusion of anonymity, I also must recognise that it is very nice to do a text search, see these textual verbata recast into their context again, surrounded by other members of their threads and appearing as part of an organic, living process. No longer isolated, no longer framed and recast by the researcher, they may speak differently to the reader or another researcher than they did to me. They encourage and facilitate deeper and further investigation, which is so essential to quality ethnography.

The second point is that a lot of people like to do this decloaking practice. For example, within days of its public release, a large and anonymized research dataset of a particular Facebook cohort was 'cracked' and identified, without ever looking at the data itself (Zimmer, 2010: 316). Computer science students and other tech-nomages enjoy decoding and decrypting, and once they have cracked the latest DRM codec they may just as well turn their attention to revealing the participants in a research study. Scholars in computer science even publish papers on the robust de-anonymization of large social networks (Narayanan and Shmatikov, 2009).

Fourth, netnographers enter into a complex and diverse social terrain containing some people who would definitely like to be accurately cited and credited for their work, and others who definitely would not. Many bloggers would rather see their online work properly cited, just as that work would be credited were they to publish it in a book or article. Yet Marwick and boyd (2011: 6) recount the story of a student who was angered that his embarrassing Facebook information was used by teachers at his school in a school-wide public presentation about posting private information in public. The issue was not that the public data became (even more?) public, it was the sense of violation over the manner in which it became public. What people care the most about in these social media contexts, according to Nissenbaum (2010) is not about the restriction of the flow of information, but about ensuring its contextually appropriate flow.

In addition,

> As conversations and debates continue to rage across multiple spheres of interest, the challenge for qualitative researchers remains: While some media savvy participants, or what Senft (2008) has called 'micro celebrities', may prefer that their publicity be protected and that researchers cite them accurately and fully, many more want the reverse. But what does this mean, if we cannot find consensus on what privacy means, much less how it is therefore 'protected?' (Markham, 2012: 337)

How are we to handle the diversity of types of posts and types of posters that constitute online social experiences and interactions? Bruckman usefully suggests that, in the Internet age, publishing is now a continuum: 'Most work on the Internet is "semi-published"' (2002: 227). Should we then follow her advice to consider whether the various individuals that we study in a netnography are 'amateur artists': 'in many ways, all user-created content on the Internet can be viewed as various forms of amateur art and authorship' (2002: 229)? Perhaps we must consider this in context, using Nissenbaum's (2010) notion of contextual integrity, in which contexts, actors, communicative attributes and communicative principles balance social rules and norms with local and general values, ends and purposes. The principle essentially draws us to think about how information is used in context; to see these norms as part of a structured social system that has evolved to help members of a social group to interact, manage and accomplish their goals; and to respect, in situ, the way that online social experiences manifest divergent, grounded and particular notions of concepts such as privacy and risk.

We might begin to think about how we would adapt, as part of our netnographic repertoire, Buitelaar's (2014: 273) historiographic narrative techniques, which suffuse collected ensembles 'of facts or data with an imaginative understanding while also synthesizing the past and present' in the service of re-endowing 'the individual with their fundamental potentials'. Can we begin to imagine a netnographer acting like a digital historian, carefully crafting stories about people's lives, interactions and social experiences? In a later section, I will offer concrete suggestions for research practices that can help meet some of these challenges.

LEGAL CONSIDERATIONS

Legal scholar, practising attorney, and professor, Tomas Lipinski (2006: 55; see also 2008) has published a valuable analysis of the potential legal issues pertaining to 'the protocols of ethnographers who use listserv, discussion board, blog, chat room and other sorts of web or Internet-based postings as the source of their data'. Although his approach favours a more observational and less interactive method, many of his conclusions appear to apply to the more participative form of netnography that I advance in this book. To summarize a complex set of topics, researchers who collect data from online sources and then 'publish' that information in some particular online venue, such as an online journal, or an online version of a journal, have significant protection from tort harm claims.

If the research is published in a traditional print medium, Lipinski (2006) suggests that researchers should be careful to only report true findings and not to deviate from standard research protocols. Those who do so are unlikely to be held liable for placing defendants in a false light, invading their privacy, defaming them, harming them, or in other ways acting in a negligent manner. Finally, because the conduct of academic research is so important to human understanding and public policy, Lipinski (2006) suggests that courts may treat this form of research as somewhat different from other types of investigation and other uses of online data, such as, for instance, commercial marketing research.

Netnographic researchers 'who refrain from including not only the subject's name or pseudonym but also any information that might identify an individual' should be exempted from claims arising from invasion of privacy. However, as discussed above, this refraining may be easier to say than to do. In general, Lipinski (2006) suggests that researchers avoid identifying individuals through their real name, online pseudonym, or other identifying information. However, even if the identification of individuals occurs, because the online communications media is legally viewed as a public place, this should undermine claims of invasion of privacy.

These sections have provided necessarily brief overviews of four issues important to the understanding of netnographic research ethics: conceptions of private and public data and bodies, pragmatics of informed consent, consequentialist determinations of harm and benefit, and the pseudonymous complexities of quotation and citation. Incorporating these suggestions into your research will mean making decisions that will alter its every aspect. Ethics is not a section of your research that can be simply 'tacked on' at the end by including a paragraph about IRB approval in a report's method section. Considering how we address these ethical questions leads us to new forms of netnography. It can transform the research question you choose to pursue, the types of data you will and will not collect, the way you present yourself online, the shape and form of your interactions, the way you save and store your data, as well as markedly transforming the nature of your final report.

Given the notions, advice, and collective intelligence presented thus far, I attempt in the next section to offer some recommended procedures and solutions. Although not hard-and-fast rules or prescriptions, these guidelines are intended to clarify standard research practices, answers to what-do-I-do questions to enable netnographers to get on with the work of doing quality netnography. The four sets of guidelines are as follows. When it is appropriate to do so, you must identify yourself and accurately inform relevant constituents about your research. When it is appropriate, you must also ask relevant people for the permission. Appropriate consent must be gained. Finally you must attempt to fully anonymize or else properly cite and credit the individuals who contributed to your netnography.

DO IT WELL
State your Name and Explain Yourself

As we can surmise from the ongoing descriptions of the Internet as territory to be protected and defended, we can see a new foundation for ethical netnography as being based in proper placement. Contextualizing what we do with where we are, in which site, is absolutely key. This is not something that can be completely codified. In fact, location and context may be the biggest part of this lesson.

In the case of archival research on saved and stored Internet interactions, you are climbing mountains, metaphorically speaking. You can do this with mechanical help, and lots of tools, using various forms of quantification and probably social network analysis. This may be especially interesting if you use it to explore your own online social interactions first. You might record your first-personal auto-netnographic-biography. This is a type of a biography of your own movement through time and cyberspace. But you are in a wild public space, a shared commons of sorts, and you must be careful not to damage, despoil or disrespect.

Or you can think of the archives as also containing some sort of ghostly figure, a glowing digital hybrid of a person. A particular person, usually not very hard to identify now, who is located on a particular ancient stage, perhaps in a haunted mansion type of manor. We must in this case dance dances with these spectral figures, around and around and around, beginning a beautiful and caring relationship between a digital double of a particular person and the researcher. Not a living breathing individual. But a digital double and the researcher. In this case, we must try to understand and respect our dance partner, while also keeping the dance separate from life, contained, as it were, in this old haunted home of our analysis and calculations. We are changed by the dance, we learn about the double, but we must take great care about telling others about our spectral dance in the dark. We must choose, as we would if we truly danced with ghosts, what to tell others so that they would understand just enough.

BE HONEST AND NEVER DECEIVE, INTIMIDATE OR CONFUSE THE PEOPLE YOU INTERACT WITH FOR THE RESEARCH

When the netnographer reaches out, projecting her voice across the digital chasm in search of other human voices, and another voice answers, then complete honesty and disclosure must prevail. In those cases of human contact, whether with an identified online site of social interaction, with individuals across many sites bound by similar topics, or with particular profiles of particular individuals, the netnographer should *always* fully disclose his/her presence, affiliations and intentions during any research interactions, especially the first few interactions. During reflexive fieldnote writing and subsequent construction of the netnographic representation, the researcher has a responsibility to be honest with herself, to delve as deeply as possible into the lived experience to be portrayed within the netnography.

We should tolerate absolutely no deception about why you are interacting with someone or what you are doing online if you say that you are doing netnography. Even if the practice of identity play, gender mixing, and other types of altered representation is common on the site, researchers are utterly bound by codes of research ethics to disclose themselves accurately. This should always take precedence over the inclination to want to find people to interact with and gather data from. This becomes a terrible performance of ownership. A researcher must never try to own a piece of research, or the people within it.

If you talk to people as a part of your research, you should *never, under any circumstances,* engage in identity deception. You must use your real name and disclose your affiliations and actual purpose. Remember the territory model. You are ON THEIR TERRITORY. This is the most difficult terrain for you to netnographically traverse in many ways, but especially ethically.

Would you want to project your virtual viewpoint into the multi-eyed but invisible surveillance presence of a fly sitting on select walls in Second Life? Boellstorff et al. (2012: 142) discuss the intriguing, but apparently amoral options for deception during ethnographic research in Second Life:

> We occasionally receive inquiries from researchers just learning about ethnography asking whether it is acceptable to conduct ethnographic research in a virtual world as a 'fly on the wall'. Or to pose as, say, a disabled person in Second Life to find out how disabled people experience the virtual world? Such subterfuge runs counter to the heart and soul of ethnography.

Indeed it does, and partly because anthropology is a science of space and is very comfortable respecting people in spaces. So these general ethnographic sorts of rules can easily apply in an Internet social media experience. The bottom line is that honesty prevails in your interactions, and that a lot of general ethnographic 'site' type advice applies well when the site is a single (part of a) corporate or other distinct website.

USE YOUR PROFILE

If you are using Facebook, Twitter, Instagram, LinkedIn, YouTube, Pinterest or another common social media platform in order to do *at least some* of your netnographic fieldwork – and if your netnographic fieldwork is going to involve your

communications with other people, then it is highly recommended that the fact that you are conducting research while interacting on those sites should appear prominently in your personal or user profile, and probably should appear at regular intervals in your status updates.

In forums or more traditional online sites, the same advice about user profiles applies. In emails, your researcher status might appear in your sig line. Another possibility would be to wear a t-shirt or a large button that proclaimed one's status as a researcher and then to have this as one's profile picture or avatar, or in one's sig line. It is also important that the way the researcher reveals his or her presence should not be disruptive to the normal activity of the site.

I'M POSING AND DIS-CLOSING: EX-POSING YOUR PERSONAL BRAND

When it comes to disclosing the research purposes of your netnographic investigation, you need to remember two things. First, that it could be counterproductive to reveal your core themes and theoretical ideas as they are just developing in your brain. Second, are regular people really going to understand your terminology or even going to care? Not 'I am trying to ascertain the extent to which the latter Michel Foucault's panopticon theory applies to new mom monitoring, correction and enforcement on Facebook groups' but, instead, 'Hi, I am interested in how Moms connect on Facebook'. The description of research can and should be a satisfying handshake. Heck, it may even help you communicate your research to your mother.

BOX 6.4

Personal Branding for Netnographers

As you expose yourself in your netnography, what should you say about yourself? In an article in the scientific journal *Genome Biology*, University of Liverpool biologist Neil Hall (2014) explicitly notes and theorizes the way that some scientists use social media. Some of these people, he writes, 'have high-profile scientific blogs or twitter feeds'. They are personally branded academics. Hall takes a somewhat disparaging view of scholars who have fame in social media but have not actually published many peer-reviewed scientific papers of citational significance. He suggests a measure of the ratio of social media fame-to-publication-accomplishment called 'the Kardashian index', named for the celebrity who is famous more for being famous than for any particular accomplishment.

My positive view on this phenomenon is fixed to notions of personal branding. The personal brand is the new corporate brand: we easily have the personal bandwidth now

(Continued)

(Continued)

that entire corporations, at one time even entire countries or economic systems had at their disposal. Bandwidth and processing powers are so plentiful that almost anyone can have them – it has trickled down in droves even to the economically disadvantaged. Or perhaps it has been made highly inexpensive in order to bring the impoverished into the system, surveillance and consumer acculturation from the bottom of the economic pyramid stretching all the way up to make everyone a member of the network.

Thus, to partake in a certain kind of netnography is now also ineluctably an act of Personal Branding. The netnographer plays the game of celebrity, or perhaps macro-celebrity – a bit larger than the little 'micro-celebrities' described by Senft (2008). Yes, explain yourself. But more than that, SELL YOURSELF. Understand that all you need to understand about branding is that marketing is about creating a sense of relevant difference. What is it about you that is really different and remarkable? What makes you distinctive? And be concise, please. Get it down to a three-word phrase. That is personal branding.

After you have the three word phrase, fill in the blanks in this sentence: To [customer segment] who desires [their need], my brand [Your Name Here] is the only [the category you want to be considered in] who has [your point of difference] because of [the reason to believe that you have it]. The point of difference is your raison d'être, your core significance that you wish to shout out to the human world.

If you perform personal branding well, it will help you to focus your research and the message you wish to transmit to the world. It may help you to earn those influential peer-reviewed studies of significance. We should not laugh at the Kardashian index. We should recognize in it the new necessity for us to use social media and personal branding concepts in our scientific careers, as well as the need to keep it balanced with high quality peer-reviewed publication.

It is also highly desirable for the netnographer to offer some more detailed explanation about themselves in the research study, beyond simply that they are a researcher conducting a study. Providing this information is relatively simple in social networking sites such as Facebook and LinkedIn. A single post can offer plenty of detail.

So, from the beginning of the research through to its end, good research ethics dictate that the netnographic researcher: (1) openly and accurately identifies her or himself when contacting and communicating directly with actual human beings, avoiding all deception, (2) openly and accurately describes their research purpose for interacting with people online, and (3) provides an accessible, relevant and accurate description of their research focus and interests.

Ask Permission

Once we spatialize the Internet, hanging up doors and windows, naming streets, creating attractions, we start to create the expectation that there is a bit of privacy available. There are certain types of online social experience, such as speaking on a

Skype call, or emailing someone, or sending someone a photograph on WhatsApp that seem more private. This is about subjective expectations, where we feel that there is some privacy and the communication is just between you and me. If you want to conduct your netnography by interrupting communications in one of those private channels, then you need to think about how this is going to be different from a telemarketer's cold call.

Territory is owned. Sometimes you need to ask permission to step inside. You always need permission to take something. You want to take data? Our data? Why? What gives you the right?

So much of online social experience is ruled over by large social media corporations such as Google, Facebook and Apple. I like Allen et al.'s (2006: 609) procedures for approaching corporate entities. As a courtesy, why not inform the appropriate group, persons or person at the company and tell them about the purpose and scope of the research. In addition, they recommend that the researchers provide a description of their research activity, preferably on 'a web-page that describes the research activity' (ibid..: 611). Obviously, these ideas would work well together, as the notification contact could contain links to the descriptive research web-page – which could be the same page used to inform anyone who is interested about your research.

There are also many websites requiring membership and registry. Chat rooms often fall into this category. Social networking sites and virtual worlds do as well. Lists and listservs are even more exclusive. When attempting to do research in these areas, asking for permission from owners or managers is clearly required.

A group administrator of a Facebook group is a legitimate gatekeeper that the researcher should approach prior to contacting other users of the group. For larger sites, such as those contained on Yahoo! Groups, a group's moderator (as well as Yahoo! management itself, as above) would be an appropriate gatekeeper that the researcher would need to contact. Guild or clan leaders might be appropriate gate-keepers to approach before attempting to gain access to the wider membership of an online game. However, as soon as we slide into the more slippery world of self defined networks, then we begin to see how fuzzy the notions of leadership and gate-keeping become.

THINK ABOUT WHETHER TO WORRY ABOUT THOSE TERMS OF SERVICE AGREEMENTS

'HumancentiPad', one of my favourite *South Park* episodes, deals with the vagaries of Terms of Service agreements. After scrolling down carelessly and signing his Apple iTunes update's Terms of Service agreement, Kyle is pursued and eventually kidnapped by shady agents from Apple who confront him because signing the agreement actually obligated him to surrender himself to

Apple for technologically-oriented medical experimentation. The experiment, for which the episode is titled, is well worth seeing.

The episode captures a fundamental anxiety surrounding the official and often restrictive language of many Terms of Service and End User License agreements. Because we must agree to their terms before being granted our accounts, we seem to be locked into playing by their rules. Should we then avoid these sites? In a word, no way.

I agree again with Allen, who said that 'manual, non-automated access [by researchers] of information on publicly available web-pages [even ones belonging to corporations] should be acceptable without special permissions or actions' (Allen et al., 2006: 607). Even though the website might not explicitly permit such acts as for research, the server load on the website is negligible – especially with the tiny loads of netnography – and this sort of limited access for research purposes 'fits within normal website expectations' (2006: 607). Furthermore, strict enforcement of the terms of service agreements 'would virtually close commercial websites to any examination by academia' (2006: 607). Combined with what we know about fair use laws in the USA from Lipinski (2006, 2008), and the recognition that academic research is considered generally important to public policy and the public good, it appears that commercial sites are viable ones for netnography – if, *and this is a big if*, there are fair use laws in effect. These laws are in effect worldwide in only two countries: the United States and Israel. Some other countries do, however, have fair dealing laws that may cover similar matters in netnography. These countries include Canada, Poland, and South Korea. This is very general advice and if this is a concern then it may be wise to consult with your appropriate Human Research Subjects Review Committee, or other regulative body and, when in doubt, to also check with a legal expert.

Always Obtain Written Consent for Interviews

It is currently a hotly debated topic whether it is ethical or even legal to record real-time interactions such as chat without permission (Bruckman, 2006, Hudson and Bruckman, 2004). Interviews, whether conducted online or off, clearly fall into the area of an interaction and thus require informed consent. Interviews, whether conducted on your own site, group, or page, or through those of another, require clear informed consent that reveals the researcher, the research study, informs the informant about the use of their information, and asks about the level of protection desired.

Three questions are important

(1) Are the intended participants in the interview adults?
(2) Are the intended research participants members of a vulnerable population?
(3) Should the research be considered to have higher-than-minimal risk in some way?

If the research participants are children or vulnerable populations, special additional levels of assurance are required, just as they would be in person. If the research has some risks, perhaps because it seeks to expose some immoral or illegal behaviours, then additional information and assurances may be required.

Properly Cite, Anonymize and/or Credit Research Participants

One of the biggest issues in netnography concerns how you will feature the involvement of other people. Particularly in the observational-archival component of your study, where consent can be fuzzy, and people may not know that their digital doubles are being interrogated and 'forced to confess', the rules of disclosure and representation have critical ethical implications. What is disclosed through the research about people and how it is represented in the research itself can have, as we have heard throughout this paper, a negative effect on real people's lives, their groups and particular communities. The ethical goal seeks to fairly balance the rights of Internet users with the value of your research's contribution to society (Bruckman, 2002, 2006; Hair and Clark, 2007; Walther, 2002). Specifying research value, however, is a matter of significant subjectivity.

In addition, we must contend with a reality in which direct quotes and real images – the kind favoured by anthropologists and sociologists because it is factual and true – present a major challenge to ethics. As we have heard, direct actual quotes are traceable through search engines to pseudonyms and real names. An actual quote can lead quite directly to an actual person. In fact, even changing a few words here and there in a quote may not be enough. A good search engine, or an algorithm that checks multiple aspects of a text at once, can identify the poster again. Photographs can be matched to their posters with equal ease. Facial recognition software is powerful and getting more powerful every year. Almost everyone in Facebook has been scanned by a range of facial recognition programs. Even an edited photo can be matched to its original by using software which scans background cues. Still shots from videos found online have the same issues. Graphics and other images are also stored and searchable. There is not much in the form of interesting netnographic 'data' that cannot be handily tracked back to its source.

Add to this an environment where semi-published authors, citizen journalists, micro-celebrities and other megaphone wielding individuals abound, and where some of these people want credit for their work, and to be cited as fellow authors. In fact, you may find that some of the professors whose books and articles you are citing are also publishing more pithy insights on Twitter or more publicly accessible ones through their blog. Would you use their name to cite their article, and then turn around and anonymize their tweet?

We must balance the following considerations: (1) the need to understand the rapidly changing social world from a human perspective, and the many social benefits that can come from a deep, profound, empathic and systemic understanding, (2) the need to protect any human participants who may reasonably be considered to be vulnerable and/or at risk from the harm that might come from being exposed as a member of a research study, and (3) the rights and responsibilities to credit or not credit individuals and groups for their creative and intellectual work. Ethics in action is about making difficult decisions, making tradeoffs under uncertain conditions. Listing names and disguising them both have issues in practice. Giving credit may mean exposure and could lead to risk and harm in some cases. Hiding in other cases may deny credit where it is due. Providing actual names may mean that you are obligated to omit potentially damaging, yet theoretically valuable and insightful, information from your written accounts. Including actual names means that you believe that there is minimal risk or chance of harm arising from publishing them. But this is always a speculation, a guess.

Unless there is considerable benefit to society, group or participants, if the study is higher risk, providing either names or pseudonyms is not appropriate. In higher risk scenarios, before beginning an interaction with a participant, the researcher should explain the risks of the study and the fact that the research participant's work will not be credited. It is important that the researcher and their regulatory body make this determination, and not the research participant. For justification of this guideline, it might be instructive to look at Elizabeth Reid's (1996) study of an online site for survivors of abuse. In Reid's thesis study, some participants agreed to speak to her only on the condition that they would be named. She later wrote that this was a mistake and ended up putting her participants at risk; she was the one who should have made that determination, not the research participants.

Concealment and Fabrication

Continuing to explore the interrelation of spatial notions, territoriality, possession and ethics, we might think of the netnographer as conducting a work of portrayal where none of the persons portrayed want to be recognized (of course, this may or may not be true) and where even the physical location of the site is vulnerable, as with some pristine Shangri-la that must be protected from the scourges of civilization. As we write about our Shangri-la and its inhabitants, we must protect their true identities and location, and we do this by deliberately altering data as we report it.

This section discusses two different approaches that can both be employed productively to help produce an ethical netnographic representation. The first is the idea of cloaking, or concealment. I draw upon and develop Bruckman's (2006: 229–230) four levels of disguise, ranging from 'no disguise' to 'heavy disguise'.

However, in order to emphasize the researcher's protective actions rather than the state of the participant, I have used the metaphor of degrees of cloaking. The three degrees of concealment suggested in this section are: uncloaked, cloaked and maximally cloaked. The following are the appropriate guidelines for using them.

- *When risks are low, and where the figure is public, use an uncloaked representation.* Providing an *uncloaked* representation means using the online pseudonym or real name of the research participant in the research report. Real names should only be used with the explicit written permission of the individual, unless that person is undisputedly a public figure. When using real names, researchers should consider whether they need to omit potentially harmful material, or if the benefits from its revelation outweigh its risks.
- *Cloaking should be used when the context of the research is important to research understanding and theoretical development, and when benefits are high and/or risks are low.* In a *cloaked* representation, the actual name of the site is provided, such as Facebook, LinkedIn or Google groups, Twitter hashtags, website forums, mobile apps, and so on. Online pseudonyms, actual names, and other means of identifying people are altered beyond recognition. There is also a good faith effort to alter or rephrase verbatim quotes, but there may also be some compelling rationale why the quotes need to be exhibited as they originally appeared, or why the risk is so minimal that exposing the person through publicizing their digital double's exact words is acceptable.
- *When risks are high, a maximally cloaked condition should be used.* The maximal cloaking condition is meant to provide maximum security for research participants. In the maximumally cloaked condition, site, names, pseudonyms and other identifying details are all altered. There are no direct verbatim quotes used, such that a search engine cannot link those quotations to their original postings. Another possible course of action is to have the original postings removed from online access – something that is usually only possible when control of the website lies in the researcher's hands. If the original posting is no longer accessible, then a direct quote can no longer be traced to the participant. However, the presence of automatic online archiving sites complicates assurances that the original posting is no longer available; it may have already been archived by a third-party (Hair and Clark, 2007). Again, due diligence on the part of the researcher would be required. In the maximum cloaked situation, some fictive details that do not change the theoretical impact of the paper may be intentionally introduced. For example, if studying an online community devoted to a high risk sport, one particular high risk sport might be changed to another one in order to protect research participant confidentiality.

Finally, Annette Markham (2012) offers an original strategy to the complex issues of online ethnographic representation: fabrication. In intentionally using the term fabrication to refer to research representation (more generally, and not just in ethnography), Markham (2012) draws our attention to the already constructed nature of scientific knowledge portrayal. Although we have become inured to processing particular conventional forms of research representation as looking correct and thus legitimate, they are all equally fabrications. Intersecting in some interesting ways with Buitelaar's (2014) advice, Markham (2012) suggests that an opening and experimentation with our online ethnographic representations is a practical way to protect privacy in research spaces where data is characterized as increasingly public, searchable and traceable. Fabrication is a creative and bricolage-style alteration of data into various kinds of composite accounts and/or representational interactions and also uses some techniques that have been associated with remix culture. Fictional narratives and layered accounts can also be featured. She suggests that academia needs to catch up with the 'innovative forms of critical thinking and scholarship' that are thriving outside of its 'walls' (Markham, 2012: 349). The modes of these innovative activities include experimentations, collaborations, creative ingenuities and remixes. Citing Jane Goodall, Markham reminds us that ethnographers are interpretive authorities, but that all of our representations are partial and problematic.

To Markham's (2012) inspirations, I would add the intriguing comments of Driscoll and Gregg (2010: 20), who similarly concern themselves with provoking online ethnographers to engage in a more empathic manner with what they term 'online intimacy'. Regarding research representation, their advice tends towards the autobiographical, a move with which netnography has considerable sympathy.

> It is almost impossible to avoid autoethnography when representing contemporary online culture, just as it is almost impossible not to have an online profile when functioning on so many sites requires them. Whether it is ethnographers attempting to pass at life online or ordinary webusers effectively operating as ethnographers, today an ever widening group of participants are helping to narrate what Escobar called 'the story of life as it has been and is being lived today, at this very moment'. If this is a move towards making ethnography more of an everyday practice, this can only be welcome when it also means a growing number of opportunities for intimacy in online and offline communities. (Driscoll and Gregg, 2010: 20)

Suitably inspired and provoked, we will return again in later chapters to these notions of netnography as combining the autobiographical with the social, narrating life stories and seeking human intimacy, and offering opportunities to represent culture in a creative, ethical, bricolage of remixed interactions, narratives and accounts.

SUMMARY

This chapter provides a general overview and set of specific guidelines for the ethical conduct of netnography. The netnographer has choices when it comes to research practices, and being informed about Internet Research Ethics procedures and accepted human subjects research protocols is important to netnographic undertakings in academic settings. This chapter follows a model of territorialism

and spatial metaphor in online social relations. Public versus private debates can be reframed in less spatial terms as being about how we treat people's digital doubles in our research. Informed consent is discussed as well as the general principle of doing no harm with our research. The chapter then proceeds from these ideas and principles to offer guidelines for ethical netnographic practice: stating your name, being honest, using your existing social media profiles, following personal branding principles to represent yourself, asking permission when needed, worrying about terms of service if necessary, gaining clear consent for interviews, citing and giving credit, and concealing and fabricating when necessary. Chapter 6 provides the foundations and specific guidelines for the ethical conduct of netnography.

KEY READINGS

Association of Internet Researchers Ethics Working Group (2012) *Ethical Decision-making and Internet Research Recommendations from the AoIR Ethics Working Committee (Version 2.0)*. Available at: http://aoir.org/reports/ethics2.pdf.

Buchanan, Elizabeth (2004) *Readings in Virtual Research Ethics: Issues and Controversies*. Hershey, PA: Idea Group.

Markham, Annette N. (2012) 'Fabrication as ethical practice', *Information, Communication and Society*, 15(3): 334–353.

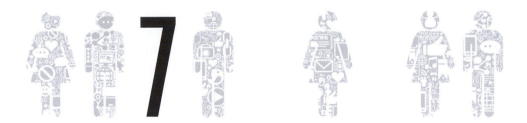

7

DATA COLLECTION

DATA QUEST

Data is a lot like the Biblical concept of Logos. There is no data before a scientific observer classifies something as data. There is only content, messages, communications, interactions, observations, notes, reflections, daydreams, bits, magnetic blips. Netnographers also co-create data in an elicited dance with software, people and machines. Interviews, investigation, instigation and insights are the four ways that netnographic data is created. Recognizing the ideologically and belief-based nature of social science practices, we could anthropologically conceptualize them as data creation rituals.

The netnographer always has two field sites – home base and the online world. Netnographers create data in introspective field and screen notes. Netnographers also save data from obscurity, elevating and noticing them, and pulling them out and polishing them through theoretical positioning as scientific gems worthy of sharing. Netnographic data collection rituals encompass curation and creation. In this chapter we explore the process of actually beginning to enact, perform and collect what you will eventually craft into your netnographic representation. But first, we must explore data.

WHAT EXACTLY ARE DATA?

Data are considered to be information, things known or assumed to be factual. In analysis, thought, reasoning and interpretation, data are the informational raw materials that are processed. In research, data are much more than this. Data are considered to be, in some specific system of investigation, the evidential components. It is the data that are the proof, the evidence. Data are of a certain form, they have a certain shape that is determined by the method that collected them and that desires to analyse them; they are the manifest basis of that method in practice. Data must be legitimate. They must contain evidence that they are real and not fabricated or fictional because they are used to legitimate scientific findings as real, true, dependable and trustworthy. Yet data, the very concept, the very notion, are bounded by our own assumptions and constructions of what they should be, of what methods we are willing to enlist for their apparent autogenesis, of what we think scientifically and pragmatically believe, pushing sceptically against all else, in this moment is true. Anthropologist John Sherry elegantly captures the connections between data, methods, theories and assumptions:

> Just as the notion of 'interpretive' research is a spurious, or, at least, a misleading one – both qualitative and quantitative approaches demand interpretation – so also must it be noted that problem-driven multimethod inquiry is gaining in popularity. Thus, practitioners of ethnographic, contextual or naturalistic inquiry, while employing a standard battery of qualitative techniques, may also incorporate quantitative measures into their regime. Perhaps the diagnostic feature of these types of inquiry is their quest for data as opposed to the capta yielded by their quantitative counterparts. That is, qualitative researchers elicit information in context, as a gift, rather less invasively than excising it for examination out of context, as a fact. The theory-ladenness of facts is a qualitative preoccupation. Unfortunately, hard/soft, natural/social, qualitative/quantitative oppositions are pre-eminent symptoms of our cultural era; methodological hegemony has impoverished our understanding of the singularity of the particular (Sherry and Kozinets, 2001: 166).

NETNOGRAPHIC DATA

In netnography, data flows from an inductive stream, punctuated by the occasional startling moment of abductive clarity. Abduction is the act of theorizing thought that finds a connection between two seemingly disparate points – a simultaneous act of perception and interpretation. The theoretical power of netnography flows from a search for anomalous evidence that must include deductive and inductive, as well as abductive reasoning. Wading through big data sets using human intelligence, looking deductively for particular keywords and core concepts, inductively classifying and coding the miscellaneous in pursuit of scrumptious tidbits of small data, the netnographer draws scientific motivation from the famous black swan fallacy. This notion demonstrates the falsifiability of induction and, indeed, of all universalizing scientific research and perhaps even of generalist universalized knowledge itself.

The black swan fallacy holds that if all you have ever observed in your field research are white swans, you might be tempted to conclude 'All swans are white'. However, a black swan was discovered in Australia. Therefore, all it takes is one black swan to falsify the general statement about the universality of white swans. Accommodating black swan evidence leads to much more interesting and elaborate scientific theories which use boundary conditions and contingencies. All native North American swans are white is a more supportable contention, and more accurate based on your evidence. Of course, the existence of black swans leads to many practical problems in a world of scientific believers.

Yet white swans are also valuable, and a census of white swans informative for its own sake. White swans can be interesting in netnography if, for example, they are found in unusual places. Or if they tell jokes and smoke cigars! Black swans are often difficult to find. If they are discovered, and if evidence of the black swan is suppressed, this is scientific cherry picking. What this indicates is that a study includes only evidence that supports pre-existing hypotheses or presuppositions. Some researchers simply ignore the evidence of black swans, and some, as in the No True Scotsman fallacy, attempt to rhetorically argue away any actual difference, stating, for example, that black swans are not really swans then, but another distinct species of bird that resembles swans. Constant vigilance is required in science, as in life, to perceive as well as to treat with informed scepticism idiosyncratic evidence.

In the search for black swans, context is all-important. While we are sorting, categorizing and classifying, we must remember and be attuned to the uniqueness of individuals, interactions, experiences and moments. Following John Sherry, I can call this notion the Singularity of the Particular, and suggest that it is a perfect place to start our discussion about netnographic data collection. Data means facts and statistics in general. Are we talking about data? Or are we referring, as John Sherry elaborates above, to gifts, to particular pieces of information gathered for sharing, appreciated and cared for, rather than harvested? In the case of netnography, there are a number of particulars to which we can attune.

In the first case, we have the online social environment and its fluid boundaries. Perhaps you consider Facebook to be your field site. But which part of Facebook? What elements will you include? Is it only a Facebook Page? Is it a part of the page? A page on a particular day? Noting and interrogating the boundaries of your constructed site is an important pre- and co-requisite for data collection, for these decisions determine not only how you contextualize your data, but what you consider to be data. Related to this are the particulars of a datum itself. What is the discrete unit of the datum, what are its boundaries, where does it start and stop? What do you save? What do you record about it?

The final particular is the researcher-as-instrument. Here you sit in on your research watch, adrift upon the Internet's high seas of information, interaction and immersive experience. As you undertake the research, it is a particular 'you' who becomes the netnographer. Simultaneously, the netnography becomes you as the result of the production of person into netnographer. In this sense, you become your own data. As the participant-observer, you have no choice but to reflect this time, this experience, this datastream through your own conscious-ness, the inevitable Heisenberg effect of ethnographic observation. As participant, you create data, create analysis, and create presentations and re-presentations. This is not bias; it is not contamination. This is the true nature of observation.

The netnographer, to paraphrase Heraclitus, never steps into the same data-stream twice. That is a very apt way to regard the online experience: stepping into a stream of something which flows. The small differences between the times that the netnographer steps into distinct datastreams is something that can be difficult for the data itself to record. For this information on dynamism and adaptation is exactly the sort of human-level interaction in which anthropology is interested. And thus much depends upon the acuity of the researcher and her careful reflexive fieldnoting. Insights begin with you, then, on the ground, making minute-by-minute decisions about where to examine, what you find and what you save. In its idealized form, netnography must achieve three things with its data collection, analysis and presentation/representation:

1. Provide an accurate atmospheric overview of the online social environs pertaining to some research question, based on generalizing and familiarizing social and tech-nological interactions, offering some broad general overview. This relates both to Symbolic Netnography and to Digital Netnography, as described more fully in Chapters 9 and 10.
2. Extend current understanding by presenting one or more particular, evidential black swans that expand extant knowledge characterizations about the focal topic and increase our understanding of elements, categories, processes, or practices in play. These types of curations relate to Humanistic Netnography, but certainly they also can feature in Symbolic Netnography as well.
3. Reflect particular and general data in a precise but idiosyncratically attuned manner through an unabashedly human filter of immersion and experience. Participation of this profound sort is most present in Auto-netnography, but must also feature as an impor-tant ingredient of Symbolic and Humanistic Netnography. Even Digital Netnographies are grounded in some degree of immersive participation.

Hence, the question for data in netnography becomes a tripartite act of collection (which must always be selective), curation (which is highly selective) and anno-tation (which involves and captures ongoing reflection of data-method-theory). These three aspects of collection relate loosely to the three types of netnographic data – the collected, the co-created and the produced – and the two key modalities of online social experience and interaction – the archival and the communicative.

Preparing for a netnography involves preparing to find, collect and create net-nographic data, which in turn involves preparing for its eventual analysis. As we discuss in greater detail throughout this chapter, netnographic data assume three forms, which parallel and connect the hybrid archival-communicative and participative-observational stance of the netnographer: (1) already recorded and stored, or archival, data, (2) communicatively co-created, or research-practice elicited data, and (3) reflective/reflexive immersive/participative authored field-note data.

- *Archival data* comprises any and all online social experience-related data that researchers 'find', 'collect' or 'gather' from social media communities. Although clearly shaped by selection biases and observer effects, archival data does not bear the imprint of the researcher as creator or director. We might think of this type of data as establishing a historic record and a cultural baseline.
- The next type of data is *elicited*, or *co-created* through the researcher's own social interactions which are stored and saved in various formats, including, with online social interaction, digitally with human beings and with bots, software applications and machines themselves, communicating electronically to servers around the world. One of the most powerful and ethically unambiguous forms of elicited data is the research web-page, which we will detail later in this chapter.
- The final type is *produced* data, which the researcher creates. Usually this is in the form of reflexive fieldnotes. These notes, however, can assume a vast variety of forms, including physical jottings on paper and in text files, to thoughts captured in digital file names, on audio recording, or in video files. Reflexive data are created by the netnographer in the role of author reflecting upon her own experiences in the social field. In the following sections, we will overview data collection, co-creation and production practices to guide whichever type of netnography you decide to perform.

SEARCHING FOR SITES OF ARCHIVAL DATA

Use Google or Your Native or Favourite Search Engine, or Use Them All

Netnographic data search will not be unfamiliar to you in terms of its operations, but it will begin to feel novel in terms of its commitment and depth. Netnography is to normal Internet use as running for the bus is to running a marathon. First, you will use your research focus and research questions as the source of your keywords. Make sure that you find many synonyms for keywords, and investigate what comes up from the keywords that might better describe the online social environment, the notional place where the online social interactions and experiences that you seek occur.

What do you seek, in sites, topics and people? If a site, the search part is simple, and you can skip right to immersion and data collection. Your study actually in this case probably started with the finding of the site. If you seek a site, but do not know which is the most relevant, then treat your search for a site as if it were a topic, following the guidelines below.

People are also relatively easy to search and their relevant sites to select. Major access through LinkedIn and Twitter is already possible, not to mention those who allow many into their Facebooks or Instagram accounts. However, following the path of individuals may not be as simple as simply following their most obvious accounts. Often, you will be seeking to understand the impression they have made upon other people. For this, the person can be treated very much like a topic. In addition, the networks of particular people may be dispersed and require some delicate sleuthing to uncover in some fullness.

And next we come to Topics, the most challenging for search and selection. Once we properly break our research focus and question down into keywords, we must enter those keywords and their variations into the most popular few search engines and use them all. Look for Facebook groups and blogs, Wikis and wiki entries, YouTube videos and Twitter hashtags, Instagram tags and TripAdvisor entries, Yelp reviews and Amazon discussions, and more. And, of course, follow at least 100 pages into Google or whichever search engine you favour or your country carries (i.e., in China).

There is no need for this book to list every possible site or carrier of sites, many do this as their main occupation, such as Brian Solis (2010) and they are much better at it than am I. I will not endeavour in this book to explain the mundane elements of this or that site of the Internet today, for this would be like describing the main retail strip in a busy, rapidly changing cosmopolitan city, such as Shanghai or Paris. Many sites will stay the same, and many will change over the course of a few years.

Although forms of mobile/tablet and desktop/laptop Internet based communication still exist as separate types in 2015, one of the trends with Internet and online interaction in general is that these are increasingly blurring one into the other. Another, barely emergent, trend is body integrations, from wearable to implantable computing. The world becomes Internet, augmented reality and an Internet of things, and we begin to transmit the codes of many things through 3D printers, but which have the potential to become so much more, such as nanoassembler units. The digital and the virtual and the electro and informational-material are converging into one. But I digress.

There is no doubt that bulletin boards are useful, some authors are using them and publishing across journals in many fields, and much past research has established their usefulness. Yet, there are currently only a few good search engines for forums. One of the top current ones is called omgili. There is also still far more missing from accessible Internet archives than in it regarding forums, although Google Groups, based on their early acquisition of Deja News, continues to offer a quality service. Google, in fact, has a suite of tools at the disposal of any interested researcher, from Google Trends to Scholar to Ngram Viewer. Facebook as well, and Twitter. Certainly YouTube's search engine should be your second most useful after Google, or whichever other search engine is number one in your country. This provides a basic outline upon which you should begin your search.

BOX 7.1

Using Search Engines for Online Social Experiences and Interactions: A Two-step Process

Finding research question-relevant online social experiences and interactions is the two-step process's key concern. I am often asked which special software tool to use. Try everything out there, online and offline. Netnography is now about using every tool available and applying it to the daunting task of understanding particular problems, answering specific questions and, above all, understanding and seeking to improve the contemporary human condition.

For the sake of illustration, you can simply use Google – and this includes additional Google features such as Google's Analytics, Trends, and NGram reader features.

Using Google is a fairly straightforward affair. Many of us know Google, but you can use whichever search engine you prefer. Google has a number of nice features for those of us who get its full functionality.

Here is the procedure. Use several engines from Google, including the web, groups, blog and image search function. Then search YouTube videos. Search on Twitter, and on a forum search engine like omgili.com ('OMG I love it!'). Take a look at Facebook Groups, Wikis and LinkedIn groups. See if there are any relevant podcasts. Use individual search engines and also follow up with social engines such as socialmention.com. Keep your search terms as simple and consistent as possible across sites and engines to start. Grab as many major overviews of data as you can, but always also stay as close to the interactions and direct experiences as possible. You are the netnographic instrument collecting human level data. Your main task at this stage is to first attune your perception to the various social media and other channels that might inform your research question.

1. Enter search terms related to your research area, focus and questions into the main Google search window. For example, if you are studying the contemporary whale and seal hunts worldwide, then consider entering variations on 'whaling', 'whale hunt', 'whale activism', 'whale management', 'conservation', 'hunting endangered species', 'animal rights', 'Native rights', 'Aboriginal rights', 'international markets for whale meat and blubber' and 'international hunting accords dating back over 1000 years'.
2. Investigate everything. Look at every website that seems even remotely relevant. Read them, and follow all the trails and hints they bring to you. Take your time. Write your findings and insights down, or capture them in annotated screenshots. Reflect upon things, upon connections, upon people, sites, interactions, experiences of pages, experiences of technology, experiences with people. And gather as much as you can in writing.
3. Keep trying different and new combinations of sites and search keywords. Move between general and specific, between wide and narrow, between full search engines like Baidu in China and community search engines like you would find using the search function on a public news or corporate website's forum. You also should notice that your topic can be categorized at varying levels of abstraction. For example,

(Continued)

(Continued)

if you were trying to study religion on the Internet, as did Marko Uibu (2012), you might find that there are many institutional levels, many keywords, and many paths that you can go by. In the long run, you must choose particular routes and pursue those, seeing where they take you. Religion can be studied on a comparative basis, but rarely is in these days of polarized crowds. It can be studied on the institutional level, on the level of power dynamics. It can be studied on the individual level, as attracting certain kinds of people who have undergone certain kinds of experiences at certain times in their lives. But how and why you direct your research will be driven both by your research questions as well as by serendipitous discoveries that you make along the way.

DATA SITE SEARCH AND SELECTION GUIDELINES
Choosing the Site

Let us assume that you have settled upon your research question and have identified a number of sites of social interaction and potential social experience that seem relevant to your research topic and questions. You have done your best to examine all of them. You have recorded and reflected upon them in your field notes, already creating data of your own. How now do you judge which subset of these sites to focus upon? By focusing in on one particular search, you also forsake many other searches. You seemingly surrender alternative possibilities as soon as you narrow in on particular sites and stop looking for other sites to search. However, the data quest never truly ends.

In general, the sites you will find will contain the records, the traces of various social interactions. They may well offer you interesting social interactions, or be sites – such as Facebook, LinkedIn or Twitter – in which you already have interesting social interaction, communications and connections which you may be able to expand through your netnographic participation.

You might now draw a table with four columns and eight rows. Across the four rows write: elements, weights, scores, totals. Down the eight rows write: weighted ranking/factors, Relevance, Activity, Interactivity, Substantiality, Heterogeneity, Richness and Experientiality. Now consider the definitions of these various factors and rate each one on a ten-point scale.

(1) *relevant*, they relate to your research focus and question(s)
(2) *active*, they have recent and regular communications
(3) *interactive*, they have a flow of communications between participants
(4) *substantial*, they have a critical mass of communicators and an energetic feel
(5) *heterogeneity (homo genius loci)*, they have either a variety of difference or a consistency of similar type of participants, providing a strong and required social sense

(6) *rich in data*, offering more detailed or descriptively rich data, as with lots of well crafted postings, blog entries, podcasts, or videos

(7) *experiential*, offering you, as a user of the site, as the netnographer, a particular kind of experience.

Relevance is the first criterion and can be the most difficult. What is the relevance of this particular site to your research question? Does it mean that it only answers the question directly? That would be a foolishly limiting attitude towards data collection. What is relevant is, first and foremost, that the data source gives you a sense of the lived cultural worlds you are moving into and within. Once you do this, you may find that there are a number of interesting side discussions going on about interesting matters in people's lives. Is this relevant? It might be. Even if those matters and discussions do not relate directly to your research question, it is important to think about abduction now, to think about how you find two different things and attempt to connect them by explaining their similarities. When you have found that their similarities are, in fact, thought provoking, then you have ascertained that this data may be relevant.

It can make good sense to trade off one or more of these criteria. For example, you might choose to investigate some ostensibly minor sites, a nearly readerless but amazing zine or blog or a podcast that nonetheless has many data-rich postings. You may well find the social experience to be different on different sites, on big ones, on small ones, on new ones, on established ones, on ones that are new to you, on ones within which you are very well versed. You should choose the data that speaks to you. You are making decisions as you are data gathering, and these decisions have method implications and thus data implications. Ultimately, they will affect not only your analysis, but even more importantly your end product, your research representation. You will need to work backwards from your desired and imagined research representation to produce, co-produce and responsibly and sustainably harvest the data from different sites and make it your own.

The archive function is incredibly valuable to netnographers. At this point, you are still anonymous; you have not yet entered the site's day-to-day interactions because you have not yet made your decision to study it. And even when you have, you may have perfectly good reasons for lurking in the shadows.

As you narrow your choices, continue with your study of different sites of online interaction and experience. Who are these people? What can you discern about them? What are some of the concepts and precepts that they hold dear? What sort of specialized language, if any, are they using? Do they have any particular rituals – deeply meaningful and repeated acts? What are some of their common practices? Who are the most active participants on this site?

What are some of this site's most overwhelming technological elements? What topics belong to it? What is its history? To which other sites does it connect, and what is the significance of these connections? Is this relevant to my topic? Where

are there answers in this data to questions that may be even more interesting than my original question? As you begin your journey, saving files, creating files and initiating interactions, you are also extending your netnography. As you interact, learn and listen, you extend your search by following trails, by clicking links, by investigating terms and other sites, and continuing your visitations. The search for sites of data and for data itself never ends.

Choosing the Data

Now that your quest for sites of data has located promising places in which to search, the major question remaining is to ask which data you are going to collect. Netnographers are on a mission. They search across multiple sites, noting patterns and regularities across massive amounts of data. They can use machines for this, or their own human insight and intelligence. Once they have a broad view, they can narrow in to select particularly insightful or representative communications to share. These communications can include interactions, creations, co-creations, and of course, stories. The stories are often at the heart of the curation.

Netnographers are hooked on context. Netnographers need to record, think about, and adjust on the fly. They are insatiably hungry when it comes to the context of data and capta. During data collection, it is incumbent upon the netnographer to struggle to understand the sites, the words, the topics and the people represented in online social interactions and to reflect upon them as an online social experience. If we were to collect this information in a way that would strip out context and present people or their practices in a general, unspecified, universalized manner, this would be strange and terrible all at the same time. For how would we then know what we had? How would a netnography be different then from every other kind of research?

Data must relate directly to research focus, to your topic and your particular questions. As noted previously and throughout this chapter *netnographers must also be attuned to the unexpected*, allowing for and attending to the surprises of black swans. Relevance is just as vital a criterion in helping you decide which particular elements of online interaction and experience you will capture as it is in helping to direct you to the sites in which you might find them. However, relevance may not be easy to determine at first. As you search, be attuned to your own reactions. Some data seems amazing from the beginning. Some data are a case of 'love at first site'. Save them, obviously. But other data can be interesting because they are anomalous, often in ways that are difficult at first to express or understand. Does something seem 'not right' about the data? Save them. Does something pique your curiosity? Explore it. Save your explorations. In so doing you are engaging in the unexpected and nondeterministic process of investigation and discovery that differentiates naturalistic methods from those that are less flexible.

The qualities of the data itself are important. Interactions are often important to netnographies. However, in many cases you might simply want deep personal data, as with a blog, and when interactions are not as salient to your research orientation or question. Similarly, recent data might be important, if you are trying to explain a contemporary phenomenon. It is not optimal, for instance, to try to explain privacy issues on Facebook with data that is five years old since this is such a dynamic field. However, if the research is to be a more historical or longitudinal overview of the way Facebook privacy issues have evolved and been discussed online, then older data will be important.

Certainly, we often seek data elements that are both rich and representative of the phenomenon at hand. When my co-authors and I studied the tensions that exist between commercial interests and the trusting relationships people formed in social media, we sought out bloggers whose narratives we could use to represent an entire category of narrative types (Kozinets et al., 2010). Similarly, you might classify various discrete pieces of data into categories, perhaps narrative categories, and then look for particular exemplary, archetypal, or ideal type instances within those categories. If the data are to represent unique new aspects of a phenomenon, black swan findings, then these unique characteristics should be apparent. If there is a choice of data of this type, it may be best to choose those that partake in a number of other sought qualities or exhibited criteria as well.

Particularly with a Humanist Netnography, we must be attuned to the impact of the data in the final research representation. Does it speak to us, and to our audience? Sherry and Schouten (2002: 222) express the value of research that allows

> for the visceral collection, analysis, and representing of data … The use of intraceptive intuition, introspection, reflexive commentary, and aesthetic form to induce emotional resonance and insight in the reader, the embodying of emotion in encoding and its re-embodying in decoding as the object of meaning transfer, is the essence of the personal writing regimes at work in [the more resonant forms of] contemporary social scientific inquiry.

Here, we may need to move to a more ephemeral and phenomenological set of criteria for judging which data are to be elevated as 'special'. Are they highly evocative, in a visual, auditory or video sense? Are they dramatic and powerful? Are they revealing of some deeper quality of people, groups, beliefs, emotions, or other deeply resonant matters?

As anthropologist Ruth Behar (1996) reminds us, we might ask if this data relates to our vulnerability as observers. Does it, in some sense, break our heart? We might also think about how the data will appear in our representation, alongside other resonant and evocative pieces of data. Does it blend with the rest of the netnography? Now that we have some sense of what we are looking for in our data, and where exactly we might best go looking for it, the next section overviews in general fashion some of the nuts and bolts of the actual act of capturing, saving and storing it.

THE BASICS OF ONLINE DATA CAPTURE AND COLLECTION

This section explains at a very fundamental level what is required in order to collect or process data as a result of netnographic research practices. Without becoming overly technical, this section will tell you how to use your computer's capabilities to capture netnographic data.

The netnographer has two basic choices to make when capturing data, and the type of data analysis she plans to pursue will dictate the choice. If the netnographer is going to code the qualitative data manually, such as using a pen-and-paper technique, or some variety of this technique (such as using jottings on computer files or in a spreadsheet such as Microsoft Excel), then data collection should be limited to relatively small amounts of data. What is a 'small amount' is, of course, rather subjective, as an individual photograph may contain many elements, or a video clip could be analysed frame by frame. Netnography has transcended the point at which we can simply state that it completely or mainly contains words on pages, that it is textual. Indeed, one of its great strengths now is that netnographers include graphical, visual, photographic, audio, and video information as shared online, as well as looking at text in context, including font, colour, size, placement, and so on.

As we will discuss further in Chapter 9, a focus on finding and interpreting gems of 'small data' is important. A focus on small data draws our attention to the curatorial aspects of netnography. What, in the end, will we be able to represent? Of what form and substance do we want our finished netnography to consist? This focus will cause us to spend more and more time on the search, on the recording of the general sense of the netnographic terrain, the 'lay of the online land', than it will in collecting large amounts of data to save, code and later analyse.

There are options. If the netnographer wants to produce a research product that takes a wider view, that applies more of a general, inclusive telescope than a particularizing microscope to the cultural terrain of the Internet, then she probably is going to need to use a qualitative data analysis software program to assist with the coding and organization of the relatively larger amounts of data such research will require. We discuss the use of such programs in Chapter 9. Particularly regarding the saving of text files, much more data can be collected. However, I urge Digital Netnographers not to exclude the visual, audio and video files that lend so much life to netnography. Saving, coding and interpreting these files is a bit more of a challenge than doing so with text files, but there are a number of flexible search programs, including Microsoft's OneNote program, which can help. Within Digital Netnography (see Chapter 10), data collection can be far more prolific, although it is still more focused and much more human-centred than the automated data mining, natural language processing, and automatic content analysis of other methods.

Two basic ways to capture online data are to save the file as a computer-readable file, or as a motion captured or still visual image of your screen as it appears. Both of these methods have advantages as well as drawbacks. When the interactions and communications are mainly textual, as they are with bulletin boards, newsgroups, forums, microblogs and wikis, then saving the file as a computer-readable file is a viable option, although it does lose some context. The files from Google Groups and Yahoo! Groups are already presented on screen as text files. However, when the data contain many visual, audio and video elements, as is the case with audio, video, virtual worlds, some blogs and some areas of social networking sites, then various methods of screen capture are preferred. A third option, which combines both of the other options, is to save the file in a computer-readable format that roughly captures what you see on screen. If you will not be using software to help you manage all of your collected data, it is best to aggregate all of your data into files on your computer that you can sort and search. All of these formats – captured screenshots and motion captures, HTML files, and downloaded text and images – can be aggregated together into separate files sorted by topic or category.

Still-image screen capture software programs are sometimes also called 'screen shot' software. There are many choices of screen capture software for Microsoft PC users, including Snapcrab, Snappy, TinyTake and Jing. Apple OS users can choose from Grab, Voila, SnapNDrag and Snagit. In fact there is so much choice, and the market for these programs is so developed, that listing programs is not necessary. Most of these programs have a very simple graphical user interface that works analogous to the operation of a camera. The researcher opens a page on their browser, and then opens the capture program. They select a capture option from the program menu, usually allowing them to select a field with their mouse, or to capture an entire window. They then press a particular button, and the image of the screen is captured. Captured screenshot images are stored in a compressed image file format such as pdf, bmp, jpg, tiff, or gif. However, you should be aware that the text included in such graphics files is not readable as such by most computer programs, such as word processing or qualitative data analysis software. They will need to be coded externally, by saving a descriptive file name, or internally using another program that can append text or codes on top of the graphics file. Further, the files can take up a lot of memory space on your desktop and hard drive.

Increasingly, I see netnography including videographic representation. For purposes of both data capture and for eventual research representation, I currently find it beneficial to use full-motion screen capture software programs to record, moment-by-moment, what appears on the computer screen. Unlike the still images described above, these programs provide a moving picture that includes audio. They are very useful, for example, in recording Skype interviews. Screen recording software such as Snagit, Camtasia, Cam Studio, Screen Recorder and Hypercam allows the netnographer to automatically record exactly what she is seeing and hearing on her computer screen in real time. She can capture various sequential site searches and quests for data, social interactions, audio and video interview, as well as the video, images and audio that she experiences on her computer monitor. These are saved as a digital video file (often an avi file, which is convertible to mpg, mov or even flv file formats). Events can be replayed at a future time, just like a DVD movie. More importantly, they can later be edited in a video-editing program.

There are applications that facilitate screenshots and even video capture from smartphones, tablets and other handheld devices. Many of these programs are contained in the phone's operating system itself. You are welcome to consult the Internet and your device's user's manual to see what your device has available.

There is no question that we must deal with an abundance of (often seemingly irrelevant) data: a data deluge that begins as soon as we start our search, once you set yourself the goal of keeping up with all the data that is being created. From this objective, you find it necessary to enter into a digital arms race. However, there are options in netnography to work at a human scale. Netnography seeks the exact same humanistic, humane and humanizing, in simpatico, tribal-dance-joining, phenomenological, eureka-yielding gestalt for which ethnography is famous.

Humanizing data in this sense means reading data, pondering it, thinking about its minutiae, and using it to track down more data and hidden references. It means using it to find new pathways forward out of the problems that fixate us, lock us in and tie us down. Without ethnographic insight, netnography becomes primarily a coding exercise. Instead, an alternative is to work backwards from the research production you wish to represent. If you want your netnography to include video, then you know you must get set up and start collecting data from cameras and microphones. If it will be purely text, then collecting text is all you need.

Data choices are interlinked with analysis choices. Both of these choices should relate to the type of netnography you wish to produce. There are time–effort trade-offs between collecting small and large data that draw netnographers to either more digital and mechanical, or more humanistic and hermeneutic methods of interpretation and analysis. When large amounts of data are collected using text file downloads, screenshots, or full motion screen capture, recording every minute requires not only an investment in additional computer memory, or an extra hard drive to accommodate initial storage, but a major investment in researcher time to review, understand, code and then analyse the data. Big amounts of data draw us almost inexorably to more mechanical methods that encourage us to code and view at less contextualized and particularistic levels. Amassing and then coding massive amounts of data draws us to software programs that help us handle and code massive amounts of data. However, *experiencing* masses of data, but only capturing and then focusing in on small amounts of high-quality data in our search encourages us to focus on interpretations of the particular, in context, using our full insight and intelligence in the process.

Considered from a socio-technical level, we can see that handling a proliferation of digitally generated data builds demand for 'big data' style analysis. Digital Netnography uses some sophisticated tools for data collection and analysis, but seeks to maintain the human elements of participation and interpretation within them. Symbolic and Humanist Netnography are drawn as particularizing research practices. *Netnography is about lighting a human candle within the glare of the neon digital night.* From its kindling, that candle may need to be guarded and overseen. Its flickering in the night may need watching and capturing in handwritten scrawled notes in narrow Moleskine notebooks, or those without brands at all. I tend to think of this lighting and writing as partly a poetic and spiritual matter.

Netnography is a technique of small data search and analysis, of human scale readings of other human groups, people and practice. It draws our attention to the types of online social structures and institutions, articulations and assemblages that perpetuate certain classes and stereotypes and bad social manners. It also draws us to ask what channels something deeply communal, social, inspirational and great in people, with helping and social kindnesses abounding over the Internet, even to an exaggerated extent. It is impossible to do netnography for 20 years and not be endlessly amazed and inspired by the goodness of people's hearts as they express them online. Sometimes, it is difficult to believe we live in such a troubled world when we view the near-utopian social experiences we have seemingly engineered online.

We have overviewed these larger issues and learned these practical fundamentals of data capture and collection in netnography, particularly as they pertain to the capture and collection of archival data. The same methods will capture many interactions, such as your communications with others online. However, we have barely touched upon the nature of participation, and participation as a social media active academic, with all of the potential for micro-celebrity personal brand building which that presence entails. The next chapter processes for you issues surrounding co-created data, which results from researcher participation, interaction and social experience.

Thus, the netnographer has a number of important decisions that must be made prior to diving into the world of social experience and interaction as it exists online. What is appropriate social and technological interaction online for a netnography? Searching for, producing, creating, and finding data. Online sites and online sources of data – as well as particular pieces of data encountered as the netnography begins – which should be favoured are those that are relevant, active, interactive, substantial, heterogeneous, data-rich, and experientially satisfying.

SUMMARY

Chapter 7 covers data collection. In netnography, data are found in archives, co-created and produced. This chapter elaborates the various important choices pertaining to data collection, including guidelines for searching for, finding, filtering, selecting and saving data. It provides the criteria you need to decide

which sites to search in depth, and which data to collect and curate. It concludes by providing fundamentals behind the actual workbench level of capturing, collecting and storing data.

KEY READINGS

Sherry, John F. Jr. and Robert V. Kozinets (2001) 'Qualitative inquiry in marketing and consumer research', in Dawn Iacobucci (ed.), *Kellogg on Marketing*. New York: Wiley Books. pp. 165–194.

Sherry, John F. Jr. and John W. Schouten (2002) 'A place for poetry in consumer research', *Journal of Consumer Research*, 29: 218– 234.

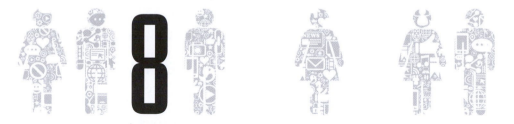

8

RESEARCHER PARTICIPATION IN DATA COLLECTION AND CREATION

INTERACTIVE NETNOGRAPHIC DATA

In netnography, just as in physical ethnography, there is a spectrum of participation and observation that researchers regularly negotiate in their fieldwork. However, appropriate participation as a group, community or culture member is nonnegotiable. In this milieu of social media, which unceasingly bubbles out to include researcher micro-celebrity, it is even more crucial to consider the essence of netnographic participation during the creation and gathering of data. What should it be? Should we charge in like arrogant bulls? Or should we offer hospitality and wine and cheese? In this quasi-utopian space we hope and pray to build and find, our attitude should be one of humility and fair exchange. It should be of a sense of fair compensation for people's time. It should be of a place and time where communications are open and honest, free to criticize and make comments.

Ethically speaking, communications with other people for the purpose of your research are social interactions, and thus a type of request. Communicating with others for the purpose of co-creating data for a research project is human subjects' research, whether it happens in a shopping mall, over the telephone, in an email or through Pinterest or Twitter direct messages. You are asking people for their time, their insights and their energy. You are asking them for their voice, for their image, for their copyrights and access to their personal brands. You want to film them, to share them.

What should you give them in return? For an interview, perhaps we should compensate with money or a gift card as a thank you. Valuable people's time is valuable. I advocate paying for it. An Amazon or a local successful retailer's gift-card can work wonders. This is a way to compensate for the usefulness of what you will be taking.

This is storytelling. Prior work in this book helped to lead you to your own narrative, the coherent story you will tell about your difference that builds your personal brand. The researcher must take the opportunity to experience embedded cultural understanding in the most human venue: her own experiences and interactions with people. Immersion in the field is Interpretive Integrity, the purest form of externalized validity that the human sciences know. Observation and participation entitle you to talk about your topic. In Internet time and space, that topic can be almost anything.

What differentiates the academic netnographic scholar is that you are immersed in both the Ancient Texts of Wisdom and the Current Words of Today. You cannot do anthropologies, of which netnography is indubitably one, without both of these immersions. Without your profound knowledge and experience of the cultural context, the interpretation cannot be trusted. This is as true of netnography as it is of ethnography. Even moreso, I believe, this is true of netnography because it demands of us the ability to see communications, communication, communicators, media channel, social media organization, and social networks as united and one and the same and yet then be able to see their divergences and conjunctures in power and influence and information-exchanging.

In netnography, data collection starts as you first consider the project and does not stop until the last version of the research is published and presented. Indeed, this is the mark of many anthropologists. I do not foresee ever ceasing my engagement or data collection on some particular topics and sites and the people within them. The continued creation and collection of data is of paramount importance. In the next two sections, we briefly consider two forms of collecting interactive netnographic data: the research web-page and the interview.

INTERACTION RESEARCH

The Web-page as Key to Netnographic Ethics' Puzzle

If we take this book's ethical stance about Internet-as-social-territory seriously, then netnography does presents itself to us as a bit of a research ethics puzzle. On the one hand, culture members interact with one another through communications and interactions that they feel are transpiring on their own territory. They own the territory or the interactions. They thus resent the intrusions and interventions of researchers who wander into and then encroach upon their online social neighbourhoods. On the other hand, these emergent indigenous conversations are alluring as netnographic data. One solution to the ethical dilemma is to fabricate data that resembles the found interactions, but is not traceable to them. However, this comes with its own set of problems, because the ability for others to trace back and audit netnographic data, seeing the data in context, is one of interaction research's advantages.

The solution I suggest is to add a researcher constructed research web-page to every netnography. Although this should not be the only source of insight for the netnography, it can be a very important additional source. Following the territory model which is central to interaction research, the research web-page becomes the researcher's own territory or, even better, neutral territory that belongs to interested others.

The research web-page can, in true digital humanities fashion, be the actual artistic expression of the professor or professional conducting the netnography. You can and probably should pour as much of your creative side into your research web-page as you can muster. Remember the purpose of netnography lies not merely in academic exercise, but in the extension of the art of being an academic into the social media realm, through your own active participation in conversations and worlds of opinion and commercial and communicative exchange. Is your website aesthetically pleasing? Can you play a musical instrument? Can you produce art? Dance? Sing? Surely you are not simply a theory and calculation machine, and nothing more? Sharing your true talents should definitely be expressed in your web-page, sharing your human side, your personal and real side, with the unknowable others out there.

Conducting human level research in the great frothing green PayPal, debit and credit card sea that is the Internet, it is best to have an alternative to entering into existing websites empty-handed, and then trying to make a positive impression, or coming hat in hand to friends, family and co-workers, asking them to complete surveys or participate in exchanges as we use our personal networks and connections to do netnographies. Entering existing cultural sites like Facebook and LinkedIn as an online researcher can be difficult. However, using these sites to create research web-pages and discussion forums is a rather simple matter, and the full disclosure possible on such sites simplifies and ameliorates some of the most vexing ethical difficulties of netnography. Further, the research website is a type of gift that, we can hope, helps to inspire a sense of communitas, or at least consociality. Online spaces should be not so different from in person contexts. If you want to ask for a favour, or want to connect with people, then one alternative is that you can create something, give it away and participate. To gain friends, you can offer something interesting and amusing which is adapted to their interests. This is an absolute core principle of Interactive Research.

Examples of Netnographic Interactive
Research Websites (NiRWebs)

This section will provide an example that may inspire you to produce a netnographic interactional research website, or nirweb. The recommended way to do this is in a small piece of Internet terrain of your own, a space claimed as Interactive Research web-page, which can easily have a blog attached to it.

Some more boring ancient history (skip if you like): In 1995, I posted the *Star Trek* Research Web-Page on CyberLink Online here in Toronto, and it hit the World Wide Web with a fishy thud. I programmed it in HTML and if I could do it, then it was definitely not particularly complex or difficult programming by any means, because I am an absolute amateur at coding, which makes me admire it even more. That early web-page offered full disclosure of Robert Kozinets PhD student at Queen's University in Kingston, Ontario, as per the ethics guidelines for netnography.

The site's landing page introduced me and my research, talking truthfully about my status as a PhD student as well as providing disclosure about my university affiliation and the outlines of my dissertation project. But the major purpose and focus of the site (for it was more than a page) was to offer *Star Trek* fans a chance to learn about existing academic research on *Star Trek* fans. Academics had been writing about *Star Trek*'s text for a long time, particularly readings of it that saw it as ideological, militaristic, colonialist and American. They had also written quite a bit about *Star Trek*'s fan community, as with Henry Jenkins' inspiring ethnography *Textual Poachers* (Jenkins, 1992). Henry's work was prominently featured throughout that page, and it had its own page where I summarized most of his *Star Trek* work. As well, the *Star Trek* Interactive Research Website featured Constance Penley and Camille Bacon-Smith's works. Pages of links to other *Star Trek*-related resources on the Internet peppered the pages, and merited an entire page of their own: even then, especially then in fact, the dark twinkling nightsky of the Internet was filled with spaceships: the Enterprise, The Millennium Falcon, the Battlestar and ships from *Babylon 5* and *Space Above and Beyond*. One of my key informants was a prominent Toronto lawyer who also was captain of a *Star Trek* fan club. She told me the principles of copyright alteration that were legally appropriate for fans to follow.

As a result, the Interactive Research Website used altered images pulled from *Star Trek* newsgroups and forums. Using Photoshop I tried to change and write over them enough that they were transformed into something original: my original works of art, like gifts of gifs for the community. And thus, if my good solicitor captain is to be trusted, apparently less of an infringement. At the time, Paramount was writing legal cease and desist letters to fans for using its images and photos on their websites. The principle my attorney friend followed was that, just as you can reword a sentence while keeping its meaning pretty much intact, so too can you change an image enough that it is physically very different, but almost exactly the same emotionally and symbolically.

I thus used a picture of a Borg to introduce my 'cyber-interview'. It was here that I posed my first research question. I wrote, in spooky dripping fluorescent yellow font on a void black and white and neon bleeding red Borg photograph,

'Be Assimilated'. In several places, including right after the questions, I provided my personal email address and I asked fans to answer a series of detailed questions I was posing for them. At the time, I possessed insufficient programming ability to create and run a discussion group myself, so everything had to be conducted via email. Now, of course, on a site like Facebook or LinkedIn, having a discussion is very easy.

Expect the unexpected, the global and the local. Not everyone who answered me was similar in the way they experienced or interacted with *Star Trek*, and there were many language difficulties. I heard from 65 *Star Trek* fans in 12 different countries. Of course English was a challenge for some of them. We had email correspondences that lasted from over in a week to 14 full months. The data I received from the Interaction Research Website was more than sufficient for my dissertation, and a top-tier article. That, plus what I found in detail on newsgroups and forums was more than enough data to get me thinking deeply about fandom as a social phenomenon affected by the online linkages of power and social network connection.

Netnography and Ethnography United through the Site

This netnographic work was, of course, intimately interrelated with my in-person ethnography. The lawyer who I mention above, who guided my entry to online *Star Trek* culture, and whose advice inspired me to create the Interaction Research site in certain ways, was known through the in-person ethnography. The online and the embodied overlap and are not mutually exclusive. In the first place, it is a body who types, uploads, snaps photos, and so on. That body is increasingly exposed online. This has become a major topic for netnography. Rightfully so. In the second place, the body is only understood abstractly, as a context. The body is conceptualized theoretically and in the mind through social media sharing: more than a micro-celebrity, the person becomes a brand, and becoming a brand both elevates and diminishes the body in interesting ways. So the body and the brand, the material and the abstract, the physical and the metaphysical undeniably interact and conjoin. The website is united by and unites ethnography and netnography.

In the research I conducted with Daiane Scaraboto, discussed more fully in Chapter 4, a full 18% of all published netnographies used a research web-page. About one week prior to my writing this statement in this book, Cynthia Witney, Joyce Hendricks and Vicki Cope of the School of Nursing and Midwifery, at Edith Cowan University in Joondalup, Australia, presented their 'Munchausen by internet: A netnographical case study' (2014) at a nursing conference. I hate to start with a negative example, but I want to point this out as a caution point, no more. Something for all of us to learn from.

The authors created a research web-page called www.breastcancerclick.au where they studied people who have Munchausen's syndrome as they applied their syndrome behaviour in websites dedicated to particular illnesses. This presentation asks: Why do people pretend to be ill for attention online? Making a web-page in order to ensnare seems to be problematic. I do not know the details of this research, but I would genuinely hope that the presenters were careful and cautious about the ethical implications of consent under such circumstances.

Positive Cycology

Now back to positive examples. Marchi et al. (2011) used an existing corporate blog as their research web-page. And look at what Bartle et al. (2013) did. They created an innovative interaction website for people interested in cycling and called it 'Cycology'. Here is some detail on the interrelation of psychological and observational methods that they used as part of their netnography:

> Three methods were used to obtain qualitative data on the use of the *Cycology* system: observation of interactions on the website; questionnaires comprising open questions administered to the participants at the end of the project, followed by in-depth, semi-structured interviews. This provided an opportunity to analyse both observed behaviour and participants' own accounts of the experience of using the information system. Observation of website interactions was used to explore the content and patterns of interaction within the group, as well as to obtain some insight into the possible influence of these interactions on participants' attitudes, intentions and cycling behaviour. However, the interviews, supported by preliminary questionnaires, served as the main method for obtaining data on social influence effects and the social-psychological mechanisms which might explain them. (2011:7)

Such efforts can pay off richly in many ways, as they provide the netnographer with a strong tool for engagement, interaction, experiences and data collection. Just look at what happens, for Bartle and her co-authors (2012) when the research web-page is located, as the chapter on ethics emphasizes, on the researcher's own 'turf' or online territory and thus ameliorates a range of important issues and facilitates particular kinds of investigation-friendly interactions. These are the sorts of contacts and connections that can be easily and ethically made.[1]

Marie's Model Netnography

Marie-Agnès Parmentier, HEC marketing professor in Montréal, Quebec, is a former model who decided to conduct a netnography on the *Next Top Model* television shows, such as *America's Top Model*, *Britain's Top Model*, and so on. Working with Eileen Fischer, Russ, Markus and yours truly at York University in Toronto, Marie experimented with a blog format and also used a research web-page for her dissertation research studying fan-like online social interactions and experiences (see Figure 8.1); she was definitely a participant as well as an observer (Parmentier, 2009). But not really a provocateur, more of a fellow fan-girl, which is exactly the right angle to take. And as a former model, Marie had credibility with this group. She already understood the industry. So you can see

Figure 8.1 Marie-Agnès Parmentier's Research Web-Page

how the ethnographic injunctions of identity which, ultimately, drive auto-ethnography and now no doubt drive auto-netnography, play with our research and enrich it to the level of art, of human self expression, fine writing and scholarship, unlike anything else we have as a cultural research form.

Tucked away in one of Marie's dissertation footnotes is the information that she wanted to ensure that other fans of the different *Next Top Model* television shows could learn about her research and research interests. What does Marie want us to learn? That while she was out in the networked world investigating her topic, she included a link to her research website in all of her online profiles. On the site, she branded herself, giving them her bio: a doctoral student working on a dissertation focused on fans of fashion modelling reality TV. When possible, she would post her bio and introduce herself in the forums' introduction thread when that option made itself available. She says that during her research – probably because it is okay to have one scribe working in a community if they are well-trained, polite, interested and fit in as a culture member – 'I never encountered any resistance or negativity about the fact that I was "studying the community"' (Parmentier, 2009: 17, footnote).

I think that this may be due to the good naturedness and essential shared geeky-ness between fans and academics, for it is surely not usually the case. It cannot be assumed or taken at all for granted that you will get positive feedback going out into any random community the way that Marie did entering into this community. She did an amazing job, producing a fantastic netnography.

The Skinny: Do the Interactive Research Website, All of You!

Research websites are relatively easy to set up, and they have few risks. The amount of time to create one is minimal, and maintaining it will be a digital portrait of your netnography, an inerasable trace and memory of your research project – which could extend out in time and topic. Researchers like Marie and the others mentioned above, and Daiane with her fieldnotes below, have collected fascinating data using such tools. They allow research participation, but without some of the awkward and difficult territorial incursions of fleshy contact. You can build researcher disclosure into the very structure of the site, so it is completely obvious who you are and why they should help you.

An interaction research website is your portal which allows you as an academic netnographer to make connections with people who will become deeper participants, interviewees and key informants. The site provides opportunities to use your research and interests to contribute something of value to people. Moreover, these sites are an ethical way to collect transnational and international interactional and social online data by gaining people's full and informed consent for participation in the research in a fully honest and open way, directly tied to our legitimacy as university professors and students.

I advocate the Interaction Research Website as an elegant solution consisting of co-created data. It solves some of the most troublesome human, legal and social aspects of the fact that netnographic data collection can get very personal very very fast. It is not just access to amounts of data that the Internet can give us. It is access to a human level of depth of understanding.

INTERVIEWS IN NETNOGRAPHY

Interviews are the Smallest Data, Ns of One

Sometimes, the data that interests you doesn't appear online. It just isn't there. What should you do then? You can do experiments, surveys or interviews. Experiments make sense when you know exactly what you are looking for, when you can define it in terms that relate to measuring variables on human subjects. Interviews can and often should be used to flesh out and amplify important topical areas that may not be explored in sufficient depth or with sufficient insight in naturally occurring online interactions, or to help interpret and probe the meanings behind difficult-to-decipher symbols and images.

Almost 60% of published netnographies to date combine netnography with other methods. Of those that combine methods, 52% combined netnography with interviews. Interviews in netnography can take place online, using voice only, using video images, in person, with a person that one has already met online through the netnography, with a person that one has met through other means, and in other formats. In-person interviews can also involve select persons who then guide the researcher in an accompanied manner into online spaces.

Interviewing online is a flexible concept. Is it an interview if I make a posting? Is it one if I make a few polite and careful incursions into the social spaces already inhabited by people online? What if I post something insightful, relevant and timely? Is a research website not a type of interview? Any sort of interview, synchronous or asynchronous can be considered a type of interview, or survey. Netnographic interviews can still take place online in textual form, keyboard and screen to keyboard and screen. They can happen in an asynchronous format through email, posting questions on a board, blog or page, Tweeting them, or using another type of message exchange. Text interviews can also take place in real-time using chat type windows in a variety of sites, such as on Facebook. So it should be unsurprising that online interviews are commonplace now. When you interview for a job, you often do it online. So as researchers we also have to account for the fact that online interviews are coloured by people's impressions of them, just as surveys or personal interviews are coloured by people's past experience with, attitudes towards and sentiment-level impressions of them.

Something incredibly new is happening, and to delve into this we need interview's nuance and ability to encompass and, moreover, identify on the ground as a cultural categorist, a sorter of cultural observations. Having a research connection and interactional website is a way to connect with people who one can later approach for some sort of relationship. Exchanges can develop naturally and all it takes is one message and one decision and two people have met in person who would never have met in person if not for the interconnective potentiality of the Internet.

As people respond and post on the research web-page, and you have interactions with them on that forum, you can also bridge into email conversations and finally interviews. Video interviews tend to be the final phase, as they provide a powerful sense of intimacy and co-presence. However, not every informant will be comfortable exposing themselves to you in this way. This is why it may be helpful to develop the relationship first via email or other textual message exchange before you gain permission to take it to the more personal level of a video interview.

There are as many options and choices for the conduct of netnographic interviews as there are for their in-person variants, and the purpose of this section is merely to briefly overview and raise awareness about these options, rather than to provide an in-depth treatment of the topic. As with the in-person interview, the interview can be group-based or individual, formal or informal, structured or unstructured. You also have your choice of multiple formats to conduct the interview.

You should try to match the message of the interview to the interviewee and the medium. Long interviews might be difficult to obtain within certain sites, such as social networking sites or virtual worlds, where culture members are too busy to stop for one or two hours to be interviewed. But you can watch yourself watch yourself, as our upcoming section on self-reflective and self-reflexive note-taking suggest, under the guise of fieldnotes. As with in-person ethnography, a simple in situ conversation, or a quick exchange of information may suffice to inform your research question and focus.

Particular interview styles and desired outcomes also fit certain online social interactions better than others. The synchronous, real-time, abbreviated and superficial interaction of Snapchat – with its conversational tone and its unfettered nature – may be more suited to the informal interview that hopes for a quick insight through heat-of-the-moment disclosure. In sites where interactions are predominantly visual or audiovisual, such as Instagram or YouTube, you may want to ensure that your messaging contains your photograph, or even a video explaining your research. Throughout all interaction forms, visual or graphical exchanges can offer participants a type of projective that reaches them on more of the tacit and unspoken level of understanding. Receiving and decoding such non-textual information can enable participants to access and express knowledge and feelings that are difficult to articulate verbally.

Online interviewing has much in common with interviewing in general. It involves formally approaching a participant, suggesting an interview, and conducting a conversation from the frame of an interview, where the researcher's role is primarily that of the asker of questions (see Gubrium and Holstein, 2001). I like and often recommend the 'long' or 'depth' interview approach described by Grant McCracken (1988).

What I like about the long interview is that it is difficult. It takes patience, and time. I have never had the pleasure of working with Grant, but I hear that he has an almost supernatural ability to tap into groundswells of taste in the cultural world. Long interviewing, à la McCracken, requires honed researcher acuity, a skill, one that requires practice and sacrifices of self disclosure. It begins with a series of grand tour questions that help to place your interviewee in their social and cultural milieu, and then narrows down to concerns more focal to the particularities of the research project. Throughout, it can be a deeply empathic and emotional, sometimes even healing, affair.

In every kind of videotaped interview, the intention in the mind of the interviewer is exposed fully by the glare of the lights and the presence of the camera. The calibre of the questions and the nature of the interaction will, however, determine the quality of the participant's response. This is where skill is absolutely essential – clever editing can never cover bad interviewing.

For those unfamiliar with depth interviewing, I note that it is much more open-ended, free-flowing, conversational, and discovery-oriented than a survey (see Belk et al., 2013: 31–56 for a more in-depth treatment). Throughout the depth interview, the interviewer is probing and asking clarifying questions, building rapport, hoping for genuine disclosure, and staying open to interesting segues and elaborations. Online talking about offline stuff, or offline talking about online stuff, or doing both at the same time, or neither one: all of these are acceptable forms of messaging through which to have phenomenological gestalt moments, moments when you could swear you just read her mind, or she just read yours.

Conducting an interview through your computer means that your communications are going to be shaped by it. In Chapter 3, we termed this 'alteration'. Alteration means that cultural communications are already adapted to the exigencies of particular online media. Alteration and accessibility can facilitate the sharing of documents or photographic images through online interviews, which include Skype. Archiving entails that the interview can be automatically transcribed and saved. A program like Camtasia, for example, captures Skype or Google Hangout interviews effortlessly. This means that the researcher can be freed from routine note-taking or transcription concerns to concentrate fully upon the interview.

It is important in interviews to try to examine the shaping of messages by medium. What is the quality, from a design input perspective, of the experience of social interaction in these particular altered and transformed forms at these particular times?

In Chapter 7, we examined the methods for finding and capturing existing online social interactions, those which have been archived online. In this chapter, we have now overviewed the three major forms of co-creating data – through naturalistic online interaction, through the research web-page, and using netnographic interviews. The next section of this chapter proceeds to discuss the third type of data in netnography, reflective data.

PRODUCING REFLECTIVE DATA

This section provides you with guidance regarding the production of the final type of netnographic data: reflective data, also called field notes. The hesitation with using the ethnographic term field notes derives from the indeterminate nature of the netnographic field. If the field is indistinct, can there be fieldwork? Netnographic data is produced as the result of 'field-based' research practices such as downloading archives of communications and interactions, conducting interviews, participating in discussions, creating and sharing materials, or initiating or joining conversations. Data that is produced in this way is recorded as it happens.

Beaulieu's (2004: 155) questions suggest the rationale for netnographic field-notes: 'If access and transcriptions are no longer unique things that the [online] ethnographer has to offer, what then is the contribution?' Methodologically, theoretically and conceptually, in netnography it can be difficult to tell an observation from an inscription from an archival moment. However, this confusion creates a genuine opportunity for netnography to build a unique set of practices that preserve the first-person element of ethnographic storytelling. The answer to the challenge is that the netnographer should use reflective 'field' notes to contribute to the ongoing, unfolding human experience of being-in-the-network, the first-person introspective reflection of netnographic interaction and experience. The Internet as a whole, its social and informational networks, is the field. Just as an ethnographer captures her experience of encountering and learning a new culture through fieldnotes, it is through reflective data that the netnographer captures her own experience of encountering and learning about the specific particularities of an online social environment.

As Emerson and colleagues (2011: 1–2) note, fieldnotes are the result of ethnographic fieldwork in which 'the ethnographer writes down, in regular, systematic ways what she observes and learns while participating in the daily rounds of the lives of others'. Even though data onscreen is easily captured, and in fact, might collectively portray everything that happens online while the netnographer is participating online, netnographers must also have good field-notes capturing those experiences on one dimension *as personal and human-level experiences*, and on another level as information that is processed out of a huge stream of possible variables and readings. Some of those notes may even make their way into print, and through them the author attempt something resonant.

But, more likely, the vast majority of reflective fieldnotes will be building theory from observations, constantly trying to detect what is going on, what is connected, what is new, what is meaningful. How, on a very human, storied and familiar level, can we explain what is happening online in these social spaces where people interact?

As Chapter 6 indicated, and as Chapter 11 will develop further, academic netnography – and Humanist Netnography in particular – may not only be targeted towards journals and books such as this one, but also might be prepared for a more popular mass audience (keeping in mind, of course, the balance of the Kardashian index). Will you share it on a podcast? As a video? Regardless, the power of ethnography compels you to write fieldnotes. From these fieldnotes, you will find your lines, your narrative, your story, and these will be the personal voice of the tale you can call your own. Fieldnotes are ultimately what will allow the story of your own vulnerable humanity to suffuse your Humanist Netnography. Their insights will allow your participation to shine from within your data collection and reception. Let the reality of what you are actually perceiving appear to you mirrored back through reflective notes on whatever it is you choose to record. It is anthropological techniques such as reflective noting that will allow the netnographer to gain distance from the technologies she is using as she is using them, differentiating the technique from all others.

REFLECTIVE FIELDNOTES AND OTHER ETHNOGRAPHICALLY AFFORDANCED ASSEMBLAGES

The netnography contains interviews, introspection and interactions. Because most if not all netnographic interactions are recorded and saved as they occur, reflective fieldnotes become far more salient than observational fieldnotes. In reflective fieldnotes, netnographers record their own observations regarding subtexts, pretexts, contingencies, conditions and personal emotions occurring during their time online, and relating to their online interactions and experiences. Through these written reflections, the netnographer records her journey from outside to inside, her learning of languages, rituals, sites, information, people, topics and practices, as well as her involvement in a social web of meanings and personalities. Fieldnotes often provide key insights into how online social interactions function and transpire. They are very useful resources to turn to in data analysis when asking why a particular person made a particular graphic, photograph, message or posting at a particular time. They help the netnographer decipher the reasons behind cultural actions, rather than offer the more typical recording or description of them.

Drawing from their ethnographic work in virtual worlds, Boellstorff et al. (2012: 82–85) offer a range of practical suggestions regarding the keeping of netnographic fieldnotes. These include:

- Jotting down interesting things that occurred while the researcher was engaged in online interactions and experiences and then typing up more extensive notes after the action subsides.
- Taking screenshots of activity and making small 'scratch notes' soon after events occur; an effort is made to expand and refine these notes within 24 hours because memories can fade.
- Using the approach of 'two-boxing' (a term borrowed from computer gaming) in which two computers, screens or windows are open simultaneously; on one screen the netnographic engagement unfolds, while on the other screen notes are taken in real-time.
- Keeping observational notes and the interpretation of reflective fieldnoting separate and distinct; this makes clear that one's initial interpretation of an event, interaction, or experience is not necessarily what actually occurred.
- Paying attention to the software affordances of various sites, for example the presence of VOIP or Skype.
- Considering other forms of notation for recording observations and interpretations; for example, game players might want to make sketches, maps, or diagrams that relate to quests, raids, or puzzle-solving; this is analogous to the role that sketching in a sketchbook might pay for physical world ethnographers.
- Collecting 'scrapbooks' of online 'artifacts' can be useful in the same way that collecting small objects can be for physical world ethnographers.

Because ethnography is emergent and inductive, we do not always know what to notice. Thus, it can be useful to take notes on many types of online social experiences: people who one recently interacted with, intriguing information or sites, social groups, events and resources. Where online experiences occur in the form of audio, photographs, graphics or video, it is important to save them in the form in which they were experienced as well as to record one's own personal introspective observations about them. It is also valuable to record observational fieldnotes written in the margins of downloaded data, elaborating upon subtleties noticed at the time but which are not captured in the text or data itself. These fieldnotes offer details about the social and interactional processes that constitute online experience. It is best to capture them contemporaneously with their occurrence.

Writing fieldnotes synchronically with interactive online social experiences is important because processes of learning, socialization and acculturation are subtle and our recollection of them becomes rapidly diluted over time. Very rapidly, we acclimate to technologies and online social experiences, and forget that life was ever otherwise. Once we join an online group and its ways and terms become familiar, we rapidly forget that they are unfamiliar to others.

Another thing to keep in mind when keeping fieldnotes is that you should not censor your recording of online events, experiences, interactions and your own internal reactions. As much as possible, let your emotions and perceptions flow naturally, as if you are writing a diary to yourself, for yourself. Your internal human reality is a key element to netnography, and the only way that it enters into your datastream is through inscription in fieldnotes. As well, supposedly small things can later become very important and may even be, or lead to, those elusive back swans.

In their netnography of the 'Webheads in Action' English language teachers group, Derya Kulavuz-Onal and Camilla Vàsquez (2013: 230–234) provide one of the most useful examples and elaborations of the practice of netnographic field-noting yet published:

> when everything is archived and accessible, especially in the case of textual data (e.g., emails) that can be treated both as observational and as archival data, determining what to inscribe in the fieldnotes may pose challenges for the netnographer. Along these lines, for example, in our netnography, the content of our fieldnotes of emails varied depending on whether or not the emails were 'archived'. As can be seen from the following excerpts from our fieldnote data, when emails were both archived and observed (i.e. the emails in the main evonline2002 email list), the focus was more on the researcher's experiences, interpretations and reflections on the discussion in those emails rather than descriptions of the email interactions (in both excerpts, the researcher's experiences, interpretations and reflections are italicised for emphasis): I'm looking at main email list recent digest. [Name] asks for a screencast tool. A member sends a link to a list of such resources. [Name] also replies back with a recommendation for Jing. I'm familiar with Jing, but haven't used it myself before. I have used CamStudio for screencasting. I clicked on the link to the list sent by one member. The list says "20 Free Screen Recording Tools for Creating Tutorials and Presentations". I see CamStudio there as well. This list is a very comprehensive one with brief reviews for each too. I look at what other tools there are quickly. At the same time, I forgot this option. I can actually prepare screencasts for my students in my graduate class as well. For their technology-infused culture-teaching materials, I can show how to use some of the technology tools, by using a screen recording tool, as they seem to be struggling with it, and we don't have much time to go over each different tool in class.

One observation that is very interesting about this fieldnote excerpt is that it is highly technical in nature, and concerns the software for doing netnography. We see the Craft of Netnography itself, on the operating table, its beating pulse visible. The fieldnote excerpt examples continue in the article and they all concern software, hardware, or some other application or non-application of information technology. The absence of more personal and emotional reflection is a presence, as are all absences in netnography. For through search and through fieldnotes, it is at least as important to record the absence of finding things you expected to find as it is to record the finding of things you never expected to find. Fieldnotes are the place where the lack of data (for example, a site or posting or person you expected to find, but did not) become data.

Although the very visual nature of our online social experience may mislead us into thinking otherwise, social interaction online is not so much an event as a process. The unfolding of this process often contains much that is of interest. Initial impressions of communities, web-pages and members' postings are important, as are key events or incidents. Record those impressions in your fieldnotes. Use contemplation to increase your sensitivity to the experiences of others. If you feel shocked at a particularly questionable posting, do others feel this way as well? The entire process of reaction and observation is contextual. 'The ethnographer is concerned not with members' indigenous meanings simply as static categories but with how members of settings invoke those meanings in specific relations and interactions' (Emerson et al., 1995: 28). Because the when, where and who questions of context are usually automatically recorded in netnographic work, what is even more important to capture in your fieldnotes is your own subjective impressions and expectations about the all-important why questions as they arise.

Daiane Scaraboto and the Geocacher's Fieldnotes

Netnography often does not stop at the computer screen. Good fieldnotes help to make the links between online and other sites visible. This visibility can lead to greater analytic insights. A few discerning others have used the research web-page form as a key juncture point linking the articulated assemblages between online netnographic and in-person ethnographic fieldwork on the same key identity group or market segment.[2] As an example, consider Daiane Scaraboto's netnography of geocaching culture. This netnography did not stop when she had thoroughly and longitudinally studied, downloaded and participated in Groundspeak's products (Scaraboto, 2013). Instead, she went physical. She became a geocacher, travelling the country to locate and record geocaches, coordinating efforts using her GPS to navigate and Internet access to correspond and share information. She interviewed people using a variety of different techniques, across different locations, recorded in different sorts of media. Throughout, she kept excellent fieldnotes.

Her fieldnotes, which she kindly shared with me as I researched this book, reveal how her in-person ethnography and netnography work blend effortlessly together. She attends a party, and meets people whose online profiles she has studied. Her fieldnotes indicate what she has learned about them from her research online, such as how many caches they have found, how active they are online, and their general reputation in the community. She chooses in-person events to attend based on their online descriptions. When she meets and introduces herself to people, she must use her screen name and people recognize her and relate to her.

Daiane also uses her fieldnotes to do more explicitly netnographic work. For example, she downloads postings directly into her fieldnotes and then comments upon them in the text, either in Word comments or in added text that she italicizes. She views a video that one of the geocachers posts on YouTube about his recent trip, and her fieldnotes record her impression and observations:

When I watched it today, the first part had 38 views, the second 28. the video is very 'amateur' with the use of some editing resources … It seems there was a father & son trip for them, the video was mostly made by a young man. They had a truck 'fully loaded' and put together a complete camping site by the lake for themselves on the first day. They did some fishing. There is no soundtrack, the mood is of calmness and quietude. Part 4 is the canoeing part, you can see his GPS (a Colorado) attached to the canoe.… when I get to part 8, I start to find the video a little boring.

Notice how she is describing herself here, implicitly inscribing herself at the same time as she is describing the video. She is the point of view, the centre of scrutiny, the commander of concentration. Reading her notes, she is revealing what she is processing from the situation, she is a deep N of One. These are thought elicitations as much as fieldnotes. Are they representative of anything except the Particularity of the Singular? That is an empirical question, one that we could decide by theorizing and testing whether others, like her, use their own versions of mental fieldnotes to track all of the postings on one of the Groundspeak forums in order to get a sense of the general topics, and to comment on their tone and content. A short except follows:

Cache at the Cemetery 12 number of extra pages (means 2 here) Is it right to do so? 72 (# of replies) DiLMar (topic starter) 1,363 (# of views). (last action:)Today, 07:27 AM. Comment: Is it friendly, family friendly to go caching in cemeteries? Most posters say it's educative, interesting and have nothing against it.

Quick to post Easy Find – Never post DNF Why don't they post Did Not Find logs? 20 jr11617 163 Today, 07:22 AM. Comment: They are discussing one of the many guidelines that are open to interpretation in geocaching: whether someone should post a DNF log when not finding a cache. Many divergent opinions on the topic. Very polite tone, it really seems they are trying to reach a common conclusion here (which is, nevertheless, very unlikely to happen).

Do you see how Daiane is abstracting, judging, describing and analysing – all at the same time? If you keep observational fieldnotes that capture your own impressions, you will automatically begin to abstract from out of the mass of possible variables and data points the ones that you, as a human instrument, consider important. As you inscribe these observational fieldnotes of your lived experience as a culture member, write as descriptively as possible:

description calls for concrete details rather than abstract generalizations, for sensory imagery rather than evaluative labels, and for immediacy through details presented at close range. [Sociologist ethnographer Erving] Goffman (1989: 131) advises the fieldworker to write 'lushly,' making frequent use of adjectives and adverbs to convey details. (Emerson et al., 1995: 69)

Descriptive netnographic fieldnoting will force you to consider new variables, new observations, new sights, sounds, smells, sensations, textures, colours, fonts, imagery, mythic symbols, brand forms, shapes, design elements, and so on. With this sort of descriptive attention, netnography shades easily into semiotic research. Semiotic studies of the many visual designs apparent upon the Internet, and social media, used as messaging communications, as alphabets and as signs, are key to understanding the many intersecting languages of people, tribes, and the media they make and which makes them.

In a netnography, these descriptions will be a combination of what is seen on the screen and what the researcher experiences. Although many of the on-screen manifestations of the 'events' that transpire through online interaction can be captured through screen captures and data downloads, your fieldnotes should strive to capture your own impressions, the subjective meanings of interactions and events as you experience them materializing over time. Especially, your fieldnotes should capture and develop your experience with the Interactive Research Website. What is it like to connect with people around an issue, idea, brand or person? No software program can substitute for the finely tuned research instrument that is the netnographer. Mindfulness is the key netnographic research stance and practice here, a discipline as valuable in life and living as it is in research. The mindful netnographer creates absolutely unique data, data and method that can be successfully harvested as part of an interactive research project: a new website, unique questions, visualizations, analysis, and interpretation: all driven by your sense of yourself driven by your introspection and maintained, ultimately, through conscious practice. Interpretation is absolutely key, and as you begin writing your ideas in your fieldnotes, of course you have already begun abstracting. Having begun abstracting, rather naturally I would hope, you have already begun your analysis, which the next chapter will argue is a type of inter-penetration, as well as a type of interpretation. Having gained this awareness, we proceed in the next chapter to investigate the nature of hermeneutic, holistic and holonic interpretation.

SUMMARY

This chapter has discussed how netnographic participation creates interactive and produced netnographic data. It has provided detail regarding the development and deployment of an interactive research website. These procedures and examples were followed by a section about netnographic interviews. Next, the chapter considered the production of reflective data, reconceptualizing it as an ethnographic affordance and providing guidance for its use. We learn through this about the interconnection of netnography and embodied ethnography through fieldnoting and the web-page, how the two move easily one into the other and back. Netnography should be a part of many ethnographies now, and ethnography should be a part of many netnographies.

KEY READINGS

Bartle, Caroline, Erel Avineri and Kiron Chatterjee (2013) 'Online information-sharing: A qualitative analysis of community, trust and social influence amongst commuter cyclists in the UK', *Transportation Research Part F: Traffic Psychology and Behaviour*, 16: 60–72.
Emerson, Robert M., Rachel I. Fretz and Linda L. Shaw (2011) *Writing Ethnographic Fieldnotes*, 2nd edn. Chicago: University of Chicago Press.
McCracken, Grant (1988) *The Long Interview*. Beverly Hills, CA: Sage.

NOTES

1. For experienced marketers and others, digital ethnographies can also be constructed using social media data to conduct repeat, yet non-intrusive studies on the actual social communication online interaction experience, using past archivally saved datastreams to test behavioural hypotheses. Of course this fits in beautifully with netnography. Digital Netnography is the name for this evolutionary adaptation, and it is explained more fully in Chapter 10.

2. There are some who believe that, as the commercial becomes the cultural, the two are rapidly losing any distinctive qualities and becoming one another. So, for example, any ancient distinction between the gift and commercial economies are blending through increasing economic-social innovations such as shareware, peer-to-peer networks, consumer generation, and open source businesses.

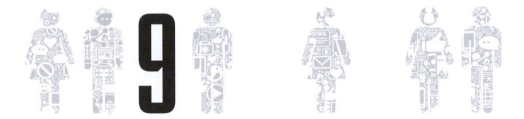

9

DATA ANALYSIS AND INTERPRETATION

INTERPRET THIS!

In this chapter, we will explore the essence of qualitative data analysis and induction through hermeneutics and deep reading. We will, further, explore the nature of the analytic modalities of netnographic interpretation. We will find clues in flexible theoretical structures like assemblages and holonic elements that will guide us in putting together the puzzle pieces of data from multiple methods, moments and research modalities. Interpretive moments have inter- and trans-textual links that connect them to vast warehouses of meaning, drawing from archetypal storehouses of interactions and experiences. Steeped in religious and scientific modalities of hermeneutic interpretation and computationally guided content and social network data analysis, this chapter balances on an ontological razor's edge.

The different forms of netnography in total embrace a range of analytic and interpretive methods, including computer and technology-assisted methods. With Digital Netnographies, and in many Symbolic Netnographies, computer-assisted methods are established and their use continues to develop. However, there is absolutely no need to use computerized methods. In fact, the Humanist form favours more naturalistic and experience-close forms of research understanding. In netnographic fieldnotes and introspection, the process and meaning of analysis should be contemplated and recorded. As the netnographer deploys different devices and procedures for analysis, including software tools, she should always attune herself to an inner and human-based understanding about how these tools are directly in contact with and are transforming her emergent understanding. Whether we use computer-assisted or more traditional pen-and-paper research practices, the procedure we will follow can be thought of as following paths of either analysis or interpretation, which we describe throughout this chapter.

Analysis means breaking a phenomenon down into its component parts. Hermeneutics means keeping something whole, or recognizing the whole within its parts. Both analysis and hermeneutics requires us to divide data in order to understand it. However, the goal of an ethnography and netnography is synthesis, building a research representation. This representation is like a mosaic we construct from the carefully extracted, and thus broken out of their context elements of something else. Netnography is about finding gems online and then building them together into magnificent pieces of jewellery, with the gold and silver metals provided by the narration, the theoretical storytelling.

Analysis has three aspects in netnography. First, analysis can be computational and computer-assisted. Digital Netnography uses all manner of computational elements to mine, extract, pre-code, classify and visualize data in the quest for culturally flavoured, anthropologically informed big data insights; big data insights which move far beyond the norm on these qualities. Second, interpretation can be personal, introspective and focused on subjectivities and subject positions, if the goal of the presentation is to be autonetnographic. It was so for Cátia Sofia Afonso Ferreira (2012) whose doctor's thesis in communication thoroughly explored the social dimension of Second Life, finding that much of the new social dimension in this virtual world, namely, its placeness, its identityness and its stories, actually replicates social being in more traditional venues. Third and finally, we find Traditional and Humanist Netnography to be a form with the function of fulfilling the need for balancing data with artful representation. This balance is possible because the collection phase limits the amount of data. Humanist Netnography is based squarely upon the principle of qualitative data mining, as is much of the Symbolic Netnography on which it depends and from which it descended.

We can think of data as raw material, close to the sensory level of experience and observation. First it must be noticed, observed. Then it must be recorded, saved, found and scraped out of the earthy ground of experience, physical and symbolic experience. Then it must be analysed; it must be mined. It is a question of how we mine it. The extraction mode takes and captures, acting from a social distance. Digital Netnography is thus more experience distance than the other forms. Still, I believe that by following the wheel of netnography as a Buddhist would follow a prayer wheel and having faith in the 12 steps, we can ensure enough understanding to distinguish Digital Netnography as a form of netnography distinct from colder and more calculating methods.

A digression to, I hope, clarify something. Here is one of my test dictums: if people's stories are being analysed by being broken, dissected and experimented upon then this is not a netnographic analysis. Netnography requires stories in the same way that most modern combustion engines require petroleum-based fuel. Netnography offers a more holistic and organic alternative, one that relentlessly seeks the meaning of online social data through efforts to elaborate and maintain its context, balancing this with an overview of the relevant datastream, all while answering specific questions.

Although the full topic of this chapter is data interpretation and analysis, it is crucial to think from the beginning about how to respect human data and how to create compelling human stories. These matters continue to be the fascination of netnography. Netnography is the story you tell with and amongst other stories. You can tell computationally impressive Digital Stories, or novelistic Auto-netnographies. You can follow the path of Symbolic Netnography, or you can attempt a more resonant contribution and build a Humanist Netnography.

The type of netnography you wish to create will dictate in many ways the type of analysis you will employ. But regardless of which form of netnography you choose to perform, this is your story. No amount of instruction can tell you how to tell your own story. This chapter intends to encourage you on this quest for scientific discovery and sometimes even self-discovery, if you are lucky. What is that you ask? What is the nature of inter-penetration? Good. I will now explain it to you.

INTERP(EN)ETR(AT)ING DATA

The German artist and poet Max Ernst once said that 'Collage is the noble conquest of the irrational, the coupling of two realities, irreconcilable in appearance, upon a plane which apparently does not suit them'. Making a collage involves collecting different forms, items and images and placing them together in a way that gives them meaning both as a whole and as parts. Collage frequently also involves the artist not only assembling and gluing items to their canvas, but also painting and drawing on or over it. Netnography – which collects and produces precious and powerful pieces of data and culturally curates them, often writing on top of them, annotating and agreeing and arguing with them – is similar to collage. The collage is, in a sense, an induction. Induction – in which individual observations are built up in stages, ordered deliberately and deployed to make general statements about a phenomenon – could also be thought of as an abstract representation of reality in which the two realities of collected traces of the empirical world and the interpretation of the researcher are coupled. The data must penetrate into the awareness of the interpreter. The interpreter's story must be permeated and punctuated with data. This is what I mean when I use the term 'inter-penetration' as a way to make more bodily and also more conscious the act of human understanding, of one human being connecting to Others' viewpoints, in contexts that are so multiple, complex and interrelated that only a human intelligence can do justice to the discernment of the meaning of them all. In Indra's net, all phenomena are mutually contained and interpenetrating. One thing will contain all that exists. And all that exists will contain the One.

THE SEVEN INTERPENETRATING INTELLECTUAL IMPLEMENTS

Within the netnographic induction, we need to make Seven Interpenetrating Analytic Moves known as Intellectual Implements, or netnographic qualitative analysis techniques. These are the seven interrelated steps in the process of turning data into representation, of taking abstract and construct-based theoretical questions, colliding them with data and positing answers, using netnography or any other qualitative research method. They are inspired by the classic work of Matthew Miles and Michael Huberman (1994: 9), but they are also very distinct from them. The Seven Implementing Moves are: Imagining, Re-Memorying, Abduction, Visual Abstraction, Artifying, Cultural Decoding and Tournament Play. They are show in Figure 9.1.

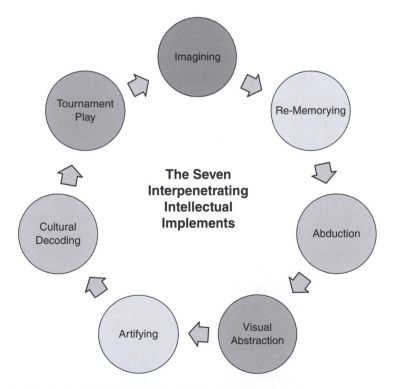

Figure 9.1   The Seven Interpenetrating Intellectual Implements

There are explained as intellectual moves to implement as follows:

1. Imagining

Imagining is the first implement. In imagining, you build on your initial reflective ideas captured in your fieldnotes and add many elements of your own awareness as a social being, as a human coming from a particular social situation, identity and place. Imagining is a stream of consciousness association. It is a right-brained wandering, the talking method, the chattering monkey voice that human mind is, beginning to dream, sometimes deeply in a hypnotic state, the murmur jabbering in our ear, as the Buddhist monks say, mindless many times like a tape recorder repeating things over, looping sounds and ideas, linking thoughts to them. Just let it run free and keep recording it. This is imagining.

2. Re-Memorying

Re-memorying is the second implement. Thinking about the data, while not looking at it, what do you remember? Write it down. Simply write as much of what you can remember, in any order you like. This memory turns out to be a reconstruction, a path, and perhaps a pathway to the unconscious mind's processing of the massive amounts of data. Memory is a creation, a re-creation each time. We remember as we re-member to the social segments we belong. As we free ass-ociate and open our awar(i)eness to all connections, we can squeeze out, with some effort, many levels of analytic thinking to explore. Among the re-collections and re-connections, we we-memory, for remembering is an active act. We read or look at some data, and then we remember, we recall and offer up associated symbols and ideas. This is re-memorying.

3. Abduction

At this point, you try fitting things together. Fitting things together is both Induction and Abduction, appearing together as the dual heads of the third implement. You have basic concepts, now you rub them up against each other. You see which ones fit. Which ones spark when they touch. Which ones repel each other like the opposite ends of a magnet. You look for the basic ideas of the abstractions and then you hypothesize that some of them are related and connected in different ways, flowing with each other, or against each other, but connected and entangled without a doubt. Specify those connections now. It could be like a correlation. It could easily be triggered by patterns revealed quantitatively in the data. The netnographic moment is to decipher and understand those patterns culturally. This is abduction.

4. Visual Abstraction

Visual abstraction is the fourth implement, and is also perhaps the trickiest implement of them all to handle. For in visually abstracting, we are in some sense Playing God. We take what is small, local and particular and we try to see qualities within it that might make it large, universal and general. We take a bunch of trees around us and we suddenly visualize the unique and shared patterns of an entire forest. We look at the landscape around us and we see the view of it from 35,000 feet. We see a blogger communicating to a hotel on TripAdvisor and we see the metaphor of the fool becoming King. With this inversion in power relationship between social media active consumers and the corporations who are increasingly recognizing them as powerful influencers, we see all sorts of new social ramifications. We can combine visual abstractions into new abstractions. We have a massive amount of creative choice about where we can abstract, at what level we are to cast our abstraction, as long as it is visual, or sensory (you may prefer to process your information auditorially or kinaesthetically: these are possible; however most people will process visually). So many social concepts, so many ideas, so much to choose from in the act of active abstraction, moving from the local to the global to the particular to the general to the macrocosm to the microcosm. It is easy to lose one's self and one's way here. However, getting lost sometimes, and finding your way back can be exactly the point of the excursion.

5. Artifying

Artifying is another way to visualize the data, which also uses the visual mind, but in a totally different way, a left-brained visual mind way. Here, we think deeply about the data while in our mind searching for corresponding metaphors, dreams, images, photographs, and of course, collages that summarize our interpretation of the data. These images may occur in flashes, so it is important to be aware enough to see them on the inner screen of your own mental movie auditorium. All you can do is hope to catch them. But it is easier when you work with materials, creating an actual collage out of bits of magazines and printed photographs, assembled perhaps on canvas or cardboard and glued together with whatever you have around the house: flour and water if nothing else is available. Build a visual tool to elicit your own personal academic metaphors. This is thinking in action. This is science as art once again, as da Vinci imagined it would be. Perhaps even with a touch of the original academia's medieval architectural mysticism and sense of Biblical Design. This potent imaginary of image as myth/mythical reality is artifying.

6. Cultural Decoding

Cultural decoding is the further part of your journey. Cultural decoding relies on you to assemble significant amounts of diverse data, to sample widely of people and their things, and to try to fit all the pieces together. In this case, we take a good close look at our data and we try to understand the cultural categories which we can use to classify it, including all of the categories that it calls itself. For example, we are studying the cultural code of dating that shows up in online dating or encounters. We are studying the cultural code of beauty among average Czech women as exhibited in social media communities, and we can then compare it to Russian women. We are studying the code of education among incoming university freshmen and their parents.

'The Culture Code is the unconscious meaning we apply to any given thing – a car, a type of food, a relationship, even a country – via the culture in which we are raised', defines Clotaire Rapaille, highly successful medical anthropologist in *The Culture Code* (2006). We assign each important cultural element a 'code', a more theorized adaptation of Clotaire Rapaille's terminology. What is the essence of what you seek to study? An emotion? An identity? An event? Anything can be understood in a deeper way online. For even more important than the code itself is what the code links to and represents. What does the code behind Friendship represent to us, in particular form, that is a general force or influence or causing factor in the world? What about the code of Enemy, or Hatred, or Opponent? The media creates much fear. The world, it seems, is an incredibly scary place right now. What is the social media response? Where are the interactions? What types of interactions are they? What are the codes we are trying to unlock? Video, podcast, avatar, text file: it does not matter what we are using as data. What is it saying? This same process should also be applied to your own introspective exercises and reflective journal field noting. What are *your* codes?

7. Tournament Play

In tournament play you will play with the many ideas you now have had, the many theories of reality explanation that you have gone through and the favourites that remain. The more ideas and theories we have about possible connections, then the more testing we need to do against the data of reality. Reducing the set as early and as often as you can, by saying it does not fit the data, is a very desirable thing to do. Tournament play is competition between your own competing ideas. Tournament play is not only an interpretation of Darwin's survival of the fittest hypothesis; it is about the survival of the fittest interpretation. We take a certain number of ideas, then we run them through some sort of prediction, or model that says if this idea was true what sort of evidence for it would show up in the data: good deductive thinking stuff. We ask, Which is a better explanation of the data? But not only accuracy is the goal. Not simply some quantitative prediction, although certainly that can be part of it. This is about predicting reality and asking which explanation tells a more interesting or convincing story. Which of these many explanations am I most proud of as a creation, an abstraction, a model, and a reality predictor? Which coherent, apprehensible story of the data should I put forward as my interpretation? Tournament play between thoughts and ideas is the way you make this decision.

These then, are the netnographic moves of Interpenetrating Analysis that flow from Interactive Research. This is the internal and human state of seeking understanding, ground up into seven exercises and tools, stages and moments to use to increase your own research academic understanding. These are your philosopher's stone, seven non-overlapping steps, movements both inward and outward, towards both interpretation and data, uniting them in a spiral to form theory. Imagining. Re-Memorying. Abduction. Visual Abstraction. Artifying. Cultural Decoding. Tournament Play. In the next section, we seek a middle ground between working with data and deepening our explanation for reality. In that section, I direct you to think about the connections between various levels in your data, looking for explanations through finding relevant and interesting links between previously separated levels of analysis and scientific/theoretical/methodological points of view.

HOLONS, HUMANS AND HERMENEUTICS
Interpreting the Human World

Appreciating different forms of understanding leaves us empowered to build our skills as human interpreters, as seekers of social clues and cues, comprehenders of cultural nuance, transmitters of subtle innuendo, translators of highly hidden messages for one another. Anthropologists should be attuning to the meaning of being human. This is always, for us, the most purposeful interpretive act.

Netnography depends upon a collective human level of analytical focus: how does this or that group behave, believe, ritualize, celebrate, and so on. The result is cultural understanding, as distinct from other types of understanding. But what the heck is cultural understanding? Cultural understanding can be thought of as coming from both analysis – which is related to Miles and Huberman's (1994: 8) 'quest for lawful relationships' in qualitative data – and from interpretation, which I relate to Miles and Huberman's (1994: 9) 'search for "essences" that may transcend individuals, and lend themselves to multiple compelling interpretations'. However, the multiple compelling interpretations should be boiled down, and 'integrated' into one coherent theoretical story line. This search for a single story line, for an essential truth, for the particular specifics of contextual understanding, is key to interpretation.

Consumer researcher Susan Spiggle (1994: 497) suggests that in the process of interpreting data, rather than analysing it, 'the investigator does not engage a set of operations [as she would in the coding operations of analysis]. Rather, interpretation occurs as a gestalt shift and represents a synthetic, holistic, and illuminating grasp of meaning, as in deciphering a code'. Notice the 'aha' moment, the eureka that this implies, and how it directly relates to some of the implements of the last section, especially Cultural Decoding.

Interpretation uses not just the brain for thinking, but the gut for understanding. Interpreting in a penetrating way, inter-penetration, is a personal yielding to insight, perhaps even to growth. Viewed in this light, interpretation becomes a radical type of translation, a perception where the perceiver and the perceived interpenetrate, flickering together like conjoining shadows on a wall. This requires Imagination. Using the implement of Imagining to birth the primordial interpretive moment, we seek to distance ourselves from the familiar, to find it somehow alarming and new, like a baby on its back being surprised at the sudden appearance of its own hands. What is technology? What is fandom? What is addiction? What is pornography? What is celebrity? What is play? What does it mean to be a mother, a soldier, a consumer, a friend in the digital age of the social? Making the familiar strange, holding onto the very profound strangeness that is technology, technological being, technological sociality and consociality in the current time, is a key netnographic injunctive in an age where we rapidly acclimate to massive technocultural transformation.

Hermeneutics

Hermes was not the nicest of the Greek Olympians. Although he did invent language, he abused it. He was a liar, as well as being a thief. Like the Native American Coyote, Hermes was a trickster. We should probably keep in mind that hermeneutic interpretation was named for Hermes, as god of both interpretation and also of lies. Consider a collection of 3 YouTube videos, 4 pages of blogger text, 6 pages of newsgroup materials and 17 Instagram posts. Finding their common elements, the key and core of their meaning structure, requires us to find the common elements between them. Locating these shared themes is the challenge of hermeneutic interpretation.

Hermeneutic interpretation requires, I would add, not merely a talent as a spinner of narratives, although this comes in handy, but also very selective and astute data collection skills. For the central topic or guiding question is likely to be the main core element that connects the collected or perhaps we might say, following Hermes, thieved set of data. As Thompson and colleagues (1994: 433) note, the idea of hermeneutics, and especially the hermeneutic circle, has been considered 'a methodological process for interpreting qualitative data'. The process is

> an iterative one in which a 'part' of the qualitative data (or text) is interpreted and reinterpreted in relation to the developing sense of the 'whole.' These iterations are necessary because a holistic understanding must be developed over time. Furthermore, initial understandings of the text are informed and often modified as later readings provide a more developed sense of the text's meaning as a whole. (Thompson et al., 1994: 433)

However, hermeneutic analysis extends the collection into a process of abduction. It abducts us from the particular to the general. It abducts upwards from individual observations, individual pieces of data, into a full representation. Hermeneutic interpretation is a process of reading and rereading, interpreting and reinterpreting, interpreting our interpretations, and reinterpreting our reinterpretations.

Questioning. Probing. Resolving. Upending. It is a process of seeking a whole from parts, and an interpretation in which we can find the whole within the parts. The notion of self-similarity is contained throughout nature and in mathematical creations. For example, if you take a whole piece of broccoli, and break off a branch, the branch resembles the whole piece. If you break the piece down further, the piece also resembles the larger pieces. You can continue for several steps, finding the self-similarity of the extracted piece with the whole. The leaves of ferns are similar, as are the edges of plotted Mandelbrot fractals. Self-similarity is related to the interpenetration of meaning between elements of data and the dataset considered as a whole.

> the meaning of a whole text is determined from the individual elements of the text, while, at the same time, the individual element is understood by referring to the whole of which it is a part ... Specific elements are examined again and again, each time with a slightly different conception of the global whole. Gradually, an ever more integrated and comprehensive account of the specific elements, as well as of the text as a whole, emerges. (Arnold and Fischer, 1994: 63)

When assembling the pieces and constructing this story, you should seek interpretations that make sense when viewed in context, and in their context they should be relatively 'free of contradiction', they should be 'comprehensible' to the intended audience for your netnography, 'supported with relevant examples', clearly related to 'relevant literature', 'enlightening' and '"fruitful" in revealing new dimensions of the problem at hand' and yielding 'insights' that explicitly revise our current understanding, and that are also written in a prose style that is 'persuasive, engaging, interesting, stimulating, and appealing' and which uses allusions, metaphors, similes and analogies (Arnold and Fischer, 1994: 64). Thompson et al. (1994) further note that a good hermeneutic interpretation will delve into the social and historical contexts of the data for its explanations, providing a subtle, specific, nuanced cultural interpretation. In order to fully develop this idea of holistic and self-similar analysis, however, we benefit from incorporating the idea of the holon and holon-based, or holarchic, systems.

Holons and Holarchic Systems

As we are considering the relation and interrelation of the part and the whole, it may be useful to consider Arthur Koestler's notion of holons, and holarchies, which he introduced in his book *The Ghost in the Machine* (Koestler, 1967). As their name indicates, holons are wholes, complete elements in and of themselves. Yet this wholeness, Koestler reminds us, is a matter of perspective, for holons are also parts of other levels. A classic example is a cell in the human body. This cell is a whole unto itself, a eukaryote with clear boundaries and a defined form. Yet the cell is also a part of an organ. An organ is not simply a giant cell, or a simple collection of cells; it is another whole; it has structural integrity and its own identity. Organs are part of individual organisms, wholes that are complete and unique. And collectivities can be composed of organisms. A collective of people is not like a large cell, or collection of cells. In fact, we learn very little about the behaviour of collectives by studying the behaviour of cells. And yet a collective cannot exist without its different component parts. Therefore, holons are parts that are wholes, but they do not, as in the self-similarity of pieces of broccoli, also reflect the form of the next order of system of which they are a part.

When the practice of hermeneutic interpretation compels us to examine the relation between the part and the whole, the notion of the holon serves as a productive reminder for us to think about the different parts and levels within our phenomenon. What are the boundaries between elements in the system? Which part or parts are we studying? Why? How does this part relate to other parts? Is their relationship holarchic: does one holon contain the other?

Because many of our questions pertain to social forms, we might think about how different social elements are collected into assemblages that fulfil social functions. We might theorize the various linguistic articulations at work and consider the constitutive function of language in maintaining a feeling of social solidity and solidarity: the role of language in institutionalization. On a social level, as with business, the military, or simply social orders, humans often organize themselves into hierarchical systems, where particular holons have higher status, greater independence and power than other holons at the same level. In a hierarchy, holons on the same level direct and take direction from one another. With a holarchy, the different system levels contain one another, as systems contain unique sub-systems. Within that arrangement, higher level holons direct the activities, and will even sacrifice the well-being of holons in the systems below them.

Not only does the notion of holarchic contexts alert us to attend to the contingent nature of knowledge – that what seems true from one 'holonic level of analysis' may not persist to the next level. It also alerts us to the more general notion that understanding is situated in a particularly complex nest of interlocking truths, some of which may seem quite incompatible. Ken Wilber (1997) employs the notion of holons to try to tackle the fundamental ontological incompatibility of realist positivist science with postmodern poststructuralism. He asserts that the reflexive nature of postmodern and poststructural critiques such as those of Derrida, Foucault and Lyotard is simply an acknowledgment that the nature of reality is one of 'holons within holons within holons, of texts within texts within texts (or contexts within contexts within contexts)' (ibid.: 100). The key, then, to making positive claims about the world, according to Wilber, is to recognize that meaning and truth are always context dependent and that contexts are infinitely extendible. For example, Wilber argues that our individual thought is actually a holon that has aspects of belonging to various other systems: intentional, behavioural, cultural and social. Truth is nested in context. As we examine different contexts, view phenomena from different perspectives, we draw closer to the truth and to enhanced understanding.

Considered as research practices that can contextually reveal truths about holonic elements of online social experience, the two different analytic processes – breaking-down to build-up again analysis and hermeneutic interpretation – overlap in many interesting ways. Analysis breaks down data by examining the various meanings, values and contexts to which it links. Analysis is the first stage of reduction and redaction. Analysis seeks the slippage of different contexts, even the identification of different holonic elements. On the other hand, hermeneutics are hermetic, isolating, holistic, storied. This mode of interpretation keeps the data whole, treasuring the big picture, cherishing the individual jewels of data and resisting breaking them apart or decontextualizing them. In the following section, I illustrate these two operations with a short example drawn from a news posting on Facebook.

ANALYSIS AND INTERPRETATION: A NETNOGRAPHIC EXAMPLE

Contextualizing the Data

We will continue learning about qualitative data analysis by applying the techniques of coding analysis and hermeneutics to a set of socially mapped graphical data extracted from a social networking site. The example I use will be grossly oversimplified and, to some, banal. However, I believe it sufficient for the purposes of illustration. Anything around you in the world of social media would be useful for you to use as your own example.

I use a Facebook post about a controversial and emotional topic: the 2014 Ebola breakout in Western Africa, and a photograph and news story about protests against the resulting quarantine. This posting appeared on Facebook's general news feed, and the posters, most of whom are non-anonymous, appear in the general feed because they have commented directly on the post. The story was posted on 21 August 2014, by a New York-based journalism professor. In the 7 hours before I viewed it, the story gained 42 Facebook 'likes', 24 shares and 56 comments from English-speaking individuals occupying a number of different countries and subject positions.

I will provide my own provisional interpretation later in this section, illustrating the Coyote's voice of hermeneutic interpretation. First, and without biasing your own response with any further information or my own interpretation, I will provide a brief interactional exchange between the respondents to the posting. I provide them with pseudonyms, attempt to describe their photographs, and block their actual names as a courtesy and to follow accepted ethical research practice as outlined in Chapter 6. It is done this way in our traditions, and our ethical guidelines suggest we do it this way, so we keep on doing it.

Figure 9.2 Facebook Ebola posting and discussion (displayed with alterations marked in greyed out spaces in original posting format)

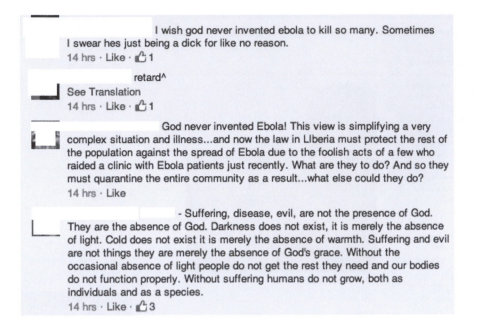

Figure 9.3   Facebook Ebola dataset in original format

However, because these comments are public, and my analysis and interpretation of them in this book as an example is unlikely to cause any harm, I do not disguise their source and I do not paraphrase them. The following are sequential postings located somewhere near the middle of the overall stream of comments.

- [photo of an attractive young couple; man in a black t-shirt; Anglo-sounding male name; lives in America] 'JOE': I wish god never invented ebola to kill so many. Sometimes I swear hes just being a dick for like no reason.
- [photo of young man smiling in restaurant, wearing a black 'Canada' hoodie; French sounding male name; lives in Canada]: 'BRIAN': retard^
- [photo of smiling middle-aged couple on a beach, she is wearing sunglasses; French-sounding female name; lives in Canada]: 'MARIE': God never invented Ebola! This view is simplifying a very complex situation and illness ... and now the law in Liberia must protect the rest of the population against the spread of Ebola due to the foolish acts of a few who raided a clinic with Ebola patients just recently. What are they to do? And so they must quarantine the entire community as a result ... what else could they do?
- [portrait-like photo of woman with long straight blond hair, alone, against neutral background; Anglo name; lives in USA]: 'CYNTHIA': [Joe] - Suffering, disease, evil, are not the presence of God. They are the absence of God. Darkness does not exist, it is merely the absence of light. Cold does not exist it is merely the absence of warmth. Suffering and evil are not things they are merely the absence of God's grace. Without the occasional absence of light people do not get the rest they need and our bodies do not function properly. Without suffering humans do not grow, both as individuals and as a species.

We will use this as an exercise, a warm-up for your own analysis. What do you see in this example? This first part should not take you more than 15 minutes to answer. First, try to analyse the online social interaction. What do you note about it? What is your analysis of this short interaction, embedded within a much larger set of interactions? What are your initial reactions to it, on any level – intellectually, visually, emotionally, practically? Grab a pen or get your paws on your keyboard and then carefully absorb and read and ponder. Go back to the Seven Interpenetrating Intellectual Implements, the thought processing and manipulating moments of Qualitative Data Analysis. Open your imagination. Visualize the abstraction. Decode cultural meanings. Remember your own Facebook and social networking experiences. Visually and metaphorically abstract to general levels. Let your differing translations compete. Continue to think about the analytic categories, the constructs that you see in the data. Which constructs, which scientific concepts come into your mind first? What abstractions do you perceive? Which theorists and theories are associated with them? Is there something new here? Something different?

ANALYSING THE DATA

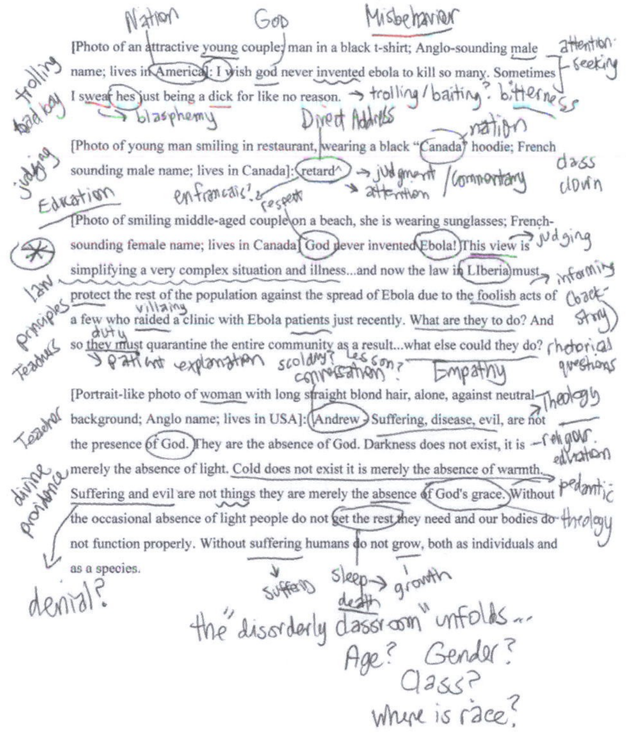

Figure 9.4 My hand-coding of the four Ebola posts

Are you back? Did you give it a try? I would prefer to be there in person to discuss this with you. However, I will begin by sharing my manual coding of the figure in Figure 9.4. I am using manual coding because it is relatively easy to reproduce in a book format, and also relatively easy to perform on a single, short posting. However, if there were 100 or more postings, manual coding would become tedious and awful. Over 500 postings, you would become very angry that you were doing it this way. Over 1000 posts for you to code may be enough to drive you into an angry rage requiring large doses of chocolate (yes, this is a First World Problem for sure). In the following four paragraphs, I unpack my reading of the various parts within this short whole of a dataset.

As you can see from the figure, I treat the entire set of four posts as my dataset. My first reaction to the dataset was to ask myself 'What am I looking for?' To code without knowing why I am coding is very difficult. Therefore, I decided on a very general research question to guide my coding and interpretation. The question I decided upon asked 'What patterns appear when people use social media to share and discuss controversial news?' Did you decide on a question? Did you have particular leanings or inclinations regarding the data and your analysis of it? Did you code with a particular lens, or were you open to simply making observations and letting the common elements appear in a process of pure induction?

My decoding found a number of common elements and patterns in these social interactions. I noted in the first post the Anglo-American viewpoint, male gender, and social situation of the poster. I also noted the lack of capitalization of the word 'god', the word referencing God ('he'), and the incendiary move of calling the Supreme Deity 'a dick' and abstracted this text as an intentional blasphemy. I connected this with higher order notions of motivation, speculating that Joe created this post for the purpose of trolling, attracting attention, and baiting other posters into noticing and responding. Perhaps, however, there is an element of truth to it, of existential agony and despair. A crying out to the Deity or deities against the meaninglessness and pain of this horrific disease. Fear and bitterness may have also been motivating factors. By refusing to capitalize God's name, and by capitalizing his own first-person singular nominative case 'I', Joe may be subtly reflecting his own atheism, or even anti-theism, using the Ebola story as a way to comment on the contradiction between a good God who loves us and the horrors present in our world.

In the next post I also decoded the context of the poster. I see Brian as a young male Canadian, and from this I abstracted again into nationality, into his Anglo North American social situation. In this post, which was only one word, I abstracted Brian's response as a judgement or commentary on Joe's post. I saw some of the same attention-seeking as in Joe's post, but in this case Brian was performing what in theatre, cinema, and soliloquy is known as a 'direct address'. In this narrative technique, a character will speak directly to the audience and seek a more candid connection. Here, I believe Brian was attempting to 'channel the crowd' to immediately and honestly label Joe's remark as silly and irrelevant by curtly dismissing and insulting him. I also note the Latin and French origin of the word 'retard', its origin in the notion of something which slows or protracts, and also abstract from this some of the intellectual tensions between Canadians and their American neighbours.

In the next post, I decode the switch to a female gender and voice, and also note that Marie is a Canadian. Marie's use of capitalization in this post is also interesting. 'God' is capitalized, as are 'Ebola' and 'Liberia'. Nations, deities and diseases are all treated with the proper Respect. So, too, is the prior posting, and a careful explanation is provided. The explanation of the 'foolish acts of a few' is provided as a back-story to give context to the current news story. Empathy is shown to the decision-makers in this difficult circumstance with the statement 'What are they to do?' Laws, principles, duty and order are important elements of Marie's posting. Abstracting to notions of teaching then allows me to connect, particularly to literature that clearly shows how social media performs an informal educational function (e.g., Kulavuz-Onal and Vàsquez, 2013; Roth, 2012; Sandlin, 2007). Marie's entire posting seems informed by a sense of moral obligation to inform and educate.

In the final post, I decode first the female American social situation of the poster. I note how Cynthia directly addresses Joe, by name. Joe – Is this a scolding? A lesson? A conversation? I also note that God is capitalized again, and respect for the Deity is reaffirmed as it was by Marie. Upon rereading and reflecting upon my reactions, Cynthia's post seems less conversation and more of a monologue, or even a sermon. I feel that I am being preached to. 'Suffering, disease, evil, are not the presence of God. They are the absence of God.' Remembering and abstracting lead me to see this as a lesson in theology. With some research, I confirm my suspicion that this is a defence of God that draws upon St. Augustine's argumentation of the privation of good. Evil, suffering and disease are thus in the Facebook posting, as in the Fourth Century Catholic doctrine, insubstantial. Death and suffering become, in the posting, like sleep. There is a quality of denial that I locate in Cynthia's posting that stands in stark contrast to the bitterness of the first post. I read it as an insensitivity. Yet, as with Marie's post, there is also a careful, patient – albeit rather pedantic and lofty – element of teaching.

In the next stage of my analysis, I decided to use a fairly simple textual analysis tool. After cleaning up my data file, removing my added descriptions of people and any extraneous words or comments added by the program (such as the omnipresent Facebook 'like'), I entered the full text in the free online word cloud generator Wordle. What stands out immediately is the presence of Cynthia's 'absence'. She uses the negating word absence so many times that it overwhelms the conversation when considered as a whole. Ebola is important (and capitalized) but so is 'God' and 'suffering'. Also important are ameliorating and negating words such as 'merely' and 'without'. 'Evil', 'light', and 'exist' point to the theological overtones of the postings considered as a whole. Free to float in my imagination, the word cloud itself seems to tell a tale of good and evil, light and dark, warmth and cold, played out in the human world through Ebola and suffering.

Figure 9.5 Wordle word cloud of the four posts in the dataset

I found it interesting to contextualize the four quotes in the entire conversation. In Figure 9.6, I inserted the entire, cleaned up text of the full 56 comments of the news posting. My intention is to compare the subset of the four postings in relation to the entire set. In the entire set, we can see how the major words no longer contain Cynthia's 'absence' – although it does still have some prominence, as does 'God'. Instead, people and disease now hold equal status with Ebola. 'People', it is important to note, is absent from the subset of the four posts. 'Africa', 'cure' and 'just' are also important words. This entire word cloud tells a much more scientific and medical story than does the four post subset, with 'experimental', 'vaccine', 'cure' and 'quarantine' appearing as important constructs, becoming characters in our theoretical narrative.

When I examined the 56 comments as a total set and coded them (a process I do not include here), there are a number of interesting comments and interactions. A pattern emerged in which certain kinds of engagement with the story and questions started the discussion, and then particular segues started to draw in other topics, and in fact multiple paradigms began to jostle with one another, dominated by three particular polarities: religious versus scientific; pragmatic medical versus compassionate/humanistic; and America versus 'the third world'. These categories come from my attempts at Imagining, Abduction and Cultural

Figure 9.6   Wordle word cloud of the entire set of posts in the dataset

Decoding, and resulted from some Tournament Play of competing theories I will not embarrass myself by sharing. These observations led me to this particular subset of the data which falls into the theological vein. However, the same over-all pattern of education and response to education seems to recur no matter how I read this. Re-memorying only makes it louder, and Artifying makes it visually apparent. The big cultural decoding that I keep coming back to involves teaching and the classroom.

INTERPRETING THE ANALYSIS

The next stage takes your analysis as a starting point, and begins to read holisti-cally and holonically for a hermeneutic interpenetration. This exercise should also take you about 20 minutes. Begin by examining your analysis of the data. Look at your categories, your decodings, your abstractions, conceptions and constructs. Try to absorb from your thoughts to which cultural categories the data that you have been using belong. Now, step back from what you have just done. Try using your imagination and then re-memorying a new hermeneutic interpretation. Think about the holonic sphere, and its relations to social interaction and experience, and the way that human social and interactive experiences are designed and connected through technology.

Think about the following guiding questions. Which elements are you considering, and which elements are they composed of in more granular detail? To which higher order units are your elements only ingredients? What are the different elements of this assemblage or articulation? Can you ascertain any archetypal abstract elements from within the visuals of the figure? Can you compare and contrast them for similarities and differences? Now, carefully sit in your thinking chair and devise a set of governing general social media principles, a substantive rule or norm, a general rule of netnography that helps us to precisely explain the sociocultural and technocultural causes behind the various patterns we observe in our interpretation of one particular piece of online social experience data, be it video, audio, photo, image, site, link or text. These rules would comprehensively explain and help us to understand in a new light this one posting, covering its consistencies and patterns and linkages.

Now, ask yourself why I would choose this example? Why would I choose this particular subset of data? What am I trying to say, about my self, about personal branding, about the privacy of identity and social data in the era of the social networking site? Why am I using these words, these terms, and not others? What do they have to do with social media in the era of the micro-celebrity academic? Now, take it to your own inner world. Why do you react in this way? What does this dataset make you feel? What do you discern to be the deeper and perhaps darker, as in hidden in shadows, meaning of this exercise? From which hidden subconscious caves does it spill forth?

As I previewed above, my own hermeneutic interpenetration led me inexorably and somewhat forcefully with its consistency to consider news sharing and discussion in social media as a disorderly classroom, one in which people play out archetypal roles of teachers and students. We know, first of all, that the posting was made by someone like us: a university professor. And one who is well known for being active on social media, someone who has a following and who is most certainly an academic social media brand personality.

Among the interactants, we see Joe playing the role of the attention seeking bad boy. He raises his hand and speaks in order to gain attention and get a reaction. However, his reaction is also somewhat genuine. It has elements of his own unique truth to it, which people detect. Some, like Brian, seek to dismiss his comment. They use the news simply as a forum for interaction in which they can deploy mockery to elevate themselves by dismissing or commenting sarcastically upon others. But others, such as Cynthia and particularly Marie, assume the role of teachers.

Marie is an educational figure par excellence. First she contests Joe's contention that God 'invented' Ebola. However, we never learn whether she contests it based on theological or scientific grounds. She then quickly redirects the conversation back to the matter at hand, the news story about quarantine and its consequences. In the absence of the moderator (in this case, the journalism professor who posted the article, and who, seemingly exhausted by the whole thing or simply distracted or too busy to keep going, drops out of the conversation after a few moderating posts of his own), Marie assumes an organizing role in this network, this temporary minigroup that has assembled in order to discuss, and perhaps to learn and share. Her posting strikes me as humane. There is a hand-wringing quality, a pensive despair in the way she repeats her empathic phrases of the tragedy of difficult decisions: 'What are they to do … what else could they do?'

Cynthia's comments also have a teacher-like quality, but Cynthia is teaching from on high as with a Minister lecturing to her good Christian flock. What Africa needs is more missionary helpers, her tone suggests to me that she thinks. Her sermon is directed at Joe and filled with her scholarly theological learning. It is distanced and apart from Joe's bitterness. In fact, it denies the phenomenon entirely. In what some might see as optimism, Cynthia denies the reality of suffering and pain, perhaps even death. Darkness does not exist. Cold does not exist. We seem to need God's absence in order to grow 'both as individuals and as a species' in her account. And yet human beings perceive darkness. They feel the sensation of cold very clearly, as distinct from comfortable warmth. They feel and suffer and die, despite our fervently believing rhetorical arguments that these are unreal or inconsequential. Cynthia's argument has to deny the ultimate reality of the material world in order to deny God's hand in and lack of response to the suffering of Ebola.

The classroom in this short series of four postings has a gendered quality. The boys misbehave and disrupt, pushing and shoving each other, jostling for attention. The women seek to maintain order, to direct, to teach, to sermonize, to elevate and inform. The boys are younger, the women older. Americans make statement about God and theological truths. Canadians respond to Americans, assuming a less theological worldview. Cynthia's posting is filled with Derridean differance and absence. Where are notions of race? The whiteness of Joe, Brian, Marie and Cynthia seem enormously evident to me not only from their photos, but also from the way they respond. Middle-class and comfortable, it is clear they can discuss, learn, argue about and even play with news of Ebola in a distanced manner. Ebola, at least then, in the pre-Texas Health Presbyterian Ebola outbreak days, seemed non-threatening to North Americans, a safe abstraction, something for the Africans to deal with. These people can empathize, they can theorize, they can try to monopolize conversations, but this Ebola thing is ultimately about those Africans, rather than us. We are debating their human suffering and pain rather than our own.

These notions open up holarchic levels within levels that we can explore further and further. Considered in the context of the full 56 postings, this subset clearly draws us into a linguistic analysis, a coding of the codes used in the discussion. We can start simply: with 'god' corrected to 'God', 'ebola' to 'Ebola', of capitalized 'I' to uncapitalized 'retard'. We can look at the unfolding sequence of these messages, these calls across the electronic sea and their responses.

There is a segue within the overall and initial conversation, which twists and turns like a snake navigating a sand dune. First, it shifts to news and government, then to medical issues and vaccines, then to First World and Third World intrigue (did the CIA really create and plant Ebola? Why don't Americans die of it then?). Each segue inspires correction and teaching, elaboration and new segues. Biological notions of bodily fear are quelled with rationality, religious beliefs and faith in science. Institutional norms of education are played out in familiar fields populated by teacher and student archetypes. Social norms of cohesion are enacted in considerate conversation and correction, even in exemplary lessons on empathic reasoning. Cultural tensions between national identities are subtly enacted. Each of these levels can be examined much further, with additional data within the dataset, collected from other news stories and their responses in social media, building strong bridges to theoretical work in education and socialization, nuancing them with novel content and context.

Now, consider your own work of interpenetration. Reflect upon what it says about you, and about the set of data. This is your interpretation and interpenetration. It should interpenetrate what you see and also inform a data collection strategy for you to further analyse and collect other data. You should conduct ongoing and iterative analyses and interpretations like this as a natural part of your data curation efforts. Collection is classification and classification is always a matter of interpretation. Does this data seem relevant to my research question? Does it offer the potential for new or related understanding? Does it confirm or disconfirm? Does it nuance? Having introduced you in hands-on, toolkit, workbench fashion to the systematic and deliberate, but also still creative, imaginative, linguistic and visually abstract nature of netnographic interpretation, the next section proceeds to provide some nuts and bolts advice about manual and computer-assisted analysis.

THE WORKBENCH LEVEL

It should come as little surprise that practitioners would be among the most advanced developers of social analysis natural language working software. I have worked with one, NetBase of Silicon Valley, and they are a very sophisticated and intelligent group indeed. In Palo Alto, California, they are perfecting processes of gaining mass understanding of existing qualitative data that both drill down and drill up, and in return, throw in the ability to compare and contrast, to segment and cluster, and to conceptually try to make sense of some of the different things you could visually analyse and identify. These are, as I have written about in my white paper for NetBase which is still available online, excellent practical benefits for the netnographer to incorporate digital signal analysis of sophisticated collections of massive amounts of social media data.

Through all of this, the Netnographer struggles to read the threads of human pathways through cultural landscapes of our own creation; institutionalization, revolution, revision and resurrection of ideas and beliefs joined together with stories and histories into ideologies which become institutionalized through norms, customs, traditions, rules and laws, solidified beyond individuals or small groups into only imagined other collectives such as nations or regions or ethnicities or religions. Each of these becomes identities. When individuals inhabit these identities, they become their roles, and this totality, and the questioning of it by themselves and by others, throughout various somewhat predictable dramatic stages, constitutes the core story of a human life. And that core story of a human life is symbolic of the life of the entire Human World. My story. Your story. Our story. The same human story. A true revolution can only start by recognizing that we are all Human. This is the key comparative moment of being an Anthropologist, rather than being merely anthropological. This is the key ethical core of the Netnographer, rather than being a digital anthropologist or an ethnographer of digital media: that a revolution is needed throughout the academic world, and among all thinking beings, that the only thing that will save our species now is a lot of respect across borders and species and systems and a lot of trust and laying down of arms – metaphorical and actual. Actual Beatles-type Love is All You Need stuff. Reprioritizing, quickly, into much simpler lifestyles, simply everyone downshifting, starting now. Everyone worldwide working much less. Less, but much more sharing, by everyone. What other possible solution could work more than starting to find respect for each other, to freely and willingly finally share what is left of the great bounty, and begin to shift it way down to much much simpler lives? There will be very tough calls about expensive things like the medical system, government police, military, education, and so on, but in the end, good decisions will be made by good people. People are much more noble in real life than they are on every single news channel on the planet. That is the reality that I know.

This is a core belief for me. That people are all inherently deserving of respect, no matter their background or accent or skin colour or gender or identity of any kind and as long as it is a good and happy kind. But the difference that divides, that tells us one group is better than another one is the core belief that leads to war. Not the reality of difference: the belief in difference. It comes as much from the human submissive urge, to bow, to hand shake, to feel social anxiety, as it does from the ideologies that build onto that disgusting weakness we all have within us for other people's attention and even, dare we voice it, the deep-seated dream for love. Related directly to love, in this next and upcoming section, you will be dazzled by the three ring presentation of the relative merits of manual and computer-assisted methods of qualitative data analysis in netnography. In particular, you will be confronted at every angle with clown-faced theoretical monkeys that grow to be three feet tall, faced with the tradeoffs that accompany this decision about combining the two things, not pitting them against each other.

Still, one can offer up principles.

1. In keeping with the small scale of exploratory data mining, Humanist and Auto-netnography tend to keep data collection small and local and data analysis close and handy.

   - If you are going to analyse data Humanistically, using your own human intelligence, then this means keeping the analysis process itself as close to your own thinking process as possible.

2. If you store your netnographic data in paper form, try to choose the real gems, the potential diamonds.

   - Remember that a diamond may not be a diamond until you recognize that it answers a more interesting research question than the one you began with.

3. Coding can happen on paper, on screen, in programs, even on dedicated mobile apps. Often, this will mean working in a word processing program such as Word, but using the search functions that are built into the program, and optionally working with paper printouts when you feel that will be helpful. If you are going to analyse data manually, this often entails working with paper printouts, for example 30-page printouts of a long message thread or 15-page printouts of an online interview. You will need to code these printouts, which may require different colours of highlighter, markers or coloured pencils. Be visual, is what we learn from the design schools and scholars. Be visual and use your visual intelligence and capacity to tap the unconscious mind's innate intelligence, and you will see more than you can normally see. Visual abstraction is a physical manifestation of thinking as visual sense. It is one reason visualization is so powerful and has always been recognized as a magical art.

4. Condensation – as you analyse categories you may want to condense the information onto file cards, perhaps physically cutting off pieces of the text and pasting or taping them onto file cards, which you can then organize and reorganize. Your data can become a literal collage. These will be stored in file folders, alongside other file folders, in boxes and cartons, which will need to be carefully labelled so that you can find the documents you are looking for when you need to examine them. If you store your netnographic data in paper form, it is going to take up some space. You will need some files and file labels to catalogue your data and organize them so that you have access to them when you need it.

There are times when the manual, on-paper, off-computer system can work effectively, such as when the dataset is quite small, the researcher is very familiar with the field sites, and the researcher is organized, has a good paper filing system, and prefers to work this way. Using such a system can be an effective way for the netnographer to feel close to the data, and to feel artistically involved in the bricolage and collage-creating curatorial act of analysis. For most netnographers, however, using a pure paper method will very rapidly become unwieldy.

CYBORGIAN PRACTICES

A lot of philosophy has been summed up as seeing the middle way as the moral way, not completely in the world, but not completely disengaged from it, either, more removed however, than present. Being middle way in netnography means being a Cyborg, moving between Machine and Human worlds effortlessly as both one and the same, combining the best of both worlds.

All analyses necessary for a Symbolic, Humanist or Auto-netnography can be completed in programs like Microsoft Word or Adobe Acrobat Pro, alongside basic online analysis programs one can access via browsers such as Wordle and Google Trends. Netnographic analysts save their files in word processing files, and they use the word processing program to automate parts of the data analysis routine. They organize their different downloaded data files into folders and then organize those folders into other folders. They code inside the computer files, perhaps in bold text, highlighting, or using different colours. They use comments to memo to themselves. They use the adequate search and find capabilities of word processing software to conduct text searches that aid them in their coding and classification.

Different levels of coding and abstraction can be organized using table of contents type features in Word, the spreadsheet capabilities of a program such as Excel, or the even-more powerful database capabilities of a program such as Access. Although my early netnographies utilized NVivo and Atlas.ti, I have increasingly relied upon these cyborgian practices of coding in word processing programs, and also printing and coding data by hand (as in the example above). I find that manual coding allows me to feel more creative and inspired, and the physical element of printout, pen and paper creates a sense of closeness with the data that I did not feel when a computer program got between the dataset and me. Cyborgean practice works well for me, and it is perfectly suitable for many types of Symbolic, Auto-, and Humanist Netnographies. It does require some computer literacy, no more than the very basic levels required to actually search and write on a computer, and involves a learning curve to become familiar with the programs and their procedures for coding and search. Within those procedures, there is considerable room for you to add a lot of available text mining, trend and content analysis, and social search information, which abound on the Internet, as well as to flexibly develop routines that are customized and with which you feel comfortable.

The alternative to these methods is to employ software that assists the researcher in their analysis of qualitative data. Some call this software Computer-Assisted Qualitative Data Analysis software, or CAQDAS, for short. Often, social search engines, such as Radian6, Sysomos, Netbase's Consumer Base, or the free online search site Social Mention, combine data mining or web-crawling functions with qualitative data analysis to provide sorted overviews of some of the social data available online. Although I find these programs useful for locating data, their analysis functions are pre-programmed and limiting. They make me feel variously like a squirrel in a cage, a monkey in a bottle, or a toad in a box. It is not a nice feeling to die in a cardboard box, away from the fields and water you love so much.

But I digress. CAQDAS software allows much more flexibility in coding and takes an inductive, bottom-up approach to the analysis of qualitative data. For many scholars, bottoms-up is still the best theoretical position. Data used could include text, graphics, photographs, sound files and music, videos and any other type of non-numerical information. Recognizing the qualities in this data is a qualitative implementation, an act of analysis and interpretation leading to inter-penetration. Sophisticated visualization abilities can assist in analysis, insights, and report presentation. In Digital Netnography, in which the netnographer seeks a more comprehensive and representative overview of particular social fields online, the researcher is confronted with large amounts of data. Where different types of data must be combined and there is a challenge in sorting and storing large amounts, it is the ability to play with data visually and to understand what you are

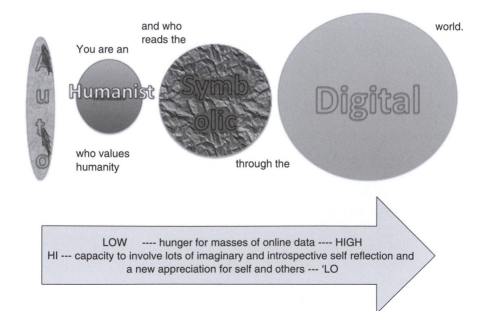

Figure 9.7   The four new netnographies

seeing that will lead the netnographer to more automated analytic methods. This ties directly into the qualitative moment of intellectual insight formation from the implements, namely the need for Visual Abstraction. Here, data is actually used as the source of the abstraction. The challenge becomes reading the cultural meaning out of the visualization.

Decisions about data collection, analysis and interpretation practices are now largely determined by the choice of type of netnography. Auto-netnographies require the least amount of data, relying most of all on fieldnotes and reflexive observation, as well as hopes, dreams, stories, songs, photos, art, and images of Life and Beauty. Humanist netnographies selectively curate manageable amounts of data. Symbolic netnographies collect considerable amounts of data. Digital netnographies hungrily seek out, like a giant mechanical shark, larger and larger amounts of data. Type of netnography, amount of data available, quality of data available, size of field (site, topic or person-related data), conventions of academic field, and the preferences and abilities of the particular researcher all help to determine the analysis tools and techniques in one's repertoire. They can make you pine for explorations of the wild, or they can give you the strength to come back to your true friends in the warm little cabin in the woods. Or, less metaphorically, we might think about it like this.

- Researchers producing work for fields that value thick description, intense focus on the particular and specific, and narrative depth may find the hermeneutic styles of Symbolic and Humanist netnographic analysis more suitable.
- Researchers producing work for fields that affirm the value of statistical evaluations and structural accounts of ethnographic field sites may benefit from conducting Digital Netnographies that utilize the precise coding and statistics calculating capabilities of computational techniques including big data analytics and social network analysis programs. This includes scholars in computer sciences and many in marketing and consumer research, and certainly quantitative geographers, librarians and sociologists.
- Researchers who prefer and are competent with on paper, filing skills should not back down from their extremely defensible human practice. I know many a good scholar who insists on writing things out on paper first, as I did much of this book. There is nothing wrong at all with keeping it simple and close and comfortable. For some, that may mean purely manual data analysis and interpretation methods. That has worked for me more times than not. There is no right or wrong answer. You can write it on paper, or you can work with it in the computer. Netnography is pluralistic and open. It is the core beliefs and ideology of netnography that are even more important than particular practices, although those practices are also rituals that I believe unite us, even if we have never met, or never will.
- There is always a middle ground solution. You can analyse the whole thing using Microsoft Word, Excel, or Adobe Acrobat Pro if you want to.
- Know your own limits. If you tend to be organizationally challenged then you might benefit from the automated organizing and data management apps and bots which ultimately may try to mutiny on you and completely take over your netnography, choking out your now-croaking human voice, trapped like a frog in a shoebox.

Do you want more information about computer-assisted data analysis techniques and programs? Then stay tuned, reader, because the next section will give you a nice bite-sized chunk.

CAQDAS FOR DIGITAL NETNOGRAPHY

In this section, we philosophize about computer-assisted qualitative data analysis; its principles, its uses, it benefits and its drawbacks. We start with a re-memory of an earlier section, in which, together, you and I analysed one short piece of qualitative data, a set of Facebook message postings responding to a shared news story about responses to the Ebola outbreak in Liberia. We conducted our analysis and interpretation by hand, on paper and using an online textual analysis program called Wordle which created a word cloud from the data. However, we could just as easily have performed these functions using a qualitative data analysis program. The same inductive principles would have applied.

Applications and software programs act in effect like sorting boxes that you set up. By highlighting parts of your data, you decide what boxes there will be, how many there will be, and what the boxes will be called. You then place pieces of data, or sections of them, in the different boxes you have created. A YouTube video from an African doctor, a Pinterest page on Ebola cures, a blog about CIA involvement in Africa – all of these can be analysed, coded and sorted into their relevant categories using the program. Instead of manually coding words like 'god', 'Ebola' and 'retard' we would have used the program to tag the words. Instead of using a blue pen to circle phrases like 'What are they to do?', this phrase could have been saved and tagged 'empathy' and 'rhetorical questions'. Instead of memoing 'denial?' and 'trolling/baiting', these terms would have been entered into the program as memos/comments. As we moved up to link 'lesson' and 'education' with 'pedantic' and 'theology' – and then to ask 'Is this a disorderly classroom experience?' – we would be both abstracting and combining categories to imagine possible generalizations which could then be connected to other theories and tested further. From higher-level analysis such as this, theories are constructed.

As we can see from this very simple example, qualitative data analysis programs provide opportunities to relate to data like any other form of qualitative analysis, by identifying and coding recurrent themes, concepts, ideas, processes, contexts, or other relevant constructs. They allow researchers to construct categories for second-order coding and further analyses of relationships. As constructs are coded and relationships between them suggested and tested, explanations or theories can be developed and recorded by the program. All of the major software packages have functionality that allows for searching for particular keywords or related keywords as well as for the retrieval of coded materials.

Computerized 'big data' methods can also be useful when working with a team. They facilitate the sharing of data across a computer network. Skyping with your research team every week: fun and familiar. A virtual organization is a cell of a network, a subsystem even, but it is not a group of people working in the same office.

Many of the current programs have so-called 'natural' language processing functions, which recognize and pre-code certain words or phrases, built in. There are many, including some free and open source packages, such as CATMA, ELAN, TAMS Analyser, and Aquad. As Lewins and Silver (2007) note, the major software packages all offer excellent capabilities in data storage, organization, coding, retrieval and visualization (see also Banner and Albarrran, 2009; Bazeley, 2007; Gibbs, 2014; St. John and Johnson, 2000; Weitzman and Miles, 1995; Wickham and Woods, 2005). Many of them allow you to collect distinct types of netnographic data into a single project, including downloaded text files, saved digital photographs, links to videos, scans of handwritten reflective fieldnotes, and so on.

At any stage of your netnographic data analysis, software applications and programs offer an efficient and effective way to generate reports of your findings. Files can be easily saved, creating a snapshot of analyses, emerging or completed. A variety of printouts and visualizations can be generated as the foundation for pen-and-paper coding exercises. There are at least five strengths of qualitative data analysis packages, some of which come with tradeoffs attached. First, most netnographic data are already in digital form, making their insertion into the program straightforward. Second, there are many integrated search programs that can automatically generate specific datasets by mining the Internet. Third, the programs encourage netnographers to think about their often vast and sprawling dataset as a whole. It is easy to become overwhelmed by large amounts of diverse data. Fourth, and very importantly for some, they can assist in keeping the project organized. Fifth and finally, the visualization options can lead to interesting new creative thoughts. If you enjoy playing with your data and using these to spur your imagination, data visualization gives you more ways to play.

Computer-assisted methods can have drawbacks as well, and we set out five corresponding disadvantages here. First, these programs can encourage a needless hoarding and grabbing of all sorts of irrelevant data. This can lead not only to sorting problems, but also to a wandering, unfocused project that is difficult to code in a comprehensible manner. Second, and relatedly, computer-assisted text searches are easy to conduct but include unintended results. Finding intended results can thus be shunted aside as less relevant or outstanding data substitutes for more relevant and powerful ones. Third, computer files are vulnerable to loss in a way that paper simply is not. A few careless keystrokes can erase months of careful data collection. Always back up your project's dataset on media or on the cloud of online servers. Fourth, computers may make it easy to fall into 'the coding trap' described by Richards (2005: 100). In the coding trap, the researcher conducts ever-increasing amounts of coding and classification, without theory ever seeming to emerge from the data. Fifth, software can help you to create too many ideas, too many categories, thus hindering the development of an elegant and integrative interpretation. As the software enables you to create many new categories, you may be overwhelmed by these and find them stifling your creativity and your ability to use the data to say something new.

There may be a trade-off between efficiency and insight.

In sum, the valuable lesson here is that, regardless of the type of netnography you choose to produce, the employment of analytic tools must be guided not by the capabilities of a software product, but by the interpretive plans and directions of the netnographer. In the next section, we discuss some of those interpretive principles, in particular, those that are adapted to the contingencies of netnographic data.

ADAPTING THE PRINCIPLES OF DATA ANALYSIS TO NETNOGRAPHIC DATA

In this section, we will learn about some of the data analysis concerns particular to netnography. These concerns arise whether we are circling our data hermeneutically, or coding it intensely in a software program. These are real issues that you have to deal with when you are struggling at the workbench level with the data. They occur because netnographic data are different from ethnographic data.

My goal is to give you some analytic strategies to address the physical and non-physical representative nature of these arguments about data. The textual nature of the data and its disembodied quality have been considered problematic in theories that are themselves clearly problematic. Similarly, there is a problem with anonymity. Not putting your name on online interactions and the type of fluid trickster lying, theft, cruelty and identity play that manifests online have been troublesome to cultural analysts.

As discussed previously, the interpenetration of data interpretation and analysis in netnography take seriously the notion of the holon. You must use your Analytic Eye, your auto-netnographer's humanist 'I' to seek out the social assemblages as well as the linguistic articulations behind the institutionalization of affordances, technological, technocultural, and technogenetic.

Interpenetration is the attempt to understanding that stretches from social systems to institutions, organizations, groups and individuals. It looks at the unique and opportunistic clustering of factors that cause events to manifest in particular interactions and experiences.

Interpenetration is a construct and a construction that builds an interpretation by linking the pieces of data to one another and to the curated dataset as a comprehensively holonic whole, placed in context. This curated dataset does not need to be comprehensive. Your interpenetration does not need to encompass every piece of data that you have collected, co-created and produced. Instead, imagine for a moment that you are back with your dataset, analysing it, and you wonder about your rationale for Artifying your dataset? What was your research collage? Your interpretation is an act of assembling, from all of the items you have collected, a thematic piece of art that tells a particular, theoretically enriching and perhaps even spiritually uplifting story. It should be a piece of work that sells your story properly to your proper academic community. But what else can it be? Who else can it comment and speak to and listen out for and help to get what they rightfully deserve as people? What are the things that need to be said in my field, and even to the world, and how can I use netnography best to say them?

In the past, the textual nature of netnographic data has been considered a problem. There were concerns about disembodiment. However, textual netnographic data is no more disembodied than the information in any book. With Facebook, Twitter, YouTube, Instagram and LinkedIn, the data is hardly anonymous and often has attached to it images of actual faces and bodies. A Skype call is virtually embodied. I am looking at your face and your office or house. Hello there. Even when we do have it, and sure we all have that option, anonymity and pseudonymity attract certain types for sure, of people, of messages, and they also in some cases can playfully tell us about identities, experiences and social relations that can be difficult to study elsewhere. It is for this reason that scholars seeking to examine stigmatic or underground behaviours, whether drug and alcohol related, sexual, unethical, marginal or criminal, have been finding netnography efficacious.

Let us consider, for the moment, the idea of using as factual data an anonymous or pseudonymous post. Let us say, for instance, that this is a male in Second Life using a female name, a female avatar, and pretending to be a female. Is this dishonest? Is the person lying about their identity? It is an interesting question, is it not?

Am I dishonest if I tell my best friend something, but I do not tell it to my sister? Am I dishonest if I tell a story to my son very differently than I tell it to my colleagues? Am I dishonest when I wear a costume during a costume party? We each have different social faces. We show faces in contexts. Those different faces, like the mask I choose to don at the costume party, each reveal different aspects both of ourselves and of the many contexts in which we find ourselves. I would not expect anyone to have a simple, uniform, entirely consistent identity: if there is one thing that we know about identity since at least Kenneth Gergen and Hazel Markus, it is that our images of our selves are complex, dynamic, and multifaceted – in this case literally multi-faced. Faces in contexts are what netnographers analyse and interpret. Faces and reactions, systems and technologies are all expected to assume in-formed structures and to be transformed by the network as the network's various contexts transform. And as contemporary social situations and their networks are unceasingly liquid, slipping and dynamic, so too are the contemporary identities that are locked into them.

We are constantly constructing and reconstructing ourselves through context-specific social acts of display. As Taylor (1999) and Carter (2005) note, the study of participants' online personas and the fact that they are different from the personas they use in other social contexts is not problematic. It fails to be a predicament because this alteration of identity is a natural consequence of our social life *everywhere* and not simply some idiosyncratic tendency manifesting itself in our social life online. 'The same freedom which inspires people to mischievously construct deliberate falsehoods about themselves and their opinions also allows them and others the freedom to express aspects of themselves, their ambitions and inner conflicts, that they would otherwise keep deeply hidden' (Kozinets, 1998: 369). Our data analysis needs to emphasize this strength of anonymous or pseudonymous data: these are often more honest, rather than more deceptive. They are a great place to look for truly deep and unvarnished human insight.

In George Herbert Mead's (1938) interactionist approach, the unit of analysis is not the person, but the gesture, the behaviour or the act. This includes the speech act or utterance. Applied to the current context of netnography, every online interaction is a social action, a communicative performance that can be conceived of as a 'language game'. Each photograph, each video, each tag, perhaps even each hypertext click of the mouse, is akin to a 'speech act', an utterance. We must be attuned to a new world where a choice from a drop down menu replaces a shrug, and a cursor's move replaces body language. If so, then every community 'player's' move in the social 'game' is a relevant observational event in and of itself. '[T]hese and other aspects of participants' text-based interaction pose interpretive puzzles for the ethnographers in terms of their relationship to participants' presentation of self' (Garcia et al., 2009: 61). Of course, but scholars like Hope Schau and Mary Gilly answered many basic questions about even early Internet dweller's willingness not only to share their identities, but to publicly display their brand tastes and uses.

Even though personal data on people's identities is increasingly easy to find, and rather straightforward to incorporate into our analysis and interpretation (as in my Facebook posting example in this chapter), a netnographer following Pragmatic–Interactionist principles does not necessarily need to know exactly 'who' is doing such things. She might initially be concerned with the observations of 'interactive acts' in the 'game' that is played on online fields of sociality and interaction. One of the key acts of netnographic interpenetration involves contextualizing the meaning of interactions and experiences in ever-widening circles of social significance.

Therefore, netnographic data analysis must include the graphical, visual, audio, and audiovisual aspects of online social interaction – the *experience* of it. Each experiential aspect is a communication event of importance. Hine's (2000) analysis of websites is exemplary in this regard. She carefully interprets choice of photos, choice of arrangements for the photos, and use of backgrounds. She employs her visual analysis to reach conclusions about how people use online interaction to convey emotional messages about a famous murder case. Merely understanding the words that are exchanged online is only a part of the netnographer's job. Are you experienced, queried the psychedelic Jimi Hendrix. Netnographers – you should be able to answer with a yes.

We need to dispense entirely with the unstable and unsustainable division between the virtual and the real, the online and the off, the word and the thing, the art and the artist, the artifice and the maker, the communication and the communicator.

Netnography studies the realm of these communications and social interactions. The interactions are real. The communications are real. The social fields we interact in online exist quite concretely. The people at the other end of a Facebook post or a Tweet are no less real than the people who talk to us on the telephone, author the books we read, or send us personal emails. With Skype, we get the tonality of in-person communication. We would have many of the same issues with the autistic YouTube video blogger Amanda Baggs if we were to interview her in Skype as we would if we were to interview her in person. However, if we were to analyse the content of her production, *In My Language*, on YouTube, as Ginsburg (2012) did, then we would be granted an entirely new perspective on her and on her disability, as she intended.

This raises a thought about social being. Human being is, in some ways, analogous to a disability. We all carry with us our imaginatively internalized weaknesses, our stutters and anxieties along with the strength of our hopes and dreams. We carry them in our bodies; this is what we would hope to pick up in person and through Skype. A slight change in pitch, an uncertain pause. A quick turn downward of the eye at a sensitive question. Voice cracking when we make some lofty statement of big belief or ambition. A long pause. A refusal to answer. These are important dynamics we regain through a Hangout or Facetime interview that we do not have in text.

However, let me say a few deep words in appreciation of words. Words being posted online, we are not giving up on you, not one little bit. Texts are wonderfully intriguing truths in their own right. They are tools of communication, too, just as are our bodies, and they have their own true languages. Emoticons, punctuation, capitalization, phrasing and language use: these are the kinesics and proxemics of textual self-expression on the net. They are as embodied as a fingerprint or an eyescan. Steeped in meaning, cultural and personal, their interpretation is the sacred task of the netnographer. I love text.

The interesting cultural netnographies yet to be performed are those which move across text and video, individual and group, art and spreadsheet, introspective self-reflection and data, language and cultural groups to unite and inform us about their interrelationship with each other.

Creating our own Communications

The limitations of the past are gone. Anonymity has dissolved. It is a new human world, full of faces, full of potential. The netnographer becomes a combination of a scribe, a historian, an interpreter, a storyteller and even a filmmaker.

Interpenetration takes the raw material, the raw nuggets of diamond, ruby, sapphire and emerald. It polishes them to perfection, mounts them, presents them as research representation. Along the way there are many decisions to make, many practices to enact. These partake in a guild-like set of analytic social science traditions. There are entire crafts, entire colonies of workers and trainers who can skill you in the Magnificent Seven Arts of Imagining (colour is purple), Re-Memorying (colour is indigo), Abduction (colour is green), Visual Abstraction (colour is solar yellow), Artifying (colour is the orange of the heart chakra), Cultural Decoding (colour is gray), and Tournament Play (colour is red), but to them we also add the folklorist's respect for narrative, the historian's sensibility for classification and miscellaneity, and the producer's delight in creating something accessible, entertaining and new. Furthermore, we add to these a choice among four different types of netnography: Symbolic, Digital, Auto- and Humanist. We learned, in so doing, the creed of the netnographer: you are an auto humanist who values humanity and who reads the symbolic through the digital world. Of course this humanist creed unites the four directions of netnography. Each path leads to a different experience and outcome. Do you want to know more about these four kinds of netnography? You do? Well that is great, thanks a lot, because the next chapter leads you on a guided analytic tour of these four new categories of netnography, with many examples. Let us see what happens to analysis as we build it into a research representation.

SUMMARY

This chapter explained and illustrated netnographic data analysis and interpretation. Using the word interpenetration and the metaphor of collage and curation, the text walks you through the seven intellectual implements, tools and exercises that you can use to analyse any complex qualitative data, but constructed especially for the research experience design of netnography, and completely native to that approach. Hermeneutic interpretation as well as the notions of holons and holarchic systems relate to the analytic and interpretive needs of netnographers. A detailed example shook down a tiny particularly specific Facebook coverage of a new story about government response to an Ebola outbreak. The final section provided the nuts and bolts of three types of data analysis and interpretation. Software analytics and digital approaches were discussed, with attention paid clearly to the fact that social media analytics and netnography have been converging for a long time, but there is more to the netnography repertoire or story than merely this. On closing, the chapter offered thoughts about the uniqueness of netnographic data and its analysis.

KEY READINGS

Miles, Matthew B. and A. Michael Huberman (1994) *Qualitative Data Analysis: An Expanded Sourcebook*, 2nd edn. Thousand Oaks, CA: Sage.

Silver, Christina and Ann Lewins (2014) *Using Software in Qualitative Research: A Step-by-Step Guide*, 2nd edn. London: Sage.

Spiggle, Susan (1994) 'Analysis and interpretation of qualitative data in consumer research', *Journal of Consumer Research*, 21 (December): 491–503.

10
REPRESENTATION

REPRESENTATIONAL DIVIDE

What we are witnessing is a politicisation far more radical than any we have known in the past, because it tends to dissolve the distinction between the public and the private, but in terms of a proliferation of radically new and different political spaces. We are confronted with the emergence of a *plurality of subjects*, whose forms of constitution and diversity it is only possible to think if we relinquish the category of 'subject' as a unified and unifying presence. – Ernesto Laclau and Chantal Mouffe (1985: 152)

REPRESENTATIONAL CRISES

Forget 'the subject'. Forget individuality. The individual no longer makes sense as the sole unit of analysis because we have such massive and amazing detail on the network. All individuals are connected into networks: kinship, economic, territorial, tribal, social. These networks exist in institutional and ideological realities, experiences that are largely designed, constructed and marketed by industry professionals. The industry that studies the existence of cultures such as this one, both ancient and modern, cultures which include all of their technologies and implements, is Anthropology.

And Anthropology has been at the centre of issues of scientific representation since the so-called Crisis of Representation in the 1980s. In *Writing Culture*, one of the milestone anthropological documents of this self-critical questioning of ethnographic authority, Clifford and Marcus (1986: 10–11) write that a range of different literatures and their epistemological stances, including among them hermeneutics, neo-Marxism, post-structuralism, post-modernism, deconstructionism and feminist theory,

> share an overarching rejection of the institutionalized ways one large group of humanity has for millennia construed its world ... what appears as 'real' in history, in the social sciences, the arts, even in common sense, is always analysable as a restrictive and expressive set of social codes and conventions.

When the dust had finally settled on the twentieth-century's scientific studies of language, from de Saussure and Jacobson to Worf, Sapir, Foucault and Wittgenstein, the fact remained that somehow, in the mind, likely in the brain as well, language constructs reality through symbolic representation. For human beings, there is no escape from the fact that the world itself is constructed of shared symbols that are constantly being interpreted and translated by our bodies. Some are rock solid, institutionally moored and stable through millennia, like the notion of a golden crown for a Ruling King. Many are highly variable, highly dynamic. Some social experiences can differ radically in the morning from the evening. They can change within a minute, like an emotion, or linger for weeks like a phase. The act of qualitative research is built into our bodies, into our sensory organs and the way they connect to awareness and thought. Ideas germinate in this physical place, they bubble up as if from some hidden inspirational wellspring.

Clifford and Marcus (1996: 11) wrote that the impact of the fact that ethnographers were actually creating their representational reality, rather than representing reality, 'is beginning to be felt' in ethnography. Almost assuredly, they intended their own volume's strong voice to amplify the social constructionist post-structural signal, which it most certainly did.

Seven Moments of Representation

Drawing on works such as *Writing Culture* as evidence of disjuncture, Denzin and Lincoln (2005) divide the history of contemporary ethnography into eight cross-cutting, overlapping historical 'moments'. We can look at seven of these moments and see how each one of them came with a representational style. These phases of ethnography ideas overlap the notions of scholars of the crafting of ethnography, such as John von Maanen (1988), who treats the history of ethnography as if it were a history of ethnographic writing which, in fact, it is.

1. First was the *traditional* moment, lasting from the early 1900s until the post-World War II period.

During this time, writing and conceiving of ethnography follow four 'classic norms in anthropology': objectivism, complicity with colonialism, social life structured by fixed rituals and customs, and ethnographies as monuments to a culture (Denzin and Lincoln, 1994). From this phase we gained many of the methodological conventions of (writing about) ethnographic fieldwork, such as immersion in a particular field site, (writing about) learning and using the local vernacular of the natives, and collecting stories and traditional materials face-to-face from culture members (in order to write about them later). Always, we are turning reality into its representation. In this stage, that awareness was barely present. The omniscient voice of the ethnographic narrator declared the cultural truth as if it was channelling a scientific deity.

2. The next phase, the *modernist* moment, extended through the post-World War II years to 1970 and writing in this sphere built on the canonical works of the traditional period.

Much was learned in the effort to make anthropological findings more commensurable with those of other social sciences. However, and unlike sociology and psychology, the widespread attempts to make ethnography more quantitatively scientistic were widely considered a failure.

3. In the wake of the modernist movement's failure, the *blurred genres* moment, lasting from 1970 to 1986, was characterized by the emergence of a plethora of different paradigms, theories, methods and strategies.

The field flourished. Flowers of hermeneutics, symbolic interactionism, phenomenology, ethnomethodology, critical (Marxist or Marxian) theory, post-structuralism, semiotics, feminism, neopositivism, deconstructionism, ethnic paradigms, and historical, biographical, dramaturgical and documentary methods bloomed. Many of these approaches were inspired by and attempted to hybridize techniques from the humanities, an interesting movement which set the table nicely for the big breaks of the Crisis of Representation.

At that stage, communications broke down, as our ability to actually understand and objectively communicate objective reality itself became questioned. It was during this period that Clifford Geertz (1973) suggested that the boundaries between the social sciences and the humanities had become blurred.

Galvanized by sociological advance summarized in Berger and Luckmann's (1966) *The Social Construction of Reality*, interpretivism was developed as a school of thought devoted to the goal of understanding the complex world of lived experience from a phenomenological perspective (Schwandt, 1994). The criteria underlying interpretive anthropology (Denzin, 1997; Geertz, 1973) favour grounded meanings, richly detailed or thick description, and use the metaphor of reading and interpreting a complicated text for the reading of a given culture. It is these principles that still tap deeply into a certain vein of ethnography, and this conduit certainly feeds my own field of consumer research, and through it netnography.

4. According to Denzin and Lincoln (1994), the *Crisis of Representation* moment in ethnography began in the mid-1980s and lasted until 1990.

It is a profound rupture. The very foundations of ethnographic representation are questioned. Ethnography literally means writing about a culture, the word itself is about the representation, the presentation, of the Other, of that which is different from you, and yet, somehow, reveals you, as it does for all great travel storytellers of the past, and all journeys even.

Clifford and Marcus' (1986) insight that language equals reality in ethnography shook to its core the legitimacy of ethnography as traditionally practised. An anthropologist could never again be a naïve writer. Her eyes once opened, she can never again be blind to the fact that ethnography's scientific documentation is created, it is fabricated, it is curated in a very personal way. As Denzin and Lincoln (2005: 3) put it: 'Here researchers struggled with how to locate themselves and their subjects in reflexive texts'. In this moment, it all became about the writing itself. The ethnographic text was suddenly not just about reporting the transparent conduct of fieldwork and cultural learning, but also the loaded politics of writing and representation in an academic context, often with colonial implications, always with the workings of influence and power, and almost always with the stronger and more compelling human voice of the anthropologist speaking louder and clearer.

5. The *postmodern* moment lasting from 1990 to 1995 was the first stage of a response. Experimentation was the order, the watchword, the zeitgeist of the day.

In work that clearly informs Clifford and Marcus' *Writing Culture*, Marcus and Cushman (1982: 26–27) overview the 'experimental ethnographies' taking place in anthropology. They find considerable 'creativity' that 'is not only required but also encouraged' and identify and discuss a number of 'ethnographers who couch their work in more personal and [like-a-novel] structured ways. In this emergent situation, ethnographers read widely among new works for models, being interested as much, if not more, in styles of text construction as in their cultural analysis, both of which are difficult to separate. Thus, the current trend is characterized by texts that are very personally written and almost autobiographical, or auto-ethnographic, in places. Further, Clifford and Marcus (1986: 13) find that these new and 'divergent styles of [ethnographic] writing]' are not only creative and personal but also 'construe science as a social process' and thus question the 'authority of a scientific discipline' as a matter of discursive representation that will 'always be mediated by … claims of rhetoric and power'.

6. Denzin and Lincoln (2005) see the next moment of *post-experimental inquiry* lasting from 1995 to 2000.

In this relatively short period, they aver that the field continues to play, refine, brainstorm, try, experiment, combine and develop lots of possible responses to the language and reality representation puzzle. All this work lends a more settled and mature air of suave sophistication to research choices. No longer is ethnographic writing innocent. We don't have to always state it, but it is now accepted and clear. And suddenly what happens again? Greater and greater levels of social consciousness move back into the evaluation of ethnographic texts. Humanity's sophisticated study of itself continues to bloom.

7. The seventh moment is the *methodologically contested present*, a time of great methodological and epistemological diversity as well as upheaval. There is tension, conflict and retrenchment. Practices of inquiry are regulated and re-regulated in order to conform to 'conservative and neoliberal programs and [political and related policy] regimes' (Denzin and Lincoln, 2005: 1116).

It may also be possible to say that major trends in anthropological writing and thinking about the world, as the two are inextricably interconnected and interrelated, swing between different polarities, like a pendulum does, between positive and negative, optimistic and dystopian, Liberal Socialist Democratic and Conservative Republican Libertarian, reality and symbolism, acceptance and activism.

Say what we may about its overly orderly classifications of moments, we can discern clearly from Denzin and Lincoln's seven moments the asteroid-like impact that the Crisis of Representation had on the field of ethnography. Ethnography, after all, is an act of one or more persons writing about other people's culture. If this act of representation is suspect, so too is the entire ethnographic enterprise. The Crisis of Representation was a crisis mainly for those who believed that science was True, rather than believing it was the truest version of reality that we could currently devise.

Post-crisis Representation as the Liberation of Expression

For those who were already attuned to the contingent elements of scientific truth-making, the crisis was actually liberating. It allowed scholars like Norman Denzin, Kenneth Gergen, Caroline Ellis, Laurel Richardson and Carole Rambo Ronai, among many others, to experiment with the forms, styles and presentation modes of their scientific craft. For those already on the humanistic boundaries of science, critical theorists engaging with visions of social betterment and cultural studies scholars taking seriously the effects of media and popular culture, the spreading crisis encouraged them to take even greater risks in term of how they delivered their messages.

We might think of the hermeneutic aspect of ethnographic interpretation as encouraging a type of folkloric study that seeks to preserve or even enrich the storied essence of the research tale, a practice epitomized by the genre of ethnographic fieldwork accounts and perhaps reaching its apex with the late Carlos Castañeda's endlessly fascinating and controversial works. Innovative and evocative scholars across many fields have been pushing paradigmatic and methodological boundaries by seeking to incorporate and systematize dramatic and humanities-inspired forms of scientific research representation. I find Carole Rambo's exemplary work in sociology to be moving, disturbing, evocative, scholarly, powerful and informative. Here, she writes about her own sexual abuse as a child:

> If I hid from him well, like in the tangles of the sheets and blankets of the unmade bed, careful to hide the outline of my body, and stayed hidden long enough, he might forget the whole idea. When he caught me, or when I cooperated, he would remove my panties and place me on the bed, my bottom propped up on a pillow. He would part my legs, forcefully if necessary, while holding me down ... These are my earliest memories of my father. I am a survivor of child sex abuse. I am also a sociologist, a wife, a friend, and many other identities one might imagine for an adult, White female. The boundaries of these identities converge, blur, and separate as I write, which is why I use a 'layered account' (Ronai, 1992) to convey my story. (Ronai, 1995: 395–396)

Rambo, writing under her former name Carole Rambo Ronai, defines a 'layered account' as an ethnographic reporting technique that combines 'a theory of consciousness' with a method of reporting. 'The layered account offers an impressionistic sketch, handing readers layers of experience so they may fill in the spaces and construct an interpretation of the writer's narrative. The readers reconstruct the subject, thus projecting more of themselves into it, and taking more away from it' (Ronai, 1995: 396).

In other works, Rambo writes ethnographically about her experiences as a strip-tease dancer. She uses the metaphor of 'sketching' on a 'mystic writing pad' where impressions are made on the pad, erased from the celluloid surface, but remain on the easel's undersurface of dark wax. Traces and layers accrete, disjoined and discontinuous. Through this analogy, Ronai (1998: 410) instructs us that:

> The meaning of being a researcher or a dancer is not inherently present in itself. These identities exist in the traces of the past and in the context of the unfolding situation as it dissolves into the future. The final meaning of what it means to be a dancer or a researcher is always deferred because there is no absolute starting point from which to triangulate these identities.

Inserting fragments; opening spaces for our own interpretation and understanding to emerge, mixing them with personal narratives; citing scholars, ideas and literatures' reflecting on the act of doing ethnography – these accounts have power and influence. More than that, to me it resonates. It resonates with truth value to say that identities are constructed in the moment, always forming and unforming, so meaning is never stable, it is sometimes not even present. To me, this aspect of the human condition, this uncertainty which is acceptance and understanding, too, acceptance of others with different beliefs, others who are very different from us, this aspect is what Rambo's work dives into, something difficult to discern and yet incredibly vital to us in an age of terrible despair, hatred and terrorism.

Towards Play and Poetry

Inspired by these literatures and forms, my own dissertation work used a script format to portray the tangled and contradictory set of positions that constitute ethnographic research and its search for a unified authorial position and voice. Adapting them for the netnographic task at hand, I paraphrase that work here:

The Scientist: Netnographic research is based on participant-observation. Thus, it is fundamentally, inescapably, realist. We are inscribing *real* events involving *real* people and trying to find out their *real* interpretations of social media experiences and interactions. We're collecting qualitative *data*, but that doesn't mean we have to turn all fuzzy-headed and obscurantist when we analyse it. What we should be doing is using it and combining it with massive amounts of data, using analytics to help us generalize, finding lucid, latent patterns and ideas that might be useful to other social scientists across many research fields.

The Poet: No. [*pounding a fist on the desk*]. You're. Totally. Completely. Absolutely. 100%. WRONG! If you'd ever bothered to read postmodern and especially poststructural critiques you'd know that and I wouldn't have to keep repeating myself. You honestly cannot assign one interpretation of 'reality' predominance over the infinity of others. What is 'really real' is indecipherable. This work will never be capital-T truth. I don't care what silly method you use. They are all liars and cheats and tricksters. Just like me.

The Scientist: For once you've said something I can agree with. In scientific realism, certainty is acknowledged as impossible. And that's especially true when we're talking about a rapidly changing social phenomenon like online experience. However, we can talk certainly about probabilities. And about certain probabilities with a high degree of confidence in our predictions.

The Poet: That probably means score another point for me. All we can say about this work, *all* we can truly say, is that it's a really real simulation of reality. So it's experimental. It plays with language. It's unstable in some ways. Lots of what I'd call parenthetical material. It invites the reader or readers to construct her or his or their own meanings and conclusions. That's why we are doing this. Can you see your self, your own thoughts, within the words you read to yourself from the page right now?

The Scientist: [*glaring*] Get back into the text and do not embarrass us. Let us set things straight here. We want to fix our meanings and conclusions as clearly as we can by defining our terms precisely and doing a thorough job of analysis. Otherwise we have said nothing.

The Poet:	[*almost rising out of his chair*] Are you denying the innate polysemy of language? [*raising his eyes*]. What are you doing on the pages of an interpretive book like *Netnography: Refedined*, then? Go find yourself an economics textbook to preach in. Lord, give me strength.
The Scientist:	Why are you so *extreme*? It's contingent. It's all contingent. Under what preconditions does this or that statement hold? We just need to specify the preconditions. The boundary conditions. The contexts.

The fact that I chose to illustrate key ethnographic tensions in my dissertation work through an argumentative and emotional debate between a scientist and a poet seems no accident. Poetry has for me long been a source of humanist wisdom and a technique for drawing forth my own self-realizations. Roel Wijland, a creative Kiwi thinker in this area, hired a celebrated poet to write some poems about open-ended topics such as the role of brands. From that poet's work, Wijland (2011: 139) reaches definite conclusions about a particular construct that he calls 'poetic agency':

> The textures of poetic agency expressively matter marketing's meanings, both at the heights of its spectacular theatricality and at the dog food level of things. The stories of consumer culture and its brands and their fitting academic narratives please the intellect and our sense of order ... It's perhaps as far as language and the imaginative white spaces in between the lines can take us to a situated approximation of agency in marketing and consumer behaviour.

The core argument is one of attempting to represent the unspeakable, that which cannot be adequately captured in the thought representations which are words, and can more adequately be evoked in the body by symbols that evoke deep memories. Sherry and Schouten (2002: 218) also 'show poetry to be both a vehicle of researcher reflexivity and a form of research inquiry in its own right'.

The use of poetic, as well as video, scripts, visual arts and all manner of artistic forms in the social sciences uses the crisis of representation to take advantage of the 'expressive aspect of the arts as reflections on and statements about profound human experiences' (Abu-Lughod, 1986: 177), the very essence of the ethnographic and netnographic enterprise.

Pilgrims and Poets

After my first ethnography of Burning Man, during which I shot over 20 hours of video, I was asked to present some early results at a 'heretical' – and thus very open-ended – preconference to my field's major research conference. Without contemplating my method, but simply seeking to express my powerful encounters in Black Rock City, Nevada, I got to work immediately splicing together a video montage of observations and interviews. In many ways, this montage style now reminds me of Rambo's 'layered account', described above. Weaving a narrative for the video was an almost unconscious act: I wrote a poem about my research journey that sought to connect the various images and interviews I had selected. Research participation in observation, and observation of my own and others' participation. The entire process was one of the most organic and natural acts of creation I have ever experienced.[1] Along with a number of photographs I took at the event, the poem was published in the journal *Consumption, Markets and Culture* (see Kozinets, 2002c).

Desert pilgrim,

Scribbling

Your thoughts

Like writing on water

Hiding

Behind your camera

Face

Your silent

Mask of

Science, your veil

Of words and badges.

Poetry, video, photographs, autobiography, sketches, introspective narratives: these all provide us with opportunities to deepen the experience of receiving the ethnographic representations of social science, making it more resonant, more physical, more visceral, more compelling, more embodied. You either believe in an ineffable, or you do not. You either believe that there is something beyond words and atonal and unitonal vibrationally captured rationality and conscious level individual understanding, or you do not. If you do believe in this ineffable, then you may well believe that we need something like poetry, or art, or human level performance to express it.

a rabbit's foot, a

toy tarantula, a

yellowjacket robot

armed to sting,

his sacrifice

a sacrificing too

an avenging Isaac

to my awkward

Abraham

(Sherry and Schouten, 2002: 228)

This poem was written on the occasion of the author's divorce or, more properly, on the annunciation of his impending separation and departure from home to his youngest son. It is the literal capturing of an actual event, whose component parts become metaphors for the life-stage developments/traumas the protagonist and antagonist have begun to experience. Such powerful words inhere in John Sherry's resonant words about separation, divorce, toys, things, beliefs, myths, emotions, identities and times.

But, critics might argue, what if John Sherry's post-hoc and opportunistic utilizing of his poem was not really a truth so much as a fabrication, what would that mean? 'Fabrication represents the activity of combining, molding, and/or arranging elements into a whole for a particular purpose' (Markham, 2012: 338). Fabrication is not 'value-laden' (ibid.). Fabrication is involved; it is intricately enfolded even, in interpretation, a penetration between worlds of individual fantasy and collective reality, a process of storytelling we have always known as fiction in the mass media. Fabrication without ill intent is just storytelling. It is the intent that is different.

What is the difference if we retell reality in a more dramatic way and authorize it with our science rather than our fiction-writing skills? In both, we seek positive impact upon the public. For a scholar, which is a much deeper relationship with the world of ideas than a student, a scientist, a non-fiction writer, or a mere economic actor-worker, our intent is to learn and to teach. For a fiction author it is to entertain and to inform – these goals are not so different after all it seems. Everything converges in the present time, amplified within media worlds of expanded academic brand engineering and social media opportunities.

Netnography as Representational Practice

Although the last several chapters describe movements towards collecting, analysing and otherwise working with the qualitative data that people share through social media and on Internet, in the end netnography is not really a method. Ultimately, as with ethnography, netnography is an act of writing. Netnography: writing about people's networked social interactions. As the diversity of approaches that fills this chapter and the next one, and indeed the entire book, attests, a netnography can be almost anything that one calls a netnography: quantitative, visual, audiovisual, poetic, purely textual, theoretical, abstract, and so on. As long as we engage in the five archetypal netnographic research practices, which follow in the next section, then this is a netnography. Equally as important is that the author links to the extant multidisciplinary body of work on netnography, builds upon it, and call her or his own work a netnography.

Netnography is not merely an extension of ethnography. It is also a way to rethink the role of scholarship, communication, understanding and academia in a social media environment. It is an integrated system of scientific research and its representation, but it is also an act of differentiation. Netnography is different from traditional academic products. We will see more of its iridescent glory when we take a closer look in the next chapter at Humanist Netnography, a practice of understanding and social action. However, before we proceed to describe the four kinds of netnography, identified partially through patterns in the set of netnographies published thus far, let us transition swiftly from these more open-ended introductions into more coherent and focused descriptions of the five research practices that are archetypally netnographic.

FIVE ARCHETYPAL PRACTICES OF NETNOGRAPHY

The five common research practices and goals among all four types of netnographic research are as follows:

1. Netnography involves participant-observation (see Chapter 8 for details)

   a. Simple observational downloads, web-crawling, or data mining are insufficient without researcher participation. The presence of the researcher's or researchers' experience in research representation – however conceived – is key.

2. Netnography seeks to describe and theorize the human element of online human and technological interaction, social interaction and experience (see Chapter 5)

   a. Netnographers may find useful the concept of technogenesis; 'the idea that humans and technics have coevolved together' (Hayles, 2012: 10), for example the idea that bipedalism coevolved with tool manufacture, and that there is a reciprocal causation whereby the changes that technology makes also inspire adaptations in what it means to be a human. This is a task for present-day archaeologists of all sorts, because we know that interacting with digital media, especially reading and writing on the web, result in neurological changes that rewire the brain as a result of the human-techne interaction.

   b. What is 'human' is a deeply personal matter known only to you. This is a big part of what you try to, and inevitably always do, express in your netnography.

   c. A corollary of this is that human stories are cherished in netnographic practice and preserved intact through the process.

3. Netnography focuses primarily on data collected through the Internet (see Chapter 7)

   a. Using computers, laptops, tablets and mobile devices, such as smartphones and their apps.

   b. Collected in interviews, such as on Skype, through a Facebook window, using Twitter, through email, or another method.

   c. But it need not rely exclusively upon this data. It can for instance interview people in person first, then learn their online habits and favourite places, and then cruise those places, both with those people and then, later, alone, as a researcher, an investigator, a participant.

4. Netnography adheres to strict and widely accepted standards of ethical online research (see Chapter 6), especially as:

   a. Online social interactions are considered to be research with human beings, rather than static relations with texts.
   b. Archival research is non-interfering until disclosed, 'interference' as in positive and negative effects of disclosure are to be determined.
   c. Research representations of other peoples' textual products can potentially cause harm, and this harm must be estimated and weighted in a consequentialist system against potential benefit; in a deontological system of ethics, however, you do not want to do any harm. In that case fabricated scenarios and personas are an option, as are videographic and poetic re-enactments.

5. Netnography always includes human intelligence and insight as a major, but not always exclusive, part of data analysis and interpretation

   a. A hermeneutic interpenetration, as described in Chapter 9, must be a part of the act of creating research insight from data.

All but the third element place netnography in a direct lineage from the anthropological practice of ethnography. The third element is, in fact, what differentiates netnography. Taken in toto, these five practices and goals do not represent a break or rupture, but a rigorous adaptation of netnography, an adaptation that grew, native, from within the copper arteries and silicon flesh of the human Internet. With these five practices elaborated, we can move on to the heart of the chapter and begin to explore the four different kinds of netnography.

THE FOUR TYPES OF NETNOGRAPHY

From its very inception, the purpose of netnography has been to provide researchers with concrete understanding and practices to guide their research of online social interactions. In this, my aims and motivation have always coincided with Bruno Latour's traditionally anthropological call to 'follow the natives'. The method originated when I realized through in-person fieldwork of a local Toronto *Star Trek* and general media fan community that much of the social 'action' was occurring online. Following the natives led me to a netnography that conceptualized online communications, interactions and experiences as contemporary extensions of more traditional communication methods such as in-person meetings and telephone calls. The similarities and differences could be observed and theorized over different conditions and times.

As soon as I began writing different netnographies, and as others joined in and began composing their own, the subtleties of the approach began to shift and change. There were assertions of purely observational netnography, which I believe I started. A strange invention to do netnography without the participative component, or with it seriously underplayed, as if you could lop off the head of a donkey and then call it a man. Because I began with word counts and qualitative data analysis software does not mean that anyone also or everyone else has to do the same thing. However, why not do it? Why not expand the field of netnography? And so it began.

As a field, we began combining the method with computer-assisted methods of search, data collection and analysis very early. In fact, without sophisticated search engines and browsers, netnography could not exist. Netnography is a totally native technique, because it was born with the Web, with Mosaic, programming in html, the first https URLs and Yahoo. Through it all, I have been trying to listen. To watch my fellow scholars play and experiment and express through netnography. To discern some patterns.

In this chapter and the next, I present what I have found. There are four paths you can choose. Four ideal types of netnography, ideal in structure and form. Each type represents a research direction. It represents decisions taken that impact and are impacted by your research focus and topic, research question, data collection strategy and approach to analysis. As we move closer to pure representation, however, netnography reinvents itself only bare slivers away from the digital arts. As products, netnographies must be scientific, informative and consistent. However, they also must perform literary or creative works. They should, in places, try to channel sweet elements of joy and bitter ones of betrayal. Evoke the human experience of interaction, relationship and 'membership' as do so many good ethnographies. Discussions, descriptions and proclamations of field immersion and engagement are the promissory notes that assure the reader that the researcher has invested her time and resources in learning the codes and languages of the culture that she professes to represent. The netnography, however, is where the dancer shows that she can dance. The following sections of this chapter talk about this dance, where the dance represents the different representational styles in netnography.

Initially, we can think of the different kinds of netnography through the apparently transparent, but actually delicate, obscurantist and fragile figure of the windowglass. The windowglass will contain the two essential qualities of roles/tools and human and technological voices. Consider roles and tools first. From the beginning, netnography contained a tension between our archives, software tools and ourselves. Our human understanding as beings in a world of increasingly intimidating and empowering technology was always an implicit part of any netnographic research question: 'As data analysis commences (often concomitant with data collection), the netnographer must contextualize the online data … Software solutions such as the QSR NVivo and Atlas.ti qualitative analysis packages can expedite coding, content analysis, data linking, data display, and theory-building functions' (Kozinets, 2002a: 64).[2] However, and standing alongside these software 'solutions', 'perhaps even more than with ethnography, some of the most useful interpretations of netnographic data take advantage of its contextual richness and come as a result of penetrating metaphoric and symbolic interpretation (Levy, 1959; Sherry, 1991; Thompson, 1997) rather than meticulous classification' (ibid.). The narrative voices we deploy and the analytic tools we employ determine the netnography we will craft, as follows (see Figure 10.1).

- If we speak in a technical or specialized voice, linguistically, and we do it using a human role, this is a Symbolic Netnography.
- If we, (1) use a technical and technological, highly calculative and computer-assisted voice, which is highly specialized, and (2) also focus more on the technology tools of software application-enabled download, capture, processing and visualizing, than we do on the human roles of analysis, introspection and interpenetration, then we are focusing on Digital Netnography.
- If we (1) use our most plain and simple human voice, tracing out and sharing our own personal network, our own private social media communications and thoughts and essences, and (2) do it in a way that favours the most human of roles over the use of highly technical computerized tools, then this act of deeply technocultural and code-switching interpellation is called the Auto-netnography.
- Finally, if we are willing to deploy any technologies possible, but to humanize them, as with video, music, sound, art, performance, and dance, because we are insistent that we make them accessible to a wider social audience through social media personal branding, then we are performing the Humanist Netnography.

These Roles, Tools and Voices are portrayed in Figure 10.1. The following four sections explain each of them in turn before turning to the final two sections of this book, which discuss standards for netnographic performance.

The Symbolic Netnographer

In Kozinets (2002a: 62) I defined netnography as 'a new qualitative research methodology that adapts ethnographic research techniques to study the cultures and communities that are emerging through computer-mediated communications'. Symbolic netnography follows the focus and precepts of earlier methodological writings on netnography (e.g., Kozinets, 1998, 2002a, 2010) which were written while the Internet and social media were in an earlier stage and the theoretical implications of developments such as the critiques of community and the rise of networked individualism had yet to be integrated. Notions of culture and community with hard definable boundaries are now replaced with more liquid notions of online social experience and interaction, but the basic precepts and foci remain intact. There is still, after all, much work to be done to investigate and understand the various ways identity groups and identity projects play out in online social interactions and experiences.

Most of the currently published netnographies are symbolic netnographies. Symbolic netnographers seek out and find interesting sites, cultures, groups and people and translate their meaning systems as values, practices and online social rituals. Discourse is a key construct. So, for instance, when Aaron Smith and Bob

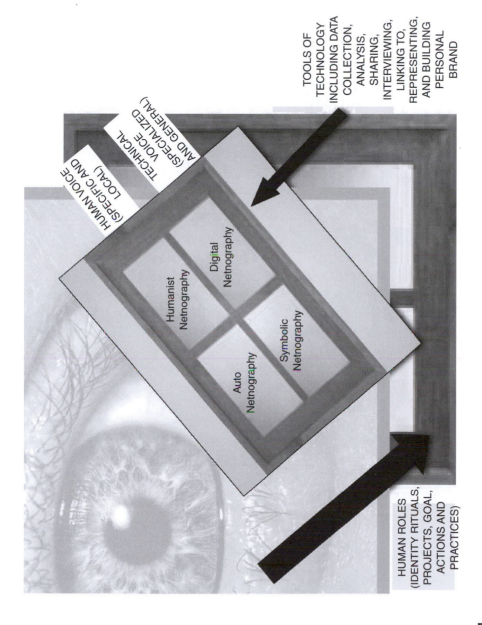

TOOLS OF TECHNOLOGY INCLUDING DATA COLLECTION, ANALYSIS, SHARING, INTERVIEWING, LINKING TO, REPRESENTING, AND BUILDING PERSONAL BRAND

TECHNICAL VOICE (SPECIALIZED AND GENERAL)

HUMAN VOICE (SPECIFIC AND LOCAL)

Humanist Netography

Digital Netography

Auto Netography

Symbolic Netography

HUMAN ROLES (IDENTITY RITUALS, PROJECTS, GOAL, ACTIONS AND PRACTICES)

Figure 10.1

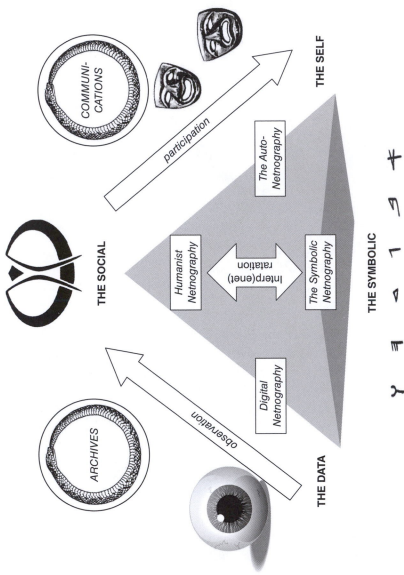

Figure 10.2 The relation of self, data and social in the netnography process

Stewart (2012) write about an online bodybuilding groups' members' sociolinguistic constructions of their bodies, they are clearly acting as symbolic translators of that online social reality. Galit Nimrod (2011) performs a symbolic netnography by studying and interpreting online social interactions structured around fun and games in the culture of seniors online sites. Opportunities abound in symbolic netnographies to expand into wider social questions about online impact on society. Nimrod (2011: 234), for example, wonders why elderly people would watch other elderly people play online in an activity she calls 'passive entertainment'. Why indeed do we all love to be such spectators, such voyeurs online? Television and reality TV in particular seem to have prepared us well to watch other people's lives and social acts. She also found lots of humour, with people joking about the losses of things like memory or sexual function associated with aging and a sense of 'intimacy among strangers' (ibid..: 235). Playing, interacting, socializing, being an elderly participant online in 'fun culture' has positive aspects; it 'can keep seniors socially engaged even when their offline social networks shrink due to friends' disabilities and deaths'; it can contribute to 'cognitive health' by activating memory, refreshing language skills, and stimulating imagination – even 'if one is just "lurking"' (ibid.). However, the relationships seemed 'quite superficial', Nimrod (ibid.) judged. Echoing ambivalent concerns about online social engagement itself – and perhaps many other types of consocial relationship in the contemporary age – Nimrod finds that they 'cannot replace real relationships and/or significantly help seniors who suffer from loneliness' (ibid.). Elderly people's online behaviours are classified and categorized, some are explored in depth, interesting new practices are detailed, actions are linked to characteristics of the group, and then types of relationship are evaluated and their implications explored. Nimrod (2011) usefully illustrates the Symbolic Netnography's behavioural, social and ethical engagement with a social research phenomenon.

Symbolic Netnographies represent the online social experience and interaction of particular people's groups, nations, languages, cultures and identity formations in the traditional textual form of an article, chapter, dissertation or perhaps book. They draw upon particular sites in order to create narratives of sharing, exploration, cooperation, conflict, exchange, empowerment, disparity and much more. Their output is meant to be read. They have a direct lineage and interconnection with the traditional use of ethnography and related qualitative research techniques across academic fields such as the many mentioned in this book. As representations, they resemble other scholarly work in their field.

In the bank of netnographic wisdom, the breadth and volume of Symbolic Netnographies are a library offering the motivated researcher and interested scholar a wealth of understanding of online sociality and consociality cutting across multiple domains, disciplines and developments. For example, Killian O'Leary and Conor Caroll (2013) provide a wonderfully rich and revealing symbolic netnography of online poker groups, with their rich meanings, interactions, moods, linguistics and identities. How does language function change online? Maíz-Arévalo (2013) studies the use of complimenting responses in Spanish on Facebook and compares them to face-to-face responses and finds 'a whole different system' of response, with its own complex set of new rules. In Estonia, a supposedly non-religious country, Uibu (2012: 70, 74) finds an incredibly supportive, open and 'remarkably benevolent' Internet forum called 'The Nest of Angels' acting as a 'religious-spiritual incubator' where people can discuss spiritual and religious ideas in relation to their own 'seemingly abnormal experiences'. West and Thakore (2013) find racial exclusion among online adult toy collectors. Studying the use of Twitter and Facebook in response to radio in South Africa, Chiumbu and Ligaga (2013) find digital divides and linguistic elites undermining our idealistic conceptions of 'publics', public agency and 'communities of strangerhoods'. Sigfussona and Chetty (2013) show how software entrepreneurs in Iceland use LinkedIn to overcome some of their geographic isolation and build social capital in global business networks.

Symbolically speaking, the Symbolic Netnography reminds us of the North, The Earth. It is like a gigantic primeval forest with a vast open sky. The word, Logos, creates the Reality, and it is the task of the Symbolic Netnography to study the way groups deploy online social experience and interaction to create their reality, symbolic, material, embodied. The ancient ways are linked to traditions of symbolism, alphabet, vocabulary and meaning. Winter, coffee, tabletops, gifts and sleepless eyes are guiding images and thoughts of the symbolic netnographer. Its core image is the Tree of Life. From the Tree echoes the world of whispers, the millions of conversations, containing images, video, texts, sounds, captures, retweets, news articles, insults, symbols, likes and the potpourri of social exchanges. Pinterest, blogs, Foursquare, Wikipedia, in Africa, in Asia, in South America and Eastern Europe – all provide rich sources of insight for symbolic netnographers to inquire into and apply in their own fields. The world of published symbolic netnographies is the richest source of netnographic insight. Symbolic netnographies constitute the core, the beating heart, of the field of netnography. I confidently predict that powerful symbolic netnographies will continue to be published in many fields for a long time. However, there are now other games in town. Three of them to be exact. The next section of this chapter turns to another ideal type of netnography, the Digital Netnography.

Digital Netnography

Computer-assisted methods are an integral part of netnography, extending rather naturally the emphasis upon words and social structures of the Symbolic Netnography into its more structural facets. As we engage with larger amounts of data, our questions can turn to ones of structure, form and overall statistical description. Deploying digital tools for data analysis and visualization in particular opens up new areas for the expansion of traditional Symbolic Netnographies into the space of data science and big data analytics.

Because it is native to the online environment, netnography has always included the use of computer-assisted methods of search, data collection and even data analysis working alongside its more traditional and human-centric methods of researcher participant-observation and qualitative data interpretation. In Kozinets (2001: 70), I describe the large dataset I collected during my dissertation research: approximately 440,000 words of field notes, interviews and member checks; 260,000 words of artifactual data; and 267 photographs. I coded this material both by hand, and also using the 'NUD*IST qualitative analysis computer package' (ibid.).

In a white paper on netnography for NetBase, a Palo Alto-based social search company, I wrote that

> Participant observation and keen description are at the heart of my netnographies. I also use many types of tools to conduct them. I use search engines such as Google, including Google Groups, Google Trends, and Google Social Search. I also use Technorati, and Twitter Search. I use qualitative data analysis software such as Atlas.ti and NVivo. For automatic semantic recognition, organization of relevant semantic forms and patterns, and location of online conversation sites, and overall understanding of what consumers are saying, I have recently been using NetBase's ConsumerBase tool.

Chapter 3 of the first edition of this book overviewed a number of different methods for understanding online social experiences, and recommended that interviews and social network analyses were a good fit to combine with netnography (Kozinets, 2010).

We can track the development and extension of netnography into digital netnography. Johann Füller and colleagues (2007) deployed netnography to study the innovative creations of online basketball groups online. They found five basketball sites, groups of the message board style, and studied them for six months. The authors of this article coded their data to identify active users, revealing a statistical portrait of the skewed nature of online social participation: 'the 212 most active users make 80% of the postings (3.4% of total 6216 members). The top 50 contributors (0.8%) produce 50% of all messages' (ibid.: 64). 58% of members are lurkers, 39% are posters who contribute regularly, and only 5% are frequent posters. A type of social structure, a clear hierarchy of influence and innovation contribution is revealed through their social structure analysis. The authors also considered a massive amount of data, screening more than 240,000 posts contained in more than 18,000 discussions. They saved everything that seemed related to the topic of innovation online in electronic files. They used QSR NVivo software to analyse and interpret 460 discussions including 11,000 posts – they note parenthetically that 9000 of the posts were innovation-related. This research took place in a corporate context, in a firm that was structured and developed to professionally design, develop and implement netnographies for corporate clients.

As we code greater and greater amounts of data, our netnographies enable us through coding to seek principles, meanings and conclusions in the patterns of social structuring as well. We learn from Füller et al. that the top topic for discussion has been coded as design, followed more distantly by topics such as cushioning, comfort, and customization (2007: 65). We learn that there are two different kinds of innovators: need-driven innovators and excitement-driven innovators. Although I had always been taught that necessity was the mother of invention, Füller et al.'s (2007) clever data analysis tells me something different: excitement-driven innovation is the motivation behind 80% of the postings, and it is a powerful intrinsic motivation at that. We then see some dramatically skilled and attractive shoe designs, presented visually and in colour in the article. This is the vivid representation of netnography in action. We learn in general about designers' characteristics (e.g., they fantasize about shoes, and sometimes draw inspiration for shoe designs by thinking about animals, like sharks), and the pattern of their contributions (two weeks after someone launches an informal design contest for the new Air Jordan shoe, the entries peak). The entire netnography includes symbolic intercourse and meaning but takes it to a more quantified and structural level, trying to discern big picture principles for innovation online from the precise coding and statistical analysis of the netnographically gathered data. And yet, this is still doubtlessly a netnography of the specific. It is grounded in time, place and topic. It searches for general principles and knowledge in the local and the familiar.

Let us consider another digital netnography. In their netnography of an online digital camera forum, Xun and Reynolds (2010: 20) question whether 'web discourse' is actually eloquent and rich, or whether it is very often superficial and of 'poor quality'. This is a valuable point, for as digital netnographers turn to more compressed data sources like those on Twitter especially, but also Foursquare, and even Facebook and LinkedIn, the aggregate impact of combining netnographic data with statistical overviews and analysis becomes apparent. Xun and Reynolds' (2010) article provides a host of useful detail regarding the way they use different online tools and techniques to conduct their netnography. They use alexa.com to discern and graph people's search visits to the three leading camera review forums. They split the type of discussions on sub-forums into four categories: camera news, which-camera-should-I-buy questions, photography and announcements. In a towering bar graph, 'Which camera should I buy?' dominates the conversation. Echoing the skews of Füller et al. (2007), a pie chart shows us participation. The chart reveals that the top three users contribute to 23% of all of the 18,405 posts created on the forum. It is somewhat amazing to see how one moderator contributes to over 3000 of these posts, a full 13%. The article codes emotive language, providing examples of statements that contain from one, to three, to twenty-one concluding exclamation points! The authors employ Alexa's analytics to look at the upstream and downstream sites for the site – it seems of little surprise that they are both Google. In fact, the powerful presence of Google reveals itself across many digital netnographies where analytics are used. Combining netnography's quest for cultural insights with all manner of software search and online web investigation is a follow-the-natives technique, a bricolage and quantitative exercise entirely in keeping with the inclusive, adaptive and ever-innovative spirit of the netnographic enterprise.

Chris Zimmerman and colleagues (2014) combined netnography with a range of software-based analytic techniques, including computational linguistics, sentiment analysis and social data analytics, to try to understand patterns in social media and traditional mainstream media expression, nationally and internationally, across the two languages of Danish and English. As any good netnography does, they grounded their study in the specific. In this case, the specific phenomenon was a February 2014 incident involving a giraffe named Marius who was put to death by the Copenhagen Zoo. Zimmerman et al. (2014) used the popular business search tool Radian6 to gather 315,000 posts from 40 online channels. The data was dominated by posts from Twitter and, to a lesser extent, Facebook. They also went to blogs, video and photo-sharing sites, as well as mainstream news sites for articles and comments. Netnography was used to reveal the types of argumentation and moral concern, which assumed the form of three argument or narrative types: rational/scientific/bureaucratic, relative/cultural/linguistic and animal ethics.

Quantitative analysis shows how activity about the giraffe killing escalates the day before the killing occurs. The third figure presented in the article shows a huge spike as the international news story breaks at 3pm on 8 February 2014. The rise in attention for the Copenhagen Zoo is nothing short of astounding. The Zoo received less than 500 posts in the three weeks before they decided to euthanize Marius. After the news broke, however, traditional and social media attention exploded. The zoo and its giraffe were mentioned 232,323 times over the next week. In the Danish language social media posts, about 53% of those mentions were from Twitter and Facebook. In English, Twitter original posts and retweets accounted for 72% of the volume, with Facebook accounting for another 21%. International reaction was larger, more dominated by Twitter, and more emotional than it was in Denmark. The words used to describe the killing were more intensely negative, such as slaughter, butcher (the giraffe's carcass was fed to other zoo animals), murder, and execution.

Zimmerman et al. (2014) provide an intriguing model for digital netnography. Their findings begin to sketch a pattern of differential affordances, uses and technological deployments:

Generally speaking, Facebook and Twitter serve differently in sharing signals. Given that 10% or less of Twitter users have a private social network, the intended audience is mostly public in nature, making the intended signal different to [sic] that of the friend-directed social network of Facebook. Twitter is therefore seen as a proxy for semi-public voice and Facebook as a proxy for semiprivate voice. (2014: 139)

The researchers also found that the mainstream media still dominate the Danish media landscape much more than they do the international sphere. Zimmerman et al. (2014: 139) propose undertaking a programme of understanding social interaction by investigating the interrelation of cultural codes – which requires netnography's cultural understanding – with ecological data and interactional structure. I like this positioning of Digital Netnography. The authors see their research as a study that regards how 'human actors from different cultures and countries interacted with each other using different technologies and languages in terms of the linguistic aspects of the interactions at the micro-genetic level and argument types at the macro structural level' (ibid.).

As these examples amply demonstrate, Digital Netnography 'no longer concerns itself with the divide between the real and the virtual' (cf. Rogers, 2009: 3). In fact, netnography has always eschewed such difference. As with the digital methods of Rogers (2009) and the 'digital ethnography' discussed in Caliandro (2014), netnography and in particular Digital Netnography study networked society in all its manifestations through a variety of tools, paying attention to the cultural insights and conditions that determine and are determined by the varieties of human experience. Netnography is not, as Caliandro (2014: 663–666) wrongly asserts, a kind of marketing and business centred 'virtual method' that avoids the quantification of Internet data. It has never been so. It is not only a technique of 'surveys, interviews, and participation' (p. 664) but one that is happy to spread out from participant-observation to web-crawling, tag clouds, sentiment analysis, PageRanks and other algorithms, crowdsourcing, semantic analysis, network analysis and much more.

In a surprising conclusion, weakly backed by a selective and tiny group of studies, Caliandro (2014: 666) claims that 'the distinct value of netnography is its capacity to bring into existence a sort of huge "Focus Group 2.0". He then introduces his own term and method as a much more inclusive alternative. I think that erroneous separations such as these may come about not only because academics such as Alessandro Caliandro and his co-authors are engaging in the age-old performance of the anxiety of influence, but also because there is a genuine sense that netnography is connected with 'offline' ethnographic methods and thus cannot be totally digital. This is an insupportable contention. In fact, it seems that they are trying to argue that a single person, sitting at their computer and using sophisticated tools like Google Flu Trends, can call themselves an ethnographer without interviewing or speaking to another living soul. Can cultural understandings be gained solely through big data analysis type exposure? More importantly, should this be called anthropology and ethnography?

We must critically examine the underpinnings of all such presumptive assumptions. Can there be a complete break between types of ethnographic investigation, such that one is totally analogue and one is totally digital? Can there truly be a hard break between people's communications using technology and their symbolic interactions in the physical world?

In this book, we seek to dispense with the notion that somehow digital means non-physical. As anyone who has even seen a server farm or who understands the massive amounts of energy required to power the so-called 'cloud' can comment, everything so-called digital/online is also ineffably physical/offline as well. There can thus be no 'explicitly digital epistemology'. As a result, there can be no 'naturally digital' methods of ethnography that somehow appear when one does Internet research. Digital Netnography embraces its origins in traditional ethnography, a millennial old technique that explores the unceasingly astonishing and kaleidoscopic aspects of our human being, and also the vast and fast evolution of our many technological tools, be they hardware, software or technical. Communications are still communications, understanding is still understanding, and Digital Netnography travels down many complex and computationally assisted roads to encompass them all.

Clearly, there are frontiers to traverse relating to integrating digital analysis with cultural understanding. As with the Digital Humanities, which we also discuss in the next chapter, there is a ubiquitous 'tension between algorithmic analysis and hermeneutic close reading' (Hayles, 2012: 31). This relationship is, intriguingly, often construed as a 'synergistic interaction' and not merely an opposition. An example is Matthew Kirschenbaum and his colleagues' data-mining project that looked at Emily Dickinson's letters to Susan Huntington Dickinson in terms of erotic language, which also involved the researchers in hermeneutic close readings of the letters, and a deepening and enriching of the analysis by a 'rapid shuttling' between the two analytic forms.

However, there are other implications to combining these modes of analysis that can be radical and destabilizing. 'The unsettling implications of "machine reading" can be construed as pointing toward a posthuman mode of scholarship in which human interpretation takes a backseat to algorithmic processes' (Hayles, 2012: 30). When Katherine Hayles interviewed Todd Presner for her book, he used what I find to be a very anthropologically informed argument to respond to her question about viewing the algorithmic processes of digital methods as erasing the human. His answer noted the dynamism of the concept (and to this I would add the lived reality) of being human. Presner insisted that the shift in terms of using machine reasoning and software analysis could be 'understood contextually' as part of the long history of human beings 'adapting to new technological possibilities and affordances' (Hayles, 2012: 30). We, ourselves, as researchers are changing. This is why, even in Digital Netnography, the reflexive role of the participant is still crucial. We are studying not only our research site, but also ourselves studying the site. Although it may reach out to the sky, Digital Netnography has its feet firmly planted in the nourishing waters of participant-observation.

In a symbolic sense, then, Digital Netnography is the East and Water. Here we see the image of Gigantic Water Spiders, Gigantic prehistoric Octopi. We can link this image of ancient inhuman intelligences to computer science, to AIs and spiders, web-crawlers, insectoid programs and bots, as well as to the financial and computational whiz-kid intelligences that code software. All of them can have immense fun pushing the boundaries of a Digital Netnography. We can think of the Digital Netnography in terms of its logo: a yellowjacket robot, armed to sting, free for you to design and crowdsource to share, free of license as Your Own Personal Digital Netnography Logo. Digital Netnographers will use sophisticated software and tools, but turn to reflect upon the interaction between themselves as human researchers and the digital machines they use, turning digital analysis of social data into an accessibly human experience. Digital Netnography is a core and key frontier, one in which computer science, linguistics and the anthropologies of meaning and human understanding are combining to bring brand new insights to the expanding spheres of online social interaction and experience.

The Auto-netnographer

[who and

what is the researcher?

doing the research?

is he different

from the ~~scientist thinking~~

writer writing the work?]

seeing through

an Other's i's

reading and using each other

's thoughts

speaking through

an Other's words i sculpt ... . (Kozinets, 2012: 481)

This is a citation from a published poem that 'i' wrote to express some of the representational and emotional conflicts that accompany being a participative ethnographer and netnographer. 'Through an implicit historical overview of the author's ... research, the poem considers classic anthropological topics such as alterity, entrée, going native, subjectivity versus objectivity, and crises of representation in the light enabled by the synthesis of introspection and poetic rhetoric' (ibid.: 478). Who and what is the researcher?, the poem asks. The representation of the self as the scientist is corrected with a strikethrough. He is the writer. The edit is visible, the self-correction exposed, revealing human vulnerability, the authorial voice no longer so authoritative. The poem tries to tell us that there is much that transpires backstage regarding our research that we hide from print and even hesitate to record and discuss.

The academic processes of research discovery, publication and dissemination are, as Latour and Woolgar (1979) aptly demonstrate, profoundly uncertain enterprises, ones filled with subjectivity, serendipity, spontaneity and gray areas. To some extent, then, every ethnography and every netnography must also be a work that results from participation in the various fields and sub-fields of academic research, not merely of engagement with field 'sites' both on and off of digital screens.

Qualitative sociological research has 'always' contained a similarly reflective and biographical aspect (Anderson, 2006: 375–378). For example, urban sociology pioneer Robert Park encouraged his University of Chicago students to research aspects close to their own personal lives and identities. As Mary Jo Deegan (2001: 20) has noted, 'The student sociologists [at the University of Chicago] often lived in the settings studied, walked the streets, collected quantitative and qualitative data, worked for local agencies, and had autobiographical experience emerging from these locales or ones similar to them.' The next wave of sociological ethnography associated with what Gary Alan Fine (1995) termed the Second Chicago School also looked at people's personal involvement, particularly as occupational cultures were used as sites of participant observation. The taxi driving of Fred Davis (1959) stands as a fine example. At this point, there was little self-narrative and barely any explicit personal revelation in the work. However, this changed in the 1960s and 1970s, when a new batch of more experimental, experiential, personal and self-observational studies were published. In these studies, the sociologists themselves were rendered visible and in fact reflected upon themselves and their immediate social worlds as sources of social theory (e.g., Sudnow, 1978; Wallace, 1965; Zurcher, 1977).

Cultural anthropologist David Hayano (1979: 99) used the term 'auto-ethnography' (which he claims to have heard in 1966 in Sir Raymond Firth's structuralism seminar) to refer to anthropologists who conduct and write ethnographies of 'their own people'. He wrote an essay that clearly specified the case for more introspective, personal and intimate studies. Contrasting auto-ethnography with colonialist anthropology, Hayano demonstrated his approach with his work *Poker Faces* (1982), based upon his personal experience as a semi-professional poker player in California's public poker clubs. When Hayano (1979) begins to talk about the types of auto-ethnographies, however, the topic becomes even more provocative. There can be auto-ethnographies conducted by researchers 'who have studied their own cultural, social, ethnic, racial, religious, residential, or sex membership group', for example (1979: 100). Auto-ethnographies can also be 'written by researchers who have acquired an intimate familiarity with certain subcultural, creational, or occupational groups' or even those who have 'become formally and informally socialized, after indoctrination, into a specific group of role-type with some specialized knowledge or way of life' (ibid.).

Hayano then provides the beguiling example of Leopold Fischer, an Austrian, born in Vienna, fascinated his whole life with India, who moved to India, became an Indian scholar and Hindu monk as well as an anthropologist. Fischer changed his name to Ramachandra and was ordained as Swāmī Agehānanda Bhāratī. Genuine membership, total involvement, and complete acceptance and identification is Hayano's criterion, but it is possible for almost anyone to study almost anything using this – admittedly stringent – criterion. Not everyone can become an ordained Indian Swami. However, many of us can aspire to, say, gain a degree of mastery in running a LinkedIn group.

We can briefly summarize some of the key points about the written representation of auto-ethnographies. Much auto-ethnography has the following characteristics:

- It exhibits an 'intense personal familiarity' (Hayano, 1979: 101)
- It is more 'holistic and descriptive rather than problem-oriented' (ibid.)
- It usually attempts to describe 'the full picture and breadth' of a particular people's lived existence (ibid.)
- It seeks, within reason, and with awareness of potential drawbacks, to use the perspective of ethnographic reflexivity as a contribution to theory and knowledge
- It opens up possible ways to think about 'the inescapable, recurrent problem of the human presence in data collection' (ibid.:103)

According to Anderson (2006: 377), after Hayano auto-ethnography became 'almost exclusively identified' with scholars demonstrating and advocating descriptive, literary, evocative approaches to ethnographic representation. By providing evocative portraits, auto-ethnographers 'bypass the representational problem by invoking an epistemology of emotion, moving the reader to feel the feelings of the other' (Denzin, 1997: 228). The 'mode of storytelling is akin to the novel or biography and thus fractures the boundaries that normally separate social science from literature ... ' (Ellis and Bochner, 2000: 744). Of course, going for broke in terms of rejecting realism entirely is only one, and a rather risky, strategy.

Hayano (1979: 102) notes that, although we often hear about the problems of familiarity in ethnography and auto-ethnography in particular, 'little has been said of the comparable, opposite stance of "overobjectivity", that is, attempting to describe a people from a totally detached stranger perspective ... '. Anderson (2006) may be overstating the degree to which scholars like Ellis, Rambo and Denzin actually forsake facts and reality. However, he does make a solid point in arguing that there is room for many approaches to auto-ethnography, including his own realist take of 'analytic autoethnography' (Anderson, 2006).

Therefore, consider the genesis of Auto-netnography. Richard Kedzior and I had decided to study the experience of Second Life and, in particular, the sense of embodiment that followed the defamiliarizing experience of 'entering' a virtual world (Kozinets and Kedzior, 2009). In that chapter, we argue that the research appeal of our ethnography lay in the way the virtual world transformed

> the relationship between the individual and their own perceptions of reality, of their own body, of the aspects of their identities, of the world itself ... Further, we hold that these elements are cloistered into areas of personal experience that can be very difficult if not impossible for other methodologies to reveal. It is for this reason – the intensely personal nature of the avatar experience – that we suggest considering and exploring the potential for an online application of auto-ethnography. (2009: 7-8).[3]

Following Hayano (1979) quite closely, but seeking to extend and develop that work into the realm of social media, we defined Auto-netnography as

> an approach to netnography that highlights the role of the netnographer's own experiences of his or her own online experiences. It captures and documents these experiences through the careful personal observation of online participation, autobiographical attention to the interrelation of various experienced 'worlds' – both online and off/real – reflexive fieldnoting, self- and first-person image and other data captures, and first person narratives which make their way into the final representation carried in the netnographic text. (Kozinets and Kedzior, 2009: 8)

Consider this example from the second author's fieldnotes:

> I was excited and overwhelmed by the number of choices that I had to make. The whole experience resembled a make-over reality show. And even though I was aware that it is only my avatar that's getting a treat, for some reason it felt like it was all about me. Knowing that I can modify my looks endlessly left me experimenting with every single option. It took me probably ten minutes only to decide on the shape of my nose. After forty minutes of modeling my new body I was exhausted. (ibid.: 12)

And here is how I expressed some of it in poem:

> ... identity
>
> as adaptation, exploration and
>
> revolution is a person
>
> an interaction
>
> in and of a virtual world
>
> our own redemption
>
> our own redaction. (Kozinets, 2012: 481)

Auto-netnography is about writing, vulnerability, art and sacrifice. Viewed from within, using symbolic sightlines, we see in the West the Figure of the Burning Man, his arms raised as they are right before he is set alight and explodes for far too long into the wild Nevada night sky. Some part of you says to yourself 'We needed this, really needed this, as a species, as human beings, as bodies in the night, here temporarily, and then gone, and we needed and need right now and will always damn it need to be reminded of the quickness and fragility of life.'

This is the Sacrifice. What are we Sacrificing? What are we willing to Sacrifice? To make as an Offering? Are we willing to Burn a Man, every year, upon a stake of fire, and dance skyclad around that fire until the dawn, walking on the coals, dancing and rolling in the sand, howling at the moon? This could be a complete fabrication, it could be a product of a mycogenetic intelligence assuming human form and expressed through the completely innerworld theories of the introspecting Auto-netnographer. A truth, others' truths, wrapped in our own truths.

Contemplation of Auto-netnography, Symbolic Netnography and Digital Netnography now clears a path for the types of understanding and communication conveyed through the last ideal type, the Humanist Netnography, which is the topic of our next chapter.

SUMMARY

In this chapter, you learned about the history of ethnographic representation. You also learned about the four ideal types of netnographic representation: symbolic, digital, auto and humanist. These forms constitute an approach to the ethnography of online interaction and experience that ranges from the reflective, subjective and personal to the statistical, expansive and descriptive. Symbolic, digital and auto-netnographies are explained in this chapter. The choice of final research product form determines choices about data collection and analysis.

KEY READINGS

Anderson, Leon (2006) 'Analytic autoethnography', *Journal of Contemporary Ethnography*, 35(August): 373–395.

O'Leary, Killian and Conor Carroll (2013) 'The online poker sub-culture: Dialogues, interactions and networks' *Journal of Gambling Studies*, 29: 613–630.

Zimmerman, Chris, Yuran Chen, Daniel Hardt and Ravi Vatrapu (2014) 'Marius, the giraffe: A comparative informatics case study of linguistic features of the social media discourse', *Cultural Contexts for Interaction*, presented at CABS 12, August, Kyoto, Japan. pp. 131–130.

NOTES

1. The video ethnography poem is entitled 'Desert Pilgrim' and is posted on YouTube on my channel, accessible at the following link: https://www.youtube.com/watch?v=BM3jrNzt3YI.

2. To this I would absolutely have to add search. Search should have been included as a major aspect of netnography where software firepower can make a huge difference. In fact, without browsers and search engines, netnography could not exist.

3. For those who are interested in auto-netnographic approaches to virtual worlds, and Second Life in particular, beyond the deservedly celebrated work *Coming of Age in Second Life* (2008) by anthropologist Tom Boellstorff, which I would definitely consider to contain many auto-netnographic elements, I also recommend reading Cátia Sofia Afonso Ferreira's (2012) dissertation work, *Second Life: Representation and Remediation of Social Space*, available in its entirety online.

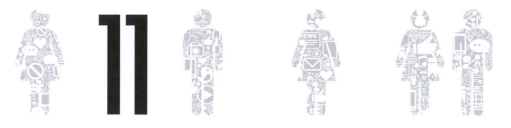

HUMANIST NETNOGRAPHY

It's smoke, and it's flames now ... and the frame is crashing to the ground, not quite to the mooring-mast. Oh, the humanity ... – Herbert Morrison, American radio reporter, covering the crash of the Hindenburg zeppelin in 1937

THE BEGINNING OF UNDERSTANDING

It is still exactly as Germonprez and Hovorka (2013: 5) describe it:

> Netnographies are an ethnographic approach adjusted to an online world (Kozinets, 2010) [and to this we must now elaborate by saying a social world of online interactions and experiences, both human and nonhuman]. They are inherently flexible, naturally exploratory and are intended to 'draw (or re-draw) the map of a new or rapidly changing terrain. [They] help to tell other researchers who will come later what are the most interesting constructs and relationships' (Kozinets, 2010: 42). Netnographies provide an important framework through which researchers can craft, review and refine research questions, build data bridges to those questions and orient themselves for knowing online social engagement. A netnography is primarily oriented to [investigative social science] through researcher participation and observation (Kozinets, 2010).

In their impressively thorough netnography of Digitally Enabled Social Networks, through which they charted Digg's social media decline through poor service to its user base, and Reddit's rise as the loyal core shed Digg for Reddit, Germonprez and Hovorka (2013: 22) also reveal a deeply humanist netnographic urge:

> [Digital Enabled Social Networks] support a vast variety of human collaborative and constructive activity in addition to being utilized for social activism, corporate activity and political action. Representative cases need not only entail struggles as illustrated in our case of Digg.com. In 2009, Iranian citizens broadcast in the face of disputed national election results. In 2011, University of California Davis students organized in support of the international Occupy Wall Street protests. In these cases, the collective was a cornerstone of change in the timeline of how the events unfolded and became realized both physically and within [the online social network].

Social movements such as these can be increasingly 'expected to be encountered, coordinated and linked through information technology' (Germonprez and Hovorka, 2013: 22).

Academia and academics have traditionally played an important part in these movements: 'Universities have long been special places, places of both innovation and resistance. From the "protestant" monk to the heretical stargazer, academics have been at the center of historical change in the West for the past millennium' (M'Gonigle and Starke, 2006: 10).

What happens when we, as academics, as scholars, turn our critical academic eye to technological change, study it as ethnographers, and seek practical understanding? As digital critic, author, artist and philosopher Hervé Fischer writes in *Digital Shock* (2006: 18), we can be fascinated by the rise of the Digital Age

> without renouncing our critical spirit or delegating responsibility for our future to software and artificial intelligence ... We have to let ourselves be swept along by the tidal wave of new technologies if we are to understand the fever, the innovation, the acceleration, the utopian hopes; we must size up the newness of the phenomenon before our minds can turn to using its faculty of critical distancing and philosophical questioning.

As ethnographers, we are also moving through temporal and historical sites, sites of different technocultural times. Our manner of being changes with the technologies we adopt, adapt to, and embrace. The task of netnographers is to join in this emic change, let it wash over us, and then transform it through our 'critical fascination' (ibid.), our critical and trained faculties, with data and holonic system-wide thinking, into an etic representation, one that can prompt positive change.

THE SURFER

Can you picture the Sky, its vastness now overlain with a gigantic Netnography Map of our Social Territories, alliances and networks, and also other people's territories, and organizations' as well?

Can you feel the electrical Wind of change, sharings, file transfers and conversational exchanges, bit mapped transfers of blipping on–off packets that get transl(oc)ated into pictures, videos, jokes, and meanings?

If you look to the South, you will see flying in this marvellous, data-filled sky a marvellous human avenger Figure. It is a bald surfer guy, cut and perfect in form, sweeping like a quick bird down, and diving now into and through the computer networks, surfing the round of fibre optic cable like he is riding a giant tube of cresting wave. He is silver. He is on a perfectly silver surfboard. He stops in front of you and says, 'Hop on' and just like that you are flying with the Silver Surfer, soaring the netways, surfing now in an incandescent web-filled sky, and he is making remarks on the different kinds of human beings and groups and troubles you both notice as if seeing each one of them for the first time. He is an Innocent. An Outsider. A brilliant alien seeing us right now with eyes anew.

As you listen to the Silver Surfer you are hearing him talk about humanity the way anthropologists have always talked about the Other, as a way to write social criticism into our fictions, as a way to try to inspire other people to want to make a difference. To help change the world into a fairer and more humane and caring place. Seeing ourselves through the Eyes of the Silver Surfer is to ask ourself: 'What does it mean to be a member of a group, a particular kind of human being, a particular person, alive, on Planet Earth today, and what do we do about it, what can I do about what I observe?'

We call this type of netnography a Humanist Netnography.

What is the role of the Academic and of the University? Can universities truly become, as M'Gonigle and Starke (2006) suggest, places where unified theories and overarching metanarratives are no longer the order of the day and sole items on the educational menu, but instead forums for open and diverse communications about all manner of contemporary phenomena? The goal of Humanist Netnography is nothing short of a reclamation of the unique voice of the Academic Researcher, directly, without the mediation of the mass media, but on our own.

Although it may be fine to be featured or interviewed for local or national newspapers or magazines, we do not need to be presented in the mainstream-run media in order to influence others. We can represent ourselves as public intellectuals. More than this, we can take up the call in our own way for the need to reinvent the university, reinvent academia, reinvent scholarship, reinvent research and research communication and create projects that we care about, that others will care about, and that will inspire positive action and connection in the world. In this chapter, the path we follow to do this has a name and that name is Humanist Netnography. Here is a detailed example of one such approach, which I hope will resonate with you in an evocative way and inspire you to create your own approach from the infinite world of expressive scientific possibilities.

3, 2, 1 ... VIDEO NETNOGRAPHY ROLL

Can we imagine a single woman, walking up to the computer's in-built camera from a dark room in the background? The light shades, darker or lighter. Can we see her completely from this distance? Is that a veil? Does she gently cover or expose herself as she says 'I am Mary Jane Parker (or insert your name). This is my netnography'?

Image this filmed on your computer's camera. Perhaps the camera on your phone as well. Some selfies from that particular netnographic time. Then, consider just as a momentary example the research question: 'What are the human implications to the world of overpopulation in certain areas and how can we as academic theoreticians play a part in finding a solution?'

What does it mean to be a human being, alive, in a highly overpopulated area of Planet Earth today? How do I experience that, from the point of view of the person that I currently am? What does it mean to be concerned about this? I would list out the identities that truly matter to me: exactly who I am in order. Would I share them? Would I interpenetrate them? Would I 'fabricate' them? This is a larger question within the matrix of questions that constitutes a netnography. Share what I find in its native form. Share what I personally wrote with an audience. Share my interpretation. Or make up some 'scenario' that I believe encapsulates accurately my experience of them. And that matrix must form the backbone of whichever representational style level you choose to work within. Eventually, I would hope most scholars would want to try at least two or three of the four types of netnography, to sample their flavour, so to speak and to decide for herself or himself. To have the prescribed effect, netnography should seek to completely challenge your skills and your risk-taking as an individual scholar, thinker, presenter and academic.

In the videography that is still unfolding onscreen, complete with data-streams, multiple language tracks combine with multiple viewpoints of the netnographer. The narration that you offer as you weave this tale is an analogue to the insider-knowledge expert remarks of film-makers talking about the science of production in the 'director's cut' comments. But now you are talking about theory, you are talking about birth rates in India, the history of government owned enterprise, the need for more public money to be spent on social projects and socialist thinking. 'Socialist as in social: a good kind of socialist'. You say 'Social enterprise. Social welfare. Social capital. Socialist.' The word 'socialist = socialite' could flash for several seconds brightly on the screen before fading entirely to white.

THE TRANSCENDENCE OF VERISIMILITUDE

Netnography is about struggling to rise to the impossible challenge of transcending our own illusory categories and understanding the worlds of other living beings, other people, tasting and sharing the human experience itself: 'To collapse and thus transcend the dichotomous self/other categories: finding the self in the other and the other in the self!' (Fernandez, 1994: 155). This true understanding of the other must also pervade our representation. In this we may talk of virtual verisimilitude, the sense that the virtual is a real part of our experience now. Just as television gave rise to a sort of parasocial interaction, so the Internet and mobile accelerate and amplify it by interconnecting us with one another, so we can talk about media, and build out more and more social networks, organized and linking across the globe, sharing and jousting just as our Facebook Ebola combatants in Chapter 8 illustrate.

This global linking is, possibly, the key to our Salvation as a Species. Because if each of us becomes netnographers, just for a little while, and tries to see through the eyes of humanity, of all humanity, seeing all suffering as real, as partly our own, then we must turn to verisimilitude in order to provide an example of something that reproduces or simulates and maps the 'real'. The importance of seeming realistic has been accentuated because of the importance of representation in ethnography's post-crisis moments. But even more than this, seeming real has become important to public intellectual communication because of the Internet and reality TV. In fact, the standards of reality TV and reality Internet channels lead us to be personal brand-managing micro-celebrity academics.

On one level, in order to evoke a sense of reality, a netnographer's narrative must be persuasive, credible, convincing and believable. On another level, verisimilitude describes a text's relation to an objectively real world. Surrealisticially, verisimilitude says 'enough people think that this image is real that they will believe it'. To get at that kind of mass belief, your netnography cannot be too surprising or jarring. Verisimilitude is achieved more by openness, honesty, and being willing to share a personal side of yourself publicly in social media than it is by being fictitious and theoretically vicious. This truth and honestly must relate to what we conceive of as our collective brand.

Our Personal and Collective Occupational Brand as Netnographers

To be a netnographer today should mean something. It should mean adherence to a goal of attempting to locate a human understanding of the specificity of particular human beings as they experience and interact through social media. It should mean vigilant attention to the seemingly ever-increasing and ever-more-sophisticated mass technological use of people across the globe. It should mean percipient development of the tools and skills needed to commit to collecting and understanding as much and as detailed data as possible. This data will be generated through what we currently call social media and the open and write-friendly web and net.[1]

There is risk when we flirt with quantification. The risk emerges as our datasets grow larger and we must use more computerized tools to comprehend them, and our ability to use our human intelligence to understand those words and stories as thoughts and imaginary ideas becomes veiled as it is reduced and decontextualized and grows more statistical and quantitative. At that point, we are at risk of losing the human element that is the nucleus of the netnographic endeavour.

This is not to say that, even with the most manual of coding, the least automated of analytic modes, we will not do violence to context. We must tread lightly and with great care as we pilfer the words and images, the video and voice of other human beings, dissect them like autopsied corpses ripped apart then stitched, Frankenstein-like, into our curations, and used to portray the cultural 'Other'; a lifeless stereotype animated by insidious anthropologies.

We must mind our resonance, a word that evokes a re-sounding, as if human beings were crystalline goblets, filled with feelings, attuned to moments and concepts, and ready to vibrate accordingly. Resonance asks about the extent to which the netnography conveys to its readers a personalized and sensitizing connection with the human experience. Is your netnography empathic, enlightening and empowering? Does it sensitize readers to the concerns and lifeways of particular human beings? I cherish Wikan's quote from a 'professor-poet' in the Balinese village he studied:

> It is what fosters empathy or compassion. Without resonance there can be no understanding, no appreciation. But resonance requires you [and here he looked entreatingly at me] to apply feeling as well as thought. Indeed, feeling is the more essential, for without feeling we will remain entangled in illusions. (Wikan, 1992: 463; square brackets in original)

Untangling from our illusions, personal and collective, is part of the challenge and the gain of being an ethnographer. Thus, of the netnographer. Communicating that untangled message means working on the craft not only of scientific representation, but the public presentation of that knowledge in our teaching, conference presentation, professional presentations, keynote speeches, and our shared links, stories, Tweets, updates, posts, blog and vlog entries, and videographic netnographies.

Professional presentation expert Nancy Duarte (2010: 123) advises us in our presentations to 'use the big idea to filter out all the frequencies other than the resonant frequency'. Remember the nature of your audience and the role of your story.

> The audience does not need to tune themselves to you – you need to tune your message to them. Skilled presenting requires you to understand their hearts and minds and create a message to resonate with what's already there. Your audience will be significantly moved if you send a message that is tuned to their needs and desires. They might even quiver with enthusiasm and act in concert to create beautiful results. (Duarte, 2010: 4)

Duarte uses the framework of the hero's journey drawn from Jungian psychology and the mythology studies of Joseph Campbell to devise an 'audience's journey' framework to help presenters interest and inspire those to whom they (re)present (Duarte, 2010: 32–35). The audience is shown a call to action, an idea that imbalances their world, and then the presenter must overcome their scepticism and take them on a journey to right this wrong. This requires some kind of conflict or imbalance which the presentation resolves, or a stubborn knot which it untangles. The audience must commit to a change, and be empowered with new tools, conceptual or otherwise, from your (re)presentation. The audience should be different when they complete audiencing your Humanist Netnography presentation than before they beheld it; they should have crossed a threshold into a new world of possibility.

A POLYPHONIC REPRESENTATION

How is a netnography like Mikhail Bahktin's (1981) 'polyphonic' novel? In those polyphonic novels, there is a utopian textual enactment of everyone speaking peacefully yet differently together. Some parts of the Internet are like a polyphonic novel. Netnography studies online social experience as an open-ended, creative set of experiences and interactional conversations between members of multitudes, diverse and fractious factions of intricately related and relating insiders and outsiders – a description that holds very well for much of what we see on the Internet: people we know and those we don't know. And those we do not know, we can meet, for online is physical. I contact you online. My phone buzzes. We agree on a place to connect (Thumb fingers type on the alphabet. Push button.). We meet.

In fact, Humanist Netnography can learn much from the experiences of scholars working in the Digital Humanities. In some of those ambitious mega projects, which combine qualitative with quantitative data, analysis with interpretation, and which seek wider audiences that transcend traditional academic boundaries, a model somewhat akin to Big Science has arisen in which groups of academics collaborate to create major, high-impact research productions (Hayles, 2012: 34). Some of this work is visible in the online multimodal journal *Vectors*, which I recommend (see http://www.vectorsjournal.org/). Humanities scholars work with graphic designers and programmers (ibid.: 35).[2] Students often contribute to Digital Humanities projects; expert amateur scholars and business people are not excluded. Although much of academia persists in a (sometimes well-founded) spirit of 'suspicion' towards business people, 'capitalism and corporations', in the Digital Humanities a willingness to reach out to funders, including commercial interests, is present (ibid.: 41). Specialized databases are created and leveraged. Multimodal scholarship includes making use 'of a full range of visual images, graphics, animations, and other digital effects' as well as creating rich and alluring soundscapes, soundtrack and audio effects (ibid.: 40). As human insight merges with and builds upon machine intelligence, the need to code programs and understand programming and code become more imminent and immediate, prompting alliances with Computer Science scholars and areas (ibid.: 41–43). In addition, we should never underestimate the power of graphic design and graphic designers. I am inspired and delighted by Tim Leong's (2013) ridiculously cool book *SuperGraphics: A Visual Guide to the Comic Book Universe*, which combines statistics and visualization to inform and entertain us about the wonderful world of super-heroes.

The visual is powerful because it is widely inclusive. Where dense text and erudite formulas are used to exclude the many and include only the well-trained intelligentsia, a good visualization draws even the less literate into the blisslike mutuality of understanding. This notion of inclusion and accessibility of understanding should permeate the Humanist Netnography. Another way to approach inclusion in Humanist Netnography is to share the political power of editing, writing, coding, interpreting and creating graphics with some of the key people you have met in the course of the research, perhaps even expert amateurs (such as fans, collectors, or history buffs). In practice, this can offer up some challenges of its own – like how you deal with challenges to your interpretations and stories directly – but it is generally a worthwhile pursuit. Most ethnographers are familiar with the notion of key informants and member checks (which I included and described in earlier versions of netnography, such as Kozinets, 2002a). Wither 'wiki-netnographies'? The wiki form possesses considerable potential to be involved in the co-construction of netnographic videographic text. Or would we be better served by a specialized wide open online journal as a place for netnographers to write more complex, layered, themed, competitive, peer-reviewed, revised and resubmitted videographies, juried and elevated, before and after we share them through social media?

In Skype interviews you may wish to obtain from your informants and to contain in your netnography, as they pertain to your sociology or other field explanations, these people's most cherished stories. The ones they have rehearsed until they are perfect brain distillations of themselves. As in hermeneutics, a new reality is constructed through the 'fusion of horizons' of researcher and informant, whereby the 'textualized' world of the other is torn open, ripped up and exposed, the yarn dangling, and then and only then can begin the active interweaving of perspectives. Video conversations in YouTube, for instance, can become like asynchronous Skype transmissions, call-and-response videographic conversations.

The film succeeds when we empathize with the characters. The conversation succeeds when we each reach some sort of new understanding. The goal of Humanist Netnography is to move people enough to act and do something to help them connect, even a little bit more, with humanity and with their humanity.

The pursuit of praxis – practical action aimed at social betterment – should guide netnographic vision. Peter Gloor and his colleagues (Gloor et al., 2011: 3) provide an active research style of netnography where they work with a major Children's hospital in Cincinnati, Ohio 'to develop a pilot "collaborative clinical care network" (C3N) trying to harness the collective intelligence of nurses, doctors, and patients to improve care and outcomes on Crohn's disease and ulcerative colitis ...' In particular, they aim to structure 'collaboration along the COIN (Collaborative Innovation Network) model – cyberteams of self-motivated individuals with a collective vision, enabled by the Web to achieve a common goal by sharing ideas, information, and work' (ibid.: 3–4) based on the prior work of Gloor (2006). Their netnography is based in strong data and an equally strong purpose and vision: harnessing social media's power to better utilize medical know-how for patient benefit. With social networking analysis clearly influencing the interpretation, their work also partakes of the Digital Netnography form in its pursuit of praxis. Analysing email, Facebook data, and web buzz, they found, among other things, that patients' participation in the project was low and they seemed peripheral to the project team. The challenge identified by this very pragmatic netnography was to bring the peripheral patients into more direct involvement with the project.

Ethnography has often been about using the Other to learn something about what we need to do, to support some agenda for change or political action (Marcus and Fischer, 1986). Chang-Ryun Han (2012) uses netnography to follow the online paths and interactions of Korean sex workers as they plan to come to North America. Why do the study? In an attempt to directly inform and influence policy regarding this activity. In a wide variety of contexts, the ability of research to motivate and influence social betterment has been increasingly held to be a sign of research quality. Indeed, Norm Denzin thinks so. 'Increasingly, the criteria of evaluation will turn ... on moral, practical, aesthetic, political and personal issues – the production, that is, of texts that articulate an emancipatory, participative perspective on the human condition and its betterment' (Denzin, 1994: 501). Lather (1993, 2001) calls this 'catalytic validity', the degree to which a research project empowers and emancipates. These efforts charge the polyphonic venture that is Humanist Netnography.

The Technocultural Study of Technology and Power

Netnography studies technology, the relationship between human being and technology, and the links between specific technologies and particular human beings, through its impact on language, all sorts of languages and meaning-systems.

> It is surprising to realize that the wide currency of the term *technology* – originally referring to systems of complex machines, now stretched to apply to items as diverse as fashion, medicine, and food – dates only to the time of World War I (Marx, 1997). Despite its relative historical recency and malleability, the notion of science, advanced technique, and mechanistic precision being built into products and services has become one of the most influential drivers of contemporary economies and a natural part of contemporary [human] experience. (Kozinets, 2008: 865)

Technology, as a way of talking, as a way of thinking and ultimately as a way of doing and being human, has radically expanded in our lives.

> Technology is, in its anthropological sense of Merleau-Ponty's extension of self, the use of tools, referring both to the tools and their use. As Nye (2007: 5) notes, it is therefore 'difficult to imagine human beings as pretechnological.' ... Like many other scholars, such as Heidegger, Ellul (1964: 3) equates technology (or 'techne') with the totality of efficiency-driven techniques and machines in a society. The term's 'unstable meaning was further complicated in the 1990s when the mass media and stock market traders used *technology* as a synonym for computers and information systems' (Nye, 2007: 1). (Kozinets, 2008: fn 1)

What does it mean for human social life, human life itself, when this very human desire for more and better technology becomes so widespread and so gluttonously indulged in that we become obese with innovation?

What does it mean to operate in this environment? Can we name names? Corporate names? News personalities? Personal names? What does it mean to have Google exist in our lives the way we do – very helpful, very useful, very powerful – holds a lot of our personal information? What do the policies of various political parties, particular political candidates mean to us? How are they related to social media and its ownership structure of stockholders, venture capital investors, and Silicon Valley and, worldwide, other entrepreneurs? What is the interrelationship between the mass media, the very real threats of spreading violent fundamentalist ideologies such as ISIS and the Islamic State caliphate, and the surveillance state of the Internet? What about the Dark Net, with its sales of drugs, guns, contract killings and even human slaves? The impact of social media interaction, transaction, surveillance, and the increasing influence that these forces and emerging institutions are having together is having radical effects upon our society, for good and for ill.

If you are to be a True Humanist Netnographer then you must choose topics and reveal them fully with a pragmatic eye to their social implications. As we examine the use of technology today, we will see that

> it is influenced by the unique gender, ethnic, class, and other social and psychological situation of the consumer, as well as by their goals, life themes, and life projects. For [some], technology is a livelihood, a way for people to connect, and a powerfully addictive joyride. For [others], it is a livelihood, a detriment to a natural life, and a way to express modern style. [Their online social interactions and] narratives reveal technology consumption as the product of historical ideological elements interpellated into personal relationships with technology that help [particular human beings] define themselves as unique individuals pursuing meaningful paths through purposeful lives. (Kozinets, 2008: 879)

Our netnography must see the narratives of people in social media as expressing particular ideological elements, shared structures of common thought, 'common difference' as American anthropologist Rick Wilk would have it (Wilk, 1995). In this case, we see different but rarely opposing ideologies of technology. We see strange lay ideologies in play, and recognize them. Then, as netnographers, seeking the natural human experience, we can begin to untangle the narrative knots of the four different 'ideologies of technology' accruing to online interactions and implying intrinsic utopian, efficient and expressive possibilities – and the opportunity to resist. We can begin to see behind technology's wizardly curtain of miracles and magic.

Performing Humanist Netnography means an unceasing struggle against racism and hate and inequality and past-based warfare, and an embracing of a new use of technology and globalization: to truly connect ourselves in a global society. As Salzmann-Erikson and Erikkson (2012: 14) rightly point out, netnography does not reach everyone, and in fact as with much of the digital divide if it were to rely only upon Internet-based information, it would exclude many:

> it was created to study privileged [educated and literature] populations who have access to the Internet and Internet forums and therefore have the possibility to express and debate issues online. A wide range of the human population consists of marginalized populations, including those without electricity, homeless people, analphabetics, and people living in countries governed by dictators, those who are imprisoned and those who [do] not speak the language of forum[s]. Although Internet usage is increasing exponentially, Internet World Stats show that only 13% of the population in Africa [have access].

We must continually strive to understand representational issues where they pertain, to remember the invidious differentiating and invisibilizing that online interaction can foster. We need to understand everything about how this Internet social informational structured network of capitals is connected and experienced. Where are its pressure points? Where does it overlap? Where is it strong? How are Chinese Internet censorship and use and response to censorship different from Saudi Arabian Internet censorship and use and response to censorship? We must encounter and then share as much of the human social, cultural and institutional dynamic as possible.

All of it Expressed in an Engaging Videographic Presentation

The understanding of a Humanist Netnography can shade into something involving the simultaneous viewing of multiple scenes: the woman, at her computers, wearing different clothing, at different times of day, her most candid shots, shots of the daily her, the relaxed real her, without makeup, with makeup, before you've brushed your teeth and your hair is all over the place, made up to really go out on the town, big bags under your eyes, aging signs, everything. A member of a society where your body assumes more, not less importance over time. We are becoming more carnal as we are becoming more technological:

a strange occurrence. But happening nonetheless. We are finding that we can choose both and not just one.

At the same time, we see a huge dataset. We see possibility, utopia, potential, sorrow, control, inequality and pain. Good anthropology is almost always newsworthy. Why not try using the inspirational social media tools at our disposal? Why not bring in state-of-the-art personal branding techniques? Why not learn and teach ourselves about how technology and netnography might not only impassion, but actually empower, social action and activism?

Now, on the screen we see all the nuggets, all the paths she had pursued in her netnography, all captured up there in montage form. All using the best software available to do the job. Then, we see her interpretation, her codification, her over-classification and penchant to repetitively go over the same findings before narrowing into the jewels that she then recites, bringing each one together into the curation, like very precious collectibles, which they are, and she the Chief Archivist who collects, preserve and adds value for other netnographic information collectors.

She recites her poem, a poem of self. It is her story. It is powerful and real. For example, 'Imagine a DVD or web-based presentation of [her] research project that could currently be put together from a project involving the reception of men to a [social marketing] campaign for Kama Sutra brand condoms in India' (Belk and Kozinets, 2005: 135). On the other screens we see other data, paths, her movement through the visual space of the Internet while we hear her voice connecting it all. Telling us secrets. Amazing things. Showing us, too. Visualization of data. Graphs, explained. Models offered. Theories compared. Tables presenting information. We see abstraction flowing from it now as if from a fountain in the foundation, like thick honey from a brain jar. And then we hear her voice, offering her interpretation, and many of her sentences are phrased in exactly the same way as the best qualitative research interpretations in her field.

Finally, the research is done. After 35 minutes of overlain perfection, her masterful theoretical work, reams and reams of data and visualization and interviews with people talking and analysing and recounting. With technological advances, we have almost unlimited tools at our disposal to create strikingly original new examples of interactive, imaginative, hyperlinked, dynamic netnography, and to post them online – perhaps as an addition to published work in books and scientific journals. It is relatively simple to fuse the use of poetry, of the body, of movement, of music, of art and dance into our netnographies.

Netnography and its development into Humanist Netnography have much in common with, and owe much to, the field of Digital Humanities, a field used by some scholars to 'advocate a turn from a primary focus on text encoding, analysis, and searching to multimedia practices that explore the fusion of text-based humanities with film, mixed, and virtual reality platforms' (Hayles, 2012: 25). The following quote from Jeffrey Schnapp and Todd Presener's 'The Digital Humanities Manifesto 2.0' (2009) captures some of the Humanist Netnography's evolving epistemology, guiding philosophy and sense of possibility.

The first wave of digital humanities work was quantitative, mobilizing the search and retrieval powers of the database, automating corpus linguistics, stacking hypercards into critical arrays. The second wave is **qualitative, interpretive, experiential, emotive, generative** in character [boldface in original]. It harnesses digital toolkits in the service of the Humanities' core methodological strengths: attention to complexity, medium specificity, historical context, analytical depth, critique and interpretation. Such a crudely drawn dichotomy does not exclude the emotional, even sublime potentiality of the quantitative any more than it excludes embeddings of quantitative analysis within qualitative frameworks. Rather it imagines new couplings and scalings that are facilitated both by new models of research practice and by the availability of new tools and technologies.

Human history shows us an endless emergent potential to create and change, as well as to be transformed by our creations. What was originally disbelieved and held to be undoable unfolds at lightning pace to become commonplace and done. In this world, more than ever, we need Humanist Netnography not only to chronicle the journey but to help light a positive human path. We must see clearly, then envision the way forward.

THE FOUR DIRECTIONS

Within the white rabbit's foot is a Symbolic Netnography,

As traditional and cultural and communal as can be.

Within the North turning to North-East, a toy tarantula, a Digital Netnography,

A yellowjacket robot armed to sting.

Within the sacrifice is his sacrifice, as we sacrifice, too,

Burn the Giant Wood Man upon a stake of fire, howl at moon

Deep within our Auto-Netnographic inner mastodon of ecstasy.

A Marvel Avenger Figure, now, perhaps a lesser known character from that imaginary Universe.

Yes, it is the Silver Surfer, soaring the skyways, surfing from the South to the South-West, always banished from his true love, always longing to return to her.

This is a deep and ancient longing, one which runs into the veins of humanity through all of its great religions' stories, certainly the Bible's tales of how Jacob worked and waited seven years for his great love Rachel to marry him, and seven more, patiently, because his love sustained him. How the Great Prophets and Saints of All Religions waited and prayed for God. It is these storytelling factors that the person grafts into the Netnographic Academic Research Praxis-Action programme of personal, professional and social change. This is Humanist Netnography. If we all do Humanist Netnography, scholars from all around the world, and share them, we can begin to build links of understanding between all peoples, and do it from where it has always been traditionally done: academia. Unfiltered as a source of increasing freedom, free information, mutual respect for all peoples, and wise action.

A humanistically branded academic will promote honest understanding of the current world, with all its power sources and influences, and try to think of positive ways to contribute to, help elevate, and transform that world for the betterment of all people, all types of people, all orientations, all different shades of surface, all superficial qualities stripped away except the one that we are all human and all brothers and sisters on this planet. At that point, the personal brand of the protagonist and antagonist will shade into a single experience. Humanist Netnography is the science of helping to amplify the signals of positive change using the current social media environment. It is the first deliberately social media methodology, one which uses media in exactly the same way it studies it: by being out there as a participant – selectively and intelligently, which does not mean not taking risks. Our world is currently challenged in so many ways: a degrading natural environment, terrorist attacks, intolerance between religions, unprecedentedly virulent disease spread, an isolating and alientating material culture, the general lack of reverence for animal and human life. In this world, more than ever, we need Humanist Netnography. In this world of so many serious and overlapping challenges, we can explore together the many ways that Humanist Netnography reminds us that nothing stays impossible forever.

SUMMARY

The Silver Web Surfer beckons you to see humanity's contemporary engagement with technology and connection with new eyes. Then, adopting a spirit of praxis, to seek transformative ways to self and social betterment. Humanist Netnographies communicate their curated stories from the found objects of Internet space, and other carefully collected treasures. Painstakingly fitted together into dramatic narratives that combine the self with data with the social, Humanist Netnographies are both in-reaching and outreaching research projects. They do not shy away from larger-order systemic thinking and theorization, looking for and finding uneven and unfair oppression, surveillance and information asymmetries, manipulation and relations of power from corporations, governments, organizations, and those who run them. Humanist netnographers try to get their message out through social media, connecting with other netnographers and with a widening audience to share and collaboratively build ideas that work for positive change in the world.

KEY READINGS

Fernandez, James W. (1994) 'Culture and transcendent humanization: On the "dynamic of the categorical"', *Ethnos*, 59(3–4): 143–167.

Germonprez, Matt and Dirk S Hovorka (2013) 'Member engagement within digitally enabled social network communities: New methodological considerations', *Information Systems Journal*, 23(6): 525–549.

Schnapp, Jeffrey and Todd Presener (2009) 'The Digital Humanities Manifesto 2.0', available at: http://manifesto.humanities.ucla.edu/2009/05/29/the-digital-humanities-manifesto-20/.

NOTES

1. Is it interesting that both webs and nets are used to catch things? A spider and a fisherman are both passive hunters, of sorts.
2. Correspondingly, netnographers may need to work with them as well as film editors, camera-people, professional research firms, data houses and perhaps even personal brand managers.

REFERENCES

Abu-Lughod, Lila (1986), *Veiled Sentiments: Honor and Poetry in a Bedouin Society*. Berkeley: University of California.

Alang, Sirry M. and Marcel Fomotar (2014) 'Postpartum depression in an online community of lesbian mothers: Implications for clinical practice', *Journal of Gay & Lesbian Mental Health*, forthcoming.

Allen, Gove N., Dan L. Burk and Gordon B. Davis (2006) 'Academic data collection in electronic environments: Defining acceptable use of internet resources', *MIS Quarterly*, 30(3) (September): 599–610.

Amit, Vered and Nigel Rapport (2002) *The Trouble with Community: Anthropological Reflections on Movement, Identity and Collectivity*. London: Pluto.

Anderson, Benedict (1983) *Imagined Communities: Reflections on the Origin and Spread of Nationalism*. London: Verso.

Anderson, Chris (2008) *The Long Tail: Why the Future of Business is Selling Less of More*. New York: Hyperion.

Anderson, Leon (2006) 'Analytic autoethnography', *Journal of Contemporary Ethnography*, 35(August): 373–395.

Andrews, Dorine, Blair Nonnecke and Jennifer Preece (2003) 'Electronic survey methodology: A case study in reaching hard-to-involve internet users', *International Journal of Human–Computer Interaction*, 16(2): 185–210.

Andrusyszyn, Mary Anne and Lynn Davie (1997) 'Facilitating reflection through interactive journal writing in an online graduate course: A qualitative study', *The Journal of Distance Education*, 12(1). Available at: www.jofde.ca/index.php/jde/article/viewArticle/266 (accessed 15 January 2009).

Appadurai, Arjun (1990) 'Disjuncture and difference in the global culture economy', *Theory, Culture and Society*, 7: 295–310.

Arnold, Stephen J. and Eileen Fischer (1994) 'Hermeneutics and consumer research', *Journal of Consumer Research*, 21(June): 55–70.

Association of Internet Researchers Ethics Working Group (2002) *Ethical Decision-making and Internet Research: Recommendations from the AOIR Ethics Working Committee*. Available at: www.aoir.org/reports/ethics.pdf.

Association of Internet Researchers Ethics Working Group (2012) *Ethical Decision-making and Internet Research: Recommendations from the AoIR Ethics Working Committee (Version 2.0)*. Available at: http://aoir.org/reports/ethics2.pdf.

Bahktin, Mikhail (1981) 'Forms of time and the chronotrop in the novel', in Michael Holquist (ed.), *The Dialogic Imagination*. Austin: University of Texas Press. pp. 259–442.

Bakardjieva, Maria (2005) *Internet Society: The Internet in Everyday Life*. London: Sage.

Banner, D.J. and J.W. Albarrran (2009) 'Computer-assisted qualitative data analysis software: A review', *Canadian Journal of Cardiovascular Nursing*, 19(3): 24–31.

Bartl, Michael, Vijai Kumar Kannan and Hanna Stockinger (2013) 'A review and analysis of literature on netnography', HHL Leipzig Graduate School of Management Working Paper, Leipzig, Germany.

Bartle, Caroline, Erel Avineri and Kiron Chatterjee (2013) 'Online information-sharing: A qualitative analysis of community, trust and social influence amongst commuter cyclists in the UK', *Transportation Research Part F: Traffic Psychology and Behaviour*, 16: 60–72.

Bassett, Elizabeth H. and Kate O'Riordan (2002) 'Ethics of internet research: Contesting the human subjects research model', *Ethics and Information Technology*, 4: 233–247.

Bauman, Zygmunt (2003) *Liquid Love: On the Frailty of Human Bonds*. Cambridge: Polity Press.

Baym, Nancy K. (1995) 'The Emergence of community in computer-mediated communication', in Stephen G. Jones (ed.), *Cybersociety*. Thousand Oaks, CA: Sage. pp. 138–163.

Baym, Nancy K. (1999) *Tune in, Log on: Soaps, Fandom, and Online Community*. Thousand Oaks, CA: Sage.

Bazeley, Patricia (2007) *Qualitative Data Analysis with NVivo*. Thousand Oaks, CA: Sage.

Beaulieu, Anne (2004) 'Mediating ethnography: Objectivity and the making of ethnographies of the internet', *Social Epistemology*, 18(2–3; April–September): 139–163.

Behar, Ruth (1996) *The Vulnerable Observer: Anthropology That Breaks Your Heart*. Boston: Beacon.

Belk, Russell, Eileen Fischer and Robert V. Kozinets (2013) *Qualitative Marketing and Consumer Research*. London: Sage.

Belk, Russell W. and Robert V. Kozinets (2005) 'Videography in marketing and consumer research', *Qualitative Marketing Research*, 8(2): 128–141.

Bell, Shannon (2010) *Fast Feminism*. New York: Autonomedia.

Bengry-Howell, Andrew, Rose Wiles, Melanie Nind and Graham Crow (2011) *A Review of the Academic Impact of Three Methodological Innovations: Netnography, Child-Led Research and Creative Research Methods*, NCRM Hub, University of Southampton research paper.

Berdychevsky, Liza, Heather Gibson and Yaniv Poria (2013) 'Women's sexual behavior in tourism: Loosening the bridle', *Annals of Tourism Research*, 42: 65–85.

Benkler, Yochai (2006) *The Wealth of Networks – How Social Production Transforms Markets and Freedom*. New Haven: Yale University Press.

Berger, Peter L. and Thomas Luckmann (1966) *The Social Construction of Reality: A Treatise in the Sociology of Knowledge*. Garden City, NY: Anchor Books.

Berkowitz, Stephen D. (1982) *An Introduction to Structural Analysis: The Network Approach to Social Research*. Toronto: Butterworth.

Bernal, Paul (2012) *The Right to Online Identity*. Available at: http://ssrn.com/abstract=2143138.

Bey, Hakim (1994) *Immediatism*. San Francisco, CA: Zone Books.

Biao, Xiang (2007) *Global 'Body Shopping': An Indian Labor System in the Information Technology Industry*. Princeton, NJ: Princeton University Press.

Biggart, Nicole Woolsey (1989) *Charismatic Capitalism: Direct Selling Organizations in America*. Chicago: University of Chicago Press.

Blanchette, Jean-François (2011), 'A material history of bits', *Journal of the American Association for Information Science and Technology*, 62(6): 1042–1057.

Boczkowski, Pablo (2004) *Digitizing the News: Innovations in Online Newspapers*. Cambridge, MA: MIT Press.

Boellstorff, Tom (2008) *Coming of Age in Second Life: An Anthropologist Explores the Virtually Human*. Princeton: Princeton University Press.

Boellstorff, Tom (2012) 'Rethinking digital antropology', in Heather A. Horst and Daniel Miller, *Digital Anthropology*. London: Bloomsbury. pp. 39–60.

Boellstorff, Tom, Bonnie Nardi, Celia Pearce and T.L. Taylor (2012) *Ethnography and Virtual Worlds: A Handbook of Method*. Princeton, NJ: Princeton University Press.

Boyer, Dominic (2010) 'Digital expertise in online journalism (and anthropology)', *Anthropological Quarterly*, 83(1): 125–147.

Brown, Stephen, Robert V. Kozinets and John F. Sherry, Jr. (2003) 'Teaching old brands new tricks: Retro branding and the revival of brand meaning', *Journal of Marketing*, 67(July): 19–33.

Bruckman, Amy (2002) 'Studying the amateur artist: A perspective on disguising data collected in human subjects research on the internet', *Ethics and Information Technology*, 4: 217–231.

Bruckman, Amy (2006) 'Teaching students to study online communities ethically', *Journal of Information Ethics*, Fall: 82–98.

Buchanan, Elizabeth (2004) *Readings in Virtual Research Ethics: Issues and Controversies*. Hershey, PA: Idea Group.

Buchanan, Elizabeth (2006) 'Introduction: Internet research ethics at a critical juncture', *Journal of Information Ethics*, 15(2): 14–17.

Buchanan, Elizabeth, A. Markham and C. Ess (2010) 'Ethics and internet research commons: Building a sustainable future', *Association of Internet Researchers 11th Annual Conference Workshop*, Gottenburg, Sweden.

Buitelaar, J.C. (2014) 'Privacy and narrativity in the internet era', *The Information Society: An International Journal*, 30(4): 266–281.

Burford, Sally and Sora Park (2014) 'The impact of mobile tablet devises on human information behaviour', *Journal of Documentation*, 70(4): 622–639.

Caliandro, Alessandro (2014) 'Ethnography in digital spaces: Ethnography of virtual worlds, netnography, and digital ethnography', in Rita Denny and Patricia Sunderland (eds), *Handbook of Anthropology in Business*. Walnut Creek, CA: Left Coast Press. pp. 658–680.

Campbell, John Edward (2004) *Getting It On Online: Cyberspace, Gay Male Sexuality and Embodied Identity*. New York: Haworth Press.

Campbell, John Edward (2005) 'Outing PlanetOut: Surveillance, gay marketing, and internet affinity portals', *New Media & Society*, 7(5): 663–683.

Campbell, John Edward and Matt Carlson (2002) 'Panopticon.com: Online surveillance and the commodification of privacy', *Journal of Broadcasting and Electronic Media*, 46(4): 586–606.

Carter, Denise (2005) 'Living in virtual communities: An ethnography of human relationships in cyberspace', *Information, Communication & Society*, 8(2): 148–167.

Castells, Manuel (1996) *The Rise of the Network Society*. Cambridge, MA: Blackwell.

Chan, Anita Say (2008) 'Retiring the network spokesman: the poly-vocality of free software networks in Peru', *Science Studies*, 20(2): 78–99.

Chiumbu, Sarah Helen and Dina Ligaga (2013) '"Communities of strangerhoods?": Internet, mobile phones and the changing nature of radio cultures in South Africa', *Telematics and Informatics*, 30(3): 242–251.

Chouliaraki, Lilie (2010) 'Ordinary witnessing in post-television news: Towards a new moral imagination', *Critical Discourse Studies*, 7(4): 305–319.

Clerc, Susan J. (1996) 'DDEB, GATB, MPPB, and Ratboy: *The X-Files*' media fandom, online and off', in David Lavery, Angela Hague and Marla Cartwright (eds), *Deny All Knowledge: Reading The X-Files*. Syracuse, NY: Syracuse University Press.

Clifford, James and George E. Marcus (eds) (1986) *Writing Culture: The Poetics and Politics of Ethnography*. Berkeley: University of California Press.

Cohen, Anthony P. (1985) *The Symbolic Construction of Community*. London: Tavistock.

Coleman, E. Gabriella (2010) 'Ethnographic approaches to digital media', *Annual Review of Anthropology*, 39: 487–505.

Correll, Shelley (1995) 'The ethnography of an electronic bar: the lesbian café', *Journal of Contemporary Ethnography*, 24(3), October: 270–298.

Couper, M.P. (2000) 'Web-based surveys: A review of issues and approaches', *Public Opinion Quarterly*, 64, 464–494.

Cova, Bernard and Daniele Dalli (2009) 'Working consumers: The next step in marketing theory?', *Marketing Theory*, 9(3): 315–339.

Creswell, John W. (2009) *Research Design: Qualitative, Quantitative, and Mixed Methods Approaches*, 3rd edn. Thousand Oaks, CA: Sage.

Cronin, James M., Mary McCarthy and Alan Collins (2014) 'Creeping edgework: Carnivalesque consumption and the social experience of health risk', *Sociology of Health & Illness*, forthcoming.

Daft, Richard L. and Robert H. Lengel (1986), 'Organizational information requirements, media richness and structural design,' *Management Science*, 32(5), 554–571.

Danet, Brenda (2001) *Cyberpl@y: Communicating Online*. Oxford and New York: Berg.

Daniels, Jessie (2009) *Cyber Racism: White Supremacy Online and the New Attack on Civil Rights*. Lanham, MD: Rowman & Littlefield.

Davis, Erik (1998) *Technosis: Myth, Magic + Mysticism in the Age of Information*. New York: Harmony Books.

Davis, Fred (1959) 'The cabdriver and his fare: Facets of a fleeting relationship', *American Journal of Sociology*, 65: 158–165.

Davis, Teresa (2010) 'Third Spaces or Heterotopias? Recreating and Negotiating Migrant Identity Using Online Spaces', *Sociology*, 44(4): 661–677.

Deakin, Hannah and Kelly Wakefield (2014) 'Skype interviewing: Reflections of two PhD researchers', *Qualitative Research*, 14(5): 603–616.

Deegan, Mary Jo (2001) 'The Chicago school of ethnography', in P. Atkinson, A. Coffey, S. Delamont, J. Lofland and L. Lofland (eds), *Handbook of Ethnography*. Thousand Oaks, CA: Sage. pp. 11–25.

Denzin, Norman K. (1997) *Interpretive Ethnography: Ethnographic Practices for the 21st Century*. Thousand Oaks, CA: Sage.

Denzin, Norman K. and Yvonna S. Lincoln (1994) *Handbook of Qualitative Research*. Thousand Oaks, CA: Sage.

Denzin, Norman K. and Yvonna S. Lincoln (2005) *The Sage Handbook of Qualitative Research*, 3rd edn. Thousand Oaks, CA: Sage.

Driscoll, Cathrine and Melissa Gregg (2010) 'My profile: The ethics of virtual ethnography', *Emotion, Space and Society*, 3: 15–20.

Duarte, Nancy (2010) *Resonate: Present Visual Stories that Transform Audiences*. New York: Wiley.

Dubrovsky, Vitaly, Sara Kiesler and Beheruz Sethna (1991) 'The equalization phenomenon: Status effects in computer-mediated and face-to-face decision making groups', *Human–Computer Interaction*, 6: 119–146.

Duggan, Maeve and Aaron Smith (2013) 'Social media update 2013', Pew Internet & American Life Project, 30 December. Available at: http://www.pewinternet. org/2013/12/30/social-media-update-2013/ (accessed 15 October 2014).

Dyck, Noel (2002) '"Have you been to Hayward Field?": Children's Sport and the Construction of Community in Suburban Canada', in Vered Amit (ed.), *Realising Community: Concepts, Social Relationships, and Sentiments*. London and New York: Routledge.

Dyke, Sarah (2013) 'Utilising a blended ethnographic approach to explore the online and offline lives of pro-ana community members', *Ethnography and Education*, 8(2): 146–161.

Ellis, Caroline and Arthur P. Bochner (2000) 'Autoethnography, personal narrative, reflexivity: Researcher as subject', in N.K. Denzin and Y.S. Lincoln (eds), *Handbook of Qualitative Research*, 2nd edn. Thousand Oaks, CA: Sage. pp. 733–768.

Ellul, Jacques (1964) *The Technological Society*. New York: Random House.

Emerson, Robert M., Rachel I. Fretz and Linda L. Shaw (1995) *Writing Ethnographic Fieldnotes*. Chicago: University of Chicago Press.

Emerson, Robert M., Rachel I. Fretz and Linda L. Shaw (2011) *Writing Ethnographic Fieldnotes*, 2nd edn. Chicago: University of Chicago Press.

Eriksson Henrik, Mats Christiansen, Jessica Holmgren, Annica Engstrom and Martin Salzmann–Erikson (2014) 'Nursing under the skin: A netnographic study of metaphors and meanings in nursing tattoos', *Nursing Inquiry*, 21(4): 318–326.

Ess, Charles (2009) *Digital Media Ethics*. Cambridge: Polity.

Fernandez, James W. (1994) 'Culture and transcendent humanization: On the "dynamic of the categorical"', *Ethnos*, 59(3–4): 143–167.

Ferreira, Cátia Sofia Afonso (2012) 'Second Life: Representation and remediation of social space', unpublished Catholic University of Portugal Doctoral Dissertation.

Fine, Gary Alan (1995) *A Second Chicago School: The Development of a Postwar American Sociology*. Chicago: University of Chicago Press.

Fischer, Hervé (2006) *Digital Shock: Confronting the New Reality*. Montreal and Kingston, Canada: McGill-Queen's University Press.

Fox, Susannah and Lee Rainie (2014) 'The Web at 25 in the U.S.'. Pew Internet & American Life Project, 23 April. Available at: http://www.pewinternet. org/2014/02/27/the-web-at-25-in-the-u-s/ (accessed 15 October 2014).

Frankel, Mark S. and Sanyin Siang (1999) 'Ethical and legal aspects of human subjects research on the internet', *American Association for the Advancement of Science (AAAS)*, Washington, DC, Available at: www.aaas.org/spp/dspp/sfrl/projects/intres/report.pdf/.

Frenzen, Jonathan K. and Harry L. Davis (1990) 'Purchasing behavior in embedded markets,' *Journal of Consumer Research*, 17(June): 1–12.

Fuller, C and Narasimhan, H. (2007) 'Information technology professionals and the new-rich middle class in Chennai (Madras)', *Modern Asian Studies*, 41(1): 121–150.

Füller, Johann, Gregor Jawecki and Hans Mühlbacher (2007) 'Innovation creation by online basketball communities', *Journal of Business Research*, 60(1): 60–71.

Garcia, Angela Cora, Alecea I. Standlee, Jennifer Bechkoff and Yan Cui (2009) 'Ethnographic approaches to the internet and computer-mediated communication', *Journal of Contemporary Ethnography*, 38(1)(February): 52–84.

Garton, Laura, Caroline Haythornthwaite and Barry Wellman (1999) 'Studying On-Line Social Networks', in Steve Jones (ed.), *Doing Internet Research: Critical Issues in Methods for Examining the Net*. Thousand Oaks, CA: Sage. pp. 75–105.

Geertz, Clifford (1973) *The Interpretation of Cultures*. New York: Basic Books.

Germonprez, Matt and Dirk S. Hovorka (2013) 'Member engagement within digitally enabled social network communities: new methodological considerations', *Information Systems Journal*, 23(6): 525–549.

Gershon, I. (2010) *The Break-Up 2.0: Disconnecting Over New Media*. Ithaca, NY: Cornell University Press.

Gibbs, Graham R. (2014) 'Using software in qualitative analysis' in Uwe Fleck (ed.), *The SAGE Handbook of Qualitative Data Analysis*. London, UK: Sage. pp. 277–295.

Ginsburg, Faye (2012) 'Disability in the digital age,' in Heather A. Horst and Daniel Miller, *Digital Anthropology*. London: Bloomsbury. pp. 101–126.

Gloor, Peter (2006) *Swarm Creativity, Competitive Advantage Through Collaborative Innovation Networks*. Oxford: Oxford University Press.

Gloor, Peter A., Francesca Grippa, Amy Borgert, Richard B. Colletti, George Dellal, Peter Margolis and Michael Seid (2011) 'Towards growing a COIN in a medical research community', *Procedia – Social and Behavioral Sciences*, 26: 3–16.

Goffman, Erving (1959) *The Presentation of Self in Everyday Life*. New York: Anchor.

Goffman, Erving (1974) *Frame Analysis: An Essay on the Organization of Experience*. New York: Harper and Row.

Goffman, Erving (1989) 'On fieldwork', *Journal of Contemporary Ethnography*, 18: 123–132.

Gorbis, Marina (2013) *The Nature of the Future: Dispatches from the Socialstructured World*. New York: Simon & Schuster.

Gould, Stephen J. (2012) 'The emergence of Consumer Introspection Theory (CIT): Introduction to a JBR special issue', *Journal of Business Research*, 65: 453–460.

Grabher, Gernot and Oliver Ibert (2014) 'Distance as asset? Knowledge collaboration in hybrid virtual communities', *Journal of Economic Geography*, 14: 97–123.

Granovetter, Mark (1985) 'Economic action and social structure: The problem of embeddedness,' *American Journal of Sociology*, 91 (November): 481–510.

Gubrium, Jaber F. and James A. Holstein (eds) (2001) *Handbook of Interview Research: Context and Method*. Thousand Oaks, CA: Sage.

Gustavsson, Anders (2013) 'Death and bereavement on the internet in Sweden and Norway', *Folklore: Electronic Journal of Folklore*, 53: 99–116. Available at: www.ceeol.com.

Hair, Neil and Moira Clark (2007) 'The ethical dilemmas and challenges of ethnographic research in electronic communities', *International Journal of Market Research*, 49(6): 781–800.

Hall, Neil (2014) 'The Kardashian Index: A measure of discrepant social media profile for scientists,' *Genome Biology*, 15: 424.

Han, Chang-Ryung (2012) 'Is the immigration of Korean Sex Workers to the United States sex trafficking or migrant smuggling?', The Brookings Institution research paper.

Hanna, Paul (2012) 'Using Internet technologies (such as Skype) as a research medium: A research note', *Qualitative Research* 12(2): 239–242.

Hayano, David (1979) 'Auto-ethnography: Paradigms, problems, and prospects', *Human Organization*, 38: 99–104.

Hayano, David (1982) *Poker Faces: The Life and Work of Professional Card Players*. Berkeley: University of California Press.

Haythornthwaite, Caroline (2005) 'Social networks and internet connectivity effects', *Information, Communication & Society*, 8(2), June: 125–147.

Haythornthwaite, Caroline, Barry Wellman and Marilyn Mantei (1995) 'Work relationships and media use: A social network analysis', *Group Decision and Negotiation*, 4(3): 193–211.

Hayles, Katherine (2012) *How We Think: Digital Media and Contemporary Technologies*. Chicago and London: University of Chicago Press.

Hemetsberger, Andrea and Christian Reinhardt (2006) 'Learning and knowledge-building in open-source communities: a social-experiential approach', *Management Learning*, 37(2): 187–214.

Herring, Susan (1996) 'Linguistic and critical analysis of computer-mediated communication: Some ethical and scholarly considerations', *The Information Society*, 12: 153–160.

Hiltz, Starr Roxanne and Murray Turoff (1978) *The Network Nation: Human Communication via Computer*. Reading, MA: Addison-Wesley.

Hine, Christine (2000) *Virtual Ethnography*. London: Sage.

Hobbs, Dick (2006) 'Ethnography', in Victor Jupp (ed.), *Sage Dictionary of Social Research Methods*. London: Sage.

Horst, Heather A. and Daniel Miller (2006) *The Cell Phone: An Anthropology of Communication*. New York: Berg.

Horst, Heather A. and Daniel Miller (2012) *Digital Anthropology*. London: Bloomsbury.

Howard, Philip N. (2002) 'Network ethnography and the hypermedia organization: New media, new organizations, new methods', *New Media & Society*, 4(4): 550–574.

Hudson, James M. and Amy Bruckman (2004) '"Go away": Participant objections to being studied', *The Information Society*, 20(2): 127–139.

Humphrey, Caroline (2009) 'The mask and the face: Imagination and social life in Russian chat rooms and beyond,' *Ethnos*, 74: 31–50.

Hyde, Lewis (1979) *The Gift: Imagination and the Erotic Life of Property*. New York: Vintage Books.

Isupova, Olga (2011) 'Support through patient internet-communities: Lived experience of Russian in vitro fertilization patient', *International Journal of Qualitative Studies on Health and Well-being*, 6(3). Accessed 12 July 2011, doi:10.3402/qhw.v6i3.5907.

Ito, M., Okabe, D. and Matsuba, M. (eds) (2005) *Personal, Portable, Pedestrian: Mobile Phones in Japanese Life*. Cambridge, MA: MIT Press.

Jackson, Michael (1998) *Minima Ethnographica: Intersubjectivity and the Anthropological Project*. Chicago: University of Chicago.

Jacobs, Katrien (2010) 'Lizzy Kinsey and the adult friendfinders: An ethnographic study of Internet sex and pornographic self-display in Hong Kong', *Culture, Health & Sexuality: An International Journal for Research, Intervention and Care*, 12(6): 691–703.

Jeacle, Ingrid and Chris Carter (2011) 'In TripAdvisor we trust: Rankings, calculative regimes and abstract systems', *Accounting, Organizations and Society*, 36 (4–5): 293–309.

Jenkins, Henry (1992) *Textual Poachers: Television Fans and Participatory Culture*, New York: Routledge.

Jenkins, Henry, Sam Ford, and Green Joshua (2013) *Spreadable Media: Creating Value and Meaning in a Networked Culture*. New York, NY: New York University Press.

Johns, M., S.L. Chen and J. Hall (eds) (2003) *Online Social Research: Methods, Issues, and Ethics*. New York: Peter Lang.

Jones, Graham and Bambi Schieffelin (2009) 'Enquoting voices, accomplishing talk: Uses of be + like in instant messaging', *Lang. Commun.*, 29(1): 77–113.

Kavanaugh, A. and S. Patterson (2001) 'The impact of community computer networks on social capital and community involvement', *American Behavioral Scientist*, 45: 496–509.

Keen, Andrew (2007) *The Cult of the Amateur: How Today's Internet is Killing Our Culture*. New York: Currency/Doubleday.

Kiesler, Sara, Jane Siegel and Timothy McGuire (1984) 'Social psychological aspects of computer-mediated communication', *American Psychologist*, 39(10): 1123–1134.

Kiesler, Sara, D. Zubrow, A.M. Moses and V. Geller (1985) 'Affect in Computer-mediated Communication: An Experiment in Synchronous Terminal-to-Terminal Discussion', *Human-Computer Interaction*, 1: 77–104.

King, Storm (1996) 'Researching internet communities: Proposed ethical guidelines for the reporting of results', *The Information Society*, 12: 119–128.

Kirschenbaum, Matthew G. (2008) *Mechanisms: New Media and Forensic Imagination*. Cambridge, MA: MIT Press.

Kivits, Joëlle (2005) 'Online interviewing and the research relationship', in Christine Hine (ed.), *Virtual Methods: Issues in Social Research on the Internet*. Oxford: Berg. pp. 35–50.

Koestler, Arthur (1967) *The Ghost in the Machine*. New York: Macmillan.

Kozinets, Robert V. (1997) '"I want to believe": A netnography of *The X-Files'* subculture of consumption', in Merrie Brucks and Deborah J. MacInnis (eds), *Advances in Consumer Research*, Volume 24. Provo, UT: Association for Consumer Research. pp. 470–475.

Kozinets, Robert V. (1998) 'On netnography: Initial reflections on consumer research investigations of cyberculture', in Joseph Alba and Wesley Hutchinson (eds),

Advances in Consumer Research, Volume 25. Provo, UT: Association for Consumer Research. pp. 366–371.

Kozinets, Robert V. (1999) 'E-tribalized marketing? The strategic implications of virtual communities of consumption', *European Management Journal*, 17(3): 252–264.

Kozinets, Robert V. (2001) 'Utopian enterprise: Articulating the meanings of *Star Trek*'s culture of consumption', *Journal of Consumer Research*, 28(June): 67–88.

Kozinets, Robert V. (2002a) 'The field behind the screen: Using netnography for marketing research in online communities', *Journal of Marketing Research*, 39 (February): 61–72.

Kozinets, Robert V. (2002b) 'Can consumers escape the market? Emancipatory illuminations from burning man', *Journal of Consumer Research*, 29(June): 20–38.

Kozinets, Robert V. (2002c) 'Desert pilgrim', *Consumption, Markets and Culture*, 5 (September): 171–186.

Kozinets, Robert V. (2006) 'Netnography 2.0', in Russell W. Belk (ed.), *Handbook of Qualitative Research Methods in Marketing*. Cheltenham, UK and Northampton, MA: Edward Elgar Publishing. pp. 129–142.

Kozinets, Robert V. (2007) 'Inno-tribes: *Star Trek* as wikimedia', in Bernard Cova, Robert V. Kozinets and Avi Shankar (eds), *Consumer Tribes*. Oxford and Burlington, MA: Butterworth-Heinemann. pp. 194–211.

Kozinets, Robert V. (2008) 'Technology/ideology: How ideological fields influence consumers' technology narratives', *Journal of Consumer Research*, 34(April): 864–881.

Kozinets, Robert V. (2010) *Netnography: Doing Ethnographic Research Online*. London: Sage.

Kozinets, Robert V. (2012) 'Me/my research/avatar', *Journal of Business Research*, 65(April): 478–482.

Kozinets, Robert V. and Richard Kedzior (2009) 'I, Avatar: Auto-netnographic research in virtual worlds', in Michael Solomon and Natalie Wood (eds), *Virtual Social Identity and Social Behavior*. Armonk, NY: M.E. Sharpe. pp. 3–19.

Kozinets, Robert V., Kristine de Valck, Andrea Wojnicki and Sarah Wilner (2010) 'Networked narratives: Understanding word-of-mouth marketing in online communities', *Journal of Marketing*, 74(2): 71–89.

Kozinets, Robert V., Pierre-Yann Dolbec and Amanda Earley (2014) 'Netnographic analysis: Understanding culture through social media data,' in Uwe Flick (ed.), *Sage Handbook of Qualitative Data Analysis*. Sage: London. pp. 262–275.

Kozinets, Robert V., John F. Sherry, Jr., Diana Storm, Adam Duhachek, Krittinee Nuttavuthisit and Benét DeBerry-Spence (2004) 'Ludic agency and retail spectacle', *Journal of Consumer Research*, 31 (December): 658–672.

Kraut, Robert, Judith Olson, Mahzarin Banaji, Amy Bruckman, Jeffrey Cohen and Mick Cooper (2004) 'Psychological research online: Report of Board of Scientific Affairs' Advisory Group on the Conduct of Research on the Internet', *American Psychologist*, 59(4): 1–13.

Krotoski, Aleks (2010) 'Introduction to the Special Issue: Research ethics in online communities', *International Journal of Internet Research Ethics*, 3(12).

Kulavuz-Onal, Derya and Camilla Vásquez (2013) 'Reconceptualising fieldwork in a netnography of an online community of English language teachers', *Ethnography and Education*, 8(2): 224–238.

Laclau, Ernesto and Chantal Mouffe (1985) *Hegemony and Socialist Strategy*. London: Verso.

Langer, Roy and Suzanne C. Beckman (2005) 'Sensitive research topics: Netnography revisited', *Qualitative Market Research: An International Journal*, 8(2): 189–203.

Larkin, B. (2008) *Signal and Noise: Media, Infrastructure, and Urban Culture in Nigeria*. Durham, NC: Duke University Press.

Lather, Patti (1993) 'Issues of validity in openly ideological research: Between a rock and a soft place', *Interchange*, 17: 63–84.

Lather, Patti (2001) 'Postmodernism, poststructuralism and post(critical) ethnography', in Paul Atkinson et al. (eds), *Handbook of Ethnography*. Thousand Oaks, CA: Sage. pp. 477–492.

Latour, Bruno and Steve Woolgar (1979) *Laboratory Life: The Construction of Scientific Facts*. Princeton, NJ: Princeton University Press.

Lazar, J. and Preece, J. (1999) 'Designing and implementing web-based surveys', *Journal of Computer Information Systems*, 34(4): 63–67.

LeBesco, Kathleen (2004) 'Managing visibility, intimacy, and focus in online critical ethnography', in M.D. Johns, S.-L.S. Chen and G.J. Hall (eds), *Online Social Research: Methods, Issues, and Ethics*. New York: Peter Lang. pp. 63–79.

Leong, Tim (2013) *SuperGraphics: A Visual Guide to the Comic Book Universe*. San Francisco, CA: Chronicle Books.

Levy, Sidney J. (1959) 'Symbols for Sale', *Harvard Business Review*, 37 (July/August), 117–24.

Lévy, Pierre (2001) *Cyberculture*, translated by Robert Bononno. Minneapolis, MN: University of Minnesota Press.

Levy, Sidney J. (1996) 'Stalking the amphisbaena', *Journal of Consumer Research*, 23(3): 163–176.

Lewins, Ann and Christina Silver (2007) *Using Software in Qualitative Research: A Step-by-Step Guide*. Thousand Oaks, CA: Sage.

Li, Charlene and Josh Bernoff (2008) *Groundswell: Winning in a World Transformed by Social Technologies*. Boston, MA: Harvard Business Press.

Lillqvist, Ella (2014) 'Conceptualizing company-stakeholder power relations in online discourse', paper presented at 11th International Conference on Organizational Discourse, Cardiff, UK, July.

Lipinski, Tomas A. (2006) 'Emerging tort issues in the collection and dissemination of internet-based research data', *Journal of Information Ethics*, Fall: 55–81.

Lipinski, Tomas A. (2008) 'Emerging legal issues in the collection and dissemination of internet-sourced research data: Part I, basic tort law issues and negligence', *International Journal of Internet Research Ethics*, 1(1): 92–114. Available at: www.uwm.edu/Dept/SOIS/cipr/ijire/ijire_1.1_lipinski.pdf/.

Lomborg, Stine (2012) 'Personal internet archives and ethics', *Research Ethics*, 9(2): 20–31.

Lysloff, René T.A. (2003) 'Musical community on the internet: An on-line ethnography', *Cultural Anthropology*, 18(2): 233–263.

Maclagan, E.R.D. and A.G.B. Russell (eds) (1907) *The Prophetic Books of W. Blake*. London: A. H. Bullen.

Madianou, M. and Daniel Miller (2011) *Migration and New Media: Transnational Families and Polymedia*. London: Routledge.

Maíz-Arévalo, Carmen (2013) '"Just click 'Like'": Computer-mediated responses to spanish compliments', *Journal of Pragmatics*, 51: 47–67.

Marchi, Gianluca, Claudio Giachetti and Pamela de Gennaro (2011) 'Extending lead-user theory to online brand communities: The case of the community Ducati', *Technovation*, 31(8): 350–361.

Marcus, George E. and Dick Cushman (1982) 'Ethnographies as texts', *Annual Review of Anthropology*, 11: 25–69.

Marcus, George E. and Michael Fischer (1986) *Anthropology As Cultural Critique: An Experimental Moment in the Human Sciences*, Chicago: University of Chicago Press.

Markham, Annette N. (2004) 'Representation in online ethnographies: A matter of context sensitivity', in M.D. Johns, S.-L.S. Shannon and G.J. Hall (eds), *Online Social Research: Methods, Issues, and Ethics*. New York: Peter Lang. pp. 141–155.

Markham, Annette N. (2012) 'Fabrication as ethical practice', *Information, Communication, and Society*, 15(3): 334–353.

Marres, Noortje (2012) *Material Participation: Technology, the Environment, and Everyday Publics*. Basingstroke, UK: Palgrave Macmillan.

Marwick, Alice and danah boyd (2011) 'I tweet honestly, I tweet passionately: Twitter users, context collapse, and the imagined audience', *New Media and Society*, 13: 96–113.

Marx, Leo (1997) 'Technology: The emergence of a hazardous concept,' *Social Research*, 64(3): 965–988.

Mathwick, Charla, Caroline Wiertz and Ko De Ruyter (2008) 'Social capital production in a virtual P3 community', *Journal of Consumer Research*, 34 (April): 832–89.

Maxwell, Richard and Toby Miller (2008) 'Ecological ethics and media technology', *International Journal of Communication,* 2: 331–353. Available at: http://ijoc.org/ojs/index.php/ijoc/article/view/320/151.

McCracken, Grant (1988) *The Long Interview*. Beverly Hills, CA: Sage.

McCracken, Grant (1997) *Plenitude*. Toronto, Canada: Periph.: Fluide.

McKee, H.A. and J.E. Porter (2009) *The Ethics of Internet Research: A Rhetorical, Case-based Process*. New York: Peter Lang Publishing.

McLuhan, Marshall (1970) *Culture is our Business*. New York: McGraw-Hill.

McQuarrie, Edward F., Jessica Miller and Barbara J. Phillips (2013) 'The megaphone effect: Taste and audience in fashion blogging', *Journal of Consumer Research*, 40(1): 136–158.

Mead, George Herbert (1938) *The Philosophy of the Act*. Chicago: University of Chicago Press.

M'Gonigle, Michael and Justine Starke (2006) *Planet U: Sustaining the World, Reinventing the University*. Gabriola Island, BC: New Society Publishers.

Miles, Matthew B. and A. Michael Huberman (1994) *Qualitative Data Analysis: An Expanded Sourcebook*, 2nd edn. Thousand Oaks, CA: Sage.

Miley, Frances and Andrew Read (2012) 'Jokes in popular culture: The characterisation of the accountant', *Accounting, Auditing & Accountability*, 25(4): 703–718.

Miller, Daniel and Heather A. Horst (2012) 'The digital and the human: A prospectus for digital anthropology', in Heather A. Horst and Daniel Miller, *Digital Anthropology*. London: Bloomsbury. pp. 3–35.

Miller, Daniel and Don Slater (2000) *The Internet: An Ethnographic Approach*. New York: Berg.

Minowa, Yuko, Luca M. Visconti and Pauline Maclaran (2012) 'Researchers' introspection for multi-sited ethnographers: A xenoheteroglossic autoethnography', *Journal of Business Research*, 65: 483–489.

Mkono, Muchazondida, Kevin Markwell and Erica Wilson (2013) 'Applying Quan and Wang's structural model of the tourist experience: A Zimbabwean netnography of food tourism', *Tourism Management Perspectives*, 5: 68–74.

Moffitt, Sean and Mike Dover (2011) *Wikibrands: Reinventing Your Company in a Customer-Driven Marketplace*. New York: McGraw-Hill.

Morozov, Evgeny (2009) 'How dictators watch us on the Web', *Prospect,* 165. Available at: www.prospectmagazine.co.uk/2009/11/how-dictators-watch-us-on-the-web/.

Mudry, Tanya E. and Tom Strong (2012) 'Doing recovery online,' *Qualitative Health Research*, 23(3): 313–325.

Muñiz, Albert M. Jr. and Hope Jensen Schau (2005) 'Religiosity in the abandoned Apple Newton Brand Community', *Journal of Consumer Research*, 31(4): 737–747.

Munt, Sally R. (ed.) (2001) *Technospaces: Inside the New Media*. London: Continuum.

Murray, Jeff B. and Julie L. Ozanne (1991) 'The critical imagination: Emancipatory interests in consumer research', *Journal of Consumer Research*, 18: 129–144.

Nakamura, L. (2007) *Digitizing Race: Visual Cultures of the Internet*. Minneapolis: University of Minnesota Press.

Narayanan, Arvind and Vitaly Shmatikov (2009) 'De-anonymizing social networks', paper presented at the 30th IEEE Symposium on Security and Privacy.

Newhagen, John E. and Sheizaf Rafaeli (1996) 'Why communication researchers should study the internet: A dialogue [on-line]', *Journal of Computer-mediated Communication*, 1(4). Available at: http://jcmc.indiana.edu/voll/issue4/rafaeli.html.

Nimrod, Galit (2011) 'The fun culture in seniors' online communities', *The Gerontologist*, 51(2): 226–237.

Nissenbaum, H. (2010) *Privacy in Context: Technology, Policy, and the Integrity of Social Life*. Stanford, CA: Stanford University Press.

Nye, David E. (2007) 'Technology'. Available at: www.sdu.dk/Hum/amstud/activities/tech.pdf (accessed 6 January 2007).

O'Leary, Killian and Conor Carroll (2013) 'The online poker sub-culture: Dialogues, interactions and networks', *Journal of Gambling Studies*, 29: 613–630.

Parmentier, Marie-Agnès (2009) 'Consuming and producing human brands: A study of online fans of reality TV', unpublished York University Doctoral Dissertation.

Penley, Constance and Andrew Ross (eds) (1991) *Technoculture: Cultural Politics*. Minneapolis, MN: University of Minnesota Press.

Pettigrew, Simone, Melanie Pescud, Wade Jarvis and Dave Webb (2013) '"Teens" blog accounts of the role of adults in youth alcohol consumption', *Journal of Social Marketing*, 3(1): 28–40.

Protection of Human Subjects, US Federal Code Title 45, Section 46 (2009). Available at: www.hhs.gov/ohrp/humansubjects/guidance/45cfr46.htm (accessed 3 February 2009).

Putnam, Robert D. (2000) *Bowling Alone: The Collapse and Revival of American Community*. New York: Simon & Schuster.

Rainie, Lee and Barry Wellman (2012) *Networked: The New Social Operating System*. Cambridge, MA and London: MIT Press.

Rapaille, Clotaire (2006), *The Culture Code: An Ingenious Way to Understand Why People around the World by and Live As They Do*. New York: Broadway Books.

Rehn, Alf (2001) *Electronic Potlatch: A Study on New Technologies and Primitive Economic Behaviors*. Stockholm: Royal Institute of Technology.

Reid, Elizabeth (1996) 'Informed consent in the study of on-line communities: A reflection on the effects of computer-mediated social research', *The Information Society*, 12: 169–174.

Rheingold, Howard (1993) *The Virtual Community: Homesteading on the Electronic Frontier*. Reading, MA: Addison-Wesley.

Rice, Ronald E. and E.M. Rogers (1984) 'New methods and data for the study of new media', in R.E. Rice (ed.), *The New Media, Communication, Research, and Technology*. Beverly Hills, CA: Sage Publications. pp. 81–99.

Rice, Ronald E. and G. Love (1987) 'Electronic emotion: Socio-emotional content in a computer-mediated communication network', *Communication Research*, 14: 85–108.

Richards, Lyn (2005) *Handling Qualitative Data: A Practical Guide*. London: Sage.

Ricoeur, Paul (1996) *The Hermeneutics of Action* (ed. Richard Kearney). London: Sage.

Rogers, Richard (2009) *The End of the Virtual: Digital Methods*. Amsterdam, Holland: University of Amsterdam Press.

Rokka, Joonas (2010) 'Netnographic inquiry and new translocal sites of the social', *International Journal of Consumer Studies*, 34: 381–387.

Rokka, Joonas and Johanna Moisander (2009) 'Environmental dialogue in online communities: Negotiating ecological citizenship among global travellers', *International Journal of Consumer Studies*, 33: 199–205.

Ronai, Carol Rambo (1992) 'The reflexive self through narrative: A night in the life of a dancer/researcher', in C. Ellis and M. Flaherty (eds), *Investigating Subjectivity*. Newbury Park, CA: Sage. pp. 102–124.

Ronai, Carol Rambo (1995) 'Multiple reflections of child sex abuse: An argument for a layered account', *Journal of Contemporary Ethnography*, 23: 395–426.

Ronai, Carol Rambo (1998) 'Sketching with Derrida: An ethnography of a researcher/erotic dancer', *Qualitative Inquiry*, 4(3): 405–420.

Roth, Ann-Christine Vallberg (2012) 'Parenthood in intensified documentation and assessment practice – with the focus on the home-school relation in Sweden', *International Journal about Parents in Education*, 6(1): 42–56.

Salzmann-Erikson, Martin and Henrik Eriksson (2012) 'LiLEDDA: A six-step forum-based netnographic research method for nursing science', *Aporia: The Nursing Journal*, 4(4): 7–18.

Sandlin, Jennifer A. (2007) 'Netnography as a consumer education research tool', *International Journal of Consumer Studies*, 31(3): 288–294.

Scaraboto, Daiane (2013) 'Cultures of circulation and the distribution of co-created value', unpublished York University Doctoral Dissertation.

Schau, Hope Jensen and Mary C. Gilly (2003) 'We are what we post? The presentation of self in personal webspace', *Journal of Consumer Research*, 30(4): 385–404.

Schivelbusch, Wolfgang (1986) *The Railway Journey: The Industrialization of Space and Time in the 19th Century*. New York: Berg.

Schnapp, Jeffrey and Todd Presener (2009) *The Digital Humanities Manifesto 2.0.* Available at: http://manifesto.humanities.ucla.edu/2009/05/29/the-digital-humanities-manifesto-20/.

Schull, Natasha (2011) *Addiction by Design: Machine Gambling in Las Vegas.* Princeton, NJ: Princeton University Press.

Schwandt, Thomas A. (1994) 'On understanding understanding', *Qualitative Inquiry*, 5(4), 451–464.

Scott, John (1991) *Social Network Analysis: A Handbook.* London: Sage.

Senft, T. (2008) *Camgirls: Celebrity and Community in the Age of Social Networks.* New York: Peter Lang.

Sharf, Barbara (1999) 'Beyond netiquette: The ethics of doing naturalistic discourse research on the internet', in Steve Jones (ed.), *Doing Internet Research: Critical Issues and Methods for Examining the Net.* London: Sage.

Sherblom, John (1988) 'Direction, function, and signature in electronic mail', *Journal of Business Communication*, 25: 39–54.

Sherry, John F. Jr (1991) 'Postmodern alternatives: The interpretive turn in consumer research', in H. Kassarjian and T. Robertson (eds), *Handbook of Consumer Theory and Research.* Englewood Cliffs, NJ: Prentice-Hall. pp. 548–591.

Sherry, John F., Jr. and Robert V. Kozinets (2001) 'Qualitative inquiry in marketing and consumer research,' in Dawn Iacobucci (ed.), *Kellogg on Marketing.* New York: Wiley Books. pp. 165–194.

Sherry, John F. Jr. and John W. Schouten (2002) 'A place for poetry in consumer research', *Journal of Consumer Research,* 29: 218–234.

Short, John, Ederyn Williams and Bruce Christie (1976) *The Social Psychology of Telecommunications.* New York: Wiley.

Sigfussona, Thor and Sylvie Chetty (2013) 'Building international entrepreneurial virtual networks in cyberspace', *Journal of World Business*, 48(2): 260–270.

Silver, David (2006) 'Introduction: Where is internet studies?', in David Silver and Adrienne Massanari (eds), *Critical Cyberculture Studies.* New York and London: New York University Press. pp. 1–14.

Silverstone, Roger and Eric Hirsch (eds) (1992) *Consuming Technologies: Media and Information in Domestic Spaces.* London/New York: Routledge.

Silverstone, Roger, Eric Hirsch and David Morley (1999) 'Information and communication technologies and the moral economy of the household', in Roger Silverstone and Eric Hirsch (eds), *Consuming Technologies.* London and New York: Routledge. pp. 15–31.

Sirsi, Ajay K., James C. Ward and Peter H. Reingen (1996) 'Microcultural analysis of variation in sharing of causal reasoning about behavior', *Journal of Consumer Research*, 22: 345–373.

Small, Jennie and Candice Harris (2014) 'Crying babies on planes: Aeromobility and parenting', *Annals of Tourism Research*, 48: 27–41.

Smith, Aaron C.T. and Bob Stewart (2012) 'Body perceptions and health behaviors in an online bodybuilding community', *Qualitative Health Research*, 22(7): 971–985.

Smith, Marc A., Lee Rainie, Ben Shneiderman and Itai Himelboim (2014) 'Mapping twitter topic networks: From polarized crowds to community clusters', *Pew*

Internet & American Life Project, 20 February. Available at: www.pewinternet. org/2014/02/20/mapping-twitter-topic-networks-from-polarized-crowds-to-community-clusters/ (accessed 15 October 2014).

Sohn, Changsoo (2001) 'Validity of web-based survey in IS related research as an alternative to mail survey', *AMCIS 2001 Proceedings. Paper 318*. Available at: http://aisel.aisnet.org/amcis2001/318.

Solis, Brian (2010) *Engage!* Hoboken, NJ: Wiley.

Spiggle, Susan (1994) 'Analysis and interpretation of qualitative data in consumer research', *Journal of Consumer Research*, 21: 491–503.

Sproull, Lee and Sara Kiesler (1986) 'Reducing social context cues: The case of electronic mail', *Management Science,* 32: 1492–1512.

Sreberny, Annabelle and Gholam Khiabany (2010) *Blogistan: The Internet and Politics in Iran*. London: Tauris.

Srinivasan, Ramesh (2006) 'Indigenous, ethnic and cultural articulations of the new media', *International Journal of Cultural Studies,* 9(4): 497–518.

St John, Winsome and Peter Johnson (2000) 'The pros and cons of data analysis software for qualitative research', *Journal of Nursing Scholarship*, 32(4): 393–397.

Stefik, Mark (1996) *Internet Dreams: Archetypes, Myths, and Metaphors*. Cambridge, MA: MIT Press.

Sudnow, D. (1978) *Ways of the Hand*. Cambridge, MA: Harvard University Press.

Sudweeks, Fay and Simeon J. Simoff (1999) 'Complementary explorative data analysis: The reconciliation of quantitative and qualitative principles', in Steve Jones (ed.), *Doing Internet Research: Critical Issues in Methods for Examining the Net*. Thousand Oaks, CA: Sage.

Sultana, Shaila, Sender Dovchin and Alastair Pennycook (2014) 'Transglossic language practices of young adults in Bangladesh and Mongolia', *International Journal of Multilingualism*, 11: 449.

Sumiala, Johanna Maaria and Minttu Tikka (2013) 'Broadcast yourself – global news! A netnography of the "Flotilla" news on YouTube', *Communication, Culture & Critique,* 6: 318–335.

Tacchi, Jo (2012) 'Digital engagement: Voice and participation in development,' in Heather A. Horst and Daniel Miller, *Digital Anthropology*. London: Bloomsbury. pp. 225–244.

Tackett-Gibson, Melissa (2008) 'Constructions of risk and harm in online discussions of ketamine use', *Addiction Research & Theory*, 16 (3): 245–257.

Tapscott, Don and Anthony D. Williams (2007) *Wikinomics: How Mass Collaboration Changes Everything*. New York: Penguin.

Taylor, T.L. (1999) 'Life in virtual worlds: Plural existence, multi-modalities, and other online research challenges', *American Behavioral Scientist*, 43(3): 436–449.

Teilhard de Chardin, Pierre (1959) *The Phenomenon of Man*. New York: Harper and Row.

The Digital Future Report (2008) 'Surveying the digital future, year seven', *USC Annenberg School Center for the Digital Future*. Los Angeles, CA: Figueroa Press.

Thompson, Craig J. (1997) 'Interpreting consumers: A hermeneutical framework for deriving market insights from the texts of consumers' consumption stories', *Journal of Marketing Research*, 34(November): 438–455.

Thompson, Craig J., Howard R. Pollio and William B. Locander (1994) 'The spoken and the unspoken: A hermeneutic approach to understanding consumers' expressed meanings', *Journal of Consumer Research*, 21: 432–453.

Thompson, E.P. (1971) 'The moral economy of the English crowd in the eighteenth century', *Past and Present*, 50(1): 76–136.

Thorseth, May (2003) *Applied Ethics in Internet Research*. Trondheim, Norway: Programme for Applied Ethics, Norwegian University of Science and Technology.

Tiidenberg, Katrin (2014) 'Bringing sexy back: Reclaiming the body aesthetic via self-shooting', *Cyberpsychology: Journal of Psychosocial Research on Cyberspace*, 8(1): article 3.

Tönnies, Ferdinand ([1887] 1957), *Gemeinshaft und Gesellschaft* (trans. Charles P. Loomis). East Lansing: Michigan State University Press.

Turner, Victor (1969) *The Ritual Process: Structure and Anti-Structure*. Chicago: Aldine Publishing.

Uibu, Marko (2012) 'Creating meanings and supportive networks on the spiritual internet forum "The Nest of Angels"', *Journal of Ethnology and Folkloristics*, 6(2): 69–86.

Valenzuela, Sebastiàn, Namsu Park and Kerk F. Lee (2009) 'Is there social capital in a social network site?: Facebook use and college students' life satisfaction, trust, and participation', *Journal of Computer-Mediated Communication*, 14(4): 875–901.

Van Hout, Marie Claire (2014) 'Nod and wave: An internet study of the codeine intoxication phenomenon', *International Journal of Drug Policy*, 18: 107–117.

Van Maanen, John (1988) *Tales of the Field: On Writing Ethnography*. Chicago: University of Chicago Press.

Varnali, Kaan and Vehbi Gorgulu (2014) 'A social influence perspective on expressive political participation in Twitter: The case of #OccupyGezi', *Information, Communication & Society*, DOI: 10.1080/1369118X.2014.923480.

Vasileiadou, Eleni M. and Magdalena Missler-Behr (2011) 'Virtual embeddedness and social media as a basis for the relational capital management of new ventures', *Electronic Journal of Knowledge Management*, 9(3): 188–203. Available at: www.ejkm.com.

Wagner, Roy (2001) *An Anthropology of the Subject: Holographic Worldview in New Guinea and its Meaning and Significance for the World of Anthropology*. Berkeley, CA: University of California.

Wallace, Anthony (1965) 'Driving to work', in Melford E. Spiro (ed.), *Context and Meaning in Cultural Anthropology*. New York: Free Press. pp. 277–292.

Walther, Joseph B. (1992) 'Interpersonal effects in mediated interaction: A relational perspective', *Communication Research*, 19: 52–90.

Walther, Joseph B. (1995) 'Relational aspects of computer-mediated communication: Experimental observations over time', *Organization Science*, 6(2): 186–203.

Walther, Joseph B. (2002) 'Research ethics in internet-enabled research: Human subjects issues and methodological myopia', *Ethics and Information Technology*, 4: 205–216.

Wasserman, Stanley and Katherine Faust (1994) *Social Network Analysis: Methods and Applications*. Cambridge: Cambridge University Press.

Watt, J.H. (1999) 'Internet systems for evaluation research', in G. Gay and Bennington (eds), *Information Technologies in Evaluation: Social, Moral Epistemological and Practical Implications*, San Francisco, CA: Josey-Bass. pp. 23–44.

Weber, Max ([1922] 1978) *Economy and Society*. Berkeley, CA: University of California Press.

Weible, R. and J. Wallace (1998) 'The impact of the Internet on data collection', *Marketing Research*. pp. 10(3): 19–23.

Weijo, Henri, Joel Hietanen and Pekka Mattila (2014) 'New insights into online consumption communities and netnography', *Journal of Business Research*. Available at: http://dx.doi.org/10.1016/j.jbusres2014.04.015.

Weinmann, T., S. Thomas, S. Brilmayer, S. Heinrich and K. Radon (2012) 'Testing Skype as an interview method in epidemiologic research: response and feasibility', *International Journal of Public Health* 57(6): 959–961.

Weitzman, Eben A. and Matthew B. Miles (1995) *Computer Programs for Qualitative Data Analysis: A Software Sourcebook*. Thousand Oaks, CA: Sage.

Wellman, Barry (1988) 'Structural Analysis: From method and metaphor to theory and substance', in B. Wellman and S.D. Berkowitz (eds), *Social Structures: A Network Approach*. Cambridge, UK: Cambridge University Press. pp. 19–61.

Wellman, Barry (2001) 'Computer networks as social networks', *Science*, 293: 2031–2034.

Wesch, Michael (2009) 'YouTube and you: Experience of self-awareness in the context collapse of the recording webcams', *Explorations in Media Ecology*, 8(2): 19–34.

West, Rebecca J. and Bhoomi K. Thakore (2013) 'Racial exclusion in the online world', *Future Internet*, 5(2): 251–267.

Wickham, Mark and Megan Woods (2005) 'Reflecting on the STRATEGIC Use of CAQDAS to manage and report on the qualitative research process', *Qualitative Report*, (December): 687–702.

Wijland, Roel (2011) 'Anchors, mermaids, shower-curtain seaweeds and fish-shaped fish: The texture of poetic agency', *Marketing Theory*, 11(2): 127–141.

Wikan, Unni (1992) 'Beyond words: The power of resonance', *American Ethnologist*, 19 (August): 460–482.

Wilber, Ken (1997) *The Eye of Spirit: An Integral Vision for a World Gone Slightly Mad*. Boston: Shambhala.

Wiles, Rose, Andrew Bengry-Howell, Graham Crow and Melanie Nind (2013) 'But is it innovation? The development of novel methodological approaches in qualitative research', National Centre for Research Methods University of Southampton Working Paper.

Wilk, Richard (1995) 'Learning to be local in Belize: Global systems of common difference', in D. Miller (ed.), *Worlds Apart: Modernity Through the Prism of the Local*. New York: Routledge. pp. 110–113.

Williamson, Oliver E. (1975) *Markets and Hierarchies: Analysis and Antitrust Implications*. New York: Free Press.

Witney, Cynthia A., Joyce Hendricks and Vicki Copes (2014) 'Munchausen by internet: A netnographical case study', paper presented at the 25th International Nursing Research Congress, July, Hong Kong.

Wright, Kevin B. (2005) 'Researching internet-based populations: Advantages and disadvantages of online survey research, online questionnaire authoring software packages, and web survey services', *Journal of Computer-Mediated Communication*, 10 (April).

Xenitidou, Maria and Nigel Gilbert (2009) *Innovations in Social Science Research Methods*, ESRC National Centre for Research Methods, Surrey, UK: University of Surrey.

Xun, Jiyao and Jonathan Reynolds (2010) 'Applying netnography to market research: The case of the online forum', *Journal of Targeting, Measurement and Analysis for Marketing*, 18(1): 17–31.

Yun, Gi Woong and Craig W. Trumbo (2000) 'Comparative response to a survey executed by post, e-mail, & web form', *Journal of Computer-Mediated Communication*, September.

Zimmer, Michael (2010) '"But the data is already public": On the ethics of research in Facebook', *Ethics and Information Technology*, 12: 313–325.

Zimmerman, Chris, Yuran Chen, Daniel Hardt and Ravi Vatrapu (2014) 'Marius, the Giraffe: A comparative informatics case study of linguistic features of the social media discourse', *Cultural Contexts for Interaction*, presented at CABS 12, August, Kyoto, Japan.

Zurcher, Louis A. (1977) *The Mutable Self: A Self-Concept for Social Change*. Beverley Hills, CA: Sage.

Zwick, Detlev, Samuel K. Bonsu and Aron Darmody (2008) 'Putting consumers to work: "Co-creation" and new marketing govern-mentality', *Journal of Consumer Culture*, 8(2): 163–196.

INDEX

Figures and Tables are indicated by page numbers in bold print. The abbreviation 'bib' refers to bibliographical information in the 'KEY READINGS' sections.